FRANCIS CLEMENT KELLEY & The American Catholic Dream

Other Books by James P. Gaffey

Citizen of No Mean City

James P. Gaffey

FRANCIS CLEMENT KELLEY & The American Catholic Dream

Volume One

The Heritage Foundation, Inc.
Bensenville, Illinois

1980

Permission has been granted by the Manuscripts and Archives Division of the New York Public Library (Astor, Lenox and Tilden Foundations) and by Henry L. Meledin of the Mercantile Safe Deposit and Trust Company, Baltimore, for quotations from the H. L. Mencken papers.

Library of Congress Cataloging in Publication Data

Gaffey, James P.
Francis Clement Kelley & the American Catholic Dream.

Bibliography: volume II, pp. 351-65
Includes Index.
1. Kelley, Francis Clement, Bp., 1870-1948.
2. Catholic Church—Bishops—Biography. 3. Bishops—
United States—Biography. I. Title
BX4705.K35G33 282'.092'4 [B] 79-9130
ISBN 0-8434-0740-9

Dedicated

to

JOSEPH A. CUSACK

President of the Catholic Church Extension Society

of

The United States of America

(1970-1976)

History puts on her most charming dress when she decks herself as biography. Dull facts are polished for the reader when they are set around the brilliant jewel of a great life. But when biography masquerades as eulogy the charm is gone. Real biography is no eulogy: when all is said, a noble figure rises before us, the figure of a human being chosen to do a great work at a critical and trying time, whose problems were not so much different from those of today—larger in some places and smaller in others—but, essentially, as modern as our own.

—adapted from Francis Clement Kelley
in *Extension Magazine,*
XVII (November, 1922), 4

Foreword

For five short years it was my great privilege to be a bishop in Oklahoma. Slowly but surely I began to know the great men who had served and dreamed and built before me. Without doubt the best known was Francis Clement Kelley.

As I lived in the house he had lived in, browsed through his books, and moved about an expansive territory of seventy thousand square miles, my interest in Bishop Kelley grew. I also became convinced that here was no ordinary figure. It was clear that Francis Clement Kelley was a man of unique proportions and a man who made a major and unparalleled contribution to the church in the United States.

His accomplishments were remarkable. But his personal qualities were no less fascinating. I met many people who knew and loved him and who were inspired and enthralled by his abilities as a lecturer, a conversationalist, and a writer.

He was a man of broad vision, imagination and courage. He had some personal involvement in almost all of the major historical events of his mature life: the Peace Conference, the Mexican persecution, the Lateran Treaty and many others.

As I knew Kelley better I grew also in the conviction that his life and his contribution to the Church were too important to be lost. After conversations with Cardinal Cody of Chicago, and through his interest, Extension, founded by Bishop Kelley, agreed to fund the writing of the biography. The president of Extension, Father Joseph Cusack, and after his untimely death, the acting president, Father Edward Slattery, have followed the project closely.

After considerable discussion with many experts in the field of history, Monsignor James Gaffey of the diocese of Santa Rosa was asked to undertake the work. I have read the manuscript entirely and believe that its author has indeed done justice, by the quality of his work, to the importance of his subject.

Francis Clement Kelley & the American Catholic Dream is first rate biography, eminently readable, and a lasting contribution to the history of the Catholic Church in the United States.

John R. Quinn
Archbishop of San Francisco

Preface

Some thirty years have passed since Francis Clement Kelley died on the plains of the American Southwest, completing over a half century of priestly ministry. It is forty years since the publication of his autobiography, *The Bishop Jots It Down*, the literary crown of his life and one of the most durable books written by a Catholic in America. Almost seventy-five years ago, its author launched the home-mission movement in this country when he founded the Catholic Church Extension Society of the United States of America.

The anniversary of these milestones prompted two churchmen to think that it was opportune to produce a full biography of this Catholic leader. Archbishop John R. Quinn, then serving in Oklahoma, conceived the idea, and the late Father Joseph A. Cusack, president of Extension, agreed to support and finance the project.

Research began in the fall of 1976, and it took seventeen months to complete the draft. The partnership of Archbishop Quinn and Father Cusack rendered the task of researching and writing as rewarding as possible—making sources available, providing hospitality, and offering at each step their interest and encouragement. Unfortunately, the team suffered an unexpected blow with Father Cusack's tragic death in November, 1976. It is to his memory that this biography is dedicated.

If I faced one overriding problem as a biographer, it was the enormous versatility of my subject. Kelley was often told that he "had more varied experiences than any other priest in America." His interests were legion; they covered, as he himself said in the twilight of life, "pastoral, military, diplomatic, political, editorial, literary, business, directing and managing" affairs. There was one element that held this broad range of activity together: Kelley had a "dream." This dream was to make his church truly "Catholic," that is, to bring the Gospel out of "the America of the great cities" and into "the real America which feeds and sustains the other—the America of the small towns, villages, and countryside." This was the goal that drove him into becoming the greatest home-missioner of his age. It was this same goal that led him to the other great achievements of his life—his diplomatic work in Europe after World War I, his faithful service to the persecuted church in Mexico, his speaking and writing, and his episcopal leadership of a Catholic minority in the heart of America's "Bible Belt."

In doing his job, the writer often becomes a beggar, and more people than I can possibly thank have helped me in completing this task. My first expression of gratitude is to Archbishop Charles A. Salatka of Oklahoma City, who gave me months of hospitality in his home and allowed me unfettered access to the papers of the archdiocese. Two California bishops were helpful: Bishop Leo T. Maher of San Diego, with his encouragement and perceptive comments on the Equestrian Order of the Holy Sepulcher; and Bishop Mark J. Hurley of Santa Rosa, who gave me the time to do this project.

A score of friends read the early draft of the manuscript, whole or in part, and these gentle critics are, in alphabetical order: Joyce Barnes, C.S.J.; Robert Charland; J. Paul Donovan; John J. Fahey; Ernest A. Flusche; Gerald P. Fogarty, S.J.; Archbishop Victor F. Foley, S.M.; Bishop Edgar Godin; Charles J. Goentges; Hal Hudson; Harry C. Koenig; Bishop Francis P. Leipzig; Bishop Stephen A. Leven; Oscar H. Lipscomb; C. A. McGinty; Archbishop John L. May; Denis Meade, O.S.B.; Luis Medina-Ascensio, S.J.; David F. Monahan; Eileen Moriarty; Joseph F. Murphy, O.S.B.; Mary Joachim Oberkoetter, O.S.B.; J.P.E. O'Hanley; John J. O'Hare; John A. Petuskey; Charles Shanabruch; Bishop John J. Sullivan; Lawrence B. Terrien, S.S.; Robert Trisco; Georges-Henri Villeneuve; and James D. White.

I am grateful, too, to Henry L. Meledin of the Mercantile Safe Deposit and Trust Company, Baltimore, who permitted me to cite excerpts from the Mencken-Dudek correspondence.

Seven persons have been central to this enterprise, and these deserve a special acknowledgement. First, Archbishop John R. Quinn of San Francisco originated the idea of the biography. During my solitary ordeal of writing and editing the text he spared no effort in making me comfortable in Oklahoma, opening the Kelley papers, reading and commenting on each page of the draft, and bringing the completed manuscript to the attention of prospective publishers. This book simply would not exist without his patronage. Second, I am deeply in debt to Father Edward J. Slattery, acting president of Extension. This magnanimous priest continued to fund the project that had begun under his predecessor, and lent to me every possible assistance, including his home in Chicago, complete freedom with the Extension materials, and his personal commitment to the work. Third, Monsignor John Tracy Ellis, a dear friend and the model of a Christian gentleman and scholar, saw me through every step of the way. His editorial skills were applied to each page of the manuscript, as he corrected many mistakes and often suggested how the text might be strengthened. Even after the completion of the manuscript, his assistance continued in the form of recommending the biography to several publishers. My good friend, Father Charles H. Schettler of Oklahoma City, was unstinting in contributing valuable comments, retrieving obscure archival items that were related to the story, and, above all, rewarding me with the most congenial companionship during my sojourn in his city. Sister Theodore Mary Von Elm, C.P.B., organized the voluminous Kelley papers and remained ever in readiness to help further, especially by typing the entire first draft of the book. Gloria Anderson, a long-time friend and typist-editor par excellence, interrupted her overcrowded professional life in California to type the immaculate last draft in record time.

A final but special acknowledgement goes to Cardinal John Cody of Chicago. As chancellor of Extension and a student of ecclesiastical affairs, he authorized the project of writing this biography, made available the papers of his two predecessors, Archbishop Quigley and Cardinal Mundelein, and contributed a substantial gift to the publication of this book.

A score of colleagues and friends have given nobly to this enterprise; and to them all I am genuinely grateful, though I alone bear the responsibility for its final form.

James P. Gaffey
Menlo Park, California
February 1, 1980

Contents

Volume 1

Maps

List of Illustrations

Chronology

1865	February 13	Marriage of FCK's parents: John Kelly and Mary Ann Murphy
1870	October 23	FCK's "official" birthdate
1870	November 24	FCK's actual birthdate
1885	September 2	FCK enrolled in Saint Dunstan's
1888		FCK enrolled in the minor Seminary of Chicoutimi
1889	April 22	Opening of the Unassigned Land in Oklahoma for settlement and the coming of the "Sooners"
1889		FCK begins a year of private studies as secretary to Bishop James Roger of Chatham
1890		FCK enrolled in the Seminary of Nicolet
1892	December 16	Death of FCK's father
1893	August 23	FCK's ordination to the priesthood at Nicolet

1893	October 26	FCK's appointment to the church of the Immaculate Conception, Lapeer, Michigan
1898	May 17	FCK granted a leave of absence to serve as chaplain of the 32d Regiment of Michigan Volunteers
1905	October 18	Foundation of the Catholic Church Extension Society of the United States of America in Chicago
1905	December 12	Extension legally incorporated in Michigan
1907	April 3	FCK officially joins the archdiocese of Chicago
1907	June 7	Extension receives papal approval
1907	June 13	FCK awarded an honorary degree of doctor of laws by the University of Notre Dame
1907		*The Last Battle of the Gods*
1907	March 17	FCK awarded an honorary doctorate in theology
1908	November 15-18	The first American Catholic Missionary Congress in Chicago
1910	June 9	The apostolic brief, *Qua Nuper,* creates Extension a pontifical institute
1912	February 2	Appointment of Archbishop John Bonzano as apostolic delegate in the United States
1912	May 9	Extension legally incorporated in Illinois
1913	July 30	FCK dates his preface to *The City and the World and Other Stories*

1913	October 19-22	The second American Catholic Missionary Congress in Boston
1914	December 10	The Mexican bishops in exile appoint FCK as their representative
1915	March 20	William Jennings Bryan's letter to FCK, stating the Mexican policy of the Wilson administration
1915	June 22	Archbishop Bonzano appointed to handle affairs of the apostolic delegation in Mexico
1915	July 10	Death of Archbishop James E. Quigley of Chicago
1915	August 25	FCK named a monsignor, first a domestic prelate, and then a prothonotary apostolic
1915	October 19	Venustiano Carranza receives *de facto* recognition from the Pan American Conference in Washington, D.C.
1915	November 18	The Mexican hierarchy approves FCK's plan to use, if necessary, political and financial pressures in their behalf
1915	November 29	Joseph P. Tumulty's public letter on Mexico
1915	November 30	Announcement that Bishop George W. Mundelein is appointed to the archdiocese of Chicago
1915		*The Book of Red and Yellow: Being a Story of Blood and a Yellow Streak* (1st edition)

1916	February 10	The "Poisoned Banquet"—Extension's reception for Archbishop Mundelein
1916	July 10	FCK takes possession of Saint Francis Xavier Parish in Wilmette, Illinois
1917	February 8	Death of Cardinal Diomede Falconio
1917	October 17	Publication date of *Charred Wood*
1917		*Letters to Jack: Written by a Priest to His Nephew*
1918	July 4	Death of Extension's only protector in Rome, Cardinal Sebastian Martinelli
1919	February 13	A special commission at the Paris peace conference kills the article on religious freedom
1919	March 6	FCK arrives in Paris to lobby for religious liberty at the peace conference
1919	May 10	FCK's meeting with Cardinal Mercier and his introduction into the Roman Question
1919	May 6-15	FCK's tour of the Western Front
1919	May 18	FCK's meeting with Premier Vittorio Orlando of Italy in Paris
1919	May 22	FCK's meeting in Rome with Cardinal Gasparri and Archbishop Cerretti on the Roman Question
1919	May 27	FCK arranges in Paris the meeting between Archbishop Cerretti and Giuseppe Brambilla
1919	June 1	The Cerretti-Orlando talks begin in Paris

1919	June 19	Fall of the Orlando ministry in Rome
1919	June 28	Signing of the Treaty of Versailles, which contains Article XXII, Section 5, granting freedom of conscience in the former German colonies
1919	July 22-24	The meeting of mission directors at Notre Dame, during which the basic plan for the ABCM is drawn up
1919	September 24	American bishops approve the ABCM for the first time
1920	September 7	FCK's meeting with the India Office in London
1920	September 22	American bishops approve the ABCM for the second time
1920	September 22	FCK helps kill the resolution on Irish independence at the American bishops' meeting
1921	January 14	Government of India agrees to stop expatriation of German missionaries
1921	March 19	FCK relieved of duties as negotiator in behalf of the German missions
1921	April 6	Cardinal Bourne's letter to David Lloyd George on the Irish problem
1921	April 30	Appointment of Emmanuel B. Ledvina as bishop of Corpus Christi
1921	September 21	American bishops approve the ABCM for the third time
1921	December 12	Benedict XV approves the original plan of the ABCM
1922	January 22	Death of Benedict XV

1922	May 2	Propaganda's decree adds to the ABCM plan conditions that were at first unacceptable to the American hierarchy
1922	August 3	Date of imprimatur for *The Story of Extension*
1922	November 14	Release date of *Dominus Vobiscum: A Book of Letters*
1922	December 14	Appointment of Archbishop Pietro Fumasoni-Biondi as apostolic delegate in the United States
1923	January 13	President Calles orders the expulsion of the apostolic delegate in Mexico, Archbishop Ernesto Fillipi
1923	November 3	The appointment of Thomas R. Carey to Lapeer, Michigan, which marks the beginning of the "Rural-Church Program"
1924	February 21	Death of Theophile Meerschaert, first bishop of Oklahoma
1924	March 24	George W. Mundelein created a cardinal
1924	June 25	FCK's appointment as bishop of Oklahoma
1924	September 25	The American hierarchy adopts FCK's revised plan for the ABCM
1924	October 2	FCK's ordination as a bishop in Chicago
1924	October 2	Date of dedication of *The Epistles of Father Timothy to His Parishioners*
1924	October 15	FCK's installation in Oklahoma City

1924	November 7	Pius XI approves the revised ABCM plan
1924	December 25	FCK's *On Missions: The First Pastoral* as bishop of Oklahoma
1925	October 14	First Catholic use of the wireless radio in Oklahoma
1926	November 13	FCK launches his "Diocesan Campaign" to help liquidate diocesan indebtedness
1926	December 12	Publication of the *Pastoral Letter of the Catholic Episcopate of the United States on the Religious Situation in Mexico*
1927	June 28	University of Louvain grants FCK the honorary degree of doctor and master of sacred theology
1928	March 14	FCK appoints John G. Heiring to administer the preparatory seminary near Tulsa
1928	April 18	The board of trustees of The Catholic University of America nominates FCK for the rectorship
1928	July 11	James H. Ryan named rector of The Catholic University of America
1929	February 11	Signing of the Lateran Pacts in Rome
1929	March 31	The Associated Press breaks the story of FCK's involvement in the Cerretti-Orlando talks of 1919
1929	May 13	Mussolini's address to the Chamber of Deputies in which he cites FCK's role in the Roman Question

1929	June 7	Ratification of the Lateran Pacts in Rome
1929	June 8	Publication date of *When the Veil Is Rent*
1929	June 21	Agreement between President Emilio Portes Gil and Archbishop Leopoldo Ruiz y Flores
1930	January 15	Notice that Italy named FCK a Knight of the Order of St. Maurice and St. Lazarus
1930	April 2	Heiring's resignation from the rectorship of the diocesan seminary near Tulsa
1930	November 14	Title of the diocese of Oklahoma changed to the diocese of "Oklahoma City and Tulsa"
1930	November 20	Archbishop Samuel A. Stritch's appointment as vice-chancellor of Extension, marking FCK's voluntary withdrawal from its affairs
1931	October 4	FCK made a Knight-Commander of the Equestrian Order of the Holy Sepulcher
1931	March 6	Austria confers upon FCK the Golden Cross of Merit with Star
1932	April 11	"Street preaching" inaugurated in Oklahoma City
1932	April 23	FCK's address to the college and university presidents in Oklahoma on the "Greater University"

1932	September 22	FCK accepts the chairmanship of the proposed Catholic Committee on Scouting
1932	October 6	Archbishop Ruiz, apostolic delegate in Mexico, deported to Texas
1932	December 19	Publication date of *The Forgotten God*
1933	February 22	Blessing of Abbot Mark Braun, O.S.B., in Oklahoma City
1933	April 2	Governor William H. Murray accepts the "Greater University" plan as his own
1933	April 19	FCK's address to the Chamber of Commerce in Oklahoma City on the "Greater University"
1933	May 27	First meeting of the new State Coordinating Board for higher education
1933	November 28	FCK's talk, "The Great Conviction," delivered on the occasion of his 40th anniversary as a priest
1933	November 30	Ruling by the attorney general, J. Berry King, on the authority of the State Coordinating Board to incorporate itself
1934	October 10	The first Catholic Action congress in Oklahoma City opens
1934	November 13	Abbot Mark Braun given permission to confirm in the diocese
1934	December 20	FCK's address to his clergy on supporting the Catholic Action program in the diocese

1935	April 10	Publication date of *Blood-Drenched Altars: Mexican Comment*
1935	November 14	FCK elected treasurer of the National Catholic Welfare Conference
1936	July 30	Formation of the Committee of Bishops on the Mexican Seminary; FCK elected treasurer
1936	August 28	Date of imprimatur for *A Holy Hour for Priests*
1936	September 20	"Mexican Seminary Sunday": a national collection taken to launch Montezuma
1937	February	Publication date of *Problem Island*
1937	September 23	Opening of Montezuma Seminary in Las Vegas, New Mexico
1939	May 8	State Coordinating Board revived under Governor Leon C. Phillips
1939	May 10	FCK purchases the Hales mansion in Oklahoma City
1939	May 16	Publication date of *The Bishop Jots It Down*
1940	May 2	Date of imprimatur for *Sacerdos et Pontifex: Letters to a Bishop-Elect*
1940	November 13	FCK returns to Extension's board of governors as vice-chancellor
1941	March 11	The constitutional amendment authorizing "The Oklahoma State Regents for Higher Education" passes in a referendum

1942	July 26	FCK delivers "Conversations with an Electric Fan" at the University of Oklahoma
1942	September 21	Date of publication of *Pack Rat: A Metaphoric Fantasy*
1942	October 18	FCK suffers an attack of angina pectoris
1943	April 6	Publication date of *Tales from the Rectory*
1943	May 9	FCK honored by the Catholic Committee of the South
1943	July 16	Bishop Laurence FitzSimon of Amarillo named FCK's vicar general in the Oklahoma Panhandle
1943	October 26	Observance of FCK's golden anniversary as a priest
1944	November 11	Appointment of Bishop Eugene J. McGuinness as coadjutor with the right of succession and with "ordinary" power
1945	January 10	McGuinness's installation in Oklahoma City
1947	February 2	Spain awards FCK the Grand Cross of Isabella the Catholic
1948	February 1	Death of FCK

Genealogy

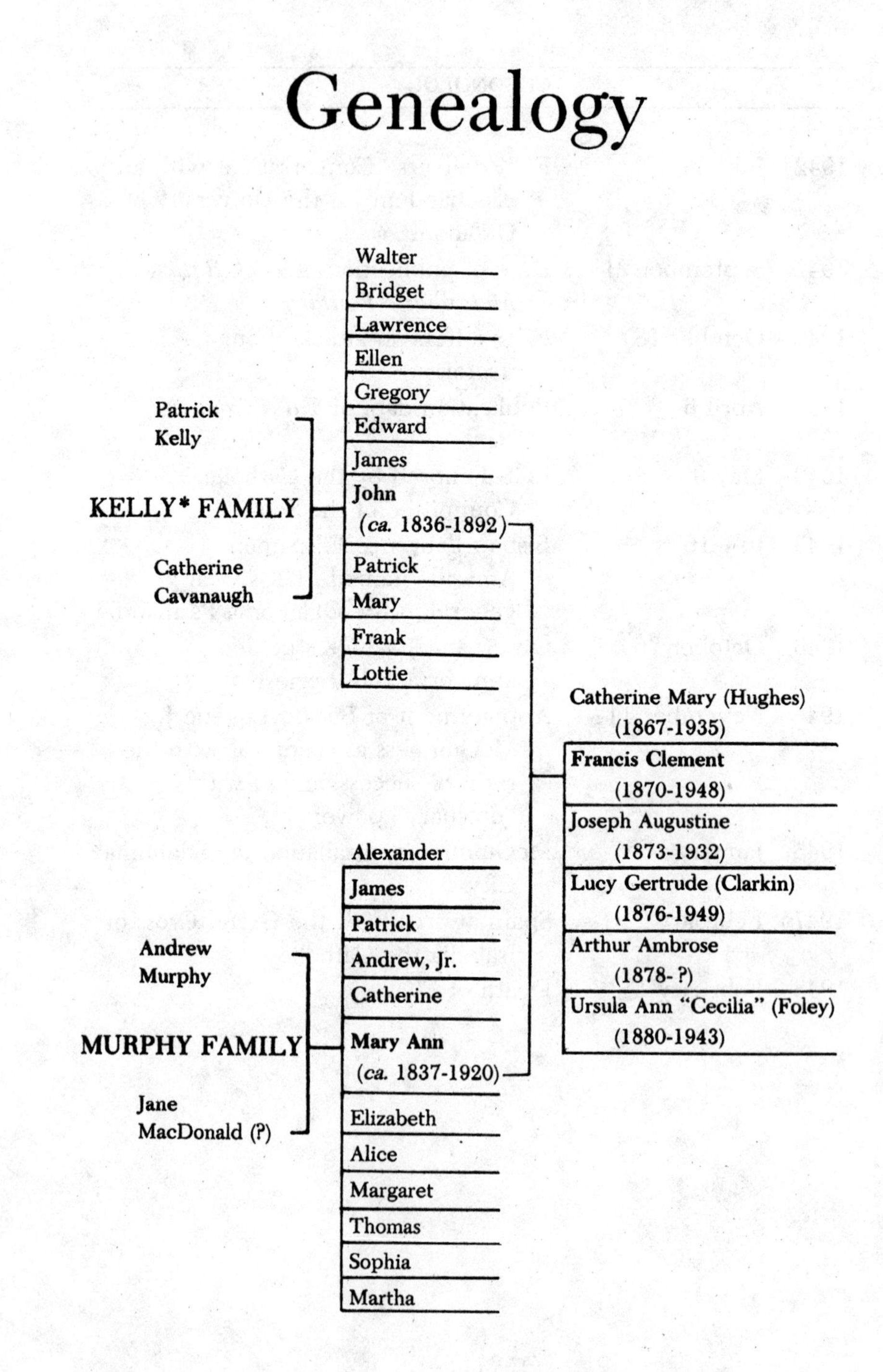

Walter
Bridget
Lawrence
Ellen
Gregory
Patrick
Kelly
Edward
James
KELLY* FAMILY
John
(ca. 1836-1892)
Catherine
Cavanaugh
Patrick
Mary
Frank
Lottie
Catherine Mary (Hughes)
(1867-1935)
Francis Clement
(1870-1948)
Joseph Augustine
(1873-1932)
Alexander
Lucy Gertrude (Clarkin)
(1876-1949)
James
Patrick
Arthur Ambrose
(1878- ?)
Andrew
Murphy
Andrew, Jr.
Catherine
Ursula Ann "Cecilia" (Foley)
(1880-1943)
MURPHY FAMILY
Mary Ann
(ca. 1837-1920)
Jane
MacDonald (?)
Elizabeth
Alice
Margaret
Thomas
Sophia
Martha

Sister Patricia Kelley, C.S.M., "The Intertwining of the Families of James Kenny and Anne Whelan, James Kelly and Catherine Kavanaugh, James Whelan and Jane Carmichael, Anthony O'Donnell and Anne O'Keefe," unpublished manuscript.

Baptism and Marriage Records at Saint Joachim and Saint Dunstan Parishes, Prince Edward Island.

Public Archives, Government of Prince Edward Island, Register of Deeds, King County, XI, 237-43.

Interview with Mrs. Catherine Praught, Vernon River, Prince Edward Island, July 6, 1977.

*On FCK's change of spelling of his surname from "KELLY" to "KELLEY," see pp. 74-75.

Prologue

Getting Acquainted

Seldom is an outsider given much more than a glimpse into the inner world of a member of the Catholic hierarchy. Usually the secret thoughts and mannerisms of these men are veiled in discreet public lives and known only to the most trusted of intimates. An exception to this rule is Francis Clement Kelley, a versatile churchman who fashioned several careers as missionary, controversialist, diplomat, bishop, and writer. Beneath the ribbons of these many campaigns beat the heart of a remarkable, private person who did not fear the full disclosure of his humanity. Perhaps the best introduction to his life and work is to study first those qualities that constituted his individuality. Like most men, he evoked a variety of reactions. A religious cynic like H. L. Mencken found him brilliant and irresistibly charming; to the idealistic Woodrow Wilson, he was nothing more than a dangerous and shifty cleric. John B. Dudek, a priest of Oklahoma who served Kelley as chancellor for two decades, viewed him as a gentleman too refined to be wasted in a frontier diocese, while skeptical Sooner newsmen were inclined to interpret his civic actions as clever Machiavellian tricks in promoting Catholic political power.[1] A preliminary inventory of his character may unravel some of these contradictions and best prepare us to weigh and appreciate an extraordinary career which helped shape Catholic America in the first half of the twentieth century.

The heat is melting me but you will naturally say that I can stand a lot of melting.

FCK to Hugh C. Boyle, August 5, 1930

If we start with the obvious, that is, with Kelley's physical attributes and personal habits, we would notice at once that our subject was portly most of his life. His physique reached some five feet nine inches in height and was crowned with a ripe Celtic face that often framed a warm, unaffected smile. As contemporaries recall, his most striking asset were his eyes—"blue and sparkling." His firm, clear voice enunciated words with care and on public occasions laced phrases together with a lilting rhythm that sometimes spellbound listeners. His homes in Illinois and Oklahoma accommodated a man with a voracious appetite for work and scholarship. While serving as a pastor in Wilmette, a suburb of Chicago, he regarded the radio as a "terrible waster of time" and moved his receiver out of his quarters to a common room where his assistants enjoyed the programs without interfering with his evenings. His apartment in Oklahoma City was likewise a workshop, paneled with shelves displaying a vast personal library. In the center of the room stood a massive desk at which he labored, beginning usually in the hours before dawn, researching and writing by hand the first drafts of his talks and books in the quietest part of the day.[2]

If his residence was a scene of serious work, it was also one of enjoyment. Kelley not only kept himself busy, but he also relished the wholesome pleasures of life. Though his table was usually simple, he was fond of a few mildly extravagant delicacies. His origins in maritime Canada had created a lifelong romance with oysters. Barrels of tangy Malpéques were shipped regularly from his native Prince Edward Island, supplemented by their Gulf cousins from Texas. Both varieties were in steady supply in his cellar until his attack of angina pectoris in 1943, when his doctor ordered him off these rich mollusks, an abstinence which, he confessed wryly, "is breaking my heart."[3] Another treat to arrive monthly was a package of *port salut.* This rich, pungent cheese was cultured at the Cistercian abbey in Oka, near Montreal, and in Kelley's home it was often served as a savory dessert with smooth golden French sauterne from the Château d'Yquem. Not only did the monks' cheese grace his own table, but he promoted its delights among his episcopal friends, several of whom joined him in becoming customers of the monastery.[4]

Francis Kelley's most notable concession to the palate consisted of a complicated recipe for what was known as "The Bishop's Salad." At special suppers, the ingredients for the dressing were assembled at the dining table—garlic, roquefort cheese, hard-boiled eggs, mashed potato, olive oil, seasonings, and bottled sauces. His guests were then treated to a surprise performance as the amateur chef measured out the elements and combined them with an elaborate flourish. Kelley attributed the recipe to a French priest, but Bishop Hugh C. Boyle of Pittsburgh could not resist teasing the Oklahoman when he unearthed an amusing century-old poem of Sydney Smith, an Anglican clergyman and wit. Smith's venerable verses narrated Kelley's recipe, though several traditional ingredients were omitted, and this discovery moved the episcopal chef to compose these playful iambs in rebuttal:

> Dear Sydney Smith! This is a meal
> But also it's a patent steal.
> An old French curé made the treat
> That you, a parson, lived to eat.
> And you forgot the olive oil
> Two large spoonfulls [*sic*] will add a smile.
> And where's the bit of garlic scent
> That leaves a gourmet all content?
> I'd mention vinegar also
> But it won't rhyme—so let it go.[5]

Kelley enjoyed tobacco too, and his tastes extended through most of its forms—cigarettes, preferably Turkish, cigars, and later a pipe. Toward the end of his life, his doctor limited him to a few cigarettes a day, too few to satisfy a lifelong habit. When his ration was soon exhausted by late morning he appealed to the German-born brothers nursing him in his last days. If they declined to slip him an extra smoke, the patient often erupted, once calling an uncooperative brother, half-seriously, "You Hitler!"[6]

Perhaps a review of a man's leisurely habits may seem trivial, but it does succeed in depicting this committed ecclesiastic as a comfortable and contented man, one who enjoyed *joie de vivre* and shared this zest with others. To this disposition, however, one should add two minor traits that bordered on eccentricity, viz., his fondness for exotic gadgets and for unorthodox health remedies. Friends were amused, even astonished, at his flirtation with experiments in parapsychology which seemed to skirt the boundaries of the occult. His interest in divination dated from 1936 when two Canons Regular of the Immaculate Conception from Europe visited him in Oklahoma City en route to their missions in Latin America. One priest specialized in "radiesthesia," a little known technique whereby a medium supplied information through the use of a pendant. He gave a sensational demonstration of its efficacy at the Catholic hospital, where he was presented with a difficult medical case and after applying a pendant came up with the correct diagnosis.[7]

The French hierarchy had discouraged this practice, but Kelley was generally open to what scientists have called the "psi" capacity in human beings, that is, higher-thought processes by which individuals of a sensitive and spiritual nature can arrive at knowledge by unconventional means; and on occasion the bishop exhibited his use of "radiesthesia." His favorite performance consisted of laying out a map of his diocese; and with a silver pendant suspended above, he claimed the ability to locate the exact whereabouts of any of his clergy at that moment. The truth of this method was never validated, and most observers ridiculed the idea as little more than a parlor game. The skeptics included Archbishop Robert E. Lucey of San Antonio, who once challenged Kelley to "use his hokus pokus to find water" for a community of sisters near the Alamo. If this sorcery produced only a dry hole, warned the Texan in mock seriousness, "it would be just too bad for Kelley." Unfortunately, there is no evidence of whether Kelley's pendant, which worked to his satisfaction in Oklahoma, ever located a subterranean spring in the Lone Star State. It was not even clear to everyone how seriously he took his hobby. When he produced the pendant at friendly gatherings, he appeared more interested in amusing his companions than in converting them to the possibilities of divination; but in private, he was deadly earnest regarding the reality of psychic phenomena.[8]

This dalliance with parapsychology was only one example of Francis Kelley's willingness to go beyond the conventions of his time; another centered on his search for relief from a chronic health problem. Through most of his life he suffered from colitis, a condition which forced him to experiment with a variety of medicines. One of his constant frustrations in this regard was that the most effective concoctions were manufactured and sold only in Europe, and their availability in the United States at that time was virtually non-existant.[9] His membership in the Knights of the Holy Sepulcher, however, brought him a benefit for which he had never bargained. This organization introduced him to the Patriarch of Jerusalem, an Italian-born churchman living in Palestine, who acquainted him with a simple remedy that soothed troubled bowels. It was garlic, that member of the lily family known to have remarkable tonic properties—chopped finely and mixed with honey. "Everyone knows," the pleased Kelley confided to another priest afflicted with the same ailment, "that the Arabians and Italians are great garlic eaters and do not call for doctors very often."[10] Though the record is not clear, one may assume that Kelley was no less faithful in the medicinal use of this powerful herb than the resourceful patriarch and many of his subjects.

> *A priest is an officer, and an officer ought to be a gentleman.*
>
> FCK, *Dominus Vobiscum* (1922), 260

If we proceed beyond these superficialities, we will discover that Kelley was far more than a sometime epicure or, according to some, a harmless crank: he was, at bottom, a man of polish and finesse. He was conscientious about his appearance, with shoes shined and clothes pressed for all public occasions; and he attended to the smallest details of personal hygiene, such as taking scrupulous care of his teeth and fingernails. He expected courtesy from everyone and reciprocated without fail. His manners were impeccable; he was always gracious in the company of women, though slightly self-conscious; and whatever he borrowed was given back promptly, including books. "A gentleman expresses appreciation for the loan of books in two ways," he once chided a seminarian: "by reading them, and by returning them when read."[11]

Endowed with an endearing temperament, he could also evoke smiles and chuckles from any audience, large and small, Catholic and mixed. His gift was less a brilliance of wit than that broader human sympathy known simply as a sense of humor. His *jeux d'esprit* were not Swiftian; they were seldom sharp or tart, seldom used to score points or to parade a quick mind. Rather, his approach was a good-natured laugh at life's absurdities —"subtle but never obscure," as contemporaries recall—which often echoed a note of pathos. This humor is especially evident in his delight in cracking jokes. Once, soon after his own health had broken in 1943, he inquired about the fitness of Bishop William D. O'Brien, president of Catholic Church Extension, the home-mission society Kelley had founded, and urged O'Brien to pace himself less strenuously, especially since there were priests in the society ready to assist him. His own recent collapse, Kelley continued, had taught him that moral, but it had come too late. He likened himself to the unfortunate black who was about to be hanged and was asked, minutes before the execution, if he had any remarks to make. "This is sure going to be a lesson to me," was the condemned man's reply, to which Kelley added wistfully: "So there you are."[12]

Seasoned a raconteur as he was, Kelley's remarks were always proper, his anecdotes never descending into the area of the vulgar. His household sometimes tested his decorum by spinning, in his presence, yarns that explored the boundaries of good taste. Invariably he gave no reaction, neither encouraging Rabelaisian humor nor signaling disapproval. His blank expression in these circumstances was so perfect that friends assumed that he had missed the point altogether. The only recorded instance in which he approached crudity was his updating of a well-known formula for longevity. This he offered to O'Brien, whose aversion to coarseness was not so developed as Kelley's. " '. . . keep your bowels open and be kind,' " recommended Kelley, "and I would add— . . . get lots of sleep."[13] Given his bout with colitis, the genteel prelate probably meant this prescription literally.

> *. . . he is a rare human being, the real Big Man. Most of us have our own particular pettinesses. We are big in some things, but small, very small in others. But I never yet knew where a priest lost anything by being a Big Man.*
>
> FCK, *Dominus Vobiscum* (1922), 116

Bishop Kelley was, above all, magnanimous; his unselfishness often staggered his friends. "Everything about him was big," commented the New Zealand poet, Eileen Duggan; and these sentiments were echoed by Archbishop Arthur J. Drossaerts of San Antonio when, on his own, Kelley raised $30,000 in 1929 to aid Mexican refugees in Texas after a recurrence of persecution in their country. "There is nothing small about the bishop of Oklahoma," began Drossaerts' tribute. "You have been good, generous and kind to the 'desterrados' in your usual big way. God bless your heart."[14] Though he succeeded in raising considerable personal income through speaking and writing, his funds were not buried in a bank account. They went freely to serve the interests of the church, such as financing his diplomatic efforts in behalf of religious liberty in Mexico, the survival of the German missions overseas, and the establishment of the American Board of Catholic Missions. Money came to him easily, but at an early stage in life he discovered that if he tucked it away in savings, he found himself becoming stingy and greedy, two qualities which he abhorred in others and smothered in himself. "For the life of me," he observed, "I cannot see why a priest should want to be a rich man."[15]

When compiling his history of Mexico, *Blood-Drenched Altars* (1935), he used the services of Eber Cole Byam, an amateur scholar who had amassed knowledge on the subject but had little inclination toward writing. Byam's health was never robust, and he was poor—"a tubercular case," as Kelley described him, "and without a penny to his name."[16] In providing the bishop with the historical background, Byam gave what he could never have used himself, and the giving was not all on his side. During the collaboration, Kelley provided a share in an important enterprise, companionship, research facilities, and a home; and afterwards he not only divided the credit and royalties but also arranged care for his assistant in a sanitarium in eastern Oklahoma, where Byam remained until his death.

To appreciate help was a strong suit in the Kelley character. "I have lots of faults," he told a Canadian bishop, "but ingratitude, thank God, is not one of them."[17] An example of Kelley's resolve to credit good work occurred when he honored the leading Catholic attorney in Oklahoma, W. Frank Wilson, who had directed the attack on the state's attempted prohibition of the use of sacramental wine during the episcopate of Kelley's predecessor, Bishop Theophile Meerschaert. From its beginnings in 1907, Oklahoma had outlawed the manufacture or sale of intoxicants, and a decade later, the legislature crowned this temperance policy with a celebrated "bone-dry" law that banned alcohol completely, except for use in hospitals and laboratories. This provision would have prevented the diocese from even possessing sacramental wine and, in effect, from celebrating Mass. Wilson and his associates scored a landmark victory in 1918, when the state supreme court allowed, as an exception, the use of wine for Catholic services. Kelley had long regretted the fact that the diocese had never recognized Wilson's contribution. To compensate for this oversight—thirteen years after the attorney's triumph—the bishop quietly engineered the conferral of an honorary doctorate of laws by the University of Notre Dame, to Wilson's surprise and profound delight.[18]

Kelley was himself no stranger to academic honors. Although he never attended graduate schools, three great Catholic universities acknowledged his achievements with honorary degrees. In 1907 Notre Dame awarded him a doctorate of laws, and a year later Laval in Quebec gave him a doctorate in sacred theology. The final degree was part of the quincentenary celebration at Louvain, one of the premier institutions of higher learning in the church. When Kelley first learned of the Belgian university's intention to honor him, he privately expressed his unworthiness. His popular books, he contended, amounted to nothing more than literary soufflés, certainly not to be classified " 'among the heavies' " in the academic world. Accordingly, if the university wanted to recognize an American, its degree should go to an accomplished scholar in the hierarchy like Bishop William Turner of Buffalo, who had published two texts in philosophy, or Bishop Thomas J. Shahan, rector of The Catholic University of America, who had made extensive contributions in the field of ecclesiastical history.[19] In any case, Kelley's modesty did not prevail, and Louvain made him a doctor and master of sacred theology in 1927.

The possession of these choice diplomas ratified the fact of Kelley's intellectualism. He read widely and respected scholarship; an author himself of seventeen books, he numbered among his friends several of the most prolific Catholic writers of his generation, the most notable being the distinguished Irish editor and biographer, Shane Leslie. Kelley attributed his deftness to his seminary education, which had introduced him to the philosophical and theological underpinnings of all specialized knowledge. This training had, accordingly, made him a generalist, and this was the secret of his reputation among the learned. "They must all go back now and then to fundamentals . . . ," he once explained, and as a priest he had "something everyone needs some time."[20] Even strangers sensed in the Oklahoman the qualities of an erudite, broadly visioned churchman. After a lengthy conversation with the bishop, followed by a tour of his personal library, a rabbi who was associated with the National Conference of Christians and Jews was overwhelmed with his host's command of subjects. On leaving the residence, the visitor gave forth a shrill whistle and exclaimed to his companion, "My, he knows his history."[21]

> *One great virtue is always needed to balance genius: Humility.*
>
> FCK, *Sacerdos et Pontifex* (1940), 162

His superior gifts earned Kelley many laurels, but he seldom succumbed to vanity or self-worship. His activities across the country brought him more than his share of attention in the press, but at the beginning of his episcopate, he firmly warned the editor of the diocesan weekly not to have his name appear too frequently. The *Southwest Courier* was to remain the vehicle of the diocese, not a personal organ of the bishop whose public appearances and views might easily occupy too much space, a weakness of many Catholic newspapers.[22] No matter how many tributes were sounded in his behalf, he did not blind himself to his limitations. When admirers tended to gild descriptions of his career, he disapproved of extravagant phrases because, as he noted, they laid the "molasses on thick."[23]

If there is a single test of humility, perhaps it is the ability to acknowledge errors, and Kelley freely confessed his mistakes. "If

I ever come to the time when I cannot admit I am wrong," he remarked privately, "I shall know that some grace has been withdrawn from me."[24] He looked upon most criticisms as early warnings to avoid future disasters—"like toothaches," as he told his nephew, "unpleasant, even painful; irritating, even maddening: but they help us and help us very materially."[25] A student of French history, he most of all admired François Fénelon, a seventeenth-century archbishop and mystical writer. An aristocrat by birth, Fénelon had been a major figure at the court of Louis XIV, but his search for spiritual peace had led him to produce a book that was condemned by the Holy See. Kelley's interest in the prelate was centered less on his mystical theories than on the spirit whereby he ended his glittering career at Versailles and humbly submitted to the will of Rome. This manly acceptance of criticism, in Kelley's view, disclosed a deeper "generosity" with which the brilliant Frenchman crushed his pride and won the everlasting respect of the American churchman two centuries later.[26] Kelley's lack of conceit, however, did not immunize him from all forms of censure. Nothing disturbed him more than a rebuke appearing in the press, an event which usually drove him into angry public debates, as will be seen, for example, when President Wilson's secretary openly accused Kelley of deceit regarding Mexico. In other words, Kelley was willing to accept corrections and to make apologies as long as his good name was not called into question openly; otherwise, his critic would have a hard fight on his hands.

> *Catholic bishops are human. . . . Left without . . . grace they would do as humans always do—make a mess of things.*
>
> FCK, *The Bishop Jot Its Down* (1939), 324

Francis Kelley was not pure gold; polished as it was, his behavior betrayed several flaws in temperament. As will be seen later, he tended to misinterpret official instructions. In 1921, without authority, he overcommitted the Vatican in his effort to save the German missions in the British Empire. Fourteen years later, he nearly ruined the American bishops' relief program for the Mexican church when he unilaterally incorporated a special committee and hired a high-voltage fund-raiser, both of which he was forced to discharge. He was also easily hurt, especially when there was denied some position which he felt due to him. An instance of this occurred in 1930, six years after he had retired as the founder-president of Extension, when he was not given the vice-chancellorship of the society. Though still a member of the governing board, he retaliated by refusing to attend meetings until that office was offered to him, an unjustifiable tantrum that deprived the home-missions of his counsel for a decade.

This brittleness not only compromised his professionalism but also complicated some of his personal relationships. As a rule, his friendships were long-term and rewarding, but his tissue-thin sensitivity could at times place a heavy strain upon his closest associates. An unfortunate chain of events nearly estranged him from the Mexican churchman whom he esteemed and helped the most during the revolution in the south. No one knew better the extent of Kelley's charity than Archbishop Francisco Orozco-Jiménez of Guadalajara. Ever since the outbreak of the Mexican persecution in 1914, relief funds had been placed at Orozco's disposal, as well as Kelley's home near Chicago, where the prelate received comfort and encouragement during the dreary months of exile. After Orozco's return to Mexico, his archdiocese was threatened with further confiscations, and this peril led him to ask Kelley to keep large sums of money for investment.[27]

This arrangement was satisfactory until 1924, when Kelley was appointed to Oklahoma, a move which took him from a major banking center. After waiting two years, Orozco abruptly asked for his money which he intended to invest in the East. This twist stunned Kelley, who gave up the funds but was mortally offended. Despite a friendship of a dozen years, Orozco had, to all appearances, lost confidence in his benefactor's ability to safeguard the interests of the church in Guadalajara. "I feel this matter very keenly," Kelley told the archbishop in grave tones, "and it has caused me a great deal of unhappiness."[28] The touchy American was nonetheless endowed with an extraordinary capacity to forgive. In 1929, three years after his break with Orozco, the latter was exiled for the third and last time from Mexico and received another invitation to make his home with Kelley, this time in the episcopal residence in Oklahoma City.[29] Not only had the wound healed; even the scar had vanished.

> *The real friend is the man who knows all about you and loves you in spite of it.*
>
> FCK, *Letters to Jack* (1917), 61

A survey of Kelley's friendships provides another angle into this complex person. The most obvious features of these relationships are their range and intensity. While he enjoyed strong connections with several bishops, especially Pittsburgh's Hugh C. Boyle, who served as his confidant in later years, Kelley also numbered among his friends a wide assortment of lay persons, many of whom did not belong to his church. Several artists saw in him a supportive and understanding colleague, including Frank H. Spearman, an author of some twenty volumes, several of whose stories had been adapted to the screen. He had published fiction in Kelley's monthly, *Extension Magazine*, and later helped the priest on several literary projects, notably the latter's allegorical novel entitled *Problem Island*. So congenial was their long association that in 1937 Spearman dedicated his last work to Kelley, *Carmen of the Rancho*, which was a romance about early California.[30] Another contributor to *Extension Magazine* who had won Kelley's affection was Francis Meehan, whose essays on English literature were standard texts in Catholic schools before World War II. Kelley had first known this eminent authority as Brother Leo, a member of the Brothers of the Christian Schools in California, who was later dispensed from vows and in 1941 left the religious community. At the time, the transition from religious life to lay status was more unusual and difficult than in recent times, and the departure of a nationally known educator like Meehan shocked many Catholics. Sensing Meehan's need for emotional reinforcement, Kelley offered him hospitality during his adjustment to a new life. This unsolicited invitation was an exceptional display of generosity, but it arrived too late. Meehan had already settled in the East and assured the bishop that his decision had been prompted "through no malign influence of war, wine or women" and that he left behind no "bitterness or misunderstanding." Nevertheless, Kelley's door in Oklahoma remained open to the former religious. "Don't forget," wrote the sympathetic prelate, "you have a friend out here."[31]

> *It is the dreamer in most men that makes them fit for human companionship. . . . I would walk miles to spend an evening with a dreamer, the less he "fits in" the greater my pleasure in his company. . . .*
>
> FCK, *Letters to Jack* (1917), 191

In addition to certain writers, Kelley took a special interest in a young Chicago architect, Barry Byrne, a pupil of the controversial Frank Lloyd Wright. Though little known outside his field, Byrne was a central figure in Catholic architecture in America. A brilliant innovator, he was one of the first religious architects to abandon the historic styles, such as the Byzantine-Romanesque, perhaps the most commonly used design for Catholic churches in this country. His seven years with Wright had taught him one fundamental lesson, viz., that buildings were not ornaments but shelters for living. According to Byrne, therefore, a church was basically a "holy enclosure" and should be planned from the "*inside out*"; it was the needs of the interior that determined the external mass and shape. This radical view both freed him from imitating antique modes and aligned him with the budding liturgical movement in America. In the 1920s, several monastic communities had begun to champion reforms in worship. The Mass, they advocated, is a communal prayer, and architects must allow the congregation to see and be close to the altar, two pleas which suited Byrne's religious and artistic temperament.[32] Encouraged by Kelley, he also experimented with the idea of a "Basic Church." This was a versatile master plan for a parish center which could fit many environments and combined practicality with simple beauty at low cost.

Despite their complexities, these ideas were successfully integrated in two stages in the Church of Christ the King, Tulsa, Kelley's favorite in Oklahoma. Completed in 1927 and renovated later to accommodate the liturgical reforms, the church met each of Byrne's stern specifications; and Tulsa was given a graceful, chaste building in which the sanctuary protruded into a wide, column-free nave, an ideal setting for focusing attention on the Eucharistic rite. This concept of placing architecture at the service of the liturgy drew rave reviews from designers, including Wright, and Byrne's creation was featured in general reference works like the *Encyclopaedia Britannica* as a model of a functional contemporary church. After this pioneering work in Kelley's diocese, the architect's influence grew steadily so that by 1941 he was regarded among his peers as the leading force in checking the spread of traditional-design churches in Catholic America. As Byrne's artistry increasingly came to the attention of the conservative dioceses of the East, Kelley continued to give him strong endorsements. "Barry Byrne is not a copyist," the bishop explained to a potential client in Brooklyn. "There is an original touch on everything he does."[33]

Kelley's closest friend in the arts was a celebrity little known in the United States. This was the poet, Eileen Duggan, the first writer in New Zealand decorated with the Order of the British Empire (1937). Her verse had been published in London, but it was practically unknown in America. In 1938, when Kelley toured New Zealand, he met Duggan, and from that moment became a champion of her work.[34] In an enthusiastic campaign to introduce her to an American audience, he not only recommended her verse to Catholic periodicals; he also published in the Jesuit weekly, *America,* a charming account of his visit with her and printed samples of her verse in his own books, including his autobiography, *The Bishop Jots It Down.* Toward the end of his active days he provided a final service in her behalf. During World War II, when New Zealand was threatened with a Japanese invasion, he generously accepted all of her manuscripts for safekeeping. It is little wonder then that the poet was touched by his attention over the years, a boundless kindness which, she said, had left her speechless.[35]

To have you near me is always a real inspiration.

Frank Phillips to FCK, December 8, 1939

Bishop Kelley's concern and esteem for people were not confined to Catholics; several outside the church were special to him. His closest friend in later life was, in fact, a non-Catholic, Frank Phillips, founder of the Phillips Petroleum Company. It was the latter's contribution of $50,000 in 1929 that sparked Kelley's dream to build a junior seminary in Oklahoma. Though the project collapsed, it illustrated the irony that over the years no Sooner, including the wealthy members of the Catholic laity, supported the diocese more than this freethinking oilman, and Kelley confided to his benefactor that it was largely his interest that kept the churchman from resigning his see.[36]

Phillips's favors extended beyond gifts of cash; he also offered his famous ranch, Woolaroc, for the bishop's use to entertain distinguished visitors. The estate was located in the Osage hills in northeastern Oklahoma, comprising some 11,000 acres of forest and lakes. A hotel-size ranch house accommodated guests, and for amusement there were good hunting and fishing, along with a museum, a private zoo, and a tour of an Indian settlement nearby. For those roughing it, Phillips furnished a menu which, according to Kelley, featured such frontier victuals as buffalo steak, bear loaf, and tender cutlets of antelope. These delicacies often made the mouth of the tamest urbanite water in anticipation, as Cardinal Dougherty of Philadelphia described his own reaction on reading the bishop's account of the place.[37] Into this rustic paradise Kelley brought on separate occasions the bishops of his province and two archbishops of New York—Cardinal Patrick J. Hayes in 1925 and his successor fifteen years later, Francis J. Spellman, soon to receive the red hat.[38]

But close as the two men were, Kelley failed to persuade Phillips to do two things. First, despite the bishop's insistence, the millionaire refused to take public credit for his charities, keeping his gifts anonymous in the fear that if his generosity were publicized he would be engulfed with appeals. "It is difficult to make money," he once told Kelley shrewdly, "but it is far more difficult to give it away intelligently."[39] The second area of resistance focused on the bishop's attempt to convert his benefactor to Catholicism. The latter's interest in the diocese testified to a lively religious sense, but he was unwilling to give his allegiance entirely to a single denomination. On one occasion, Kelley interpreted a comment as an invitation to lead Phillips into the fold. When the oilman observed that the two men seldom discussed religion, the bishop pursued the opening by offering to supply his friend with accounts of conversions, a natural overreaction on the part of the zealous churchman. But Phillips gently discouraged further developments with the remark: "I am a man of peculiar temperament and perhaps had better be left as I am."[40]

For a quarter of a century, the two Oklahomans forged the strongest bond of friendship. Perhaps the mutual respect was based partly on the fact that both were imaginative organizers. While Phillips was creating a business empire which expanded from oil production into refining and retailing, Kelley was transforming a hesitant Catholic community into a visible and respected minority in America's "Bible Belt." Aside from these similarities in vision, they admired one another profoundly. Kelley regarded Phillips as the most charitable man he knew, and the latter viewed the bishop as a vital force for raising the religious tone of the state. By the end of Kelley's active life, both men acknowledged their singular love for each other. This mutual affection probably reached its finest expression in 1940 when

Kelley observed his seventieth birthday. The highlight of the celebration came when a large bouquet of roses, seventy in number, reached the bishop's home, a present from Phillips. No gift gave the septuagenarian more pleasure that day, and Kelley divided the roses between the chapel and dining room, giving his anniversary a happily festive air.[41]

> *When Loyalty leaves this earth there will be nothing worthwhile remaining; for the joy will have gone out of life.*
>
> FCK, *Letters to Jack* (1917), 231

It is one thing to befriend talented artists and businessmen and quite another to remain faithful to those who have fallen from grace. Kelley's admirable quality was his capacity to uphold some of the mavericks of his generation. The most notable instance of this centered on his defense of Edward L. Doheny, the petroleum baron whose name was tarnished in the 1920s during the congressional investigation of the leasing of federal oil fields to private producers. The bishop's connection with Doheny dated from the previous decade through a common interest in events in Mexico and Ireland. Meeting in London after World War I, the two men found themselves in agreement over the injustices of the regime of Venustiano Carranza in Mexico, Doheny defending his oil rights in that country and Kelley protesting the persecution of the church. Turning their eyes to Europe, they were also one in the conviction that British rule in Ireland must end.[42]

Doheny's troubles arose from an association with an old prospector friend, Albert B. Fall, a cunning politico from New Mexico who headed the Department of the Interior under President Harding. In 1921 Doheny loaned the secretary $100,000 to purchase a ranch in his home state, and the next year the oilman was awarded, without competitive bidding, a federal contract to build a large naval fuel station at Pearl Harbor, Hawaii, along with drilling rights in the naval oil reserve at Elk Hills, California. An inquiry followed, climaxing with the sensational indictment of Fall and Doheny for bribery and conspiracy to defraud the government. Civil and criminal trials dragged on for years, resulting in Fall's imprisonment and Doheny's loss of his investments in Pearl Harbor and Elk Hills valued at $20 million; but the oilman was exonerated of all criminal charges.

Throughout this ordeal, no one was more faithful to the Doheny family than the plain-speaking bishop in Oklahoma. Kelley's close study of the case had convinced him of his friend's innocence. The prelate volunteered to go on the stand as a character witness and urged the defendant to publish his apologia for which Kelley had even recruited an Irish playwright to serve as ghostwriter.[43] When religious publications questioned the oilman's faith, Kelley rose sharply to his defense. This happened in 1926 when *The Acolyte*, an influential fortnightly for priests, referred to Doheny as "nominally a Catholic." In a blistering rejoinder to the editor-in-chief, Kelley cited as evidence of genuine belief Doheny's benefactions to the diocese of Los Angeles, where he lived, such as St. Vincent de Paul's Church, a jewel of a building that combined the baroque and Spanish-mission styles, and the seminary in Camarillo, which was a special object of Doheny's charity.[44] While these gifts did not necessarily make Doheny a practicing Catholic, they certainly proved his interest in religious institutions and inspired Kelley to vindicate his friend.

The personal tragedies that befell the family during their legal hassles also evoked a stream of sympathetic messages from Oklahoma. The worst domestic crisis occurred in 1929 when Doheny's son was murdered by a secretary who then committed suicide. At a loss as how to comfort the grief-stricken parents, Kelley tried to alleviate their near despair in divine providence with this advice: ". . . one thought of God may be as powerful a prayer in the intensity of it as a thousand spoken carelessly as sometimes, alas, we do. We do not know God's ways but we do know that He is love and mercy."[45] Even Doheny's death in 1935 did not end Kelley's determination to clear his friend's reputation. Not only did the bishop preach a glowing eulogy at the requiem but also paid a public tribute in his next publication, *Problem Island.* One of Kelley's most inventive works, this novel was dedicated to Doheny's memory, and one of the principal characters was patterned after the deceased oilman in the form of a generous and enlightened prospector who arranges an elaborate experiment to test the thesis of whether man is naturally religious.[46] This was not all. Five years after Doheny's death, Kelley summed up his long and steadfast connection with this family in a letter to a Methodist bishop; it was the Oklahoman's final argument for the defense before the jury of public opinion:

> Yes, I was an old friend of the Doheny's who stuck to them in their troubles; not alone, however, because of friendship but because I knew that Mr. Doheny was not the kind of a man to exercise his talents by breaking the commandments.[47]

A less celebrated instance of Kelley's attachment to discredited friends, but one no less telling, involved his grant of sanctuary to Joseph F. Hallissey, a Detroit priest who left his diocese under awkward circumstances. As young pastors in Michigan, Kelley and Hallissey had become close friends, each priest visiting the other from time to time in his rectory; and the relationship had deepened to the extent that when Kelley celebrated his first pontifical Mass as a prothonotary apostolic in 1916, he asked Hallissey to serve as the preacher.[48] A decade later, however, Hallissey's star began to wane when charges were made against his moral character, forcing him to resign his parish. His health and spirit broken, he appealed to his old comrade in Oklahoma, who responded with a ready welcome to join him. An ecclesiastical trial could have settled the issue, and Kelley actually took the case to Rome, adding a strong endorsement of the priest's integrity. The accused, however, demurred on the grounds that the expense would be too great and, more importantly, that the calling of lay witnesses in his behalf would be a source of greater scandal.[49]

Though, technically, Hallissey was never excardinated from the diocese of Detroit, Kelley, with full confidence in his innocence, assigned him to the Newman Foundation at the University of Oklahoma. The bishop's faith was amply rewarded; his friend's ministry to the campus was exemplary.[50] In 1943, after more than a decade with the academic community at Norman, Hallissey reached his fiftieth year in the priesthood, and Kelley wished to reward him with a monsignorship. The bishop confided his plan to the jubilarian's superior in Detriot, Archbishop Edward Mooney. The latter discouraged the idea, correctly suggesting that if a request for the prelacy were sent to Rome, the curia would examine the file and discover that according to the record Hallissey had been removed from his parish and had waived a trial. No papal honor would be granted until these black marks were erased.[51] This logic, although disappointing to Kelley, laid the matter to rest. But the incident shows again how devoted he could be to those who suffered reversals. While in the minds of many both Doheny and Hallissey were pariahs, this unhappy fact did not sour Kelley's attitude toward them. No matter how public opinion had scourged Doheny, no matter how serious the charges against Hallissey had been, the bishop of Oklahoma abandoned neither and did what he could to rehabilitate their reputations.

> *I made my seminary studies in Quebec and I know the people of "Our Lady of the Snows." I scrapped with them often but liked them always. I knew their loyalty to ideals and how easy it was to misunderstand them.*
>
> FCK to Eugene Exman, September 28, 1942

Kelley's courage was not limited to defending friends whose good names had been blemished; he was ready to take up some of the unpopular causes of his day. Singlehandedly, at the turn of the twentieth century, he forced the leaders of a city-based Catholicism to see the religious crisis in rural America, and founded the Catholic Church Extension Society, a story to be told later. Afterwards he devoted three decades to an intrepid defense of the church in Mexico at a time when the majority of

Americans ignored or favored the course of the revolution, including its violent anticlericalism. Equally indicative of the strength of his convictions was his sympathy for another underdog, the French Canadians.

Because he was a native of Canada and received part of his education in the province of Quebec, he understood the truncated nationalism of his *habitant* countrymen. As editor of a Catholic monthly, he openly agreed with them over an explosive issue in the final days of World War I. The length of the war in Europe had forced Canada by 1917 to abandon its traditional reliance on volunteers for fighting abroad and to impose compulsory miltary service. When the *Canadiens* objected to this change of policy, the country was divided as it had not been in nearly a century, and Kelley's editorials in *Extension Magazine* excoriated the government.[52] The issue arose again when World War II broke out in 1939. The *Canadiens* made it clear from the beginning that while they were prepared to defend their native soil, they opposed the draft for duty overseas; and the government was compelled to pledge itself against conscription. The issue slept for three years before Ottawa called a national referendum, asking the electorate to release it from its promise regarding conscription. Canada was split as it had been earlier, with the English-speaking majority overwhelmingly in favor of giving Ottawa a free hand, while three-quarters of the *Québécois* opposed the motion. This reaction was sufficient to force the government again to postpone its plan to conscript troops.

These developments alarmed patriotic Americans, who viewed the *Canadien* intransigence as no less treasonable than the active collaboration of Vichy France with the Axis powers. During the debate Kelley saw the need to explain French Canada to his puzzled countrymen and contacted a New York *Times* editor, Neil MacNeil. Like Kelley, he had spent his childhood in Canada's maritime provinces, and now commissioned a series of articles by the bishop.[53] After conducting interviews in Quebec, Montreal, and Ottawa, Kelley published his report in September of 1942. The issue, he argued, was deeper than that of military service; at the root lay a collision between two ways of life. The *Canadien* was a romantic provincial with strong ties to North America, its past and its soil. Coupled with this were a powerful religious perspective on life and a vivid sense of belonging to an oppressed minority. Arrayed against him was the paradoxical Anglo-Canadian—a modern individualist, on the one hand, relentlessly pursuing his own material success regardless of Canada's welfare, and, on the other hand, a hidebound imperialist in his blind devotion to his country's membership in the British Commonwealth. Neither his individualism nor his imperialism, Kelley pointed out, focused on Canada in its own right.

With this original twist in viewpoint, Kelley portrayed the *habitant* as Canada's true nationalist, and appealed to all supporters of the Allies for patience. "Must we go into every war great or small, that Britain wages?" he quoted one *Canadien* as having asked. "If so, adieu to our dream of nationhood."[54] As the articles circulated throughout the United States, Kelley's friends found them enlightening on a complicated topic, and some of them were genuinely impressed with his powers of analysis. In providing the best exposition of French Canada for Americans, he displayed not only his sympathy for a misunderstood minority but also his skill in handling subjects of a controversial nature. One of the leading editors of the day, Eugene Exman of Harper's, who had guided the bishop through the publication of his autobiography, judged the articles as "first rate journalism."[55]

> *No priest can win the love of his people who does not show by his every action that he is safe in the love of God.*
>
> FCK, *Dominus Vobiscum* (1922), 102

So much of Kelley's life was bound up with organizations that no picture of his person would be complete without a discussion of him as an administrator. Though his direction of a mission-aid agency like Extension and later of the diocese of Oklahoma occupied most of his time, his years in charge of St.

Francis Xavier Parish in Wilmette, Illinois, are no less revealing of his executive ability. Demands outside the parish forced him to delegate much responsibility to his assistants who became junior partners in parochial administration. "The more responsibility you put upon a subordinate," was his cardinal rule, "the bigger and brighter you are making that subordinate. It is by ruling that he learns how best to serve. The wisest ruler is he who gives the fewest orders but looks for the greatest results."[56]

In spite of the free rein given to his helpers, Kelley remained in command and cultivated an effective pastoral style. Each week parishioners looked forward to his mounting of the low pulpit in the sanctuary where, as one of his former altar boys recalls, they were "both enlightened and entertained." His sermons were instructive, clear, well-prepared, appropriate in length, and often amusing. He never harangued or pontificated; he was a preacher who was always relaxed and smiling, whose delivery was natural, sincere, and enormously persuasive. What evoked even more attention was his way with the parish announcements whereby his gentle humor could make the most humdrum item sparkle. "At least once or twice each Sunday," our witness notes further,

> the congregation was chuckling at his comments, often laughing out loud. His touch was light, always unexpected, often droll. Yet it was never of the "set-up," premeditated joke type of humor. Rather it seemed to come from a spontaneous capacity to see the humor inherent—to puncture the pompous, the overstated or pedantic. And it was local in its references, dealing with the goings on around us.

When Mass was over, he was seen regularly in the rear vestibule of the church where "it was largely a laughing exchange with the many who wanted to trade a word with him." Wilmette was not surprised in 1924 when it learned of his transfer to Oklahoma; everyone knew that he was truly a remarkable man, "a little bigger than life, . . . too special to stay long in a small suburban church." After six years as pastor, Kelley had had a unique and lasting impact on his congregation. "No one could have followed and filled his niche in our hearts," concludes Kelley's former acolyte. "The particular light, and lightness, he brought to that low pulpit left with him. . . . We loved him."[57]

Francis Kelley's relationship with two prominent households in the vicinity provides a more intimate view of his pastoral style. The first was that of Edward Hines, a lumber merchant and major benefactor of Saint Mary of the Lake Seminary at Mundelein, Illinois, whose family belonged to what Kelley called "high society." The pastor was amused by the trivial maneuverings of his wealthy friends, including the Hineses, and he was not reluctant to satirize their antics. The appearances of visiting celebrities presented the smart set with opportunities for one-upmanship, and in 1921 Kelley noted that the Hineses scored the triumph of the season when they entertained a young foreigner who belonged to one of the great sovereign dynasties of Europe. The guest was Prince René, a son of the last duke of Parma and a thoroughbred Bourbon whose sister and brother had wedded the rulers of Austria-Hungary and Luxembourg and who himself had married into the royal family of Denmark. While these pedigreed connections dazzled Chicago's society, they appeared to have had little effect on Kelley. Privately, he ridiculed all the fuss, lampooning the visitor as the "real thing, blue blood, royal descent, rings on his fingers and bells on his toes, Brother of an Empress, Brother-in-Law of a Grand Duchess, Cousin of all the Kings of Europe. Rah, rah, rah, Sis Boom Bah!" The round of receptions displaying the prince enabled the Hineses, as Kelley further noted mischievously, to "put it over their enemies in great shape."[58]

These occasions, however, in which the pastor poked fun at some of his spiritual charges were rare; his concern for them all, and the Hineses in particular, was authentic. He was present to share in their joyful milestones as when he officiated at the lavish wedding of their daughter, Loretta Hines. And he was a "tower of strength"—*turris fortis,* as the first two words of his episcopal coat of arms read—when he preached at their funerals, the saddest of which was that of Edward, Jr., the eldest Hines son who had gone to Europe in World War I as a young army officer and whose body was brought back from France and buried in a special chapel on the grounds of the seminary at Mundelein.[59]

The other notable family which knew Kelley as its pastor was that of Mr. and Mrs. Claude G. Burnham, whose three sons continued to interest him long after his departure from Wilmette for Oklahoma. The Burnhams had likewise moved from Illinois and settled in the East, where only Philip kept up with Kelley. As editor of the Catholic weekly, *The Commonweal,* Philip published several pieces by his former pastor, along with others recommended by him. Kelley's occasional inquiries regarding the family's Catholicity encouraged Philip to report in 1939 on the spiritual condition of his two brothers who, the bishop had learned elsewhere, had lapsed from the church.[60] This impression was not entirely accurate. Finding the Catholic doctrine of the Real Presence difficult, David had not received the Eucharist in years but, as Philip explained, was still "Catholic" in his allegiance, attending weekly Mass and defending the church against his agnostic friends. More intellectual and complicated than Philip, James Burnham, the eldest son, was on the threshold of becoming a leading political philosopher of his generation in America. His original views on the "managerial revolution" would in two years delineate for the world a major shift in the mechanics of capitalism. After returing from Oxford, he taught at New York University, where he blended the ideas of Aristotle, Saint Thomas Aquinas, and Karl Marx into a unique system. Though he was an avowed Trotskyist at this stage, the courses he taught centered on traditional Christian thought, especially that of Aquinas and Dante. These struggles of faith disturbed Kelley, who felt that he was still entitled to offer words of advice; and his counsel was standard fare for the day. Tell David and James, he instructed Philip, that he too had experienced doubts as a student in Canada but had discovered that nothing satisfied the mind and heart better than the church's creed and the philosophy of St. Thomas.[61] This simple recipe would hardly satisfy the subtle tastes of these two pilgrims, but it was offered in the spirit of real concern from one whose religious belief was a precious and comforting treasure to be shared with those he felt less fortunate.

If a bishop is not a pastor to his clergy, he is not going to fulfil his other duties with any high degree of merit or success.

FCK, *Sacerdos et Pontifex* (1940), 74

The gentle firmness that characterized Kelley's pastoral style in Wilmette was equally evident in Oklahoma, where he served as bishop for a quarter century. His approach to episcopal administration was epitomized in the fatherly caveat he offered to a younger prelate, Joseph F. Rummel, on the occasion of the latter's appointment to the archdiocese of New Orleans. The problems of that southern see, Kelley cautioned, required a "master hand in a very soft glove."[62] This mixture of autocrat and diplomat governed Kelley's own leadership of a diocese in the heart of fundamentalist America. First, he was a tough superior, imposing upon his clergy the highest standards of service. He would not tolerate priestly scoldings of parish congregations, badgering for money, irresponsible indebtedness, or indifference toward non-Catholics. He gravely warned a quarrelsome pastor that his temper "irritated" people, and the bishop went on to say: "When you feel these surges of anger come over you, . . . reach for your rosary and say a decade before you act—it is as good a cure as I have reason to know."[63] To another, he urged that money must never become a topic in the pulpit. A better way to increase parish revenues was personal contact, either through visiting homes in the community or mailing appeals when necessary.[64]

The casual use of funds, whether parochial or personal, also disturbed Kelley, who frequently reprimanded priests for neglecting their financial obligations. These hapless clergymen were tagged clerical fakers, "four-flushers," and the chancellor of the diocese often took pains to warn the clergy of the bishop's eruptions of temper over this matter. "He loses confidence in a man who does not pay what he owes," Monsignor Dudek explained to one offender. "Another priest in the diocese saved himself from absolute explusion only because he had the good luck to die before the Bishop acted."[65] In Kelley's view, it was a disgrace for a priest to leave creditors with unpaid bills; and on occasion the prelate went so far as to settle accounts out of his own pocket.

Coupled with this insistence on avoiding offense was his positive mandate that each priest should be actively engaged in evangelization. Ironically, the greatest disappointment of Francis Kelley, America's premier home-missioner, was the small number of conversions to Catholicism for which he was directly responsible. His years as president of Extension in Chicago and bishop in Oklahoma, although evangelical in spirit, had tied him bodily to an office at the periphery of this ministry. "I organized, I wrote, I went to conventions," he recalled after nearly half a century in the priesthood. "Did I get anything more out of it all than a transient reputation? Almost nothing. There arose a disturbing fact: my converts were few."[66] Nonetheless, he resolved to compensate for this personal shortcoming through his clergy. Midway in his episcopate, he made it clear that no pastor should remain idle in his rectory, ministering only to the members of his own parish. Certain incentives were introduced in order to encourage each priest to go out and contact non-Catholics. When there arose opportunities for promotion to a position of greater responsibility in the diocese, the first question the bishop would ask was whether the candidate was zealous in making converts.[67]

Exacting as he was, Kelley tempered this severity with a benign interest in his clergy. The essence of this solicitude was twofold. First, he was aware of the priestly heroism in many Oklahoma parishes, and second, he was able to communicate his satisfaction for work well-done. No one was taken for granted, and the bishop expressed appreciation of those in the field. "We take credit," he once confessed, "for the labor of others a thousand times more devoted, more zealous and by far more humble than ourselves, as a right due to us to whom nothing is due."[68] Dedicated priests in Oklahoma were therefore designated as "unselfish" and "self-sacrificing." If a priest's health broke down, he was given an order to seek immediate medical care, along with Kelley's promise that if his current assignment was too taxing, a substitute would be found, as well as quarters in the bishop's own home. On several occasions, Kelley fretted when he did not have a less burdensome appointment for those whose work had earned some relief. Disintegrating parishes troubled him, too, where priests labored courageously but where natural disasters, like the drought of the 1930s, destroyed their congregations—a problem which he himself had faced as a young pastor in rural Michigan.[69] Not everyone recognized his good will, but some junior clergymen openly regarded him as their spiritual father, an affirmation which strengthened his own morale. "Now and then bishops need a bit of cheering," he confided to a young chaplain, "for not many days go by without something to depress them. The bits of cheering that come in from their own clergy are always the most encouraging kind."[70]

> *Who is the Enthusiast? He is the conqueror and the king, the leader in every movement . . . the blazer in every trail, the pathfinder into every jungle. . . .He is Progress personified.*
>
> FCK, *Letters to Jack* (1917), 149-50

The clearest record of Kelley's parental attitude toward his younger associates is found in the early career of Stephen A. Leven, one of the first native Oklahomans ordained for the diocese and a future bishop in neighboring Texas. Leven was an "Enthusiast," a rare combination of apostle and intellectual. He has been trained at the University of Louvain and had become, in his early priesthood, the leading exponent of "street preaching" in America, setting up temporary pulpits in open spaces and engaging any passers-by in discussing the Catholic faith. Kelley admired this modern zealot and wanted him to pursue graduate studies in philosophy, possibly as a prelude to a university post in Oklahoma. An arrangement was made whereby Leven returned to Louvain in 1935 and earned his doctorate three years later. The academic environment abroad did not rob him of his evangelist's fervor. While taking advanced courses, he wrote articles on "street preaching," one of which Kelley had published in *America*; and during research visits to London, he perfected his forensic technique with talks in Hyde Park as a member of the Catholic Evidence Guild. As he neared the end of drafting his doctoral dissertation, he confessed to the bishop that these years in Europe had only made him "just plain homesick for . . . the outdoor platform in Oklahoma."[71]

Stephen Leven's prestigious degree from Louvain opened up avenues for appointments to national institutions in the East; and Kelley, though wishing to keep him at home, never stood in the way of his advancement. The Catholic University of America invited him to join the faculty, the overtures coming directly from the rector and from another Louvain alumnus, Fulton J. Sheen, then professor of philosophy. Though declining this offer and retaining his parish in Oklahoma, Leven accepted in 1939 the directorship of the National Center, Confraternity of Christian Doctrine, a bureau which coordinated programs in religious education with headquarters in Washington, D.C. At this time, his extroverted ways, scholarly accomplishments, and contacts in the East prompted several confreres to whisper among themselves that Leven had lost his humility. Kelley was aware of the backroom gossip but never lost faith in his protégé. In the bishop's view, Leven was a true missionary, having no desire to serve outside his native diocese and, despite a certain bravado, betraying no inclination toward ecclesiastical careerism. "He is not ambitious in any but a good way," Kelley indicated privately to a friend. "He had a wonderful chance in Washington to proceed along a path that might have led to high promotion, but his heart was in Oklahoma and its dusty roads."[72] It was an appreciative superior who framed this secret tribute to the young Sooner's fidelity to his diocese.

> *. . . you have the ability, the knowledge, the finesse, and the force of character, to get things done on a large scale. . . .*
>
> Francis Gilfillan to FCK, December 4, 1928

While Bishop Kelley was grateful to keep his talented priests at home, his own perspective was panoramic, encompassing a wide spectrum of national issues. Two projects especially occupied him in the last decade of his active life, and both illustrated not only his leadership among peers in the episcopate but also the special "Kelley touch" in fulfilling delicate assignments. The first issue involved the solvency of the National Catholic Welfare Conference. Established in 1919 in Washington, D.C., this organization served as the general staff of the American hierarchy. Though, technically, its pronouncements bound no bishop in his diocese, it offered a variety of services and executed the policies of collective action which the assembled prelates approved at their annual meetings. The heart of the NCWC was the Administrative Board, composed of ten leading bishops and governing an elaborate network of departments that ranged from Education to Social Action. Ever since his nomination to the episcopacy in 1924, Kelley had participated in the conference's deliberations at the bishops' meetings, and he entered the inner circle eleven years later when he was elected to the Administrative Board and named its treasurer. At the time of this appointment, the NCWC's financial base was deteriorating; on receiving the ledgers, Kelley discovered that the cash balance of the organization had dropped to an appalling $1.17![73] The depression had forced bishops to delay and sometimes to withhold the payment of their assessments; and these lapses created a chronic shortage of money. A seasoned fund-raiser, Kelley was expected to smooth the uneven operation in Washington by collecting the revenues on time.

The problem confronting the NCWC treasurer was that many bishops had never accepted the importance of the conference and resented their duty to support it. Kelley's closest friend in the episcopate, Bishop Boyle of Pittsburgh, himself a member of the Administrative Board, admitted having grown a "bit cynical" over its future.[74] The new treasurer recognized the need for a fresh strategy to raise money. If the NCWC merited a low priority in many dioceses, it was foolish for him to remind the bishops of their commitment by merely sending grim financial reports, the method used by his predecessors. Calling upon more positive techniques of persuasion, he blitzed his colleagues with appeals in which he exerted his considerable charm and humor. His best circular appeared in the bleak spring of 1936, when dust storms were sweeping through Oklahoma and the cash in the NCWC account had again fallen to critical levels. ". . . the outlook for the summer," Kelley wrote in mock despair, "is blacker than the dust this State is so busy exporting to its neighbors. I need a bit of encouragement." Comments like this drew the attention of all the bishops to their obligation and even brought surprise commendations from some. Archbishop John J. Mitty of San Francisco, a tightfisted administrator known to keep a sure hold on his reserves, hailed these letters as "masterpieces" that glowed with optimism amid the gloom and, at last, made the NCWC appear to be a "family affair."[75]

Kelley's most delicate responsibility was to nudge the more prominent bishops—the "big boys"—into paying on time. A consistent offender was none other than Cardinal George W. Mundelein of Chicago, one of the major sources of the NCWC's income. Year after year, the cardinal's important check would arrive at what he admitted to be the "eleventh hour" and only after a "gentle push" from the treasurer. Despite this awkward situation, Kelley kept the finances in good order, paying salaries and bills punctually, sometimes without much time to spare. To Mundelein, he compared himself to a breathless Notre Dame football coach in a closely matched game. "In the second half,"

Kelley explained, hoping to jog the Chicagoan's conscience, "one is intent and anxious just to pull through each minute of play and keep a few points ahead."[76] At any rate, the Oklahoman's six-year tenure was a striking success, a personal triumph in which he managed quietly to raise the NCWC's cash balance from virtually nothing to almost $68,000. This sum was equivalent to more than one-third of the annual budget and gave his successor a comfortable cushion with which to begin the new fiscal year. Never had the conference been more secure than it was in 1941, when Kelley was followed by Archbishop Samuel A. Stritch of Chicago, who regarded the Oklahoman's work behind the scenes no less monumental than any of his more visible accomplishments.[77]

The second project to demonstrate Kelley's special magic as a national leader concerned the integration of Catholic youth into the Boy Scouts movement. In 1916, eight years after its foundation in Great Britain, the movement had been chartered by the United States Congress as the "Boy Scouts of America," and large numbers of boys in early adolescence were enrolled in its program of citizenship training and outdoor activities. Many Catholics favored it as an antidote to the efforts of totalitarian regimes in Europe to win their youth to fascism or communism, efforts which churchmen in America feared would spread across the Atlantic and cripple their programs for young people.

Promising as the Boy Scouts movement was, however, its nonsectarian character appeared to weaken the moral training it offered. Catholic leaders, notably Cardinals Hayes and Mundelein, refused to affiliate with the National Council, BSA, until there could be arranged separate Catholic units. These would both follow the standard scouting program and develop an additional component for spiritual formation.[78] This policy created a complicated situation. The BSA was reluctant to make exceptions that would erode the unity of its program, whereas the bishops required special spiritual exercises for their youth. Only a master's touch could succeed in bringing the religious and scouting leaders together over this issue.

In 1932 the bishops were prepared to negotiate with the National Council, and Kelley was given the critical role of chairman of the Catholic Committee on Scouting. Taking command, he expanded the committee membership to fifteen bishops who promptly drafted a plan of affiliation. In March, 1933, a formal partnership was sealed when the National Council approved not only this plan but also Kelley's committee as the official liaison between the bishops and the BSA.[79] The next step was to promote scouting in the dioceses. As chairman, Kelley's key contribution consisted of persuading individual bishops to build diocesan organizations around local chaplains and commissions composed of clergy and laity. He also secured the services of a splendid executive director, Edward Roberts Moore, a New York priest in charities work who looked after the details and assisted dioceses in developing their scouting programs.[80]

Bishop Kelley's mission was virtually completed in only six years. By 1939 the number of all-Catholic units, approximately 4,000, had more than doubled, and the BSA had swung around to a full endorsement of church-sponsored troops. So widespread had Catholic affiliation been under him that some scouting executives wondered privately whether the bishops would desert the BSA and institute a separate organization of their own or whether, in the words of one alarmed officer, they simply planned to "take over the whole Scout movement in America." This uneasiness delighted Kelley, who nonetheless gave assurances that the hierarchy had no such designs. Both parties continued to cooperate and in time recognized his central role in the partnership. In 1939 the BSA honored him with one of its highest awards, the Silver Buffalo. Three years later, the bishops presented him with a jewel-studded "Ad Altare Dei" medal, marking their gratitude for a decade of managing the Catholic Committee on Scouting, and they informally dubbed him the "Eagle Scout of the hierarchy," a nickname he cherished more than either of the decorations.[81] More importantly, the NCWC confirmed the importance of his achievement in 1940 when it expanded the committee into a separate Youth Department in charge of supervising all Catholic youth activities. This development signaled, in the Oklahoman's view, that the bishops no longer regarded his work with the BSA as "one of Kelley's fads."[82]

> *Our need is for bishops who pray at their work and make their work pray.*
>
> FCK, *Sacerdos et Pontifex* (1940), 14

The final word must be reserved for the deepest and, from the outsider's viewpoint, the most elusive of Francis Kelley's dimensions, his spirituality. One must step gingerly beyond the natural into the life of grace; these probings into the secrets of the soul are no better than tentative. Earlier, we have seen how Kelley lived the gospel values in his spiritual concern for his friends, parishioners, and clergy and in his zeal to share his faith with non-Catholics and those who might have drifted from the church. As in the case of most priests of his time, this ministry flowed from the daily spiritual exercises of meditation, Mass, visit to the Blessed Sacrament, rosary, and devotional reading. This standard routine, however, Kelley adapted in two curious ways which revealed that he did not share the advanced views of his day on spirituality. Since the turn of the century in Europe, liturgical crusaders like Belgium's Lambert Beauduin, O.S.B., had condemned the excessively subjective and private character of prayer that prevailed in the church. These reformers advocated the revival of corporate worship, focusing their attention mostly on the Mass and the Divine Office, and winning many followers in America.

This movement eventually remolded the whole of Western liturgy; but, with the exception of the work of architect, Barry Byrne, Kelley appeared oblivious to it. While he offered Mass everyday, this was ordinarily done alone, without a congregation, around midnight. Insomnia kept him working until the small hours of the morning, and he slept late. This condition forced him to get permission from Rome to celebrate Mass before retiring, a practice which few diocesan priests were allowed to follow and which, to the horror of the liturgists, shifted the Eucharist from a communal rite to virtually a private devotion. Likewise, he was obliged to pray the Divine Office. Known since Vatican Council II as the "Liturgy of the Hours," the Office is the official prayer of the church, consisting of the public or private recitation of psalms, hymns, and readings at prescribed times each day. It arose largely out of the ancient monastic tradition to consecrate the course of each day to God. Priests in Bishop Kelley's time, whether in choir or not, were bound to participate in this prayer and, as ministers of the church, to keep its corporate, or "ecclesial," spirit. Though he was a voracious reader, a problem in Kelley's left eye somehow complicated his use of the breviary—the cause is vague; and he secured another indult to commute this obligation to some private prayers.[83]

Kelley's spirituality, therefore, was out of step with current trends. It was not nourished by the liturgical life of the church as such; rather, it drew its greatest strength from the personal reflection he did in preparing his sermons and books. Outmoded as it was, this religious individualism produced an authentic interior life. This is evident from a sample of his thoughts on a type of mental prayer known as "meditation," in which one, through reflection upon a religious mystery, strengthens his resolve always to act in a Christian manner. "In its best form it is like talking to God with the tongue of the spirit, and hearing Him answer with the ears of the soul. . . ," he once noted. "It is filled with consolations unknown to those who never practice it. At its poorest it is the highest form of prayer, at its best it is a foretaste of heaven's joy." Though the grace of religious ecstacy had been denied to him, this description points to a vivid inner union with God. He also found meditation to have a direct impact upon his behavior insofar as it gifted him with increasing self-knowledge. ". . . while it sends the soul exploring the heavens," he explained, "those who feed on it are the sanest and most sensible men. My follies are at their greatest when I neglect my meditation."[84]

These insights, less striking in their originality perhaps than in their eloquence, flowed from a solid prayer life and earned for him wide respect as an authority on spirituality. His retreats and devotional books were enormously popular. He conducted spiritual conferences for clergymen from coast to coast, and several of his publications were religious best sellers. What made his work so significant was his ability to blend a fresh appreciation of the Christian mysteries with bold and original applications to everyday life. Priests, for instance, were long struck by his prescription concerning how to make their sermons concrete and interesting. "Get the habit of reading every day out of the book of nature," he recommended:

> Study bugs and beetles, grass and violets, trees and frogs, flies and elephants, stars and comets, maps and vegetables, men and minerals, oceans and bath tubs, baseball and physics, poetry and brickmaking, statesmen and bolshevists, rulers and the ruins they left behind them. Now you are laughing. Please don't! I am telling you the simple truth. A good preacher must know enough about everything to summon everything to testify for God and the truth. You need examples. You must marshal your metaphors and drill your similies [*sic*]. You must advance your soldiers to the trenches, and follow your regiment, in the uniform of religion, to the shock of the battle. To do that well you must develop in you the habit of observation. Enlist your fighters. The soldiers will spring out of their barracks in your brain as soon as you need them. They are a loyal lot, these recruits you have gathered from

> your walks in the woods and your delving into books. They are anxious to serve; only you will not have them unless you go out where they live and recruit them.[85]

Observations like this one were not the banalities of one who skimmed the surface of religious truth ,or who pilfered the thought of others; they were always personal and imaginative—often described as *Kelleyesque*—and sometimes penetrating and worthy of the greatest spiritual masters.

A faint discord, however, blemishes this symphony of spiritual harmony and balance. While able to help others, Bishop Kelley was not at complete peace with himself, especially in his later years in Oklahoma. He was no stranger to suffering, physcial or emotional, and his books provide some of the wisest advice on how to cope with it. But he seems to have been afflicted with a dark wound which no remedy would heal. Even the worldly Mencken sensed in his friend a melancholy and compulsiveness that drove him into a blizzard of activity and frequent travels out of the state. Once Kelley realized that his future would end in the Southwest, his energies confined largely to a satellite diocese, he felt isolated and finished, far from the scenes of his greatest triumphs and with little to look forward to. This discovery cast him into what some might interpret as a lingering fatalism. He dutifully accepted the role that God had chosen for him, but he wondered why. "I have no enemies that I know of," he told Peter Guilday, the ranking Catholic church historian of his day,

> but then I have no friends, and I am far away from the places where friends count. I am just resigned to the lot God has given me. History may treat me more kindly, but I shall then be dead and it will not matter.[86]

Close to the root of Kelley's spirit there flowed two opposite currents—a firm trust in divine providence and a haunting bewilderment regarding its reasons. This vortex of colliding waters conjured up moods which, on occasion, pushed his stoic resignation to the edges of self-pity.

In these vignettes from the life of Francis Clement Kelley, one can detect all of the major qualities which made him an influential leader in American church—his love for the priesthood and interest in the missions, his compassion for the victimized, his sound management of men and money, his erudition and self-confidence without vanity, his ability to befriend a potpourri of tycoons, artists, and rough-hewn plainsmen, his attraction to public controversy, his receptivity to the unconventional, his generous outpouring of self and resources, his encompassing vision of the church and repugnance to what he called the "selfishness of parochialism,"[87] his ultimate faith in a merciful but mysterious God. Yet these glimpses into Kelley's life reveal a man not without defects. A zeal for quick results frequently triggered his inclination toward impetuosity. His tendency to exceed his authority in several instances led him into unnecessary struggles. Often his aggressiveness in public debate needlessly embittered his opponents and projected him as a narrow, hopelessly pugnacious bigot. The fragile shell protecting his self-esteem likewise made him vulnerable to any unexpected blow.

> *How good God is to let us regret; for by regrets we keep humble and loving; by regrets we try to do the new task better. It is only those who have made a complete failure of life who are without regrets, since only the complete failures are fools enough to think that they did all things well.*
>
> FCK, *Letters to Jack* (1917), 252

This was a complex organism, not perfect as he himself admitted, a churchman whose vivid but flawed humanity stood in full view without obstruction. Now that we have become acquainted with him, we can proceed to his life and work. This brings us to the very beginning—to Kelley's Island.

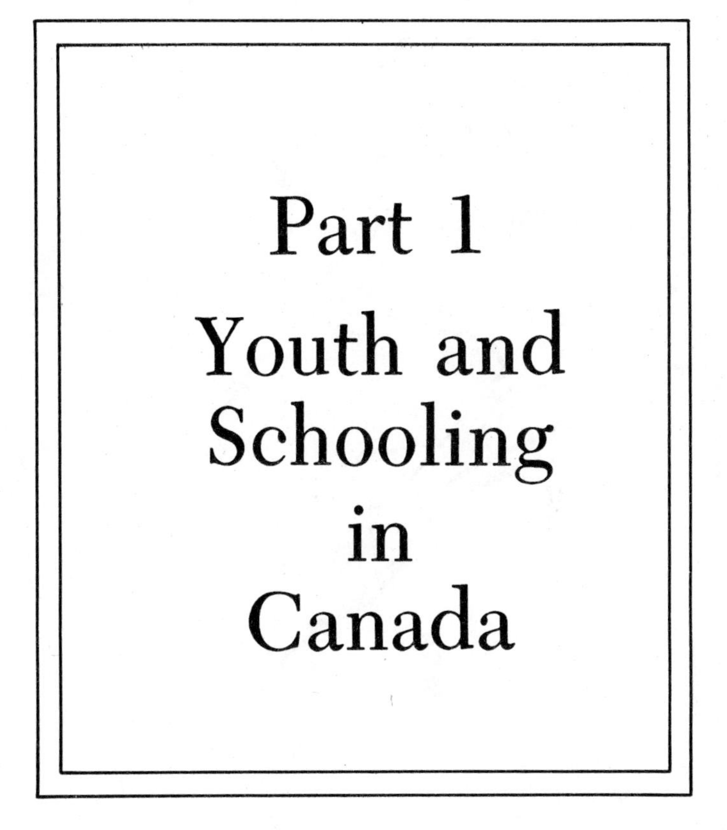

Part 1
Youth and Schooling in Canada

(1870-1893)

CITIES OF KELLEY'S YOUTH AND EARLY MANHOOD

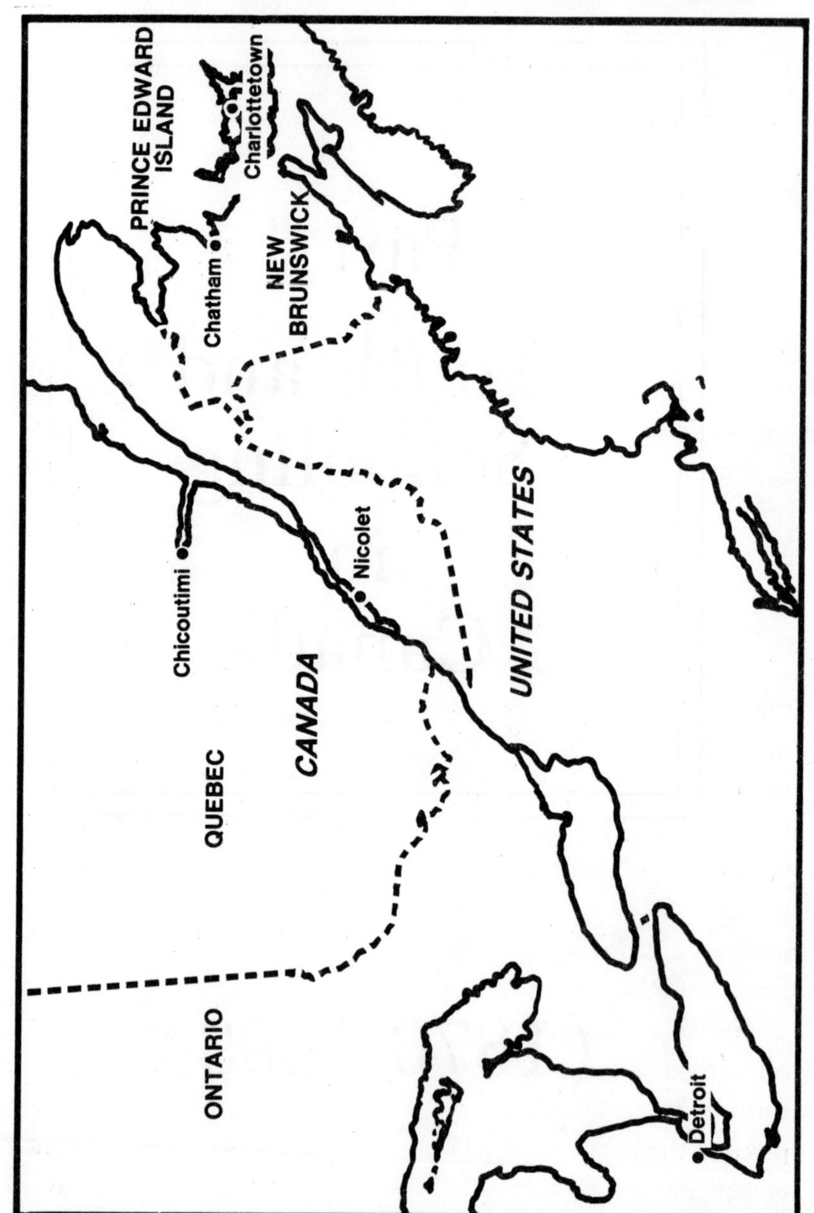

I
The Islander

Prince Edward Island is a delicate crescent scissored out of the eastern seacoast of Canada. Separated from the mainland by the narrow Northumberland Strait, it comprises some 2,000 square miles of lush farm land in the Gulf of St. Lawrence, hardly the size of the state of Delaware. History christened this paradise with a sucession of striking names. Indians had tagged it Abegweit, "the home cradled on the waves." French settlers had dedicated it to the Beloved Disciple in the Christian gospels, naming it Ile St-Jean. The British elected to use it in memorializing Prince Edward Augustus, fourth son of George III, whose sole accomplishment was to have fathered Queen Victoria.[1] In spite of these tributes, the Island never attained a prominent place in the affairs of men. It never duplicated Crete's distinction of having evolved a seminal civilization, or Corsica's by having produced a military genius whose impact ranged from Moscow to Louisiana. It never approached Manhattan's achievement as a world marketplace, or Malta's as a great and unyielding fortress.

Events seemed to pass it by. Its comfortable location had not allowed it to be a factor in the eighteenth-century war for empire between London and Paris or in the revolt of the thirteen colonies to the south. Once the Union Jack was raised over its green acreage, it was regarded more as a nuisance than an asset. Even when Canada was organizing its Confederation, the Island's leaders struggled against the national trend, resisting membership until economics forced them against their will into the new government. It was one of the last provinces to join. Its windswept beauty and charm notwithstanding, Prince Edward Island lay outside the mainstream of life, profoundly provincial and evidently unwilling to sacrifice its seclusion. Once, however, our perspective shifts from political trends to ecclesiastical life, we find a theme which breaks with the tone of insularity and reveals an expansive Catholic community in tune with the outside. A pioneer diocese since the early nineteenth century, the Island had accommodated, since 1829, the first separate see east of Quebec and the second English-speaking resident bishop in Canada. From it, too, had streamed a body of missionaries into the central and western provinces, as well as into the United States. One of these clerical immigrants was a third-generation Islander, Francis Clement Kelly, known to family and friends simply as Frank.*

His origins can be traced safely to the settlement of his two Irish-born grandfathers on farms that were located almost side by side. In 1767 nearly all the Island had been divided into townships, or lots, each averaging 20,000 acres, which were awarded to individuals with claims against the London government. These proprietors were required merely to pay a nominal quit-rent and

*FCK's surname was originally spelled as "Kelly.". The second "e" was not to appear regularly until after his ordination to the priesthood and his departure from the Island for the diocese of Detroit. See pages 74-75 below.

to provide for the settlement and development of their estates. Though it quickly discharged the government's obligations, this simple arrangement had profound social effects on the Island. First it produced a polyglot population. Indians and French Acadians had preceded the English landowners, who contributed further to the complexity of the community by bringing over as tenants waves of Britons, including fellow English, Lowland and Highland Scots, Ulsterites, and southern Irish—each group distinguished by sharp ethnic and religious identities. Frank's later move to the United States served as no introduction to cultural pluralism. On his Island, few ethnic groups blended, and the compactness of the physical environment demanded from them all a working formula of tolerance and cooperation. Secondly, this mixture of groups was organized along feudalistic lines. By the time his grandparents established their homesteads, most tillers of the soil had been forced to lease their land from proprietors, the majority of them absentee. This medieval arrangement ceased only five years after Frank's birth. When London approved the Land Purchase of 1875, most tenants were finally able to acquire as freeholds the land they worked.[2]

In this context, Frank's grandfathers located their families along the Georgetown Road in two interior townships, lots fifty-one and sixty-six, among the last to be settled and among the poorest on the Island.[3] Frank never knew his Kelly ancestor Patrick, not even his forename, but he recalled faint stories that his paternal grandfather hailed from "quite a tribe" in Kilkenny County, probably in the vicinity of the village of Inistioge.[4] A strong tradition suggests that Patrick had married Catherine Cavanaugh in Ireland in the 1820s, their first child Walter being born there a year later. With the young mother pregnant a second time, they undertook the hard crossing to Prince Edward Island by way of Nova Scotia, where a daughter was born.[5] This account conforms fairly well to the sketchy census data.

The Kellys were therefore off to a running start when Patrick leased 100 acres in lot fifty-one, and by 1841 five more children had arrived, including Frank's father John, with five more to come. Already signs pointed to Patrick's prosperity. With a good number of broad-beamed sons at his side, his tract soon featured thirty acres of "arable," or improved, land, three times more than that of his neighbors. In the next two decades, his holdings grew into two large parcels—one with 108 acres owned outright, itself an exception in those times; and another with 122 acres leased from the proprietor. Altogether he could work 160 "arable" acres, while neighbors averaged no more than twenty-two. Wheat, oats, potatoes, and cattle were his specialties. Willing to experiment with mechanization, Patrick was also one of the few farmers in the district to own a threshing machine.[6] Frank's grandfather was an illiterate, but the lack of schooling had been no barrier to success with the soil. Unfortunately, death faded the recollection of the patriarch in the mind of his young grandson. In 1874, when Frank was but four, the old man scratched his mark on a last will and testament. Soon after, the youngster, sitting on his mother's lap, viewed the funeral procession as it passed their house, wondering what the commotion was about. This was Frank's only recall of his Kilkenny grandfather. By the end of the decade, his godfather and uncle, Gregory Kelly, had succeeded to the homestead.[7]

If Frank inherited the ethic of hard work and success from the Kellys, his humor might well have sprung from his mother's side, the Murphys. Located only two farms to the east of the Kellys, in lot sixty-six, this family appeared to have enjoyed a more relaxed life-style. Frank's Wexford-born grandfather, Andrew, had settled in the Island in 1834 and married a native, Jennie, a flower of the prolific Highland Scots clan, the staunchly Catholic MacDonalds. As their offspring grew, they complemented the dozen children at Kellys. Eight daughters and four sons had arrived at the Murphys, including Frank's mother Mary Ann, while Patrick and Catherine were raising on their farm nearby eight sons and four daughters. With a younger household and fewer males to help, Andrew's success with the soil and livestock was equal to that of Patrick. By 1841, he had cleared only fifteen "arable" acres, half of Kelly's; but his farm was as productive as his neighbor's.[8] Two decades later, he was able to retire, having accumulated two parcels as his own. In addition to the family homestead along the Georgetown Road, Andrew had acquired another tract near the Stanhope Road to the north.[9]

Both sides of Frank's forebears knew hard work but what particularly distinguished the Murphys was a gentleness and lightness of spirit that was absent at the Kellys. Unlettered, Patrick Kelly was doubtless a taskmaster with his boys and frugal with his money. On the Murphy farm, however, an interest in education and the prevalence of the feminine smoothed some of the rough edges of Andrew and his sons. While the memory of the Kelly ancestor had dimmed, Andrew Murphy was long remembered as an irrepressible tease. Jennie's lively and effervescent nature delighted her husband, who was heard to have said: "She can jig any tune she can get her toes on." Frank cherished the image of his maternal grandfather as "one of the Old Irish 'well read' men." The jaunty old gentleman, he recalled, enjoyed his prominence in the district, like an "unofficial squire," each Sunday sporting a "plug" hat and a cane with an ivory knob. These evidences of self-made success made a lifelong impression on his grandson. No one, however, not even Frank, was exempt from Andrew's sharp tongue. He had studied a while for the priesthood in Ireland and would have persisted, he often said with a twinkle, if he had not been "too fond of the rum." In his tender years Frank was uncomfortable with this kind of banter. He admired the old man's natural intelligence and dignity, but these verbal daggers had stung the boy permanently.

Later, his memoirs would acknowledge the "irascible" nature of his grandfather from Wexford, a trait which he was grateful not to have inherited.[10]

Within this uncomplicated milieu—Irish, Catholic, agrarian, children growing up together—Mary Ann Murphy fell in love with John Kelly. It is not known when they began to keep company, but in 1855 both appeared at the parish church in Vernon River as godparents to Mary Ann's cousin, Lawrence Murphy. The baptism was hardly a signal of an engagement between them, but ten years later they were married in the same building, their wedding ceremony an exclusively family affair, as Kellys made up the groom's official party and Murphys the bride's.[11] The young couple followed at first the footsteps of their parents, and settled in Summerville, an interior farming community which was among the last on the Island to be developed. One reason for the late arrival of permanent settlers was the quality of the land in this district. The census of 1861 described the soil as only "pretty fair." This acreage promised relatively low yields in crops and livestock and was therefore slow in attracting farmers and their families. Another factor retarding settlement consisted of transportation difficulties. The markets in the coastal towns were distant, and the farmers of Summerville were most often forced to haul their surplus along the Georgetown Road, twenty miles west to Charlottetown or twelve miles east to Georgetown.[12]

Summerville thus offered poor Irish and Highland Scots an opportunity for hard work which they could afford, and it was here that Frank's parents began their lives together. Three years after the wedding, the two families helped to stake John and Mary Ann, who by now had their first child, Catherine Mary. In 1868 John leased for £10 a plot from his wife's uncle, Lawrence Murphy, and this was promptly followed by the purchase of a small parcel on the main road that was carved out of the Kelly homestead.[13] Two more children blessed the union. The couple's first son, Francis Clement, was born in 1870, followed three years later by Joseph Augustine. Frank's birthdate reflects the carelessness with which the registers of the time were kept. His family Bible logged it as November 24, 1870, the date which he commemorated as the true anniversary. The parish baptismal register made him a month older, listing his birthdate as October 23, 1870.[14] The earlier date gave him an advantage years later. When he was ready for ordination to the priesthood, he was below the minimal age of twenty-four. Since his bishop was required to apply for a dispensation, Frank accepted October 23 as his "official" birthday, hoping that it would expedite Rome's permission to ordain the underage candidate.[15] Frank Kelly was to lead an enormously complicated life, and one might say that the endless stream of twisting convolutions that highlight it began at the very beginning—with two birthdays.

The prevalent work in Summerville did not entirely suit John Kelly, who soon turned to commerce as a supplement to his income from the fields. There was an obvious need for an entrepreneur in the interior district. Since farmers grew cash crops in order to pay rents and mortgages, they looked to the services of a broker who could bring their produce and hides to the markets. John Kelly welcomed this opportunity. While he continued to accumulate acreage to farm, his parcel on the Georgetown Road was ideally located for a store where products of the field could be exchanged for general merchandise. His early success in business soon led him to explore locations for other outlets. In 1869 he bought a lot near Montague, describing himself on the deed for the first time as "Trader of Summerville." Montague was some eight miles southwest of his district and at the time offered the nearest and best used market of his neighbors.[16]

Frank's ambitious father thus had a sharp eye for trends in business and was willing to break out of the cocoon of Summerville. The village of Georgetown in Cardigan Bay had at the time the greatest potential to become the Island's business center. Its harbor had a longer open season than its competitors, along with easier access to the main shipping lanes, and the location was nearer to the best fisheries on the Island. In 1873 John therefore disposed of his property at Montague and in the next year bought a town lot in Georgetown, a decision no doubt preliminary to an intended family move from Summerville.[17] Other evidence of John's growing self-confidence as an entrepreneur accompanied these developments. In 1871 a property deed identified the 36-year-old promoter with the stately title of "Merchant." Another sign of his prosperity and the maturing of his rural community occurred the same year when he sold a plot to a shoemaker and teacher, James Doyle. On it was erected a one-room, unornamented building where the craftsman taught school subjects, and, after the students were dismissed, made boots for Kelly's store. In this rustic academy, little Frank mixed with dozens of older farm children, learning all the while a few letters of the alphabet.[18]

Frank was not five years old when his parents agreed to uproot the family out of the countryside. Prospects had evidently dimmed in Georgetown, and Kelly decided to stake his future in another Island village, Charlottetown. Founded between the Hillsborough and North Rivers, the provincial capital commanded a network of water and road systems that linked it with the interior. It was developing into a major shipping depot, its harbor accommodating vessels bound for mainland Canada, New England, and the British Isles. When John Kelly pulled up stakes in Summerville, Charlottetown was already funneling abroad half of the Island's export trade—mostly oats, potatoes, fish, pork, and eggs—products in which he had long specialized.[19]

Before his fifth birthday, Frank found himself in new surroundings when by August of 1875 his father had moved family and business to the bustling capital. He first secured a large building on Dorchester Street, deep in the downtown section and only three blocks from the wharf, a location in which the Kelly name would figure until the end of the century. When he signed the property deed as "Saloon Keeper," John indicated that his interests had expanded beyond the merchandising of groceries.[20] This facility served principally as an export-import warehouse and a distributing center for shippers. Aside from wholesaling, a second store was soon opened in the town center on the north side of Queen Square. This probably housed Kelly's retail operation, listing the proprietor as a dealer in "dry goods & general merchandise" as well as "groceries & liquors." In the meantime another building was bought in the residential part of town, running along Longworth Avenue and Euston Street. In this transaction whereby John described himself this time as an "Inn Keeper," the property was perhaps to serve as a home not only for his family but for a few roomers as well. During this hectic period, the arrival of three more children rounded off the Kelly family—Lucy Gertrude, Arthur Ambrose, and Ursula Ann, Frank's favorite sister who preferred to be called "Cecilia." By the end of 1880, his parents had had their last child and established their permanent home on Pleasant Street.[21]

Once settled in Charlottetown, Frank was introduced to a succession of schools. The first included a brief association with LePage's School on Kent Street. This private academy crowded nearly fifty students into a single room, a condition which disturbed school inspectors; but the program was well-conducted by a lame schoolmarm, Miss Alice Fennessey. Well-concealed beneath the folds of a black dress, this handicap did not impair her ability to teach or to dispense discipline, recalled Frank, with convincing whacks on pupils' ears with her ruler.[22] A place was soon found for him in St. Patrick's Hall, the boy's grammar school for the cathedral parish managed by the Christian Brothers. In this environment, the lad from Summerville planted the seeds of a lifelong friendship with James M. Reardon, who would later follow him to the United States as a priest and join the archdiocese of St. Paul. As Reardon recalled those classroom days, there was nothing to set Frank apart from the ordinary student. His scholarly performance was no more than average, though he was "a general favorite, genial, companionable, unassuming, placid rather than pugnacious, inclined to take things easy as far as serious study was concerned." Two durable qualities already stood out, however, one a weakness and the other a useful asset. First, Frank displayed an early disinclination for speculative mathematics. "He had no head for [the] triangle, cube root or formula of any kind," noted Reardon. "Sine and cosine were inventions of the evil one and he would have none of them." While numbers puzzled him, planning and arranging new ventures came naturally. Under his hand new student societies were organized in which the merchant's son, as might be expected, invested himself in the key office of treasurer.[23]

Before they were far advanced in their studies, the two young friends encountered a drastic change in the school administration. Private schools had proliferated in Charlottetown and, according to law, qualified for tax support. Since this arrangement impeded the development of the public-school district, the provincial government under the Liberal Party enacted in 1877 corrective legislation which had been opposed by the Catholic bishop. If, thereafter, attendance in public schools fell below 50 percent of school-age children in the district, assistance to private schools would be reduced in order to make up deficient tax revenues for the district. This awkward formula convinced the Christian Brothers to abandon St. Patrick's. Beginning on January 1, 1878, the city school board leased a portion of the building from the cathedral, and Frank ended his grammar-school years in the same structure, known then as "Queen Square School." The struggle between the bishop and the government was beyond the grasp of the young scholar, but it had an impact on the Kelly household. "I heard that my father was a Liberal in politics," recalled Frank more than six decades later, "but that he changed and became a Conservative because of that fight."[24] To all intents and purposes, however, the academy remained as Catholic in spirit as when the brothers managed it. Frank's eight years under its tutelage did not deter him from enrolling in 1885 in the institution which would become his premier *alma mater,* Saint Dunstan's College.

* * * * * * * * *

As Frank's education progressed, his father's career took on a new tone. His business in Charlottetown had led him into public responsibilities, and he soon rose as a civic leader of some importance. As a part-time saloon keeper, he qualified to serve on the liquor-licensing board, but more importantly, he succeeded in acquiring an elective office. The establishment on Dorchester Street allowed him to run for the City Council from the Second Ward. He won this office, probably for more than one term. Typical of his political success was his triumph in the election of January, 1886, in which he defeated his opponent 135 votes to 103. His numerical majority of thirty-two represented roughly a sixth of the ballots cast, a sound victory at the polls.[25]

Frank's father was therefore active in municipal government, winning elections as councillor and reportedly an active participant in official discussions.[26] His star reached its zenith when he won a city-wide election. Disastrous fires in 1886 and 1887 had made the city's water-control system a subject of concern. The use of wells had proven insufficient to provide water for the fires that threatened the growing capital, and insurance rates had climbed to prohibitive levels. The City Council was therefore urged to create a Board of Water Commissioners in charge of developing a modern municipal water system.[27] In June, 1887, when a special city-wide election was held for the new body, John Kelly won first place among eight candidates.[28] This was an enormous tribute to the respected merchant. His reputation in business and government had earned him the distinction of serving on the city's original board. In time, the commissioners upheld the public trust by building a pumping station that became a model of its kind in water supply. During these days of his father's work in government, Frank attended grammar and high schools and was no doubt an attentive student of civic affairs. This political involvement provided the Kelly household with some familiarity with the Island's leaders, and this early association with provincial politicians may have spawned Frank's later independence in dealing with public figures. There is no question that throughout his adult life John's eldest son harbored little fear of great officers of state, including governors, senators, and even presidents of the United States.[29]

While John Kelly's political future looked bright, his business had fallen upon uncertain times. Evidently one factor working against him was his willingness to accept notes secured by parcels of farm property. In 1878 he had taken on a mortgage of a farmer who had been loaned $200 at 15 percent. When the farmer defaulted, Kelly was forced to use the courts to obtain the title and to dispose of the parcel at a public auction. Though the property recovered his investment, he had lost legal expenses and two years' interest, losses that would dishearten anyone in business.[30] Political events, moreover, did not ease his commercial burdens. The Island's membership in the Dominion of Canada since 1873 had not brought the economic bonanza that had been expected. Kelly had developed strong connections with produce markets in Boston, but the new union with Ottawa had forced the Island's focus away from New England toward the Canadian mainland where he had less experience. The shift of markets was further complicated by the rise of protectionism in the United States which discouraged imports from abroad, including Canada. This latter trend gave rise in 1890 to the McKinley Tariff, which raised taxes on most foreign produce to prohibitive levels. It is impossible to measure the direct impact of these forces on Frank's father, but property transactions reveal that by 1885 he had begun to sell off his holdings outside Charlottetown, perhaps to raise the quick cash which his sagging export trade had not produced.[31]

John Kelly's business fortunes were perhaps more clearly reflected in the student years of his first son. Frank finished the program at Queen Square School in 1885 and would have gone on to Prince of Wales College, a secondary school financed by the provincial government. This was the route that his schoolmate, James M. Reardon, followed; but as the latter told it, John Kelly, still a successful entrepreneur, had the income to send his son to a private institution, Saint Dunstan's College.[32] As Frank prepared to enter, the school had fallen upon its most difficult days. Two years earlier, it almost closed its doors in bankruptcy; and in the term before his enrollment, the student body had slumped to about a dozen. But since its foundation in 1885, the college had fashioned a tradition of academic excellence. It had specialized in classical studies, training its boys for the professions and the priesthood. In this way, even though many students never planned to be ordained, the school served in part as a preparatory seminary. Its alumni were renowned as writers and public speakers, and several had attained prestigious positions in government and the press. Bishop Peter MacIntyre was therefore resolved to save the diocesan school. On the eve of Frank's admission, he built a strong faculty of clerics and laymen around a new rector, Reverend James Charles McDonald, who would one day succeed MacIntyre in the see of Charlottetown.[33]

Student registers show Frank's full-time registration from 1885 to 1888. The young scholar did not find the college perfect. It never helped him overcome his weakness in mathematics, and its library housed no more than 300 books, a paltry collection.[34] But his formative years at Saint Dunstan's were crucial because they introduced him to one of the major forces of his life, Alexander McAulay. The faculty and student body lived together in close quarters, occupying the same dormitory building and being present to each other in a daily cycle of classes, study periods, religious services, games, and meals. These conditions fostered deep bonds between an instructor and student, and Kelly found his soulmate in McAulay, an advanced seminarian, only ten years older, who taught history, elocution, and science.

A descendant from Highland Scots whose first language had been Gaelic, his teaching featured two qualities that affected Frank profoundly. A man without a trace of pretension, McAulay was, first of all, enormously erudite, an inexhaustible reservoir of information; and secondly, he imparted his learning informally and with enthusiasm. The world of Saint Dunstan's permitting little privacy, McAulay allowed the awe-struck lad to sit on his trunk while the older man read aloud selections from the classics and essays, a luxury that Kelly recalled until death. Their formal association took place in history classes, but even here McAulay's personal approach dominated. "I talked more about [history] than I made the pupils study out of books," the old professor reminisced over fifty years later. "I think history should be taught by talking it, past, present, future, rather than reading about it." No one relished these impromptu tangents more than Frank, who admitted that the diversions had not been difficult to arrange. "Any student could trap him into talking," recalled Kelly, "and most of us did." In Frank, as in others, McAulay's conversations were feeding a passion for learning, an unquenchable curiosity which amounted to the greatest success any teacher could achieve. "He was a sane enthusiast," commented the grateful Kelly, "who did not even dream that he was setting at least one mind on fire."[35]

Frank's final year at Saint Dunstan's, 1887-88, was filled with problems. The fall term opened auspiciously when he founded the student monthly, *The Collegium.* Assigned as faculty supervisor, McAulay was named editor, and Frank became the business manager. It was a perfect partnership, and the project brought the two even more closely together. The editor admired the younger man's techniques in recruiting subscribers and advertisers, noting much later: "He was a diplomat even then."[36] Meanwhile, though McAulay never taught Kelly English, his editorial duties managed to plant in Frank confidence as a writer and some craft with a pen. "I got my start as a writer on the Island," Kelly acknowledged a half century later, "chiefly from MacAuley [*sic*], who thought that he was being only a bit kind. . . . MacAuley [*sic*] was St. Dunstan's for me."[37]

Reverses in his father's business forced Frank to withdraw from the college before graduation. As John Kelly negotiated the sale of his last parcel of real estate outside of Charlottetown, as mentioned earlier, his son was picking up extra income for the family by working in a dry-goods store.[38] This interlude at home included a bout with typhoid fever which nearly took his life. There is also a trace of evidence that he took a course in commercial studies, a sign that at this point he viewed his future in his father's market and not in the sanctuary. Around this time, he enrolled in the "Charlottetown Business College," where he learned bookkeeping, business law, and the principles of brokerage.[39]

Eventually, his parents scraped together sufficient cash to return him to Saint Dunstan's, where he climaxed his final year in a spectacular threefold triumph. First, his writing continued to improve. *The Collegium* featured a reverie of a Greek philosopher in search of happiness, Frank's first article to reach print. Logius of Athens was portrayed as groping his way through the palaces of pleasure, fame, power, and wisdom—only to end his search in the modest cottage of conscience. The morality tale was contrived and clumsy but not without flair. The style bore the student's weakness for florid phrases, but already the young author displayed a command of vocabulary and the power to arrange a narrative with dramatic effect, all at the service of a traditional theme. These literary tendencies—a clean story line, straightforward expression, an orthodox message—were already well-formed and would characterize Kelly throughout his writing career. Above all, this modest success sealed the author's intention to pursue a literary career. "No one seemed to get anything out of the [allegory] but myself," he mused a half century later, "but I had the confirmation of the faith that some day I should write."[40]

Next, Frank apparently resolved a crisis of vocation. Having once prepared to succeed his father in business, he found his interest beginning to wander from the marketplace. At the end of the spring term, he was forced to cram for his final examination in religious studies. What had begun as a frantic survey of a year's work in the classroom opened the way to what he saw as a mystical event. He had stumbled upon the crossroads of his life. The experience quickened his faith as a Christian, producing what he eventually called "The Great Conviction," and no doubt laid to rest whatever hesitation he might have nursed about studying for the priesthood.[41]

Lastly, Frank all but swept the honors at graduation. Only seventeen years old, he served as valedictorian and dominated the list of prizes awarded to students for academic achievement. First honors went to him in religious studies, physical geography and geology, botany, and elocution, as well as second honors in Milton, honorable mentions in Greek and history, and a special prize for "proficiency in penmanship." The pattern not only mirrored a well-rounded competence in the arts and sciences, but it also pointed to his chronic weakness with numbers and to an indifference toward Latin. The highlight of the closing exercises occurred, however, when he was given the gold medal for excellence in English, the first one awarded since the foundation of the college thirty-three years earlier.[42] John and Mary Ann Kelly had made sacrifices to restore their oldest son to Saint Dunstan's, and his swan song at commencement had more than justified their burden.

* * * * * * * * * *

Frank Kelly's completion of high school in 1888 marked his formal commitment to the priesthood. Since the Island was not in short supply of clergy, his eyes turned across the Gulf of St. Lawrence to the diocese of Chatham. Its patriarchal bishop, James Rogers, had ruled since that see's erection in 1860, having built it from a scratch beginning of more than five counties in northern New Brunswick which were served by only seven diocesan priests. Ever in need of candidates, he adopted the young collegian from Charlottetown and sent him to the minor seminary at Chicoutimi. This was a logical choice on the part of a bishop whose diocese had large pockets of French-speaking Acadians. The school was located in a remote lumber and pulp center along the Saguenay River, much like the area where Rogers governed and Kelly planned to spend his priesthood. Founded in 1873, it had originally served the isolated northern territory of the archdiocese of Quebec and was affiliated with Laval University. Five years later, however, it had become diocesan when Chicoutimi was raised to a suffragen see.[43] The negotiations regarding his enrollment disclosed Frank's concern over his father's financial state. At Chicoutimi, his bills would be a family responsibility as they had been on the Island. The year's tuition, room, board, and laundry amounted to only $84, considerably less than the charges at St. Dunstan's. With his academic record, however, he was able to arrange not only to pursue his studies but also to earn $40 toward personal expenses by teaching English.[44]

This environment in which Frank spent his first extended sojourn away from home introduced him to the other half of Canada. On the Island he enjoyed contacts with Acadians, who had resisted assimilation, but at Chicoutimi he lived daily with *Canadiens,* whose devotion to the French language and culture exceeded any he had known. These months in the upper wilderness had strengthened his sympathies toward this minority whom recent events had progressively alienated against their English-speaking counterparts. One factor had been the fate of

Louis Riel. A leader of French half-breeds in the Northwest, Riel had sparked two abortive rebellions against the government and in 1885 had been captured, tried, and hanged. His execution had bestirred *Canadien* nationalism everywhere. Tensions had continued to mount into 1890 when Manitoba abolished French as an official language and Ontario limited its use and study.[45]

Unwittingly, Kelly contributed a minor note to these volatile times when he published on the Island an appreciation of his new home and friends in the province of Quebec. In February, 1890, the Charlottetown *Herald* featured a lengthy article narrating a trip he made from Tadoussac, at the mouth of the Saguenay River, to Chicoutimi. Readers found a friendly description of the persons and landscapes Frank had encountered, coupled with commendations of the institutions, mores, and prosperity of the settlers. Unfortunately, the author had not yet come to appreciate the fierce pride of the *Canadien* and his closing paragraph contained this mild criticism:

> Of the inhabitants too much cannot be said in praise of their good qualities, but they hold fast to the customs, language and laws of their French ancestors, which to us appear a little behind the age. As well as might you try to turn the St. Lawrence from its course as attempt to change either the language, customs or laws of this people.[46]

This comment on *Canadien* intransigence evoked tolerant smiles from the faculty at the seminary, but it thoroughly annoyed an Island priest, the Reverend Azade J. Trudelle. A native of Quebec, he had been ordained for Charlottetown seven years before Frank's birth and had long reigned as pastor in Hope River. An accident had forced an early retirement, but in 1882 he had accepted an assignment to Palmer Road, where, with disgust, he read Frank's opinion of *Québécois* stubborness.[47] The old man set about to retaliate, aiming his arrows at what he saw as a contradiction in the young author's logic. How could one admire so much of *Canadien* civilization, as Kelly did in his article, and then condemn those living along the Saguenay River for holding fast to it? "These are the miserable customs," the priest retorted further, "the damn language, the perverted laws which are found in a marvelous and charming countryside and have produced prosperity and happiness."[48] Probably never published, Trudelle's challenge was long afterwards discovered among his private papers. No doubt Frank never realized that at the age of nineteen he had engaged in his first newspaper controversy, a role that would become familiar to him in years to come.

After a year in Chicoutimi, Bishop Rogers invited Kelly to spend the next one, 1889-90, in Chatham as his "assistant secretary." Thus began the "outstanding" year of his life that is best chronicled in his autobiography. The old prelate had himself never attended a seminary, having taken his ecclesiastical studies in an episcopal household. In his judgment, this approach had strong merit, and Frank was agreeable to the idea because it spared his family the costs of seminary tuition. As he moved into the bishop's house, Rogers was nearing his thirtieth year in the episcopate, and his impact on the young man was equaled only by Alexander McAulay of St. Dunstan days. The bishop's spirit was contagious, his energy boundless, and he had endearing habits of speech, often breaking in with "Hooray, Hooray!" He was, above all, a learned, transparent, spontaneous pastor whom Frank grew to love deeply.[49]

Rich as it was, the tutorial menu in Roger's household was not ideal for priestly formation. Lessons were taken haphazardly; assignments often interrupted with outside tasks; hours were irregular; no one was available for the candidate to discuss the progress of his training; and Frank's health began to fail. During much of his time in New Brunswick, he suffered from catarrh, a respiratory ailment that inflamed his nose and throat. One year under these conditions was sufficient. As early as November, 1889, Frank confidentially inquired into the seminary at Nicolet where the theology program was more than adequate to prepare him for ordination in three years. He also hoped to negotiate an agreement whereby his expenses might be partly or fully paid for by teaching English and perhaps bookkeeping as he had done at Chicoutimi. By March, 1890, he had reached the edge of another decision. His health had so alarmed friends that at their suggestion he considered a transfer from Chatham to a diocese with a warmer climate.[50]

Frank climaxed his studies for the priesthood at Nicolet, a town of less than 4,000, about half the size of Chicoutimi, which was located near the south bank of the St. Lawrence River, midway between Quebec and Montreal. Its seminary had been founded in 1803 and since 1863 enjoyed affiliation with Laval University. In 1890 Frank again entered a venerable institution in French Canada. As before, his two jobs kept him busier than most others. He served on the faculty, teaching the commercial course, while he managed to finish his theological studies in only three years. The grades that are extant, however, are inconsistent, no doubt reflecting the heavy load he had undertaken. He scored best in the course on "Creation," winning thirteen points out of a possible thirteen, and in the "Incarnate Word," where he scored 17.5 out of eighteen. But he achieved only passable grades in the "Sacrament of Penance," getting 5.1 out of twelve, as well as in "Grace," with only six out of thirteen.[51] Though his scholastic record at Nicolet paled against that at St. Dunstan's, his proudest accomplishment lay outside the classroom. With considerable diplomatic skill, he engineered in this citadel of French Canada a remarkable celebration on St. Patrick's Day in 1891. The rector solemnized Mass in the cathedral, Frank serving as one of the liturgical officers; and the bishop was maneuvered into preaching in English on the patron of Ireland to a congregation packed with French-speaking *Canadiens,* a remarkable incident which received lavish detail in Kelly's autobiography. In any case, alumni recall that under Frank's inspiration St. Patrick's Day was a festival in Nicolet during his three years there. No doubt the Islander was the major contributor to the student plays with mischievous titles that capped these annual celebrations—"More Sinned Against than Sinning" in 1891, "The Elixir" in 1892, and "Troublesome Servants" in 1893.[52]

These last years before ordination seemed to keep Frank in constant motion. The summer of 1891 included a visit to New York and New England, where he succeeded, among many interests, in recruiting for the diocese of Nicolet two students from Amesbury, Massachusetts.[53] Furthermore, a friend had offered to pay for lessons in elocution. Determined not to let this opportunity slip by, Frank investigated the best programs in Boston and selected one from among the New England Conservatory, the Boston School of Expression, and Harvard University.[54]

The following year brought about the delicate negotiations of a transfer from Chatham to an American diocese where the climate would not impair Frank's health, a critical step regarding his future. The key to this shift was an Island priest, Thomas J. Broderick, who had left Charlottetown after high school and eventually was ordained for the archdiocese of Baltimore. During a visit to one of the Canadian seminaries, Kelly had met this priest on a tour of the campus. The two had become such friends that the younger man confessed his worries about surviving the rigors of New Brunswick. If Bishop Rogers would release him, the visitor assured Kelly, he would find a welcome in Baltimore. Rogers was agreeable, but Cardinal Gibbons declined the application on the grounds that his archdiocese had as many seminarians as it could support. Hence, Frank's name went to a former Baltimorean, Bishop John Samuel Foley of Detroit, who was Gibbons's friend and Broderick's former pastor.[55] Foley accepted the candidate, and Kelly's switch from maritime Canada to Michigan was completed by mid-1892.[56] However, a final problem remained. Though his worries regarding health were gone, Kelly's youth had become a minor hurdle to the reception of preliminary orders leading to the priesthood. In behalf of his family, he had planned to receive the subdiaconate in Charlottetown in the summer of 1892, but the bishop did not have permission to ordain him because he had not reached his twenty-second birthday.[57] His steps into major orders, from the subdiaconate to the priesthood, therefore, had to await his return to the seminary at Nicolet; and to their great disappointment, no relatives were able to attend these ceremonies.

As he began his last year of training, there appeared on the immediate horizon no obstacle to the priesthood. Expenses did not trouble him. No longer forced to double as an instructor and student, he was, as he told the superior, "ready to pay for board & tuition." Granted that his grades were somewhat erratic, his studies were well in hand, and the faculty had already judged him as a "bright and promising student."[58] Even though his new diocese was unknown to him, it at least would spare him the hardship of Canadian winters and lay to rest his concerns about health. Yet one sadness intervened before the final step to ordination, the death of his father in late 1892. Only fifty-six years of age, his health had begun to fail during Frank's last year at Nicolet, though at first there were few signs to disturb his family. He had taken a short trip abroad, conducted business in Boston, and was seen in his warehouse a week before the end. Toward mid-December his condition worsened alarmingly. On December 14, 1892, he made out his last will and testament, and a telegram was sent to Nicolet, urging Frank to return immediately.[59]

The agonizing journey took him two days, but he reached his father's deathbed an hour before he expired. Witnesses recalled the young man's kneeling by the bedside and taking his last farewell. John Kelly died at nine o'clock on December 16, 1892. He had left his mark on the community. The news of his death called forth a chorus of eulogy in the Island press, which lauded his integrity in business and service in local government. Perhaps *The Daily Examiner* best summed up his character in profiling him "as a man whose 'word was his bond.' "[60] The funeral took place at the cathedral with Frank serving as subdeacon, and the requiem was offered by his former rector at St. Dunstan's College, James Charles McDonald, now bishop of Charlottetown. His father's death signaled changes for the family, the most notable being the deterioration of the business. Frank had forsworn a merchant's life for the ministry, his two younger brothers had shown little interest, and his mother could not cope alone. In 1899 Mary Ann sold the establishment on Dorchester Street that had been in her husband's name for a quarter century—at a considerable loss. This erased the last trace of "John Kelly & Co." in Charlottetown.[61]

A man's youth shapes the character he will carry to the grave. Unfortunately, John Kelly did not live to see his son's ordination, but his death climaxed the young man's formative years. In nine months, Frank would take his leave from relatives and friends in Charlottetown and set out for his first assignment in the diocese of Detroit. His two decades on Prince Edward Island had prepared him well for the rich and productive career that lay ahead. A brief infancy in the countryside of Summerville had conditioned him to the reality of rural life. In a dozen years after his arrival in Michigan, he would be the first to act on the religious crisis in the farm belts of the United States and Canada. His parents had come from staunchly Irish households whose patriarchs had emigrated from the Old World. Perhaps his grandfathers had bequeathed the capacity to pull up stakes and to go far in search of opportunity. Three times Frank would change dioceses, transfers that would bring him from the north Atlantic coast to the heartland of Michigan and Illinois and finally to a new state in the American Southwest. From the Kellys and Murphys he certainly inherited the pride in his Hibernian ancestry. "The little drop of Scotch blood in me," he confessed later, "had long ago been assimilated by the more exciting Irish flow. . . ."[62] The *Nicolétains* had learned this, recalling his sturdy devotion to St. Patrick, and others would, too.

Above all, Frank Kelly had had superb teachers. In high school, an unheralded mentor had invaded his spirit and rooted in it a lifelong passion for study and expression. For this grace, Alexander McAulay was later immortalized in his student's autobiography, a book of literary charm and one of the most notable memoirs produced in Catholic America. As he took his first theology classes in Bishop Rogers's home, Kelly had learned not merely how to bridge gaps between generations but to accommodate himself to the irregular demands of the ministry. He had seen, too, that neither age nor the obscurity of a diocese could dim the ardor of the truly pastoral churchman, a lesson that influenced Frank until his own retirement in Oklahoma. The two seminaries in the province of Quebec had nourished a sympathy for the underdog by forcing him to live among the *Canadien* minority. After an uncomplicated boyhood on Prince Edward Island, he had entered their complex world at a time when French traditions were threatened with extinction. Their outrage had touched him, making him a ready advocate for the victim. The odds for victory neither determined his causes nor steered him from controversy. Large portions of his public life would be consumed in battling giants, as he defended the rural ministry in a city-centered church, the missions of defeated Germany against the British Crown, and the Mexican clergy and religious against the weight of American public opinion.

But Frank's greatest teacher was his father. As a broker in the marketplace, John Kelly's experience had underscored the need for initiative, imagination, and persuasion in promoting enterprises. This truth was not lost on Frank, whose special goal had been to perfect his English expression and elocution. The art of influencing others was to become indispensable in future campaigns that ranged from the launching of the home-mission movement in America to engaging the Italian government in reconciliation with the papacy. John Kelly's years in municipal government had also brought Frank at an early age into the orbit of political life. This inside view of the City Council and the Board of Water Commissioners had revealed these Island leaders to be as mortal, vulnerable, and accessible as his own father. As a priest, he would not hesitate to befriend or challenge their more lofty counterparts in governments on either side of the Atlantic. The final paternal lesson centered on the value of work. Since John Kelly's success in commerce had been spotty, his children had never known affluence, and at home the oldest son had had no privileges of rank. From the age of seventeen, Frank improvised ways of supplementing the family income and helping with the expenses of seminary training. No doubt his parents would have eased his way toward the priesthood, but money was scarce and Frank was willing to contribute. This hardship had therefore nursed a positive attitude toward work. Frank always carried more than his share of the load—whether it consisted of organizing mission-aid societies or drafting a pastoral letter on the persecution in Mexico for the American hierarchy. At Chicoutimi, he had heard his scripture professor, Louis Nazaire Bégin, later cardinal archbishop of Quebec, advise students that "the best recreation for a priest is a change of work."[63] This counsel he followed until the end, taking on a variety of tasks and often forcing friends to caution him against overexertion.

His departure from the Island occurred right after his ordination. Bishop Elphége Gravel of Nicolet imposed hands upon him in the seminary chapel on August 23, 1893.[64] Notwithstanding the loss of his father, there were special consolations for the young priest. He returned briefly to Charlottetown to offer his first Solemn Mass, at which Alexander McAulay, a priest for only three years, preached. Before the final farewells, Frank was honored with a debut in the cathedral pulpit, delivering a rousing sermon on the rosary, and later he gave a public lecture on "The Dream of Equality." The latter performance evoked an enthusiastic description of his youthful eloquence. The newly ordained priest, noted a reporter, spoke for ninety minutes "without Note or Ms.," interspersing the address with "bright anecdotes and epigrammatic sayings which frequently elicited hearty applause." Before the end of the visit, his father's friends and business associates arranged a reception at which he was presented a purse to help him start his new life.[65]

The shelter of his Nazareth was behind him. A public ministry of more than a half century awaited him in a new diocese and a new country. By the time Father Kelly crossed to the Canadian mainland on the way to Detroit, these themes had been orchestrated into his adult temperament—intelligence and a will to expand it; an enormous sense of responsibility; the energy and flair, as well as the nerve, to face public life and controversy; strong habits of work; and a willingness to follow anywhere the pastoral mission of the church. These qualities fell short of perfection at the age of twenty-three, but they portended an extraordinary career.

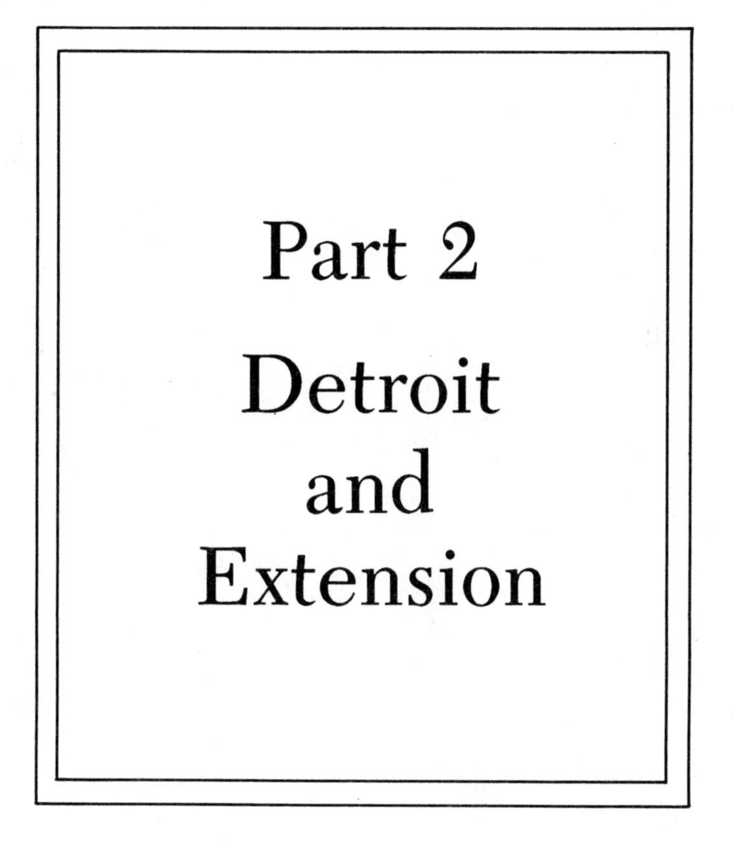

Part 2
Detroit and Extension

(1893-1924)

II
A Dream Unfolds

Great ideas have two assets: they originate from large needs and offer hopeful solutions. The young Detroit priest had such an idea, one that was central to his life and governed him through four decades. This idea would bring him from the rural fields of Michigan to the largest Catholic urban community in the country. It would introduce this parish pastor into the complexities of Washington politics and international diplomacy. It would create lasting friendships and enmities among the most powerful ecclesiastical and secular leaders of his generation. It would eventually lead him from a paneled office in the commercial center of the Midwest into a young territory in the Southwest which had not even achieved its statehood when the idea was conceived. It would transform a desk-bound theorist into a missionary practitioner in one of the few frontiers left in twentieth-century America. This idea was the Catholic Church Extension Society.

Its roots begin with Father Kelly's years in Michigan. The center of his new diocese was different from the provincial settings of Charlottetown or Chatham. Visitors would find nothing quaint about Detroit as it approached the turn of the century. Located near the Great Lakes, it had specialized in commerce and the production of heavy machinery; and it was about to take the lead in a new industry, the manufacture of automobiles. The city's experience in making carriages, along with a large pool of mechanics, had attracted the interest of imaginative capitalists who would make it the country's largest producer of motor vehicles. These currents had shaped the Catholic diocese into an urban, cosmopolitan community. French settlers and Indian converts had composed its original nucleus, but the Irish and Germans soon added to the count, to be followed by waves of immigrants from southern and eastern Europe who manned the new factories. In 1888 John Samuel Foley had been named its fourth bishop, beginning a thirty-year administration during which the Catholic population trebled.

Into this setting the Islander arrived with two distinctions. First, he was an exception from the start. At twenty-three years of age, he was known to be the youngest Catholic priest in America, having been ordained fourteen months before the minimum age.[1] His youth was, therefore, seen as proof of exceptional ability which would merit him responsibility early in the ministry. Second, he changed the spelling of his last name, a vague signal perhaps of his accepting the radical transition from Prince Edward Island to mid-America. He had traced the name to its Gaelic origins, "O'Ceallaigh," and uncovered such variations as "Kelly," "Kelley," "Kiley," and among the Scots "Kellie." Though public records show his father's exclusive use of "Kelly," Frank claimed that, as a merchant with two establishments, John had spelled his name in two ways, "Kelly" at one store and "Kelley" at the other. Most of the family continued to sign "Kelly," but Frank favored the version with a second "e." While he later acknowledged his use of "Kelley" only because "it was longer," some who knew the background considered the change an affectation. Another slight modification occurred at this time when he began to prefix the new surname with "Francis."[2] Too much might be made of these adjustments, but of themselves they represented a mild break with a past where most church and school records in Canada knew him as "Frank C. Kelly."

As challenging as the ministry appeared during the rise of "Motor City," Father Kelley discovered that he was to see very little of it. At first he had been assigned to temporary duty in an urban parish, Holy Trinity in Detroit's old Corktown, where he promptly distinguished himself as a preacher. In late October, 1893, however, he was sent to Immaculate Conception Church in Lapeer, Michigan, as administrator of an extensive country parish some sixty miles northwest of Detroit.[3] Hardly the typically quiet appointment in the country, this parish would have taxed the resources of a veteran clergyman, let alone one who had been ordained for only two months. The first pastor of twenty-eight years, John Busche, had created a crisis. During the last eight years of his administration, the practice of religion had nearly died out, largely through his apparent loss of faith. It was estimated that out of 100 Catholic families in the parish, no more than a dozen attended Mass by 1890, the year of his suspension. Refusing to reconcile with the diocese, he continued to live in the area until his death in 1905, having been married in a civil ceremony and publishing irreligious tracts in the local press. When Father Kelley arrived, he was no way prepared for the emergency he encountered. An anticlerical spirit pervaded the community: children sometimes pelted him with stones and church property was reduced to miserable sheds. The situation further darkened shortly after his appearance when the second pastor, William J. Sinn, died, and the young priest succeeded him, remaining at this outpost for thirteen years.[4]

Kelley's charm and tact quickly melted the icy hostility. Many appreciated a polished clergyman in their midst who preached eloquently without notes and was adept at making friends. An early tribute was paid to him when the first boy baptized after his arrival was given the names "Francis Clement."[5] Nevertheless, the assignment presented enormous challenges. First, on a personal level, the young priest found too much leisure and loneliness in a country parish. Later, he complained that at Lapeer he had narrowed himself to a weekend ministry, having discovered that after his Sunday work there was nothing to do.[6] This situation eventually induced him to invest his energy in study and writing. In 1894 his pamphlet on *Sacramental Confession* merited a friendly notice in the St. Dunstan's monthly, *The Collegium.* This early publication reflected the "Kelleyesque" style that would characterize the score of books and articles to follow—an argument rooted in research and cold logic, forcibly expressed, and resting squarely on Catholic tradition.[7] A more alarming handicap was the spiritual and physical condition of the parish. Not only was there little evidence of instructed parishioners, of what Kelley called "intelligent faith," but he soon uncovered serious leakage from the church. The general morale was mirrored in the condition of the plant. Immaculate Conception's main church was in Lapeer, and the parish was responsible for missions in Imlay City and Richfield. All three places had chapels in sad disrepair, as well as a crumbling rectory in Lapeer.

The deterioration, along with the ample free time, triggered dramatic action from the young pastor. He first attended to the missions, building a brick-and-stone church in Imlay City and another in Davison which replaced the old site in Richfield. A year of pleading for support in Lapeer, however, failed to move the congregation, and he took matters into his own hand. The old church was sold for $1,500, and a lot was purchased in the center of town for $2,000. Since this bold maneuver left Kelley without a church in his principal community, as well as a debt of $500, he was forced to rent the old property until the parish could build. "I felt like a gambler," he recalled, "with everything on his last throw." The risk was compounded when he began to build a stone church without a cent in the account. The parishioners slowly responded to these heroics, at first volunteering labor and materials and raising enough cash to hire professional contractors. But as long as money remained scarce, the work proceeded unevenly. Meanwhile, neighboring Methodists were engaged in a similar project, and Kelley was told that an "extension society" had assisted them with seed money. In desperate need for funds, the priest searched the Catholic directories for a similar agency and to his grief found none. The begging in Lapeer continued until the frustrated pastor was forced to halt the work, still $8,000 in debt, and moved his congregation into a shell of a building, unplastered and unheated.[8]

The Islander had been less than five years in the parish when a war changed his life. There could be no question regarding Father Kelley's loyalty to his adopted country. As war clouds gathered in 1898 over Washington and Madrid, he was asked during a public lecture what an American Catholic should do if hostilities broke out between the United States and a solidly Catholic nation like Spain. Without hesitation, Kelley retorted: "Get a gun!"[9] When war was declared, the enterprising pastor viewed it as an opportunity not only to defend his country but also, perhaps, to resolve the crisis in the parish. The only diocesan priest in the state to enlist as a chaplain, he joined a National Guard unit, the 32d Regiment of Michigan Volunteers. He did this partly in the hope that his salary—or death benefits from an insurance policy—would go toward the unpaid debt at Lapeer. He was thus forced to leave the parish abruptly, spending his last hours in shaping up the records for a possible successor and in the dual spirit of citizen-martyr left for basic training in Florida.[10]

The new role provided several lessons as Captain Kelley met some special problems of the chaplains' corps. First, there were proportionately few Catholic priests, a scarcity which was due largely to the failure of bishops to assign clergy to the National Guard. When these units were called up, fewer priests were available to Catholic servicemen on a per capita basis than ministers serving Protestant soldiers. Catholic representation in the corps thus remained for Kelley a pressing concern during the two world wars to follow.[11] He also encountered the corps' need for status among the ranks. The chaplain's attire avoided identification with the professional soldier—black instead of the color of the regular services and barely distinct from a priest's ordinary wear. Kelley resented this unique costume which was neither military nor civilian. When protests from other chaplains grew louder, the corps was permitted to have uniforms, and Kelley found an immediate improvement in his work and condition.[12]

Morale among the soldiers was another factor that troubled him. The training had been designed for fighting in the tropics, and the men were eager to engage the enemy. Kelley nursed no hesitation in sending these volunteers into combat. One of his brightest memories focused on a camp of beardless youth waiting impatiently for action. When, at last, they were told to prepare for transport to the front, he never heard such cheers as the yells from these recruits. When, as he wrote later, the shouts faded from the troops' exhaustion, a band followed with the national anthem, and the men stood "silent in the spirit of Valley Forge and Andersonville. . . . The tears rolled down our cheeks, and we felt proud that we, too, were of that company."[13] Kelley was a patriot. The length of his service did not exceed five months and included no invasion of Spanish territory, only defending his health in the fever-breeding camps of the South. Long after the war, he teased himself regarding his military record, admitting —perhaps with some regret—that his combat experience had been limited to "fighting mosquitoes down in Florida. . . ."[14] His only exposure to battle would be a tour of the Western Front after World War I. Nevertheless, he lived on to earn the distinction of being the oldest priest to have served in the chaplains' corps, a distinction that gave him much satisfaction.[15]

The Spanish-American War did not ease the crisis in Lapeer in the way that Father Kelley had planned. Instead of liquidating the debt through a hero's death benefit turned over to the parish, the war led to other unique methods to raise the money. His army horse Teddy was first raffled off, bringing in $1,500. Local fund-raisers like this one did help, but a more promising avenue lay in his war experience and the captivating manner in which he told it. Kelley had already raised some parish revenue through lecturing locally on such subjects as "The Maid of Orleans," a talk on Joan of Arc; but his recent adventures in the army ripened into a more timely address, "The Yankee Volunteer." Now that he had a topic with broader appeal, he joined a professional speakers' bureau known as the National American Lyceum. Already more than seventy years old, it had spread from New England, where it had served as a powerful force in adult education and discussions. Across the country it had featured many of the ablest orators of the nineteenth century, who were furnished to local groups on a contract basis. Kelley knew of several priests who had an income from such speaking engagements. The Lyceum therefore contracted with the Islander, sending him on a lengthy circuit, first within Michigan and then throughout most of the West. The lecture tour was a huge success. His fees soon climbed, and dates to return forced him to extend his repertory with additional topics.[16]

Kelley's years in Lapeer revealed a pattern of pastoral administration which would be repeated decades later when he would return to it as the bishop of Oklahoma. First, the parish could support neither him nor his building program, and he used his talent liberally to make up for this deficiency. The income he derived from such personal activity as lecturing went entirely to the parish. The salary of the priest assigned to assist him was paid out of his own pocket, and the rest went toward the building of the church in Lapeer. His lecturing kept him out of the state for lengthy intervals, but arrangements were made so as not to deprive the parish of any essential service or to impose on his assistant. Weekday duties were light, and he was always in the parish on the weekends, taking a regular turn in attending the mission churches. The church at Lapeer was finished after nearly eight years—a noble Gothic structure of stone, with a slate roof and tasteful furnishings inside. When he was transferred, this property had a debt of $7,300, an obligation which Kelley had tried to lessen with every dollar at his disposal. On receiving a personal gift of $1,000, he promptly sunk it into the parish debt. When parishioners insisted on a parting gift, he asked for cash which he intended to apply to the debt. Instead, they presented him with a silver service which he was forced to take with him. In this way, Kelley's assets—his talent and his money—were placed at the complete disposal of his first pastoral charge as they would again be in Oklahoma. As his successor, Patrick W. Dunigan, pointed out, "he left Lapeer without a cent, just as poor as when he came."

The second theme in his style of pastoral administration was that the warmth of his personality reached across barriers of misunderstanding. In thirteen years, while an ex-pastor lived in open scandal in the vicinity, Kelley charmed a community once embittered toward the Catholic Church. His public appearances were as popular among non-Catholics as they were among his parishioners, and on the eve of his departure, a delegation of Protestant neighbors presented as a memento a substantial gift of cash to which no Catholic was allowed to contribute. "Dr. Kelley killed bigotry in this community," Dunigan noted further, "and made the Catholic Church respected and the Priest honored.... The stamp of his work will remain on this parish."[17]

The lecture tours constituted the turning point of Father Kelley's life. They first enabled him to finish the parish construction, the climax of his work in the diocese of Detroit. More importantly, they introduced him to the central idea of his life, the foundation of an "extension society" for Catholic America. As a traveling speaker, Kelley found that his problem in Michigan was not unique. His bout with loneliness and poverty in a rural assignment was matched in dioceses of the West and South, where he discovered first-hand a fading Catholic presence. His concerns began to focus during a brief stopover in a Kansas town where he found no Catholic chapel or the means among Catholic residents to build one. This was followed by a conversation with John J. Hennessy, bishop of Wichita, who told his visitor directly: "What we need is a national society like these Church Extension bodies in the Protestant sects." Kelley agreed, suggesting further that a bishop begin the movement. "No," Hennessy retorted, "a bishop is not the one to do it. Why don't *you* do it." The bishop continued on with an avalanche of argument. The priest had seen the crisis first-hand and from a broad perspective. Great movements, Hennessy added, have been launched in obscurity, an idea that appealed to the Islander's youth and lack of ecclesiastical rank. Under such pressure, Kelley escaped Wichita only with the promise to study the concept of Extension and to write an article for Hennessy's diocesan paper.[18]

Kelley embarked on studying the crisis of the rural church, but work in Lapeer intervened. His intention to publish an article thus faded until years later, in 1905, he returned to Kansas to lecture in the town of Ellsworth. The hopeless condition of the local parish there compelled him to fulfill his promise. On the train back to Michigan, he sketched his first article on the need of Extension. "I know a little 'shanty' in the West," it began,

> patched and desolate, through whose creaks and cracks the blizzard moans and chills, cellarless, stairless and dreary. Built on low prairie land, the excuse for a garden about it floods with water when the rains come, so that the tumbling old fence, with its network of weeds, falling, fails to hide the heartbreaking desolation.

Why, he asked further, did the pastor live in such poverty? "Because his people do not care," came the answer. "The decades of neglect . . . have left the scattered few unmindful." Kelley's indictment did not fall merely upon the parishioners of Ellsworth, Kansas. The distress of this pastor was equally due, he pointed out, to urban Catholics, who possessed the wealth to arrest the religious erosion in the countryside but were blind to the crisis. He went on to enumerate the Extension societies among the major Protestant bodies which in 1904 alone had assisted 657 churches on the American frontier—the Extension Board of the Methodists, the Baptists' Home-Mission Society, and the Congregational Church Building Society. The success of these agencies, he urged, had promoted the leakage of Catholics in the West and South; and only a Catholic counterpart could repair the damage and reverse the trend.[19] Kelley's train-bound meditation had thus centered on the major contribution of his life, the idea that large regions of the United States were genuinely a missionary field as pagan nations abroad, and were therefore entitled to touch the conscience of the affluent dioceses of the North and East.

Two final steps remained. The first was to publish the article on the "little shanty," and the medium selected was the *Ecclesiastical Review,* an influential monthly within clerical circles published in Philadelphia.[20] The response to Kelley's suggestion was overwhelming, transforming, as he recalled, "a timid and half-frightened young advocate into a determined pleader." This round of applause led him to the second stage, the search for a prominent member of the American hierarchy who would sponsor a new society to aid home-missions. This required consultation of bishops who had read the article and expressed interest in Kelley's proposal. When Bishop Hennessy insisted that only an archbishop would do, Archbishop Peter Bourgade of Santa Fé appeared at first the likely choice. But the New Mexican pointed the priest in another direction. Granted that his see was historic and located in the mission field, its poverty prevented him from taking a national role in raising funds. This logic convinced Kelley to look for his patron among the wealthy donor archdioceses of the East and North.

Three leading candidates along the Atlantic Coast, however, were promptly eliminated. John J. Williams of Boston was too old to add a mission-aid society to his burdens, and Kelley's visits with John Farley of New York and Patrick J. Ryan of Philadelphia were discouraging. The priest's best hope, therefore, lay with the rising metropolis of mid-America. Chicago was a growing Catholic center, but its archbishop of only two years, James Edward Quigley, was an unknown factor, a coldly reserved ecclesiastic whose capacity to lead was as yet untested. Nevertheless, as Kelley learned, he had read the article in the *Ecclesiastical Review* and favored the proposal. This was sufficient for the Michigan pastor to search out Quigley, whom he located at a clergy retreat at the University of Notre Dame. Before the opening exercise, Kelley frantically elaborated on his scheme to establish a national home-mission society but found the archbishop uncommunicative and aloof. Nervousness forced the priest to go on chattering, almost without breath, as the prelate watched and listened without a sound. When the visitor finally paused, Quigley broke his silence with an assurance of firm support. The patron had been found and Kelley's second preliminary step completed. The historic conversation ended with the archbishop's recommendation that a board of founders assemble at his home in Chicago.[21]

"Church Extension was now assured," noted the relieved Kelley, "and I knew it." With these thoughts he approached his thirty-fifth birthday, almost half his lifetime. Four active decades remained to him, years that would be spent in implementing the proposal he had just given to the archbishop of Chicago.

* * * * * * * * *

The birth of Extension signaled a counter-trend within the American Church which was evolving into a predominantly urban body. By the turn of the twentieth century, Catholics numbered almost 11 million, almost 15 percent of the national population. Their numbers were concentrated largely in the cities of the East and Midwest. Four archdioceses alone—New York, Boston, Philadelphia, and Chicago—accounted for a third of the faithful. Since the Civil War, the energies of church leaders had therefore focused on the problems of the cities, such as trade unionism and secret societies, quarrels among immigrant groups, and the building of a network of private schools. Catholic presence was weakest in the rural communities of the South and West, where dioceses were forced to depend on outside support. European organizations, like France's Society for the Propagation of the Faith, had long subsidized impoverished bishops. American Catholics had also made some strides toward reaching certain neglected native minorities, such as the establishment in 1886 of the Commission for Catholic Missions Among the Colored People and the Indians.

However, the crisis of the rural church, where priests were scarce and leakage among the scattered laity was increasingly alarming, continued unabated; and it had not reached the attention of Catholic majority. A step to reverse this trend took place on October 18, 1905, at the home of Archbishop Quigley, where nineteen gentlemen gathered to launch a home-mission society. The founders represented the great heartland of America with three exceptions—Peter Bourgade, the missionary archbishop of Santa Fé; Anthony A. Hirst, a wealthy attorney of Philadelphia; and Father Patrick L. Duffy of Charleston, South Carolina. With this strong midwestern flavor began the Catholic Church Extension Society of the United States of America, with Quigley as chairman of the board of governors and Kelley its president.[22]

Four developments characterize the formative years of Extension under Kelley's leadership. First, the society progressively strengthened its organizational core. Headquartered at first in Lapeer, it was incorporated in 1905 under Michigan law which provided for a board of governors as its policy-making body. The articles of association specified the purpose: the society was to collect and distribute funds "in any portion of the United States." Its focus was therefore on evangelism in continental America and her possessions. The choice of its saintly patron reinforced this aim. The new society was dedicated to Europe's most celebrated home-missioner, Philip Neri, the venerated Florentine of the sixteenth century who found his "India" in the streets of Rome.[23] Thus, Kelley's idea rapidly materialized into a legal entity which had a clear purpose and could responsibly solicit and dispense money. Hearing of this sound foundation, a young priest in Indiana applauded the beginnings. Like Kelley, John Francis Noll was a writer-lecturer and sensed the need of the evangelization at home. His first contribution was small, but he pledged annual support—a promise which he and his later creation, the weekly *Our Sunday Visitor,* kept faithfully.[24]

Essential, too, was the location of the offices of the society. At first, Kelley's rectory served in this capacity, an arrangement that was more than a convenience. Since Extension's mission was to rural America, he was convinced that its center should be located in a typical small community, a condition which Lapeer suited admirably. Another advantage was the prospect of lower expenses there than in a large city. This logic, however, was challenged from afar. Archbishop Patrick W. Riordan of San Francisco, a fellow Canadian by birth and former Chicago priest, had long proclaimed the unique spirit of enterprise in the Windy City. His early experience there, he often acknowledged, had been the source of whatever success his administration enjoyed in California. In the strongest terms, he urged that the society be transferred to a large city, preferably Chicago. In December, 1906, the board accepted Riordan's recommendation, and Kelley shortly thereafter acquired offices in the heart of the metropolis.[25]

This move was a major milestone. Not only did Father Kelley leave his first parish in which he had worked for thirteen years, but he switched dioceses, having been received at the age of thirty-seven as a newly incardinated priest of Chicago. Curiously, the change in diocese was an error. Kelley had originally intended only a leave of absence, but a delegation from the board had left for Detroit before receiving clear instructions and asked

Bishop Foley that Kelley be allowed to join the archdiocese of Chicago. Foley agreed, but both Quigley and Kelley regretted the mistake. Their preference was to have the president remain a priest of Detroit, while working in Chicago, so as to emphasize the supra-diocesan, or national, character of the society. In any case, Kelley's transfer had a lasting impact on both prelates. As Quigley became progressively energetic in his advocacy of Extension, Foley, along with some of his clergy, harbored a lingering resentment. Though he was a member of the board, the bishop of Detroit never attended meetings and showed at best an indifference toward the work of the society.[26] Six years after Kelley's departure from Michigan, the transfer to Chicago was completed when a charter was granted under Illinois law.[27] Despite the initial awkwardness, Kelley never regretted the curious irony that his mission to rural America should have been centered in what was becoming the nation's largest Catholic urban community.

Incorporation and accessibility provided credibility for a mission-aid society, but the mere good will of several clergy and laymen was hardly sufficient to awaken Catholic donors. Approval by the Holy See was necessary to ensure confidence in the new movement. In drafting the petition, Kelley consulted four archbishops—Quigley, Bourgade, Sebastian Messmer of Milwaukee, and William O'Connell of Boston. On June 7, 1907, Pope Pius X granted approval to the society and special indulgences to members.[28] This action climaxed a series of careful moves in molding Kelley's idea into a visible and respectable organization, particularly one which wealthy individuals would take notice of and trust.

The working style of the board of governors marked the second feature of Extension's origins. The By-Laws had authorized this board to set the society's policies, and it was to work with an auditing committee drawn from its own membership, along with a staff of executive officers. The board comprised several personalities who deeply touched Father Kelley's life.

The chair was occupied by the quiet, self-effacing archbishop of Chicago. A former bishop of Buffalo, Quigley had been in this assignment only two years when he agreed to sponsor Extension. His silent, inscrutable manner drove the Islander to occasional fits of exasperation. To all appearances, the archbishop was ponderous and incurably passive but sensible enough to see the value of Extension. His only known relaxation was the harmless hobby of cartology, collecting and studying maps. His reluctance to act led activists like Kelley to view him as a sluggard who must be guided to decision. In time, however, Kelley discovered that beneath the soft, opaque exterior there was a surprising toughness. In face of personal risk, Quigley could fix himself to a principle and be unswervingly loyal to a comrade. The superficial limitations in temperament were eventually to strike Kelley as merely "the faults of prudence, which may not be faults at all."[29]

The second ranking ecclesiastic was Sebastian Messmer, archbishop of Milwaukee, but Kelley viewed Peter J. Muldoon as the second most important member of the board. An auxiliary bishop when Kelley arrived in Chicago, Muldoon was named in 1908 to the new suffragan see of Rockford, Illinois. Kelley entertained no doubts regarding this prelate. In contrast to Quigley, Muldoon appeared open, balanced, decisive, uncomplicated; and under pressure, Kelley was told, this bishop would give the soundest counsel because he was known as "one of the most level headed of the whole crowd and there is no yellow streak in him."[30] Muldoon's reputation had earned him the chairmanship of the auditing committee, a responsibility more important than the vice-chairmanship of the board. Nothing would have pleased Kelley more than Muldoon's promotion to a major city where his talent could be fully used and where, too, Extension could sink new roots.

The need for home-missions also drew to the board a broad nucleus of laymen. Catholic wealth and position were represented in Richard J. Cuddihy of the *Literary Digest;* Richmond Dean, general manager of the Pullman Company; Richard Kerens, former United States senator and future ambassador to Austria. Perhaps the most colorful was Kelley's lifelong friend, Ambrose Petry. An active board member, Petry donated the first Catholic chapel-car in mission service in the world and volunteered to publish in book form an appeal to men of great wealth. Throughout his turbulent life he remained devoted to Kelley, always addressing him as "Francis." A believer in the business value of display, his offices were noted for their furnishings, paintings, and Persian rugs. His splendid taste in this direction, doubtless, influenced the tone of the Extension suite located in the stylish Rookery, the same building as Petry's.[31]

Petry was, however, afflicted with two weaknesses, both of which Kelley indulged. The first was a fetish for decorations, derived no doubt from his views on image-building. In negotiating the award of Knight Commander of St. Gregory the Great for him, Kelley confided to Quigley that "Petry appreciates a thing like this more than the tongue can tell." Later, Petry sought Kelley's intervention for an honorary doctorate, a suggestion which was mercifully discouraged.[32] His second flaw was poor business sense. Speculative ventures in America and Europe soon reduced Petry to penury and forced him into hiding, one step ahead of creditors. The hounding should cease, thought Kelley, since "he is absolutely penniless. He could not help a cat to save one of its nine lives." When his mercurial friend could no longer assist the society, Kelley never abandoned him. In Petry's later years, Kelley helped him dispose of his Chicago assets, advised him firmly to abandon the money markets, and occasionally passed on commercial secrets which might restore his friend's career. Whenever "Sir Ambrose" slipped into town, a bed always awaited him at Francis's residence.[33]

Petry was a flamboyant exception. Most laymen on Kelley's board were Catholic notables who had succeeded in business or the professions. But there was one more unique figure among Extension's supporters, Max Pam. There were two reasons which made him singular: he was an Austrian Jew by birth and an anonymous benefactor. A self-educated corporation attorney who had helped organize several of the greatest trusts of his age, Pam was a philanthropist with an interest in Kelley's society. He belonged to no denomination and was acquainted with only two or three priests. But, a frankly conservative man, he saw in the Catholic Church a force in favor of order and against socialism. For political and ethnic reasons, he remained a secret donor, giving $500 a year to Extension. An intimate of President William Howard Taft, Pam was Kelley's first channel into the White House. In return, Kelley introduced this friend to highly placed Vatican officials, including Cardinal Merry del Val, secretary of state, whose picture was hung prominently in Pam's law offices. Pam's interest attested to Kelley's ability to attract well-placed non-Catholics to his cause, men of the world with no more idea regarding religion than a natural urge to promote good. With a peculiar combination of charm and conviction, Kelley was able to touch outsiders and respect their differences as few of his contemporaries in the clergy could do.[34]

Father Kelley's executive staff suggested the same diversity as his chief advisers on the board. Second in command was Emmanuel B. Ledvina, an Indianapolis priest of Czech descent who, like the president, had given up a parish for Extension work. Besides being first vice president, "Led" was the general secretary who supervised the office and departments. He earned everyone's admiration as a superb manager. "He is a man of detail," Kelley commented to Ledvina's bishop, "who understands finances and administration. I question if there is a priest in the United States who has a better grasp of business than he has. . . ."[35] This temperament also tended toward a tenacity and candor that could occasionally jolt. Kelley welcomed open discussion, and in his presence Ledvina felt no intimidation, crediting Kelley with the standing invitation to his staff to voice "sentiments straight from the shoulder." But those unfamiliar with this Hoosier could interpret his sturdiness and unblinking honesty as an inflexible literalness.[36]

Few could have been more different from Kelley and Ledvina than William D. O'Brien, a young red-headed priest from Chicago whose elfin looks and reputation as a quipster suggested the stereotype of the carefree Irish cleric. In 1907 "Willie" joined Extension, beginning a lifelong association with the society. Self-styled as Kelley's "chief cook and bottle washer," he first served as director of diocesan home-mission programs in Chicago and was given minor responsibilities, such as developing programs to reach school children. His steadiness would lead Kelley one day to recommend that he succeed Ledvina and eventually himself. On the road as field secretaries were two other priests, Alexander P. Landry of Ogdensburg and Edward L. Roe of Peoria, who worked in the dioceses that invited them. Their work was a sensitive assignment because local authorities often resented their intrusion and placed tight restraints on fund-raising. Eventually the role of field secretary was discontinued when Landry entered the chaplains' corps in 1911 and Roe died three years later.[37]

In charge of them all was Francis Kelley, whose grasp of the reins was relaxed but ever firm. Though each subordinate was expected to do his job, Kelley allowed genuine friendships to seal the bonds among the priests. Seriousness and humor alternated in their exchanges with each other; the mood under Kelley's leadership was natural and comfortable. While Ledvina supervised with the strong efficiency, Roe felt free to remind the mildly anglophobic Kelley of the mischievous "story about the lady down whose back a piece of ice was dropped at a dinner and about the Englishman trying to get it out."[38] The staff eventually became "pals," with "Led" and "Willie" providing the continuity in the office, while the others toured the field. But beneath the bustle and banter was the unmistakable presence of the president, tagged forever among these intimates as the "Boss."

Though the personalities blended smoothly, housing provided a frustrating problem for the priestly staff. On transferring to Chicago, Kelley had alerted Archbishop Quigley that a parish appointment would interfere with Extension work, but suggested that for the sake of position he should be ranked as a pastor.[39] Kelley's desire for a separate staff residence troubled Quigley, and a compromise was reached when the priest agreed to begin in Chicago's South Side a new parish named after the society's patron, Saint Philip Neri. Plans went far enough for a rectory, large enough for eight, to be built for a mixed staff of Extension and parish priests. As it turned out, the archbishop relented on the arrangement. Kelley never took formal possession of the parish, and by 1914 each Extension priest was given a living allowance and expected to arrange his own accommodations. Having acquired from the Holy See the privilege of the "portable altar," Kelley took an apartment in the fashionable University Club, where he offered Mass privately and managed to evoke disapproving glances from a score of Chicago clergy.[40]

The board and staff helped Kelley guide Extension through its infancy. As these individuals worked together, there evolved the third original mark of the society, a set of principles and strategies that governed the work for the home-missions. Extension was, first of all, a national organization. Though the majority of the board members was drawn from the Midwest, continual efforts were made to recruit along the Atlantic and Pacific seaboards. "It must be remembered," Kelley repeated throughout his years in Chicago, "that Extension belongs to the Church in the United States and not to any one diocese."[41] Quigley shared this conviction. One way whereby his archdiocese raised capital was to market notes known as "Catholic Bishop of Chicago bonds." Though these were competitive regarding security and price, Quigley discouraged the investment of Extension's funds in these bonds. No diocese, including his own, must be allowed to take advantage of the convenient location of a national organization; otherwise, he argued, suspicions would be aroused regarding the independence of the society.[42]

Another principle was to narrow the target to white missions in the United States and its possessions. Other fields had already been apportioned to foreign-missionary groups and agencies already in charge of Indian and Negro missions. Extension was not to be a competitor or intruder. Archbishop William O'Connell of Boston appreciated this. In 1923 Ledvina was able to report to Kelley O'Connell's later thoughts in this regard. "From the very beginning of Extension's existence," O'Connell reminisced, ". . . it was a very, very much needed movement, big enough to take in a scope of activities, without bothering or interfering with any other movements or activities."[43]

Thirdly, Kelley's board did everything to maintain faith with its patrons. The auditing committee was an active instrument in this regard, carefully scrutinizing accounts and monitoring expenses. From the start, Bishop Muldoon and his colleagues stabilized the Extension's finances even at the risk of becoming, in the sentiments of the board itself, "at times. . .very inquisitive."[44] There was, however, a fourth and final principle that best distinguished the spirit of the board, one that was closest to Kelley's heart and the only truly controversial one: the principle of investing some income back into the society. Desperate appeals from the field tended to press Kelley and the board to spend whatever revenues remained after expenses. So intense was the pressure that at first Kelley suggested making grants before the money was collected, a recommendation that failed.[45] Soon after, a change in attitude appeared when Kelley convinced the board that as much as one-third of the revenues be held from the missions and used for administration. Once this policy was approved, the president had substantial sums at his disposal in order to hire a lay staff at attractive salaries and to lease well-appointed offices in downtown Chicago. Kelley recognized the businessman's dilemma, either "to economize" or "to put the best foot forward," that is, either to satisfy owners with dividends or to recycle profits into expansion. "The more money we put in," he reasoned, "the more we take out."[46] This approach made Extension unique among mission societies. Here was a society which imitated, to a degree, the style and philosophy of wealthy capitalists. At the same time, however, Kelley's break with the traditional pattern of mission-aid societies made Extension vulnerable to misunderstanding and criticism.

Finally, once these four principles were crystallized in the mind of Kelley's board, they were rapidly translated into inventive programs of raising and dispersing funds. In soliciting donors, Extension depended largely on individual contacts. The methods included direct mailing, legacies, donations—the normal strategies of fund-raising open to the society. Encouraged by Kelley to be innovative, the board developed two original techniques. The first was the annuity plans whereby Extension pledged to a donor a monthly percentage for a lifetime gift held in trust, a unique arrangement among mission-aid socities in the days before widespread pension programs in America. The annuity program did not, at first, win the board's enthusiasm, and the preliminaries leading to its adoption were conducted with the utmost care. Two board members even visited the St. Bonifacius Verein, the home-mission society in Germany, to study its experience in this field. It was only after their report that objections were overcome, and in 1912 the board approved the program.[47] Not only would this be a new avenue to raise money, but it reflected the board's confidence in the long and fruitful future of Extension. The annuity program had one further long-term result. Since it appealed to people preparing for their retirement, the board was encouraged to pursue only the most conservative routes in investing the society's funds. This cautious use of revenues from the start limited the impact of the business cycle upon Extension's assets, especially during financial disasters such as the Great Depression in the 1930s.

Another original project was *Extension Magazine.* Mission-aid societies had had organs to communicate with members, but Kelley revolutionized this vehicle by expanding a mouth-piece for the missions into a literary periodical. The first issue appeared in April, 1906, as a modest quarterly, which soon evolved into a splendid monthly with mission news, appeals, fiction, articles on applied theology and church personalities—all strikingly illustrated. As subscribers increased, numbering about 100,000 in 1911, the magazine provided Kelley with an exceptional opportunity to communicate. The monthly intervals between deadlines discouraged him from commenting too extensively on contemporary issues, and his pen concentrated largely on instructing, story-telling, and reporting on broad topics. In spite of the growing subscriptions, the expenses of the magazine generally absorbed any profit to be distributed to the missions. For this reason, Kelley was forced to use every personal resource to defend its value to the society. It was the only instrument to move Extension's message beyond the limited circle of wealthy donors into contact with the less affluent masses of Catholics who could not afford the annuities and large contributions but who formed the principal support of the other societies, especially the foreign-missionary ones. As a fund-raiser, therefore, the magazine had at best an erratic record, but as a device to extend the range of the society and to test the potential of Catholic periodical publishing, Kelley's monthly was a smashing success. Within five years it reached perhaps four or five million people.[48] These figures, along with Kelley's vigorous defense, justified the overhead, and the board's tough-minded auditing committee agreed. "If we never received a dollar profit from the Magazine," it concluded in 1911, "it is still our greatest engine for good."[49]

Alongside this early ingenuity in collecting money and reaching the Catholic public, the society displayed a parallel skill in distributing funds. From the beginning, the heart of this phase was to build chapels in neglected rural areas. The board member from Philadelphia, Anthony A. Hirst, initiated the idea when he endowed the first chapel in memory of his son. Within ten years of its foundation, the society was averaging two memorial chapels every week; and, it was hoped, each would develop into a parish.[50] A more sensational device was the adaptation of a Baptist idea, the chapel-car. Approved by the board in 1906, the first car was built with fully equipped chapel and chaplain's quarters and commissioned "St. Anthony." The vehicle had many advantages. It improvised a temporary place of worship in areas where no permanent chapel could be supported, notably in the Southwest and Pacific Northwest. The car likewise stimulated such curiosity in isolated communities that Catholicism briefly touched their lives, if only as an exhibit. The program was almost self-sufficient. The plate collection on Sunday supported the chaplain; and since the car seldom moved more than thirty miles a week, the railroads were generally willing to haul it without charge as freight along branch lines. While Kelley published extravagant tributes and experimented with chapels in large automobiles and boats, the program had several little known limitations. The heat of most summers in missionary areas rendered the chapel-car useless for several months. In a sense, too, it had oversold itself. The notoriety inclined benefactors to specify the use of their contributions exclusively for this purpose, thus tying up funds. Some like Peter Kuntz, a wealthy donor from Dayton, Ohio, sponsored no other projects than additional chapel-cars, regardless of the need elsewhere. Under his sponsorship, Extension completed its fleet with two more cars, "St. Peter" and "St. Paul." However, the greatest liability of the program was that it somehow offended the sensibilities of the apostolic delegate, Archbishop Diomede Falconio, O.F.M., a complex tale to be told later.[51]

In a short time, Father Kelley tasted success. His board was enthusiastic and resourceful. Revenues were mounting, and missionaries were lavish in expressing their gratitude. A compelling sign of results was the birth of a daughter society in the land of his birth. Kelley had strong fears about the neglect of English-speaking Catholics in western Canada. From the Deputy Indian Commissioner based in Winnipeg, he had learned confidentially that the shortage of English-speaking priests was contributing to the church's decline on the frontier. Kelley's own board included another first-hand authority, Michael F. Fallon, O.M.I., a distinguished Canadian educator whose differences with the French-speaking hierarchy had forced him to move temporarily to the United States. After a pastorate in Buffalo, he had been elected provincial of the American Oblates and joined Extension's board. From him, Kelley learned further of the incompatibility between English- and French-speaking clergy along the Canadian frontier.[52] This crisis—"the spectacle," in Kelley's words, "rising up before us constantly of souls perishing on the . . . plains for the Bread of Life"—moved the president to recruit the best known priest on Prince Edward Island, Alfred E. Burke, a man of enormous talent and enthusiasm but one given to strong independence of action.[53] Eager for a prestigious appointment that would take him to the mainland, Burke accepted the challenge of organizing an Extension society for Canada, and the apostolic delegate at Ottawa, Archbishop Donato Sbarretti, endorsed his efforts. Like Kelley, Burke at first met indifference in the hierarchy, especially among several French-speaking bishops. In 1908, however, he found his patron in Fergus Patrick McEvay, the newly appointed archbishop of Toronto.[54] Burke's promising work for the home-missions, however, did not last as long as had been hoped for. Though Extension had rescued him from the oblivion of a country parish, his tactless behavior would nearly abort the society in Canada, a tragic episode which will be discussed later.

Francis Kelley had thus guided Extension to maturity with a brilliant combination of drive and restraint. The task was never easy, demanding an enormous reservoir of energy and resilience. By and large, Kelley had mastered events. His archbishop was cooperative and pliant. The board engaged in uninhibited discussion, overruling on occasion the president's recommendations; but it shared a basic vision and trusted the executive staff. Ideas were not scarce, engineered into projects that drew admiration and imitation. With Burke in Toronto, Kelley had repaid a debt to his homeland, giving to it an institutional offspring of promise. As we note these considerable milestones, we should neither forget nor underestimate the enormous difficulties which Extension had overcome in its infancy and which made its quick success truly monumental.

* * * * * * * * *

Despite its solid beginnings, Extension had one serious flaw in its foundation. The society reached individual donors but was cut off from the Catholic masses, a handicap which not even the magazine had remedied completely. In order to assure itself of regular income, the society had to penetrate the diocesan structure, especially in the populous East. It was hoped that the American hierarchy would be cooperative; but if not, Kelley was ready to enlist the Holy See and perhaps overpower the bishops into supporting Extension. Tampering with internal operations of dioceses involved great risks ahead, but the reaction to his effort to reach the Catholic masses was more than what he expected. In starting the society, he had met indifference, but in now trying to broaden its support in the eastern dioceses, he confronted for the first time strenuous opposition.

Kelley's initial contact with the national leadership was unproductive. In 1906 he led a delegation to the annual meeting of the archbishops in Washington, where he urged the metropolitans to sponsor the new society. No decision was reached, but Cardinal James Gibbons formed an investigating committee composed of the heads of four midwestern sees—Chicago, Dubuque, St. Louis, and Milwaukee.[55] To Kelley's disappointment, no churchman in the East was named to the body, and the committee produced neither an endorsement in behalf of Extension nor invitations to introduce it throughout the country. Meanwhile, field secretaries continued to contact dioceses in order to promote the appointment of diocesan directors of Extension, along with encouraging special collections which would be divided between the society and the diocese. Not only were no directors appointed—William O'Brien of Chicago being the sole exception—but these visits seemed to make Extension all the more unwelcome. Even missionary bishops in America were asked to raise token sums for Extension as an example of good faith for the East. In 1908 Kelley finally brought the issue to the board's attention. In New York and Boston, he pointed out, the Society for the Propagation of the Faith enjoyed great success for the foreign-missions because of parish organizations. In a limp gesture, the board approved the publication of a booklet which would help organize volunteer parishes for the home-missions. After two years, only one bishop responded to Kelley's call, J. Francis Regis Canevin of Pittsburgh.[56]

Just as the barrier appeared impenetrable, Archbishop Quigley offered two key suggestions. First, he recommended the convocation of a national conference as a possible lever to move the dioceses. Kelley was thereby given charge of America's first missionary congress to be held in Chicago.[57] The three-day proceedings began on November 15, 1908, and drew to Chicago the largest Catholic gathering ever held in the nation, including more than sixty bishops. It was a spectacular triumph for Kelley as an organizer, and the formal sessions were noteworthy for three reasons. The presence of Archbishops Falconio and O-'Connell represented a quickening of interest in the East. Moreover, Patrick J. Donahue, bishop of Wheeling, struck the keynote when he prophesied: ". . . over [America's] plains and across the mountains . . . , I see a vast chain of Catholic Churches. . . ."[58] This forecast of a countryside dotted with chapels articulated Kelley's dream, a projection that he would recall for a lifetime. Kelley's own address, lastly, was extraordinary insofar as he dropped all caution and took the offensive. In the hour of his strength and glory, he declared with emotion that the American Church was "missionless," sleeping comfortably, swaddled in warm parochialism. His strong words were meant to indict the sterile centers of the Atlantic seaboard.[59]

But Kelley's real purposes at the congress were not confined to accusations. During the sessions, Archbishop Quigley chaired a public meeting of Extension's board of governors. This served as a vehicle to enlighten the bishops about the society's need for diocesan support. The discussion touched on the two central issues: the distribution and collection of funds for the home-missions. This open forum gave Kelley a rare platform. Regarding the society's disbursements, he recommended that these funds be filtered regularly through bishops who would be required to account for every dollar. Next, he raised the more important topic, a guaranteed support of Extension. "Things can't go as they have been going on," he urged. "It can't be left to one or two men to do the work. It is necessary that we get the people." With several prelates attending as guests, he then raised the key question: "Will the Bishops let us into the Dioceses . . . ?" Unfortunately, when Kelley hurled this challenge, the hour was late, the subject complex, the participants tired and edgy; and Quigley was forced to adjourn the meeting, unfinished.[60] Though a golden opportunity had been lost, Kelley's candor had cleared the air, and his sentiments had directly reached many who had been antagonistic towards him and the society.

Quigley's first suggestion—a national congress—was followed by a second: Extension should become a pontifical institution. This privilege would strengthen its affiliation with the Holy See, along with its credibility in the United States. The idea arose from blasts of criticism against the society, a carping which no action of Kelley and his associates could stifle. At the center of the opposition in the East was the Society for the Propagation of the Faith located in New York City. Its national director, Father Joseph Fréri, did not welcome the intrusion of another mission agency. When Extension was first organized, he interpreted this development as an indictment of neglect on the part of his own society to assist the home-missions in America. Almost immediately, he reminded Quigley that from 1832 to 1905 the Propagation had sent $6,020,977.18 to America and planned to continue its assistance.[61] From the beginning, therefore, Fréri would question the legitimate need for Extension.

Criticism extended even to the use of Mass stipends donated to Extension for the support of missioners. This was a delicate subject which involved the apostolic delegate, Archbishop Diomede Falconio. As a former Franciscan foreign-missioner, he was inclined to share the Propagation's opposition to Extension and was, in fact, among the last to accept Kelley's movement. The delegate was prompt to warn Kelley that stipends were not a source of cash income for a mission society. Kelley's assurances that the offerings went only to needy missioners did not suppress the complaints. Accusations continued, alleging further that Extension was cutting into the support of the parish clergy and that Kelley and his colleagues were appropriating the stipends for themselves. The charges were brutal. All that Kelley could do was to investigate the matter and repeatedly assure the delegate that he and his colleagues had not abused the regulations regarding Mass offerings.[62]

The sensitive nature of these complaints in the East kept the opposition out of public notice until two midwestern Catholic newspapers took up the Propagation's cause. The St. Louis *Western Watchman,* run by the peppery Father David S. ("Doc") Phelan, perhaps commanded the greatest influence among the midwestern clergy, and his view were supplemented by Omaha's *True Voice.* Frequent editorials censured Extension's policy of engaging businessmen as financial advisers and of reinvesting a portion of the revenues into "vain display and palatial headquarters." This practice amounted to a "commercialism" that was unique among mission societies. Not only had contributions been selfishly withheld from missionaries, but it was alleged further that Kelley and his financiers had made poor decisions with their money, bringing Extension close to early bankruptcy.[63] Extension's progress and its president's forceful views, especially his impassioned speech at the missionary congress, had aroused partisanship on both sides. These beginnings have "given us strong friends," he admitted to Quigley, "but . . . also awakened a number of 'wasps' who have always been against everything that was good."[64]

While Kelley discounted this criticism as little more than a nuisance, Archbishop Quigley perceived the enormity of the crisis. Though Extension had received papal approval in 1907, it could be crippled by a handful of unfriendly bishops. Priests working on the executive staff were only on loan to the society and could be summoned home at a moment's notice. Even Quigley's successor in Chicago could deal the movement a mortal blow by recalling the priests belonging to the archdiocese and inviting the rest to leave. The best protection against such a calamity was canonical erection, that is, to have the society made a pontifical institute. This was an unusual course of action; not even the 80-year-old Propagation had received this privilege. Kelley agreed to make preliminary inquiries at the Holy See. On February 18, 1909, he took passage on the *Caronia,* his first of twenty-six crossings of the Atlantic.[65]

The Chicagoan arrived at the Holy See at a dark moment of its history. Since the seizure of the States of the Church in 1870, the popes had made themselves voluntary prisoners at the Vatican. Along with his two predecessors, Pius X never appeared outside the basilica as a protest to the presence of the king of Italy, who reigned across the city in the Quirinal Palace. Aside from the conflict between church and state, outsiders perceived a deep division within the Roman Curia and identified two factions to which they affixed old Roman names. The "Politici" referred to the progressives who favored the trends set under the previous pontiff, Leo XIII, and his secretary of state, Cardinal Mariano Rampolla. This regime had been admired for its encouragement of a renewal among Catholic intellectuals, notably in the revival of Thomistic philosophy and the opening of the Vatican archives. This movement was accompanied by the willingness to work out practical accommodations with governments unfriendly to the church. Under Leo, for example, French Catholics were encouraged to accept the Third Republic as their legitimate government, even though it had a pronounced anticlerical tone.

The accession of Pius X in 1903, however, brought many adjustments in political and theological attitudes. At the risk of painting the colors too boldly, one might say that the current pontificate was dominated by the other party in the curia, the "Zelanti." Scholars with liberal tendencies were now intimidated by a suppression of thought that was climaxed with the condemnation of Modernism in 1907. Prominent in this administration was the British-born son of a Spanish aristocrat, the magnetic Cardinal Raphael Merry del Val, who followed Rampolla in the secretariat of state. Handsome and gifted in languages, ascetic and free from personal ambition, Merry del Val had the complete confidence of the pope and helped set the reactionary mood at the Vatican. As Pius's chief counselor and a *zelante,* he earned a reputation of standing for the strictest orthodoxy, and among diplomats, his conduct of foreign policy was marked by intransigence and a cold aloofness.[66]

During his first visit, Kelley steered clear of the complex struggles within the Roman Curia, but he did make several minor discoveries regarding its operation. Perhaps the biggest surprise was that little business was conducted at papal audiences. His first meeting with Pius X forever impressed his memory, but all the pontiff could do was to execute several formalities of welcome. The real work was done in the curia, and his three interviews with Cardinal Merry del Val were productive. That the Vatican was a seedbed of countless rumors of varying shades was another key lesson for the visitor. He met Archbishop O'Connell, whose cardinal's hat, he reported to Quigley, was all but fitted for the next papal consistory, and Chicago, Kelley noted further with delight, was the prime candidate for the second. Lastly, he learned that black-robed priests have virtually no status at the Holy See, waiting endlessly in stark antechambers and finding themselves ever at the end of a queue. Testimonials from prominent figures at home were no substitute for the purple of a prelate. To be effective at the curia, he concluded, Extension's president must come next time as a monsignor.[67] Nevertheless, Father Kelley's first tour succeeded beyond his expectation, and especially gratifying was Merry del Val's reception. "The Secretary of State was more than kind," he told Burke, "In fact, Bishop [Thomas F.] Kennedy [rector of the North American College] said I had the best reception that he has ever known a man with a black cassock to get . . . . I could not possibly have done more than [what] I did do."[68]

On his return to Chicago. Kelley began work on a new constitution to be submitted to the Holy See. As the plan for canonical erection unfolded, it called for a cardinal protector in the curia, and the board of governors empowered to nominate candidates for the presidency, one of whom would receive from Rome a pontifical appointment for five years, much like a bishop's. To Kelley's chagrin, however, Quigley stalled at this point. His concern centered on future problems if the archbishop of Chicago lost the exclusive right to name the president. In this effort to protect the society, the pendulum had swung too far. Extension would be practically autonomous in the archdiocese if the officers were nominated by a board, appointed in Rome, and given lengthy terms. As Extension continued to grow, reasoned Quigley, the presidency might become a target of ambitious ecclesiastics as had several wealthy dioceses; and Roman appointments had not remedied this abuse. After two weeks of delay, however, Quigley abruptly dropped his objections. In the meantime, Kelley had slighted the archbishop's experience in these matters and became impatient at his procrastination. "I know my man pretty well now . . . ," he complained to Burke. "He will postpone and postpone over again everything of the kind. He believes in postponement."[69]

In all, progress had been rapid and uninterrupted for Extension. The only obstacle which had thus far exacerbated Kelley was not the editorial criticism in St. Louis and Omaha but the gentler pace of his patron Quigley, a man whom nearly everyone underestimated. Within a year, however, he would find the tepid archbishop of Chicago made of sterner stuff than he had imagined.

"I know my man pretty well now. . . ." The cocky Islander was in for a surprise.

III
The West Awakens

Archbishop Quigley's reluctant approval of a new constitution for Extension was but the first step toward making the society a pontifical institute. The document had to be drafted, endorsed by the board, and submitted to the Holy See through the apostolic delegate. The most disturbing unknown in this sequence was the position of Archbishop Falconio. The petition for canonical erection to Rome would be channeled through him, but his inclinations already seemed to favor Extension's critics. Events in Canada made Francis Kelley more apprehensive about Falconio's sentiments. In Toronto, Father Burke had likewise moved toward canonical erection and had the open support of the delegate at Ottawa, Archbishop Sbarretti. But when Kelley recommended in early 1910 that both societies submit petitions together, Burke was forced to decline. Sbarretti had insisted that the Canadian society act independently, and this suggested to

Kelley that Falconio was so opposed to Extension in the United States that if given the opportunity, he would use his influence to cripple the Canadian society as well.[1] These vibrations from the north raised the ironic possibility that Kelley's daughter society in Toronto had a better chance to become a pontifical institute than his own in Chicago.

An attempt to convert Archbishop Falconio to Extension began at this time when a field secretary, Father Edward L. Roe, tried to introduce Extension into New York City. His work, however, drew such complaints from Archbishop John Farley, the principal patron of the Propagation in the hierarchy, and from Monsignor Joseph Fréri who had established the Propagation's national office in this city, that Roe had to be recalled.[2] This disturbance persuaded Kelley to go in person to the delegation in Washington, in an effort to clear the air with Falconio himself. His trip to the East brought a sharp awakening. Prepared to find Falconio mildly unsympathetic to Extension, he encountered an angry churchman. Given no opportunity to defend the society, Kelley was battered by a torrent of misinformation—all obtained, the delegate confessed, at Archbishop Farley's table.[3] This encounter, no doubt, stunned Kelley into the realization that Extension could not look to the delegate for help but must seek its own representative at the Holy See. This revelation of Falconio's hostility, however, was compensated by another development: the unfolding strength of the archbishop of Chicago. When Kelley reported the delegate's attitude to Quigley, the latter calmly advised the priest to reserve his defense for the appropriate moment. "The more I see of the Archbishop," admitted Kelley, "the more convinced I am of his staying qualities. He is averse to a row, but when somebody brings it on, he is not averse to fighting it out."[4]

Falconio repeated his objections when Quigley visited Washington in early 1910. First, the delegate expressed grave doubts regarding Kelley's character and ability. The source of this comment had been, Quigley discovered, Kelley's former bishop, John S. Foley of Detroit, originally from Baltimore. Though Foley had made no accusations, his dislike for the priest had been carried to Cardinal Gibbons, who evidently relayed it to the delegate. Next, Falconio doubted the value of the chapel-cars and even questioned whether all the chapels listed by Kelley in the annual reports of the society had actually been built. As the delegate continued, Quigley sensed the sectional undertones which the fight over Extension was stirring. The two major institutions of the American Church which received national support were located in the East, each with a powerful protector: the Propagation of the Faith with Farley of New York and The Catholic University of America with Gibbons of Baltimore. But, headquartered in Chicago, Extension was a western creation, barred from the wealthy sees of the East. At this point, Quigley came forward as the society's protector when he dramatically interrupted Falconio's diatribe. "I know Dr. Kelley and I know what he is doing . . . ," he retorted angrily:

> This nagging at the President has to stop. . . . If this thing continues, we are going to fight. The Bishops of the West have some rights.

The archbishop punctuated this interruption with an emphatic blow on the table, leaving soon after with what was described as "blood in his eye."[5]

Quigley kept on the offensive, intending to return to Washington with endorsements and a committee. Back in Chicago, he summoned the board to a special meeting on February 15, 1910. A series of resolutions was passed. The first expressed confidence in Kelley as president and another endorsed the chapel-car program. A third listed the chapels built with Extension money, while a final resolution reviewed the general accomplishments since the beginning. Furthermore, to neutralize any misinformation from Washington, the board authorized Kelley to deliver personally to the Holy See this litany of resolutions, along with the draft of the new constitution which would make Extension a pontifical institute. This remarkable display of Quigley's leadership exhilarated the president. When Kelley thanked the archbishop for his heroic stand in the delegation, Quigley's reply was characteristically cryptic but pointed: ". . . the cause is worth it and the fight will now be to a finish." His unflinching loyalty, coupled with Kelley's sense of guilt for having misjudged this man, forced tears to the Islander's eyes as he departed for Rome. The archbishop "does not say much," he told Burke, "but I learned . . . that a quiet exterior does not mean weakness."[6]

At Quigley's suggestion, Extension's board had not only approved the president's trip to Rome but also selected an impressive committee to bring the new constitution and resolutions to Falconio before Kelley's departure. According to Kelley's recollection, the historic encounter combined gravity and comedy. It began as a contest of appearances. The delegate was "all decked out in his finest cassock," and the committee arrived in a fleet of splendid carriages. "They were the swellest things in Washington," chuckled Kelley to Burke. "A pair of horses each with [a] silver mounted harness. There is nothing like a coach and pair to do the work and no detail was missed." Falconio then greeted the visitors with a polite commendation of the society's plan to apply for canonical erection. He had no objection to the home-mission movement, he remarked, and was "a Father to us." His earlier criticism of Extension had been intended only to alert it of the charges that were circulating. This, he added, was the action of a friend who "never shared in them." Next, he acknowledged his previous acquaintance with the board members—the clergy as well as "all the nice lay gentlemen," as Kelley commented mischievously, who "would do no wrong." The society, Falconio admitted further, had produced splendid reports which should be published.

Once these opening courtesies had been observed, the real business began, and nearly all the laymen had their say. As Kelley remembered the episode, the group thrashed out all the issues, including the chapel-car program and the annual reports on chapel-building. After an hour, Falconio and the committee parted "good friends." Along with a promise to forward to Rome the new constitution and board resolutions, the delegate expressed his delight to meet "so many nice people." With relish Kelley recalled the lavish farewells featuring Falconio himself who led the visitors to the front door, bowing all the way and catching a glimpse at the fine carriages outside. The priest's sarcasm typified the exuberance of the committee. Convinced that the cause had been won, Quigley and Kelley found themselves that evening at the Waldorf Hotel in New York City, recounting the delicious details of the interview until two o'clock in the morning. In a moment of heightened euphoria Kelley's thoughts turned to Farley and Fréri. After this meeting in the delegation, the priest mused, " 'little old New York' will probably be in a corner that will be narrow enough to hold them in tight."[7]

To all appearances, the delegate had been converted and would dispatch the documents with no further objection. Nonetheless, Kelley made a second trip to Rome, bringing with him a duplicate set of documents.[8] In his audience with Pius X on May 1, 1910, he found the pontiff briefed well on Extension. The pontiff questioned the detailed character of Kelley's constitution, explaining that its many provisions would only harness a young organization. Extension, he advised, was too inexperienced to impose upon itself a heavy structure which would discourage adaptation in the years ahead. Instead of approving the constitution, Pius issued an apostolic brief, *Qua Nuper,* which elevated Extension to a pontifical institute and created three key positions. First, it named the prefect of the congregation of rites, Cardinal Sebastian Martinelli, as Extension's "protector" at Rome. He would not only symbolize Extension's special union with the Holy See but, as Falconio's predecessor for six years in the American delegation, he would also serve as an informed advocate for the society. Second, the chairmanship of the board of governors, known henceforth as the "chancellorship," was affixed to the archdiocese of Chicago. Quigley and his successors were to inherit that post by virtue of their appointment to this see. Third, the "president" would be a papal appointee who would be selected from a *terna* submitted by the board and given a five-year term.[9]

The apostolic brief completed Extension's adolescence. In its first five years, the society had encountered weighty opposition but managed to collect nearly $650,000 for the home-missions in America. With its new status as a pontifical institute, it had special proof of Rome's approval of its work. The simplicity of *Qua Nuper* testified to the confidence of the Holy See in its capacity to work out its own future. Kelley attributed this extraordinary trust to Cardinal Merry del Val in whose department the brief had been written; and this debt the priest repeatedly acknowledged for the rest of his life.[10] Extension had weathered a turbulent puberty and had come of age.

A dreary epilogue occurred with Archbishop Falconio's last effort to scuttle the society. Even after the apostolic brief had been promulgated, the chapel-car work continued to obsess the delegate. "He is still abusing the Chapel Car," Kelley complained to Quigley, "from one end of the country to the other." The chaplain of the car in Oregon, Kelley learned, had visited the delegation and reported to Falconio how Archbishop Alexander Christie of Portland, Oregon, lauded this program. "Does the Archbishop think I am a child?" Falconio replied. "I do not approve of the Chapel Car. I condemn it."[11]

But the delegate's unfortunate fixation was to reach even the corridors of the White House, and Kelley would know it. Montreal had been selected as the site of the International Eucharistic Congress in September of 1910. The papal legate was to be Cardinal Vincenzo Vannutelli, dean of the college of cardinals. Kelley had a special interest in the congress. At Rome he had met Vannutelli, who wanted to see a chapel-car, and Kelley spared no effort to move it from Oregon for exhibition in Montreal.[12] This afforded a well-placed member of the Roman

Curia, along with his entourage, to see the notorious item for himself. After the congress, moreover, the cardinal toured parts of the United States, and arrangements were made for a visit with President Taft at the White House. A member of the party was Monsignor Sante Tampieri, a veteran bureaucrat in the curia who worked in the secretariat of state. An early advocate of Extension, he had written the draft of *Qua Nuper* and remained a lifelong confidant of Kelley. Through Tampieri, the Chicagoan learned of a conversation between Vannutelli and Falconio, who accompanied the cardinal to the White House. To Kelley's distress, the delegate used the pause before President Taft's appearance to denounce the chapel-car program. Falconio's tenacity was incomprehensible. Viewed from Chicago, this stubbornness proved that the delegation was a virtual captive of the East. "We are face to face," reflected Kelley, "with all sorts of calumny coming from around Washington, Baltimore and New York."[13] But the delegate's impact had been circumscribed. Extension was rapidly building up a broad base of allegiance in the home-mission fields of the West and South. As a pontifical institute, it also had its own clear channel to the Holy See in the person of a protector.

* * * * * * * * * *

The difficulties between Archbishop Falconio and Extension had an important impact on the Catholic leadership in the Midwest. The delegate's persistent opposition had underscored for the society the sectional imbalance in the American Church. It appeared that the eastern dioceses, notably New York and Baltimore, had an inordinate influence in shaping the attitudes of the delegate and in setting national priorities at the meetings of the American hierarchy. More importantly, this unpleasant dispute had stimulated in Archbishop Quigley qualities of leadership which had, heretofore, escaped the notice of Kelley and others.

The placid chancellor, Kelley discovered, had shown under fire the hardness and durability of a "brick." He was also something of a strategist, leaving the errands and worries to Kelley. His two inspirations, a national congress and pontifical status, had strengthened the society enormously. These were to be followed by a third suggestion, a national collection for Extension, which was the most ambitious proposal yet. If successful, it would confirm Extension's rapid ascendancy and, in the name of home-missions, touch the pocketbook of every diocese in America.[14]

The new proposal was based upon two needs. First, Extension had yet to reach the Catholic masses. Its work rested on the generosity of wealthy individuals, but as early as 1909, Kelley urged the necessity to shift emphasis. "In my opinion," he told the board, "a struggle must now be made to get to the people who give small sums."[15] The society's contacts with this level of the Catholic community had been confined largely to personal appearances, such as visits and public speaking, and to the magazine. But both approaches were costly. The only efficient solution, Kelley was convinced, was local cooperation, especially in the use of diocesan and parochial structures. A pioneer in this approach was Bishop Canevin of Pittsburgh, whose diocese sponsored a Missionary Aid Society. At first, contributions were raised through memberships, and the revenues were divided between the Propagation and Extension. Eventually, the system evolved into an annual parish assessment, based on 0.5 percent of the gross income.[16] Such a plan increased and stabilized home-mission support, while all but eliminating fund-raising expenses.

Along with Extension's need to reach the Catholic masses through diocesan and parochial structures came a second: the need to penetrate eastern dioceses where the bulk of the Catholic working class lived. The experience of the field secretaries confirmed this. In the spring of 1909, Father Alexander P. Landry had been invited to organize Extension in New Orleans. The priest canvassed the archdiocese thoroughly, mailing over 3,000 pamphlets and circular letters; but the historic see of southern

Catholicism made a paltry showing. "The real fertile soil for Church Extension revenue," Ledvina told Kelley, "is the East, beyond a doubt, and also in the Central States, in a measure. When we go beyond that we will not find the results commensurate with the efforts."[17]

The best means of anchoring Extension in the Catholic population centers would be a national collection. This method would not, however, be readily agreeable to the bishops because it would add a collection to the five already in operation. Kelley's very first action in this direction was a miscalculation that crippled the entire effort. In October, 1910, the board approved a petition drafted by him, which was addressed to the pope and requested an annual collection for home-missions in each diocese.[18] Before going to Rome, the document was to circulate among the bishops for their signatures. No plans were made to meet with the hierarchy, and Kelley had deliberately excluded the delegate, who appeared still bent on Extension's suppression. "He takes his ideas entirely from New York," Kelley explained to Quigley, "and he will continue to nag at us as long as we exist."[19] From the start, Kelley was managing a direct appeal to the Holy See, a risky strategy which he adopted because of the society's favor in Rome and the strength of its opponents at home.

The campaign was halted when word came from New York. In acknowledging the petition, Archbishop Farley urged that a matter of this importance be submitted to the archbishops at their next annual meeting. If commanded by the Holy See, New York would do its share, but in the meantime, he added, it must protect the interests of the Propagation.[20] Kelley received a similar reply from the other major center in the East—Baltimore—where Cardinal Gibbons governed. A month later, when Father Roe reported a confidential conversation with Bishop Thomas F. Kennedy of Rome's North American College, Kelley learned of the rage which his campaign had provoked. On a recent visit, Kennedy had found the usually gentle cardinal "*simply furious*" at the way in which the Islander had ignored him as dean of the American hierarchy. The dioceses would not tolerate another general collection, Gibbons insisted, and the signatures on Kelley's petition bore little weight because they represented "those only who would be beneficiaries." Merry del Val, Martinelli, and Falconio would soon receive blistering protests, describing Kelley's "underhand methods" as an insult to the cardinal of Baltimore. With his acute sense of Vatican etiquette, Kennedy warned that the Holy See would not easily overlook the "personal" slight which Gibbons's reaction emphasized.[21]

In circulating the petition, Kelley's action was technically correct. A majority of archbishops, eight out of fourteen, had signed the document, and the cardinal was forced to denounce it principally as an affront to himself as their national leader. But the tactic was a blunder of gigantic proportions. In failing to observe the customary courtesies, Kelley had alienated a venerable churchman who commanded the loyalties of his generation. But this opening mishap did not deter the Chicagoan. As he moved further into position to engage the aging powers of the East, he was ready to challenge the master strategist of Baltimore.

At Farley's request, Kelley agreed to present the petition for a national collection to the archbishops at their annual meeting on April 27, 1911, but this did not prevent him from lubricating the machinary in Rome. Cardinal Martinelli received the document, and two weeks before the meeting in Washington, he presented it to the pope. At this point, the petition appeared unstoppable. It had reached the papal chambers; by now, almost three-quarters of the ordinaries in America had affixed their signatures to it; and Extension was a proven success in assisting home-missions, its annual revenues already approaching $300,000.[22] The minutes of the archbishops' meeting record only this innocent skeleton of the discussion: the presentation of Kelley's petition, the unanimous commendation of Extension, and the motion to defer action until the next meeting in October.[23] The postponement forced Martinelli to ask for new instructions from Chicago, and in reply Kelley provided a full commentary on the meeting. The key to the archbishops' course of action was Gibbons's concern over another national collection which, in Kelley's view, was in jeopardy. The cardinal served as chancellor to The Catholic University of America, the support of which had faded in the hierarchy in recent years. Vital to its survival was an annual collection in each diocese which, on the archbishops' recommendation, had been approved by the Holy See in 1903 for ten years and was soon to expire. Hence, Extension's petition complicated Gibbons's plan to have this permission renewed. If Extension's petition were presented along with that of the unversity, there would be a chance that the archbishops or the Holy See would either veto or combine both collections, or perhaps even shift their support from the university to Extension. Rather than take this risk, the cardinal elected to promote the university collection at this meeting and to table Extension's petition.

His first objective was won when the archbishops approved the continuation of the university collection. Following this lead, Archbishop John J. Glennon of St. Louis proposed to suspend the discussion of Extension until the university matter had been settled in Rome. This motion was opposed by Quigley, O'Connell of Boston, John B. Pitaval of Santa Fé, and James H. Blenk of New Orleans, along with proxy votes from John J. Keane of Dubuque and Alexander Christie of Oregon City. The critical turning point occurred when Gibbons—correctly—disqualified the proxies. Thus, those who carried the postponement constituted a coalition of Gibbons, Farley, Glennon, John Ireland of St. Paul, William H. Elder of Cincinnati, and—to Kelley's disappointment—Messmer of Milwaukee, the vice-chancellor of Extension. This vote led to the suggestion that a resolution be passed approving the society. Quigley rejected this, reminding his colleagues that the papal brief, *Qua Nuper,* was sufficient endorsement. The archbishop pressed for the petition again but was told that the postponement was only to assist the university. Afterwards, the cardinal promised Quigley, O'Connell, and Blenk that he would support Extension's petition as soon as the Holy See approved the university collection. Kelley momentarily accepted the outcome, fearing that pressing the issue might injure the university's interest and divide the hierarchy.[24] Frustrating as it was, the meeting had, as he told Burke, one good effect: "we now know where our friends are, and the air is all clear."[25]

To be idle while a great issue remained unsettled was contrary to Kelley's nature, and he took full advantage of the interval before the next meeting of the archbishops. First, he made several gestures of conciliation to the patrons of the university. He suggested to his benefactor, Max Pam, the establishment of a university chair with an endowment of $50,000. He also explored the possibility of combining the annual collections. A smaller number of well-managed appeals, he reasoned, could actually increase revenues for the institutions supported by the hierarchy. He even invited the university rector, Thomas J. Shahan, to go with him to Rome where, together, they could consult with the Holy See about this matter; but Shahan declined. Through these efforts, however, Kelley continued to interpret the impasse over Extension in terms of classic sectionalism. "My own position," he explained to Shahan, "is that I want peace absolutely between the East and the West. . . ."[26]

In addition to extending the olive branch at home, Father Kelley returned to Rome in order to plot strategy with the cardinal protector. The collections for the university and Extension, Martinelli urged, must be merged because the Holy See might veto separate ones. In the past decade, Kelley was told further, the university had lost prestige. Extension's petition, however, though it enjoyed greater favor at the Vatican, would fail without Gibbons's support. Thus, at the fall meeting of the archbishops, Quigley would have to reopen the issue of the university collection.

The visit with Martinelli not only formulated strategy but it also reassured Kelley of Extension's strong position in the Roman Curia. The visitor from Chicago was drawn into the inner circles of papal government. Both Merry del Val and Martinelli, he learned, appreciated Quigley's refusal to accept the archbishops' recent commendation of Extension. "Card. Martinelli," Kelley confided to Quigley, "was particularly sarcastic about the 'propriety' of the meeting offering to endorse 'the Pope's endorsement.' " Before his departure, officials even sought his views on episcopal candidates and shared some confidences regarding the current appointments of Edmund F. Prendergast to Philadelphia and of James J. Keane to Dubuque. His reception appeared so warm that Kelley even recommended his friend Burke for the newly vacant archdiocese of Toronto.[27]

Soon after his return home, the Islander suffered a series of jolts that snapped his euphoria. The first was the defeat of a national collection for Extension. As Cardinal Martinelli had proposed, Archbishop Quigley agreed to reopen the issue of the university collection at the fall meeting of the archbishops scheduled for October 12, 1911. To his astonishment, however, the meeting was abruptly called off. Quigley received word of the cancellation only when he arrived in Washington, and no reason was given. This action sealed the fate of his proposal to divide the collection between the university and Extension.

Nevertheless, the determined archbishop remained in the capital for the meeting of the university's trustees. Earlier in the year, the rector had been requested to survey the hierarchy regarding the continuation of the university collection, and Quigley now requested that a report be made to the trustees. The results were that out of sixty inquiries only thirty-five responded in the affirmative, the remaining bishops having sent no reply at all. This tally, Monsignor Shahan admitted, was "very unsatisfactory." No bishop had expressly opposed the university collection, he reported further, but many expressed strong disapproval of adding more national collections. It was plain to Quigley that, though the university's patronage was thinning, the home-missions had little chance for a similar program of financial support among the dioceses. The trustees therefore instructed

Shahan to leave for Rome.[28] When the Holy See renewed permission for the university collection in January, 1912, Kelley dropped all hopes for Extension.

Kelley received his second blow when the Holy See made its long awaited announcement of the new American cardinals. During his visit to Rome, Kelley had received strong indications that Quigley would be named the first one west of the Appalachian Mountains. Others had been mentioned, but Quigley appeared on everyone's slate. Even the Chicago papers had followed Kelley's movements in the Eternal City, describing him as a powerful insider who was advancing Quigley's candidacy. In late October, however, the official news broke that the three American citizens to receive the red hat were Farley, O'Connell, and Falconio.[29] Kelley's reaction was mixed. On the negative side, not only had the Midwest been overlooked, but two arch-enemies of Extension had been honored, Farley and Falconio. No doubt, too, Kelley was haunted by the thought that Quigley's firm advocacy of the society might have created powerful enemies who had checked his promotion. On the other hand, he welcomed O'Connell's honor, promptly wiring his congratulations to Boston and arranging a public statement by President Taft. But even this response was bittersweet because, as he told a Boston priest, it was O'Connell's "nomination which a great many people thought should go to the West."[30] This milestone therefore reinforced Kelley's belief that, in the eyes of Rome, Catholic America was still centered along the Atlantic seaboard. Along with Gibbons—as the priest's friend, Ambrose Petry, put it—there were now "Four Red Hats all within 500 miles in a North & South line."[31]

Lastly, Kelley was staggered by the fact that his opponents had nearly succeeded in discrediting him in Rome. In October, 1912, Merry del Val alerted Quigley of complaints regarding Extension's finances and requested an accounting. Assisted by Kelley, the archbishop returned a spirited and elaborate defense in which he acknowledged his awareness that the major objection centered on the society's relatively large operating expenses. Without a national collection, he explained, Extension was forced to generate its receipts by direct mail, publishing a magazine, and personal appearances by the staff, all of which were expensive techniques in fund-raising. These programs required a large central office staffed by skilled employees. Quigley then charged that behind the complaints was sectional jealousy. Leadership in the West was rapidly maturing and was willing to take on its share of national responsibilities. It was this fact, not the desire to conduct a "rivalry with the older Catholic centers," that had made Chicago the seat of the home-mission movement.[32]

The report was a remarkable performance, Kelley's hand evident in each paragraph, and it was desperately needed. Before it reached the Holy See, a sympathetic visitor in Rome sensed the crisis which threatened Extension. The curia had been told, Burke reported to Kelley, that "it takes 40% of your collections to pay expenses of maintaining your luxurious offices and your good self in the luxury of a prince." Burke's associate in Toronto, Joseph T. Roche, had gathered equally disturbing news regarding Falconio, now a cardinal of the curia, who was in strong position to undermine Extension. "He is as bitter as death . . . ," Roche noted. "You people have an implacable enemy in Rome. The University crowd are responsible for it and they have made common cause with the New Yorkers."[33] Despite the warnings, Kelley waited patiently for Quigley's report to take effect, confident that his defenders were a match for his adversaries. "It appears," he confided to Roche, "my dear friends from New York, Washington and Baltimore are getting after me pretty lively; but the big men are sticking." Martinelli was vigilant; Tampieri in the secretariat of state viewed the charges "with a grain of salt"; Quigley stood firm; and "the Boston Cardinal will not forget." Kelley's confidence was not misplaced. When Merry del Val finally studied Quigley's report, it succeeded in exonerating the society. "Your report of Extension," Bishop Kennedy told the archbishop, "has called forth the highest praise from the Secretary of State. I have never heard him express himself so enthusiastically as he did . . . the other day."[34] The crisis at the Holy See ended in triumph for Kelley, who refuted forever the charges of Extension's extravagance and mismanagement. At the same time, he could not forget that, until its climax, this emergency had brought Extension as close to suppression as it would ever come in its history.

In sum, Father Kelley's vindication was little more than a Pyrrhic victory. He had battled his opponents brilliantly through Archbishop Quigley, but the campaign was lost when the Holy See's renewal of the university collection ended hope for support of the home-missions at the diocesan level. This defeat he attributed partly to smug provincialism and partly to sectional jealousies. A major obstruction in Catholic America, he told a Roman friend, was still the "narrow parochial and diocesan spirit that has fastened itself, imperceptibly, upon us. The priest thinks only of his little parish, and the bishop only of his . . . view of things." Related to this ecclesiastical myopia was geographic self-interest which afflicted and divided the church's leadership. "At the bottom of everything," he remarked bitterly, "is the fact that the Society is new and comes out of the West." His struggles had convinced him that the established centers of the Atlantic coast continued to dominate the hierarchy and ignored the vast interior, the rich and bustling heartland which had reached "the point where it is the most important part of the Church in America."[35] At the turn of the century, many midwesterners shared his robust opinion, but Kelley was one of the handful who was willing to risk everything for it.

* * * * * * * * *

The Islander was persistent. "I suppose it is the Irish in me that makes me hate to be licked," he explained to Shahan, "and when I start out to do anything, every nerve is working until it is done."[36] Though the national collection was out of reach, the East remained his target, and Kelley explored new maneuvers in that direction. A foothold in the New York area was first suggested by Roche, who had discovered the diocesan weekly in Newark for sale. If, he told Kelley, Extension purchased it and shared it with the bishop, this would "put you into the heart of a territory, which is now practically closed to you." Kelley was interested but hesitated. "Make up you mind. . . ," Roche pleaded, "you will never amount to a row of beans in the East until you break in this way."[37] The opportunity eventually slipped away, and New York was left intact.

Kelley, however, took greater interest in penetrating the ecclesiastical domain of Cardinal Gibbons by pursuing the donation which Max Pam had agreed to give The Catholic University of America. The prominent, conservative Jewish attorney of Chicago had scaled down Kelley's original suggestion of a chair endowed with $50,000 to five scholarships amounting to $5,000, a gift still very welcome to Gibbons as the university's chancellor.[38] With Kelley's help, Pam drafted the formal letter of presentation to the cardinal, a careful document which reflected the dual authorship. First, the philanthropist explained his interest in the university as a champion of the traditional values which he endorsed. Second, Kelley included a subtle invitation toward reconciliation between Baltimore and Extension. The scholarships, the letter stipulated, would be awarded jointly by the university and the society.[39] The significance of the donation lay less in the amount than in its origin and impact. Kelley's idea not only suggested that it was time to heal old wounds between East and West but it also represented midwesterners as above sectional self-interest. The scholarships did not open the archdiocese of Baltimore to Extension, but they helped mellow the cardinal's memory of his recent struggle with Chicago over the university collection.

As it turned out, the Yankee city of Boston offered Extension the only route into the East, and the vehicle to carry it there would be the second missionary congress. The first one in Chicago in 1908 had been so successful that Extension's board had at first planned a cycle of congresses to be convened every two years. When this proposal proved to be too ambitious, the board was pleased to accept the invitation of a pioneer supporter in the East, Archbishop William O'Connell, who suggested dates in October of 1913.[40] Preparations for this gathering strengthened Father Kelley's relationship with two prominent figures in the hierarchy of his generation. The first was the host of the congress. Not a universally beloved ecclesiastic, Archbishop O'Connell was feared because of his intimate contacts within the Roman Curia of Pius X and especially because of his long friendship with Cardinal Merry del Val. During his first trip to Rome in 1909, even the inexperienced Kelley noted the New Englander's enormous influence, describing it as a " 'cinch' on the Vatican."[41] His appointment to Boston as coadjutor three years earlier had raised a storm among the American bishops because his name did not appear on any of their lists of candidates. His elevation to the cardinalate in 1911 had likewise drawn cool comments around the world. On that occasion, Burke reported from Rome that the English-speaking colony irreverently called the new prince "Big Bill," explaining further: "They don't like him. . . . He is so high & mighty."[42]

Francis Kelley did not bear such ill will toward this early patron of Extension. Disappointed as he was that the red hat had not come to Quigley, Kelley immediately carried the news of O'Connell's elevation to President Taft, who was visiting Chicago at the time of the announcement and sent his congratulations to the new cardinal. This was a courtesy that was much appreciated in Boston.[43] What Kelley admired in O'Connell was his devotion to the missions, foreign and home. From Archbishop John J. Williams, he had inherited as diocesan Propagation director, James A. Walsh, whom he encouraged in the foundation of the Catholic Foreign Mission Society of America known as Maryknoll. Walsh's successor in Boston, Joseph F. McGlinchey, had been allowed to assist the home-missions and attributed the success of his programs directly to O'Connell. Though a busy administrator, the cardinal invariably gave time and manpower to the mission director. "I seldom see His Eminence," McGlinchey told Kelley, "where there is not a sincere inquiry and cheerful word of encouragement about my work."[44] Throughout most of his episcopate, Boston's prince was looked upon as Extension's friend.

The missionary congress tightened an even closer bond between Kelley and Dennis Dougherty. The former seminary professor from Philadelphia had been among several young American bishops assigned to the Philippine Islands after the Spanish-American War. In his thirteen years there, Extension had been one of his chief benefactors. Since collections in America were indispensable to his work, Dougherty had taken a leave of absence in 1913 from his diocese in order to raise funds in America, and Kelley assigned a field secretary, Father Edward L. Roe, to assist him. Four months before the congress in Boston, Dougherty and Roe completed a triumphant tour, having collected $84,000 in cash and $70,000 in pledges. Before his scheduled return to the Philippines, the missionary bishop gratefully appeared before Kelley's board and acknowledged that no organization had helped his diocese so much as Extension.[45] In order to broaden the appeal of the Philippines, Kelley arranged for Dougherty to postpone his return and to deliver a principal address at the missionary congress. As an easterner who depended upon the generosity of Extension, the Philadelphian would have the ear of those bishops who had shut out the society.[46]

Bishop Dougherty's presence at the missionary congress was but one project during Kelley's elaborate preparations which required of him two and a half months of complete attention. At O'Connell's urging, he spared no effort in keeping expenses low so that the greater portion of the collections would go to the missions. A minor complication occured when, at this time, the Vatican department in charge of Extension had been changed from the secretariat of state to the consistorial congregation. Advised to seek a representative from the Holy See, Kelley invited Monsignor Pietro Pisani, an official in the consistorial who was described by Roche as "the noblest of Romans and. . . a true loyal friend of yours."[47] Recalling how the previous congress had "nearly killed" him, the astute Islander also found time to plan a secret getaway afterwards to the warmer parts of Europe. Quigley's tardiness in submitting the text of his speech was a lingering nuisance, but it was more than compensated by the prospect that some seventy-five bishops had signified their intention to attend, including Cardinal Farley of New York and several Mexican bishops who had recently fled the revolution in their country. These preliminaries pointed to the fulfillment of Kelley's prophecy to Burke four years earlier: "the next Congress is going to be a whopper."[48]

The three-day missionary congress opened in Boston on October 19, 1913. Facing a predominantly eastern audience, Kelley delivered a more subdued address than the one he had given at the first congress in Chicago five years before. The highlight was, expectedly, Bishop Dougherty, who carried Extension's message. His talk recounted the drama of Extension's instant cabling of a $5,000 gift for his seminary. This action had prevented his creditors from foreclosing on the mortgage, and the school was now named "The Archbishop Quigley Theological Hall." Later, he continued, when he visited the society's headquarters, he encounterd a business-like no-nonsense attitude. Without having to go through the customary ritual of begging, he was readily granted a pledge of $15,000 for an orphanage. In a conclusion that certainly pleased Kelley, Dougherty publicly chastised the Propagation for having failed to help the Philippine Islands and urged the establishment of Extension in each parish in the United States, a step, he added, that would not injure the work of the Propagation. "There is, surely," he proclaimed with a flourish, "enough room in a country as vast as this."[49] This address gave the East a raw sample of Kelley's vision, perhaps without realizing it. Bishop Dougherty had proved a forceful spokesman for Extension in surroundings where its founder was suspect. A grateful and willing partner, the future cardinal archbishop of Philadelphia had paid the first installment on a debt that he would acknowledge for a lifetime.

* * * * * * * * *

With the second missionary congress, Kelley had nearly reached the midpoint of his career as president of Extension, an appropriate moment for us to review the balance sheet. Measured by most standards, the society enjoyed a bonanza of success. When Kelley first launched his movement, the receipts for the foreign-missions alone did not average $250,000 each year in the United States. By 1912, Extension had not only passed that annual mark but altogether had accumulated more than $1 million for the home-missions. And these impressive sums were raised virtually without diocesan collections and branch organizations.

The key to this success in revenues was *Extension Magazine,* which supported the work not from profits but from the appeals that appeared in its issues. In only six years after its debut, its subscribers numbered 150,000, making it a truly "national monthly." The church-goods department had provided impoverished parishes with religious articles that ranged from altars to chapel bells. In seven years it had donated more than 33,000 items. The chapel-car program had expanded into two working vehicles, one in Oregon and the other working mostly in Kansas. Its operation reflected the close collaboration developing between the society and missionary dioceses. The host bishop usually assigned a chaplain to it, while Extension supplied a permanent superintendent who doubled as equipment manager on weekdays and organist-singer on Sundays. Each car accommodated a miniature chapel equipped with sanctuary, pews, and confessional; and the remaining space was given to the priest's quarters and library. Special attention was also planned for Mexican immigration in the Southwest, where already a motor chapel operated along the Rio Grande River.[50]

Kelley, however, failed to remedy a basic weakness. The eastern dioceses had not established branches of Extension in their parishes, a step that would have stabilized revenues and cut the expenses of fund-raising. At the Boston congress, a bishops' committee had been appointed to study the possibility of parish collections and membership in the society, and there evolved an elaborate scheme known as "The Mission Association." Kelley even arranged through Cardinal Merry del Val an endorsement by the pope. To the Chicagoan's disappointment, however, the scheme was never implemented. The only tangible outcome from this effort occurred in the archdiocese of Boston where, at Cardinal O'Connell's direction, the parishes were asked to volunteer help for the home-missions.[51]

Mixed as the balance sheet was, the credits outweighed the debits, and this raised the question of public recognition for Father Kelley. During his first decade with Extension, he was interested in papal honors for himself, such as a monsignorship; but no evidence has ever suggested that his motive was self-serving. Acknowledgement from Rome would assist his work in two ways. First, it would certify the Holy See's commendation of the society he founded, a valuable asset in cooling opposition at home. Second, it would enable him to conduct business more efficiently at the Roman Curia. Ever since his first visit to Rome in 1909, he had been impressed with how a prelate's purple, even that of a monsignor, opened doors at the Vatican.

In the same year, an official in the curia, Monsignor Jules Tiberghien, had confided to Father Roe that the Holy See was disposed to grant a monsignorship to Kelley as soon as Archbishop Quigley requested it.[52] Ironically, however, the greatest obstacle to honors for Kelley was the chancellor. While ready to defend the society's interest, Quigley was unwilling to seek special titles for its officers. There were reasons for this reluctance.

He publicly disapproved of climbers among the clergy, commenting on one occasion: "The higher they go, the worse they get." This attitude was reflected in the fact that, at the time of his death in 1915, the archdiocese listed only three monsignors out of nearly 500 diocesan priests.[53] Furthermore, the activities of Extension's priests had not endeared them to all of the Chicago clergy. In certain quarters, it was insinuated that Kelley and his colleagues used the home-mission movement in order to promote careers in the church.[54] No open criticism erupted during Quigley's episcopate, but the archbishop sensed enough of a ground swell so as to defer any notion of singling out Kelley for a dignity.

Though Quigley's attitude disappointed Kelley, developments in Canada did not allow the matter to rest. Archbishop McEvay of Toronto had agreed in 1910 to recommend to Rome that Alfred E. Burke, president of Extension in Canada, be named a prothonotary apostolic, the highest rank among monsignors; and the apostolic delegate at Ottawa, Archbishop Sbarretti, gave his endorsement. What hindered the plan was Quigley's inertia in doing the same for Kelley. It was doubtful, reasoned the Canadians, that the Holy See would honor the daughter society in Toronto without a corresponding dignity for the older one in Chicago. For this reason, McEvay and Sbarretti tabled their request until Quigley joined them in Kelley's behalf. This set of circumstances led the eager Burke to press Kelley into making a series of indirect suggestions to Quigley. With reluctance, Kelley raised the issue with the archbishop on several occasions but without success. "He is," explained Kelley in frustration, "one great, large sized mystery."[55]

This quest for honors ended in a twofold humiliation for Kelley. First, Quigley's attitude eventually forced the intervention of outsiders to obtain papal recognition for the two Extension presidents. The Canadian chancellor McEvay died in 1911. When Burke clashed with the archbishop's successor, Neil McNeil, the only chance for honors in Canada was through Burke's friendship with Sbarretti. In the meantime, Quigley remained intransigent until his death in 1915, at which point there finally appeared a sponsor for Kelley's monsignorship. In that year, members of the Mexican hierarchy asked the Holy See to acknowledge Kelley's recent work among the refugees from the Mexican revolution, a story that will follow. Ironically, it was through his efforts in Mexican relief, and not in behalf of the home-missions in the United States, that Rome began to consider personal recognition for the Chicagoan.

The second humiliation was the manner in which the honor was eventually given. Through Sbarretti, Burke received a prothonotaryship apostolic; and on August 26, 1915, Kelley was named a domestic prelate, a rank lower than Burke's. Instead of elating Kelley and his associates, this news came as a shock to Chicago, where there were plans to postpone the announcement until the memory of Burke's higher dignity had faded. Shortly afterwards, Kelley arrived in Rome on other errands to be discussed later. During this visit, his wounds were partly healed when the new pope, Benedict XV, intervened in the matter and personally replaced the domestic prelacy with a prothonotaryship apostolic.[56]

This was an extraordinary conclusion to what should have been a routine promotion. In seeking a monsignorship, Kelley seemed to have been a victim of his friends. After ten years of working for America's home-missions, his own chancellor had declined to intercede for him, and it was left to a foreign hierarchy to arrange his papal honor. Kelley's anxious colleague in Canada had forced him into all but asking for the recognition, a tactic that was distasteful to him. His Roman connections had failed to spare him the indelicacy of having at first an inferior title awarded to him. Only his presence in Rome corrected all the errors, a final touch which closed the complicated episode. Kelley's temperament, however, had bounce to it and kept him from taking the snub too seriously. On his return to Chicago, he accepted from associates many of the vestments and insignia of office, which he mischievously called "the whole 'purple smear.' " Within a short interval, he pontificated in a friend's parish in Wilmette, Illinois. At this Mass, his tall Gothic mitre stood, he remarked, "like a tree, and it feels like one." Early reports indicated that the new prelate did not "look half bad" in the regalia, and he was willing to ackowledge "a little consolation in that."[57] No doubt, the greatest advantage from the new title was that Monsignor Kelley no longer had to walk the Vatican corridors in black-cassocked obscurity.

Francis Kelley's monsignorship marked the end of the most productive decade of his life. It began when he launched the Catholic home-mission movement in the Midwest; and it ended when, under his leadership, Extension had weathered easterly storms and had become an indispensable aid for the rural ministry. During these formative years, Kelley had become a master promoter and built his vision upon a rare combination of responsibility and innovation. From the beginning, Extension's resources—money and manpower—were managed with scrupulous care, and its constitution and programs carried many original features. Funds were channeled under the vigilant eye of a unique governing board whereby, in the words of a contemporary, "the layman was invited to sit in with priest and bishop on terms of equality. . . ." Unlike other mission-aid agencies, Kelley's elegant headquarters matched those of any successful commercial enterprise. Clients, whether they were millionaire benefactors or needy missionaries, found these offices "good to look at, and . . . pleasant to visit."[58] Evangelical to the core, Extension likewise pioneered in new ways of reaching communities across the country. The timeless Gospel of the church was transported into the backwoods in temporary chapels along railroad tracks; it was also carried to the great urban centers by way of a monthly magazine of singular quality.

Besides being an inspired organizer, Kelley was a bold crusader. Careless of personal consequences, he championed two unpopular causes—the national obligation to support the rural church and the rise of western leadership in Catholic America.

These two issues gave him a quick passage to prominence, but they also provided, at best, a mixed reception in the hierarchy. His Irish persistence had pitted him against the most powerful churchmen of his generation and had transformed his own associates into partisans, including the tranquil archbishop of Chicago. At its root, however, Extension was not a force of division. Its founder proposed a unity that no one else had seen—a natural solidarity between foreign- and home-missions, between the cities and the countryside, between the East and the West.

IV
An Uncertain Dawn

Ten years in the home-mission movement had made Francis Kelley perhaps the best known priest in America. The birth of Extension had brought his name before Catholics in most sections of the country. The cities read or listened to his appeals. The countryside thanked him for their subsidies. The leadership of Catholic America attended his congresses. In a decade, he had risen from the obscurity of a country parish in Michigan to presiding over a formidable corporation in America's second city. His work touched the great figures of his generation. His partisans and adversaries were numbered on both sides of the Atlantic; and he enjoyed more than a superficial acquaintance with the occupants of the Vatican and the White House. In becoming an ecclesiastical celebrity, "Extension Kelley" had encountered his share of obstacles, but seldom had these discouraged a man who felt in command.

The year 1915 also represented a turning point. First, it inaugurated the second stage of Extension, the work of consolidating its early gains. It also introduced the Islander to personalities and situations which did not yield to the Kelley charm or persistence. The ascendant years were behind him, the years that had given him a trusting and compliant superior, along with aging opponents in the East whom death would soon silence. Kelley was not immune to transition. His dreams and effort would hereafter produce less; his spirit—and body—would endure less. The second decade of Extension was to bring a passage of years in which Kelley, above all, felt the loss of his mastery of events.

This dramatic shifting began when Extension in Canada nearly collapsed. At the center of disturbance was Father Alfred E. Burke the brilliant but erratic Islander some years older than Kelley, whom the latter had known as a lad in the cathedral parish. After a brief interval as the bishop's secretary, Burke, had been sent from the cathedral to a country parish in Alberton, a quiet fishing village where Kelley recruited him for the presidency of Extension in Canada. Thus began the most curious professional association in Kelley's life. At first glance, Burke's personality exhibited characteristics that would have kept Kelley at a safe distance. His considerable intellectual gifts notwithstanding, Burke was volatile and impatient, a stormy petrel whose very being seemed locked into strife. Unpredictable and unreliable, he demanded enormous attention and tolerance from friends; he sought out and transmitted gossip and was not averse to minor intrigue. Certainly, no one but a fool would trust him in a major scheme.

Repeatedly, Burke's behavior exacerbated Kelley. The Canadian's strong independence forced him repeatedly to scorn friendly counsel from Chicago and led him into many ruinous situations. This dangerous tendency was bolstered by a deadly pomposity against which Kelley warned continually. "Behave yourself," Kelley advised, "and do not act too supercilious with the folks you meet. A little humility mixed in with your prayers will make a Saint of the Holy Founder of Canadian Extension some day." There were other contradictions in Burke that frequently exhausted Kelley's patience. He leaked secrets, provoking the Chicagoan once to think about chasing Burke "with a club." "A man who violates confidence the way he has done," Kelley noted in a fury, "ought to have a guardian." Yet, Burke demanded news without interruption. Kelley's more careful letters to Toronto were, in Burke's phrases, worthless exercises in which Francis "spoiled. . . sheets of paper, saying nothing." When these two strong individuals spent much time together, such as in travel, there was the risk of a fuss, Kelley attributing the danger to the Jekyll-Hyde personality of his companion. As Islanders, the two did not even share sentiments regarding England, Kelley a devout anglophobe and Burke an almost sanctimonious subject of the British Crown; and these political differences fueled many a quarrel on land and sea.[1]

But Kelley admired this irrepressible crank. Burke had enormous talent and a sense of humor—qualities which Francis appreciated. Canada's nationalities—especially the rivalry between the French- and English-speaking communities—were a source of potential trouble for the home-mission movement. But Burke's early work in Extension had been careful, avoiding the pitfalls, and he had won the confidence of the first chancellor, Archbishop Fergus P. McEvay of Toronto, and that of the apostolic delegate at Ottawa, Archbishop Donato Sbarretti. Though Burke was pleased to head Extension in Canada, Kelley teased him over the fact that it was only the daughter society. In prompting a letter along, Francis quipped to the older man: "Hurry it along now, like a good boy, or papa will give you a spanking." Burke enjoyed the fun. When the two had simultaneously received from Rome their first pontifical appointments as president, Kelley's letter actually assigned him to Canada—a scribe's mistake, no doubt. Nevertheless, Francis wondered about the letter to Toronto. "Would you please look at your appointment," he asked Burke playfully, "and see if you are me, or if I am you? It will be a great relief for me to know that I am still myself. . . ." Kelley was prompt to add that if the error were not corrected, he would cheerfully take charge of Burke as his subordinate just "to keep you in the straight and narrow path for the rest of your natural life."[2] Burke understood and chuckled.

In sum, there was room for a maverick in Father Kelley's affections. Beneath Burke's eccentricity and even his conceit, Francis could see perhaps the most gifted priest in English-speaking Canada. It was Kelley's summons from Chicago that had rescued Burke from the oblivion of the Island and had given him an opportunity for national leadership in the Dominion. Faithfully, therefore, Kelley followed his friend through the first great crisis of Extension in Canada, a crisis which not only imperiled the home-mission movement in the provinces but also served, in Kelley's eye, as a prelude of his own future.

From the beginning of the daughter society, Father Burke enjoyed a more satisfying relationship with its chancellor, Archbishop McEvay, than Kelley did with Archbishop Quigley. When McEvay had come to Toronto in 1908 from the diocese of London, Ontario, he was expected to serve as a leader of the English-speaking Catholics. Unfortunately, he was not destined for a lengthy reign, and his health broke two years after his appointment. Disturbing as it was to Burke, the news was equally so to Kelley. "There is," the latter told the worried Burke, "no man on earth I admire more—not even my own Boss—and you know how I feel if any danger menaced him."[3] The archbishop of Toronto's death in May, 1911, was one of Kelley's great sorrows. Though unable to attend the funeral, he publicly acknowledged his profound gratitude to the prelate who made Extension possible in Canada.

McEvay's premature death had cast Burke into prolonged gloom over a personal loss, and it also raised the paramount issue of succession. The next archbishop of Toronto would be Extension's chancellor, and Burke worried over the prospects. The society was protected, Kelley assured him, through its status as a pontifical institution. The Canadian's five-year term as president was a papal appointment, a reasonable guarantee of independence. In spite of this encouragement, Kelley was privately troubled over the possibility that an unsympathetic chancellor could injure, if not destroy, the movement. The lengthy interregnum after McEvay's death strained Kelley's judgment and forced him into one of the boldest acts of his life. In an effort to safeguard the Canadian society, he furnished the Holy See with an unsolicited recommendation regarding the succession. In September, 1911, Burke made his first pilgrimage to Rome accompanied by Kelley; and the Chicago clergyman used the opportunity to introduce his companion as a dark-horse candidate for the vacant see. After the suggestion had been made in Rome, the travelers left for London, where Kelley reinforced his suggestion in a careful letter to the papal secretary of state. Burke, he noted, "is one of the strongest men in English-speaking Canada," and deserved to be considered. As a tactic to force attention upon Burke as worthy of the promotion, Kelley urged that the prothonotaryship apostolic be immediately conferred upon his companion.[4] It was the most sweeping strategy possible—an American priest discussing a major Canadian appointment with the second most powerful man in the church. Kelley's motive was not to advance a friend's career but to guarantee that the succession would not injure the infant movement. His bold maneuver was not impulsive because five months later he continued to promote Burke's candidacy. "Without a doubt," he told Monsignor Sante Tampieri, an intimate of Merry del Val, "Burke is the ablest English-speaking ecclesiastic in Canada, and the only man, I know, who has all the qualifications necessary."[5]

After a lengthy vacancy, the Holy See named Neil McNeil in the summer of 1912, a scholar and missionary who came to Toronto after previous episcopal experience in St. George's, Newfoundland, and in Vancouver. Almost at once, Tampieri transmitted to Chicago early warnings of Burke's distress at this appointment. "After what 'our mutual friend' wrote," Tampieri remarked, "I fear that he will not be happy in Toronto with the nomination of the new Archbishop." At first, Kelley did not share Burke's apprehension. McNeil was a veteran administrator who had governed sees in eastern and western Canada; and in Kelley's judgment, this experience would enable him to recognize Burke's enormous value.[6] Therefore, the Chicagoan prudently kept his distance from the developments in Toronto for several months until early 1913 when McNeil decided to confide in him, dashing Kelley's hopes that the succession of chancellors would have little impact on the fortunes of Extension. The Canadian clergy, explained the new archbishop, had lost confidence in the society under Burke's management. McNeil charged that, since his arrival in Toronto, Extension had virtually ceased to function; and, he added gravely, there was little hope for reviving it "for the reason that its unpopularity had sunk too deep in the Catholic public." Although the situation appeared desperate, McNeil welcomed any useful suggestions from the founder. Thus, at the archbishop's request, Kelley gingerly edged himself into this delicate affair when he proposed a secret meeting away from Toronto, where, he hoped, his friend Burke would not get wind of it.[7]

The meeting accomplished little because by that time McNeil and Burke were colliding head-on. At this point, according to Burke, the archbishop demanded control of the society's weekly newspaper, *The Catholic Register*, and Burke firmly declined. The situation had deteriorated so quickly that Archbishop Sbarretti confidentially urged Kelley, "*for God's sake*," to mediate the dispute. As a go-between, Kelley made valiant attempts, consulting authorities in Rome and in Toronto; and he explored with Burke acceptable assignments if he were to resign. This investigation disclosed an incredibly complex crisis. Convinced of Burke's singular ability, Kelley had seen his Island comrade build Extension in Canada through personal contacts and a well-edited newspaper; and in doing so, Burke had become a leading Catholic spokesman in North America. In spite of these accomplishments for the home-missions, his career seemed centered in controversy. A major factor for this was his weekly newspaper which, unlike Kelley's monthly, commented on current political topics in the Dominion. Burke's position, for example, on the explosive nationalist agitation had managed to alienate both sides. While his English-speaking slants upset the *Canadiens,* his ardent devotion to the British Crown disturbed the English-speaking provincials. Influential clergymen of Toronto likewise resented the intimacy between the previous archbishop and this outsider from the Island, and had maligned him as "the power behind the throne." Like many near geniuses, Burke was headstrong and sometimes tactless, but, as Kelley concluded from his inquiries, McNeil could have harnessed the energies of this seething volcano as had his predecessor.[8]

Kelley failed to reconcile McNeil and Burke; their quarrel became nastier. In August, 1914, World War I erupted across the Atlantic, and the blackening antipathy between the two churchmen prompted Burke's associate, Joseph T. Roche, to quip to Kelley: "I think that Europe is a much safer place than Toronto at the present time." McNeil, Roche added, had confided to him that he planned to fire Burke.[9] This remark stunned Kelley because the issue was more than the dismissal of a friend. It focused now on the constitutional rights of Extension's president, who received his five-year term from the Holy See on the recommendation of the governing board. Burke's fate would, therefore, test the authority of the chancellor acting alone, and this was a question of great importance. If McNeil's removal of Burke was upheld, then Kelley's own position *vis-à-vis* an unfriendly archbishop in Chicago would be tenuous indeed. This issue had so exercised him that he carefully examined the constitutions of the two societies and found, to his dismay, that even though the provisions favored the independence of the president, the apostolic delegate could be called in for a ruling.[10] It was unlikely that the latter would overrule the decision of an archbishop.

In any case, Burke's quarrel with McNeil had illumined the limitation of written charters. Technically, the constitution protected the pontifical terms of the president; but McNeil's attitude toward Burke had paralyzed Extension until mid-1915 when the latter reluctantly submitted his resignation. Burke's ill fortune was a key lesson for his Chicago counterpart: papal guarantees or not, it was indispensable that the society work with a benevolent chancellor.[11] Hence, in Kelley's mind, among the qualifications for Quigley's successor would be an interest in the work of Extension. So alarming was the disaster in Toronto that Kelley was prepared to take an unofficial hand in the appointment of the next archbishop of Chicago.

* * * * * * * * * *

The tragedy in Canada merely opened this interval of transition in Father Kelley's life. Two other changes promptly followed—historic shifts in Rome and Chicago which added to the confusion. The first concerned one of Extension's premier assets, the cardinal protector who served as a personal delegate at the Holy See. As a member of the Roman Curia, he was expected to represent the society's interests without the intervention of the apostolic delegate in Washington, and at first Cardinal Sebastian Martinelli had been a responsive agent. In the spring of 1913, however, Kelley had lost confidence in the protector when the Chicagoan requested the cardinal to obtain an extension for Bishop Dougherty's tour of the United States, a concession which would allow him to address the second missionary congress in Boston. To Kelley's astonishment there were no replies from Rome; and Martinelli's bewildering silence drove the priest into fits of impatience.[12] At length, the proper congregation at the Vatican granted the leave, but the experience had raised doubts in Kelley's mind regarding Martinelli's effectiveness.

What revived the issue of dependable representation at Rome were the death of Pius X in August, 1914, and the extensive adjustment to follow in the Vatican bureaucracy. This meant the departure from authority of several friends of Extension, including Cardinal Merry del Val, who was replaced in the secretariat of state. Along with the fading of an influential patron came the word that Cardinal Martinelli was incurably ill. The society had thus lost its direct access into the Holy See. Kelley inquired of Monsignor Tampieri how to proceed in getting a successor to Martinelli. This was not such a simple matter, advised the astute bureaucrat, but one of supreme delicacy. Nevertheless, he promised to make the proper inquiries, including some regarding the cardinal's health.

Until Martinelli was replaced, Kelley felt vulnerable; emergencies like this tended to strain his patience and judgment. Tampieri's tardiness in reporting his progress in Rome prompted Kelley into directly offering the position to Merry del Val.[13] He was an ideal selection: he was fluent in English, had supported Extension since its beginnings, and was interested in the post. This step commenced a lengthy campaign to have this notable named protector. In the meantime, news of Martinelli's condition worsened. The dying man, afflicted with arteriosclerosis, would never see another pope and, Kelley learned further, was unable even to offer Mass. At last, Tampieri confirmed the earlier accounts that Martinelli's malady was terminal. But he lingered, and a cardinal's prerogatives prevailed. Benedict XV himself, Kelley was told, said there would be no successor to represent Extension until the old protector died.[14] Halted temporarily by papal courtesy toward Martinelli, Kelley therefore found himself dealing with a new regime in Rome without the services of an insider, a situation that weakened the prerogatives of a pontifical institute.

Burke's resignation in Toronto and the shifts in the Roman Curia were accompanied by an equally unsettling event in Chicago, the death of Archbishop Quigley. Kelley had never blinded himself to the weaknesses of his chancellor—the slow arrival at decisions, the uninspiring and lumbering exterior, the irritating touch of ambiguity; but in the last years, the Islander discovered that beneath these qualities lay true strength and integrity. Quigley was not Kelley's ideal churchman—the lamented Fergus McEvay was that. But Quigley had established the priest in Chicago, defended him before leaders of the American hierarchy, permitted him an enviable freedom of activity, and on occasion tempered his strokes of impetuosity. In time, Kelley perceived how the two temperaments complemented each other, and his feeling for the old man ripened into genuine respect and affection. "From my own experience with you," began one of Kelley's admiring comments to Quigley, "you were a listener; . . . you do not give any 'snap judgments,' but take time to consider everything."[15]

In the late spring of 1915, Quigley was stricken with disturbing symptoms while visiting the East. The Chicago press carried reports of Bright's disease, but Kelley was relieved when he learned that the trouble was thought to be minor, perhaps only ptomaine poisoning which had acted on the kidneys. "The Archbishop is out of danger and resting easy," he told Burke, "but the doctors won't let him come home and, in fact, insist that he stay away from his work all summer." But there soon followed some alarm in Chicago when Father Thomas V. Shannon brought back pessimistic reports of his visit with Quigley in Washington. Kelley's friend was shocked to discover that the archbishop's memory was failing. The physicians suspected a slight stroke but forecast that the patient would soon be fit again. This news was sufficient to bring Kelley to Washington, where he confirmed the diagnosis of a stroke but did not detect in Quigley a lapse of memory. The situation was yet far from hopeless. The apostolic delegate, Archbishop John Bonzano, paid a visit every day, and the doctors approved Quigley's plan to leave the capital on June 1. "He must be a little better," Kelley commented to Burke, "for they would not take him out of the hospital."[16] Despite the slight improvement, the archbishop's active life was finished, a hard fact which Kelley refused at first to accept. While he looked for recovery, the outsider Burke was more detached and was the first one to acknowledge that Quigley's paralysis had ended a useful career "forever."[17]

The archbishop was strong enough to reach his brother in Rochester, where the newspapers shortly reported his utter collapse. By the beginning of July, Kelley expressed his acceptance of the inevitable. "There is nothing to hope for in the Archbishop's case," he wrote to Burke. "He may be dead before I am finished dictating." His condition had become moribund—only his strong constitution kept his heart beating. This personal loss saddened Kelley, but the future did not trouble him. "If the work is worthwhile," Burke was told, "it is going to go on and that is all I have a right to care about. Personally, I guess I can earn my living somewhere and somehow, so what's the use of worrying?"[18] But the priest's composure did not endure long: Quigley died on July 10, 1915.

Kelley's eulogy in *Extension Magazine* capped ten years of a fruitful professional and personal association. Two features distinguished his from most tributes to departed superiors. First came the broad suggestions of Kelley's own perception of the archbishop's character, a perception which did not completely idealize the deceased, as was common on such occasions, but which corresponded to Quigley's flesh and blood. The archbishop had been "a stern, and silent man, who knew how to keep his council." This exterior toughness, Kelley proposed, had rendered him impervious to influence and even to close friendship. This quality was the source of his passion for justice, an unyielding sense of fairness that emerged in disputes and could be misunderstood even by his clergy. Quigley's silent strength, as Kelley saw it, was reflected in an ability to grow and to listen. Once he selected his subordinates, he gave them his trust and "never interfered." There was more: this opaque, limited man revealed to intimates a sense of humor. "He loved a story and a joke," Kelley recalled, "but he could not tell them." Concurrently with this appreciation ran Kelley's second theme, his fear that the majority of his priests and laity would fail to appreciate this hidden man. Quigley had, unfortunately, sealed himself off from a true assessment of his twelve-year episcopate. His death appeared a trivial event in Chicago history, but, as Kelley sought to point out, Quigley's unique contributions to the archdiocese and to the national church would flower in the passage of time. Only then would Catholic America be able to arrive at a proper appreciation of his greatness.[19]

A curious postscript closed the events surrounding the chancellor's passing. Without explanation, the archdiocesan administration failed to telegraph to the Vatican the official notice of his death—probably through oversight or, as it was whispered in some circles, through a disregard for the deceased. For a month afterward, the only information at the Roman Curia regarding Quigley's death had been gathered from outside sources, and this lapse astonished the congregations. Only when Kelley sent a friendly letter to Tampieri did the Holy See receive its first word from Chicago.[20]

* * * * * * * * * *

Archbishop Quigley's death led Father Kelley into the most questionable decisions of his life. Three successive blows had jolted him—Burke's failure to survive the succession in Toronto, a cardinal protector in Rome who was known to be *"circiter mortuus,"* and the specter of adjusting to a new chancellor-archbishop. Thus far Kelley had been forced to react to events. By nature he despised passivity, a quality which he had found and criticized in Quigley. In confronting problems, his own instincts called for strategies which put him on the offensive. And now he desperately needed to recover control of the forces that governed his life. In the fall of 1915, this restlessness drew Kelley into a series of risks which were calculated to restore balance to his life and which, at the same time, aroused complaints that he meddled in affairs beyond his authority.

The most dangerous risk he took was to arrange a trip to Rome during the transition in Chicago. In six years Kelley had paid several visits to the Eternal City, and he was aware of how sensitive one's presence in Rome could be. Such movements were under scrutiny. Three years before, while relaxing after the missionary congress in Boston, he had deliberately avoided Rome, knowing that even a harmless holiday there could call forth a flood of criticism. "I love Rome," he had told Tampieri, "but I do not think it wise to be visiting without business. . . . Frequent visits to Rome might be misunderstood."[21] To the seasoned ecclesiastic, there were no innocent trips to the Tiber, especially when one's archdiocese was vacant.

After Quigley's funeral, however, Kelley had his reasons to go to Rome, and he did not care whether he invited suspicions at home. First, there was the obvious problem of the mails. The European war had made postal deliveries so irregular that few people would post important messages. Tampieri had warned Kelley to register all letters for some safety.[22] Furthermore, the tenth anniversary of Extension was to occur three months after Quigley's death, and this served as an official reason to bring Kelley across the Atlantic. The society had prepared a commemorative volume of the Quigley years with clippings, maps, photographs, and sundry documents. In August, 1915, the board authorized Kelley to present it to the Holy Father. The anniversary meant, in addition, that his term as president had nearly expired, an occurrence every five years which invariably troubled Kelley; and a trip to Rome would expedite the reappointment.[23] Moreover, the Islander had become recently involved in the issue of religious freedom in Mexico. With the approval of the Mexican hierarchy in exile, he had requested the Wilson administration to press the revolutionary factions into ending their persecution of the church. But since his efforts in Washington, D.C., had produced nothing since the beginning of 1915, he now planned to invoke the Vatican's diplomatic channels in mediating religious peace in Mexico; and this too required his presence in Rome.[24]

There were other objectives, hidden and more personal, which encouraged Father Kelley to book passage for September of 1915. He wished, of course, to pursue the question of his monsignorship and to investigate the condition of Cardinal Martinelli. He would also join Burke in arranging for the latter's successor as president of Extension in Canada. Kelley strongly advocated Bishop Michael F. Power of St. George's, Newfoundland, a former missionary who had followed Burke as acting president. His episcopal rank, Kelley reasoned, would add prestige to the society and ensure the cooperation of the other bishops.[25] Though he promoted his own nomination as a prothonotary apostolic, Kelley did not use the trip to advance himself into the episcopate despite suspicions to the contrary. He had, in fact, instructed the archdiocesan consultors not to consider him among their candidates to succeed Quigley. But the prospect of a bishop heading Extension in the United States, as was possible in Canada, interested the board of governors in Chicago. In Kelley's absence, it reviewed the advisability of petitioning Rome that he be named a titular bishop. No formal request was actually sent, but Ledvina delicately passed the word to Monsignor Jules Tiberghien, a Vatican bureaucrat and confidant of Benedict XV, that such a promotion would be supremely agreeable to the society.[26]

A number of errands would therefore bring Francis Kelley to Rome in the fall of 1915, but the major one concerned the Chicago succession because the new archbishop would be *ex officio* the chancellor of Extension. While appearing stoically self-confident on the surface, Kelley was deeply troubled about the future. His society might, he feared, face the same misfortune as Extension did in Canada when the Holy See named Archbishop McNeil, an accomplished prelate who had governed two sees before coming to Toronto but whose views collided fatally with those of the society's president. "Archbishop Quigley's successor," Kelley confided frankly to a friend in the Roman Curia, "will have the fate of the Society in his hands." This situation suggested several courses of action for the troubled priest. One was to seek the transfer of chancellorship to the apostolic delegate in Washington, D.C.[27] A more likely direction, however, lay in pressing the candidacy of a proven friend of the home-missions. The archdiocese of Chicago had a recent history of unexpected appointments. In 1902 the odds-on favorite had been the suffragan in Peoria, John Lancaster Spalding; but after a lengthy interval of six months, an easterner had been named, James E. Quigley of Buffalo, much to the disappointment of many citizens of Illinois. Thirteen years later, the hope was again that the appointment would be prompt and given to a midwesterner. Kelley's logic, therefore, led him to lobby in behalf of a compatible local candidate for Chicago, namely, Peter J. Muldoon, first bishop of Rockford and one of the founders of Extension; and Kelley's tactics were much the same as those he used when championing Burke for Toronto four years earlier. A capable administrator, Muldoon had earned Kelley's respect as chairman of Extension's auditing committee, a key unit within the board of governors. Before his assignment to Rockford, he had been a popular Chicago cleric who, it seemed, was the heir apparent. His current assignment as a suffragan bishop, Kelley felt, offered too little for this gifted leader and served only as a prelude to something higher. Kelley's decision to work for his friend's return to Chicago—after six years in Rockford—appeared only to conform to public sentiment; and the Islander did not hestitate to bring that message to Rome.[28]

On September 11, 1915, Kelley sailed for Italy, accompanied by Juan Navarrete y Guerrero, an exiled Mexican priest who served as a Spanish interpreter. His departure from Chicago released a torrent of criticism, much of which had been suppressed during the Quigley years. This outburst was the first of its kind and gave some idea regarding the impact of Kelley's person and work upon important segments of the Chicago clergy. Rectory carping was certainly not unknown to the "Boss," an outsider from Detroit whom Quigley had favored. In addition to his special relationship with the deceased archbishop, Kelley's life style contributed to the bitterness. As early as 1909, he had acknowledged the clerical complaint that the Extension officers at that time were not required to live in parishes and to do priestly work on Sunday; and this grievance no doubt led to the aborted attempt to found St. Philip Neri Church in Chicago. But, had Kelley succeeded in operating a parish, the criticism would have merely shifted to the charge that he was depriving senior members of the diocesan clergy of an appointment as pastor.[29]

Kelley, moreover, enjoyed special favors. He traveled extensively with Quigley's approval, and in Chicago his residence was the plush University Club. The privilege of the "portable altar" allowed him to offer Mass in his apartment as well as conveniently on the road. Even the daily obligation of reciting the breviary had been dispensed when Kelley explained that the nerve of his left eye was cupped and that this required him to restrict his reading.[30] These exceptions were not ignored and served handily to fuel clerical gossip. Tension between the diocesan and Extension priests therefore appeared inescapable. The undercurrent in Chicago alarmed one priest visitor from the Island who viewed it as implacable and lethal. Joseph T. Roche dubbed Kelley's enemies "stiletto men," wielders of the notorious "Chicago knife." ". . . they hold you guilty of one unpardonable offense," he warned—"You came in a stranger and got close to the throne."[31]

It was Kelley's trip to Rome, however, that focused the opposition. Until the appointment of Quigley's successor, the archdiocese was governed by the vicar general and rector of the cathedral, Michael J. Fitzsimmons. In most circles, the administrator enjoyed the reputation of a beloved elder. His coping with a "gastric ulcer in the duodenum" had become a precious tradition among the Chicago clergy. As it was recalled years later by William D. O'Brien, Fitzsimmons's health had required strict dieting. After he ate the special menu, his associates and guests—in astonishment—saw him served the regular meal, which was devoured with no ill effect. To the lasting amusement of his confreres, this heroic routine sustained the vicar for more than a quarter century.[32]

Amiable as he was, Fitzsimmons was incensed at Kelley's September departure for Rome and protested this action to the Holy See. Kelley's action, Fitzsimmons contended, had flagrantly violated church regulations. No one in authority had given him permission to go to Rome, and this had made the trip an act of disobedience. It also interfered with the succession in Chicago since, in the vicar's view, Kelley's overt objective was to lobby in behalf of a candidate for the vacant see.[33] It was not clear at what point the traveler was told of the exact charges, but his two Vatican sentinels in the Roman Curia—Jules Tiberghien and Sante Tampieri—knew of them as soon as they reached the Holy See. At first, Tiberghien tried delicately to alert his Chicago friend. During an audience with Benedict XV, the veteran bureaucrat learned that a serious charge had been made against Kelley and had reached the ears of the pontiff. Throughout the discussion, the Holy Father offered no details and displayed no anger; but as Kelley was gently told, he alluded to a mysterious "complaint of Mgr. Quigley that you were too independent." Kelley's arrival at Rome so soon after the archbishop's death, Tiberghien reasoned, was the factor that had aroused the opposition into reporting him.[34]

But neither Tiberghien nor Tampieri was content to limit his service in Kelley's behalf to mere subtle warnings. Upon learning of Fitzsimmons's accusations, each drafted strong denials to Cardinals Merry del Val, now secretary of the congregation of the Holy Office, and Gaetano De Lai, prefect of the consistorial congregation which supervised the work of Extension. Kelley's position as president of Extension, it was insisted, required a degree of independence, paralleling that of the rector of The Catholic University of America. The immediate superior of both institutions was a "chancellor"—not the rulers of the dioceses in which the university and the society were located. Archbishop Messmer of Milwaukee, they added, Extension's temporary chancellor, had discussed Kelley's trip with the board and had given his approval. Lastly, Kelley's defenders cited the accusation that his mission was to influence the next appointment to Chicago; and, continued the two Romans, this charge suggested that in his personal ambition he sought this high office for himself. It was "absolutely absurd," the Holy See was told, to suspect in this way a priest who had voluntarily announced to the archdiocesan consultors that he was no candidate.[35]

Though the two sentinels had skirted the issue of whether Kelley had pressed Bishop Muldoon's name in Rome, they improvised a persuasive case and cleared the Islander's name at the Holy See. Fitzsimmons's indictment did not seem to carry decisive weight. But an omen could hardly be missed: Kelley's secure position at home had been weakened critically. During Extension's infancy he had confronted more powerful ecclesiastics than the vicar general. But these earlier battles had threatened no disaster because the opposition had been scattered in the East and because Kelley could rely on Chicago as an impregnable base of support. Archbishop Quigley's passing, however, had altered the climate at home for Kelley. No longer would critics in the archdiocese be so guarded. His exceptional life style had made enemies, and his former accessibility to the throne had whetted, as Roche would say, the "Chicago knife." Though a national figure because of Extension, Francis Kelley was still an outsider in clerical Chicago. His effort, therefore, to transform the succession from a local issue that involved the archdiocese, into a national one that affected the future of Extension was not only unwelcome; it was also meddling in affairs in which he had no place.

* * * * * * * * * *

When Monsignor Kelley returned to Chicago in late November, 1915, he was near collapse. "The strain was heavy," he told Jules Tiberghien, "and my nerves were a little unstrung."[36] Despite the burden of exhaustion, the pilgrim had scored several important accomplishments. On his arrival in Rome, he had been given the prothonotaryship at the personal request of the pope who had manifested a remarkable acquaintance with Extension. Though the failing Cardinal Martinelli lingered, Kelley found a solution concerning a representative at the Vatican. Since Monsignor Tiberghien's recent activities regarding the Fitzsimmons episode had proven their worth, Kelley appointed him as "procurator." An independently wealthy man whose estate would be valued, at his death, at 10 million *lire,* or $400,000, he was a cultured gentleman, a world traveler, a *bon vivant* whose visit to Chicago in 1909 had nearly pauperized Kelley. But this French cleric was more: he had been one of the few Europeans who had donated to the home-missions of America. And, above all, he had the best connections in Rome, not the least of which was access to Benedict XV. "He is my friend," remarked the pontiff on learning of the Frenchman's appointment as Extension's procurator, "and therefore this will make a new bond between the Pope and your Society." Several issues remained still unsettled, including Extension's leadership in Canada and Kelley's own reappointment as president. But the most important unresolved topic was the selection of a successor to Archbishop Quigley, whose see was to remain vacant for five months.[37]

Francis Kelley could hardly be expected to remain neutral over such a sensitive issue as the appointment of the next archbishop of Chicago, who automatically served as chancellor of Extension. The Islander's top priority at this time was to promote a leader sympathetic to the home-missions, and he had been among the first to join the chorus singing the virtues of Peter J. Muldoon. Kelley took a step further: he was willing to risk an active and open partisanship in favor of the Rockford suffragan. Ten days after Quigley's death, Kelley along with another admirer of Muldoon, Thomas V. Shannon, left with the apostolic delegate, Archbishop John Bonzano, for a tour of the Pacific Northwest. A private railroad car had been provided for the three men; and en route to Seattle, the two Chicago priests had ample opportunity to air their opinions regarding the special virtues of Bishop Muldoon. Their friendly advice, Kelley confided to Burke, "I do not think . . . will do any harm." The Islander carried his appeal even to Rome. In the fall of 1915, the pope and Cardinals De Lai and Merry del Val had received verbal resumés of what the delegate had been told regarding conditions in Chicago and the merits of Muldoon. The lengthy wait for a successor, Rome was told, had splintered the archdiocese, and expectations rose steadily into the first days of winter. Moreover, the chances of Dennis Dougherty, bishop of Jaro in the Philippines, began to attract some attention, a prospect that was also acceptable to Kelley.

But the appointment of his first choice, Muldoon, seemed all but certain when, according to strong rumors, the name of the next archbishop of Chicago was to begin with an "m" and end with an "n," a Delphic clue which proved accurate—with a vengeful twist.[38] On November 29, 1915, Kelley surveyed the landscape. "The situation is very quiet," he told Tiberghien. "Very little is being said." Less than a dozen priests, he estimated, were fixed in their opposition to Muldoon. Nonetheless, these were powerful men, evidently with their hopes pinned on Bishop Edmund M. Dunne of Peoria, a former Chicago priest who openly disapproved of Kelley and his work; and Kelley was troubled over what he perceived as the blindness of Dunne's partisans to needs beyond the boundaries of the archdiocese. "I am simply hoping and praying," he observed uneasily, "that what looks like an impending calamity may be averted." That evening a historic telegram was sent from Washington to Brooklyn.[39]

The Chicago factions were abruptly united on the next day, all stunned by the news that an unheralded auxiliary bishop in Brooklyn would be their new master, George William Mundelein. When the press searched for someone who knew the appointee, only Kelley acknowledged a personal acquaintanceship, describing him vaguely as a builder and "most energetic man."[40] This statement concealed the bewilderment that Kelley shared with all of Chicago—Rome's choice seemed to offend every logical consideration. Quigley's successor was young, two years junior to Kelley. As an auxiliary, he had had no independent experience in diocesan management. An Easterner, he was an unknown. And the coming of this German-American offended the sensitivities of two large minorities in the archdiocese. "The Poles are very much wrought up over having a German," Kelley confided to a friend, "and the Irish are going around with closed mouths." Even he could not resist the silly topical humor that Mundelein's appointment stimulated. To Burke, who had just been commissioned a chaplain in the Canadian army, Kelley entrusted this message for Kaiser Wilhelm: "Tell him that he has captured Chicago as well as Serbia. . . ." But the Islander's deepest anxiety arose from the fact that, as a lifelong urbanite, George Mundelein had no known interest in America's rural missions.[41]

The confusion did not abate quickly. Even the East was dazed, including the leader of the hierarchy, Cardinal Gibbons, who had endorsed Muldoon. Disturbing letters arrived immediately at Rockford, prompting the bishop to ask Kelley to call on Gibbons on his next trip to Baltimore. "The East that writes me," Muldoon told Kelley, "is non-plussed and very much chagrined."[42] Several Romans, too, shared this reaction. Along with Kelley, Tiberghien knew of Muldoon's considerable weight at the Holy See and was astonished at the outcome. Being so close to the center of authority, he tried to find a rationale, explaining to Kelley: "I suppose that Rome, seeing the divisions, wanted to send a new man." As the dust and tempers settled in Chicago, other explanations circulated. The almost simultaneous appointment of Dennis Dougherty to Buffalo suggested to Kelley that the former missionary bishop in the Philippines had been the original selection for Chicago. The pope himself "switched" Mundelein from Buffalo perhaps, reasoned Kelley, because of a diplomatic protest from the British government against having a German-descent prelate so close to the Canadian border during wartime. Shortly afterwards, Kelley chatted with the one person who could clear up the mystery. Before Mundelein's arrival in Chicago, Archbishop Bonzano visited the city and made Fitzsimmons a monsignor. If this was partly a gesture to heal wounds, it did little to heal Kelley's.[43]

In this charged climate of grievance and waiting, Monsignor Kelley quickly absorbed the shock and sought an early exchange of views between himself and the new archbishop. What he looked for in Mundelein, first of all, was tact. This Brooklynite, he thought, might be gifted in many ways, but at this moment he had to be "one who can win his way with the clergy and people." Only a truly self-possessed, graceful man could keep the diocese from fragmenting into pockets of ethnic enclaves. Second, what Kelley was prepared to offer to his new superior was unreserved commitment. "I am disappointed, of course," he confessed to Burke, "on account of Bishop Muldoon, but what can I do since I am not the Pope? One thing is sure: the new Archbishop is going to get loyal co-operation from me."[44] In a short time, the exchange of views took place. From the East, Mundelein notified the president that he endorsed Extension and invited him to Brooklyn, an adroit gesture which flattered Kelley. This was the first of two interviews before Mundelein's appearance in Chicago. In both, he not only charmed Kelley with pledges of firm support for the society but he also allowed the discussion to range freely beyond that of the home-missions. Kelley felt invited even to raise delicately the issue of Mundelein's ancestry and was quickly assured that his host came from a proud line of American patriots. "His German name came to America three generations ago," Kelley told the skeptical Burke in London, "and his grandfather fought in the Civil war." By the time Mundelein was prepared to come west, Kelley had dropped all fears, and his uncertainty about Quigley's successor had dissolved. With renewed confidence, the "Boss" began to make plans, wide-ranging and elaborate ones. A decade earlier, he had come to Chicago, a stranger; now he was anxious to take the lead in striking a note of loyalty and welcome for another stranger.[45] Let Fitzsimmons, the administrator, introduce him to the archdiocese. Extension would unveil him to the civic leadership of the city and state.

Why not, therefore, a banquet right after Mundelein's installation at the cathedral?

Kelley's ideas crystallized rapidly. On February 10, 1916, the day following the installation, the archbishop would attend Extension's banquet in the hall of the University Club. This affair, Kelley planned, would be underwritten by twenty-five laymen and would gather from the general community some 250 guests, including a large non-Catholic representation. Of these, he calculated, a hundred would comprise leaders in government and the professions, another hundred would be drawn from the financial world, and the remainder would be members of the hierarchy who would stay over in Chicago after the cathedral ceremonies. Kelley's proposal had a noble and timely design, and it was welcomed by Mundelein, who saw in his arrival an opportunity to unite "men of all creeds and from every walk of life." Monsignor Fitzsimmons had no authority to object, and Mundelein agreed that, as Kelley had suggested, the reception would thus be shared by the archdiocese and the society.[46]

This ambitious plan, at the same time, offered an irresistible temptation to Jean Crones, a young anarchist who worked as a chef at Kelley's club. Unwittingly, the "Boss" had given him a golden opportunity of assassinating at one stroke the leaders of every institution he abhorred. During the preparations for the meal, the culprit seasoned the soup with a lethal mixture of arsenic and mercury, and fled, never to be arrested. Later at the banquet, to Kelley's horror, many guests suddenly came down with fits of vomiting; and those able to stand groped to exits where they relieved themselves. Kelley was among the casualties and had to be helped to his apartment on the third floor of the building. "I was very sick myself," he told Burke soon after; "in fact, I am just over it. It may break out again anytime." Fortunately, however, the conspiracy failed. The damage from the attempted massacre could have been incalculable if the chief steward, a forgotten hero by the name of Al Brissette, had not noted beforehand the odd aroma from the soup kettles and ordered their contents to be thrown out. The evening was, therefore, not a total disaster. No one died; and by the end, nearly everyone had returned to honor the archbishop, a remarkable demonstration of respect that was not missed by the newcomer. Meanwhile, the ailing Kelley was concerned over Mundelein's health, but the guest of honor had escaped unharmed. He was known to have favored a rule which evidently spared him from the poison: the public, he believed, was a place where one was seen and sometimes heard but where one never ate.[47]

While Chicago survived the incident in good spirit, Kelley anticipated that alarming reports would be sent abroad, specifically to Rome. Therefore, he gathered local press clippings and, with a commentary, mailed them to Cardinals Merry del Val and Falconio. Both men read English and were asked to correct any false impressions that arose in European accounts of the incident. Perhaps, suggested Kelley in a clever twist of logic, the experience served the church by teaching non-Catholics in America a great lesson regarding radical subversion. Anarchism could be seen as a respecter of no creed, Protestant or Catholic; and as the banquet victims could testify, no one was safe from its deadliness. Ever the resourceful promoter, he tried to claim this slight dividend out of his blushing embarrassment.

The coming of Archbishop Mundelein signaled an uncertain dawning. Kelley had borne a dark night of agony—the fall of Burke in Toronto, the fading of Martinelli and Merry del Val in Rome, the death of Quigley in Chicago—his beacons of yesterday, forever extinguished. A new star from the East was approaching. It was an unknown. It appeared on no one's charts; its behavior was still a mystery. It had intruded somewhat, entering a charged environment that was filled with grievance and division.

Yet Francis Clement Kelley was a decent navigator. He welcomed this new factor in the heavens as generously as any man in Chicago.

V
The Task Completed

Throughout 1916, no one in Chicago was the target of more searching scrutiny than Archbishop Mundelein. Along with many who studied the newcomer, Monsignor Kelley would have located in him three centers of gravity. Most obvious, first, were his eastern origins. A native of New York City, he had been ordained for the diocese of Brooklyn in 1895, where he promptly rose high on the staff of Bishop Charles E. McDonnell. His advancement in ecclesiastical rank had been equally spectacular. In eleven years, Mundelein had become the nation's youngest monsignor and in 1909 its youngest auxiliary bishop. The chief factor in the churchman's early success was the patronage of Bishop McDonnell. The Brooklyn ordinary had made Mundelein's episcopal promotion the focus of a personal errand in Rome. In the course of this trip in 1909, he had contacted in person the pertinent Vatican officials in breathtaking succession: Pius X, Merry del

Val, De Lai, Falconio, and others. One of his joys, he had told Mundelein, had been the anticipation of a long partnership with the young prelate.[1]

Although within the province of New York, McDonnell's diocese had not shared in the Propagation's early antipathy toward Extension. A prominent Brooklynite had been elected to Kelley's board as early as 1906, Father Edward McCarty. His impressive work for the home-missions had, it seemed, tempted Kelley in 1907 to have Archbishop Quigley ask the Holy See for a monsignorship—in spite of McCarty's protests. This occasioned the first recorded contact between Kelley and Mundelein. McDonnell had resented an effort to honor McCarty without first consulting Brooklyn, and he had asked Mundelein to help him block Kelley's proposal. The Chicagoan's trespass was not fatal, as evidenced in the following year by the active participation in the first missionary congress on the part of McDonnell and "Monsignor" McCarty.[2] Mundelein's transfer to the Midwest in 1915 did not seal him off from these contacts in the East. He preserved many of his early friendships, especially the one with another of McDonnell's protégés, Thomas E. Molloy, who would succeed the Brooklyn bishop in 1921.

In Kelley's view, however, the greatest objection at the time of the announcement had not been directed against his German ancestry: it was "the fact," Kelley told Cardinal Merry del Val, "that he was an Eastern man." This seemed curiously inconsistent with Rome's interest in developing local clergy. According to Kelley, Mundelein simply followed in the wake of so many sent to the West, while "no Western prelates [were] sent East." This pattern suggested that in making its appointments, the Holy See ignored merit and gave too great a weight to geography.[3] Quigley had come to Chicago from Buffalo and, even with his Irish ancestry, had not been fully accepted. How deeply, wondered Kelley, would the roots of this most recent transplant from New York be allowed to sink into the Illinois soil?

The second key to Mundelein was a singular devotion to the

Holy See, known popularly as *Romanità*. Like a score of promising students from the United States, he had taken his priestly studies in the Eternal City—with a difference. Instead of enrolling in the North American College, he lived at the Urban College of Propaganda Fide, a pontifical institution sponsored by the Vatican department in charge of missionary activity in the world. This experience had a profound impact on the New Yorker. Studies in Rome gave most students a broader perspective of Catholic life than that given to their contemporaries at home—through their lessons, friendships, and presence at the heart of the institutional church. The Urban College excelled in this broad formation. It gathered young men from around the globe, including Mundelein, and conditioned them for the missions. Though not destined for the field afar, he had lived their simple, even primitive life; worn their distinctive cassock and hat; and, along with his collegemates, was dubbed a *bagarozzo*—a "cockroach"—the street taunt which Romans snapped at the ubiquitous, straggling seminarians.[4] Through this hard living, the college shaped in Mundelein a universalism which exceeded that of the national colleges in Rome and prepared him for a central role in the home-mission movement in America.

Mundelein's *Romanità* comprised more than a catholicity of viewpoint; it also meant special friendships. The college had introduced him to an ecclesiastic who succeeded Bishop McDonnell as Mundelein's chief patron. This was John Bonzano, who served as rector of the Urban College during Mundelein's student years. There was from the outset the strongest attachment between the two. In 1894, when Mundelein's mother died a sudden death "unattended," that is, suddenly, without the last rites, the sad news from Brooklyn was sent to Bonzano, who was asked gently to inform the young seminarian. To spare him the tragic details, the correspondent asked the rector not to show the letter—but Bonzano passed the correspondence on to the young man, an act which revealed that there were few secrets between them and that the older man already respected the inner strength of his protégé.[5]

Each man had paced the career of the other. Bonzano had assisted in the negotiations for Mundelein's promotion as an auxiliary bishop and had been the first to congratulate him. Mundelein had likewise helped the other in the mastery of English, a skill that would contribute to Bonzano's rise in the Vatican diplomatic corps. From this there developed a lifelong practice whereby Mundelein wrote letters to his former rector in English and Bonzano reciprocated in Italian. Aside from the normal exchange of news, this arrangement was designed to give language practice to each. Regularly the rector reported his progress so that by 1906 he no longer needed to consult a dictionary. Three years later, Mundelein learned that his distinguished pupil in English was a candidate for the apostolic delegation in the United States. In 1912, after Bonzano had been named to this post, he discussed, with no one else but Monsignor Mundelein, his plans to arrive in New York City. The new delegate's preference, he confided, was to make his first calls on Mundelein and McDonnell; but protocol required him to visit Cardinal Farley upon disembarking. Since that appointment, the two friends saw more of each other—the Roman often inviting the Brooklynite to the nation's capital, in exchange for occasional holidays at Mundelein's cottage in New Jersey.[6] Bonzano's presence in Washington, however, signaled more than the opportunity to deepen a 20-year-old relationship. As delegate, he supervised the selection of American bishops, and his former student was not to be forgotten.

Francis Kelley would certainly have approved of Archbishop Mundelein's Roman connection. Under Quigley, he had built his own Vatican ties as a life line for the society. In fact, the "Boss" had developed an association with a member of the Roman Curia which paralleled the relationship between Mundelein and Bonzano. Kelley's intimate in Rome was Monsignor Sante Tampieri.

A Ravennatan by birth and eleven years older than Kelley, he had served in the secretariat of state under Cardinal Merry del Val, whom he cherished as a lifelong idol. After the death of Pius X, Tampieri was replaced in the curia, and his usefulness then centered more in his acquaintance with Vatican insiders. His access to the secretariat of state under Pietro Gasparri, Merry del Val's successor, was through the third-ranking member of the department, Giuseppe Pizzardo. Tampieri's channels into Propaganda, moreover, were two rising bureaucrats who would later serve as secretaries of this congregation, Francesco Marchetti-Selvaggiani and Pietro Fumasoni-Biondi. In 1917, three years after Merry del Val's fall in the secretariat, Kelley's friend recovered his official status in the Roman Curia when he was appointed to the Apostolic Camera, a minor bureau that administered the temporalities of the Holy See during an interregnum between pontificates. This veteran of Rome was thus an asset to have: he knew everyone and was a virtuoso in languages. As Mundelein had done with Bonzano, Kelley composed letters to Tampieri in English and encouraged his correspondent always to reply in Italian. "I discovered recently," the American explained, "that the language is better known to me than I had supposed, and I hope that I shall make even greater progess in the future."[7] Extension's president and new chancellor, therefore, appreciated the advantages of active associates at the Vatican, and in several ways the styles of these transatlantic relationships bore a striking resemblance.

The attitude of the apostolic delegate was crucial to the fortunes of Extension, and Kelley anticipated a warm relationship with Archbishop Bonzano. Even before the latter's appointment to the United States, their paths had momentarily crossed. On a trip to Rome in 1907, Quigley had enlisted the former Propaganda rector to bring the society's petition for papal approval to the Vatican. This was a key assignment, representing Extension's first official contact with the Holy See, and what followed had its moment of embarrassment. The document was properly delivered but was mislaid at the Vatican. The rector feared at first that it had been lost within the mountain of paper that accumulated in the congregations; and he was forced to postpone his report to Chicago. The petition, fortunately, was found, and, as Bonzano confided later to Quigley, the Holy Father had taken a personal interest in the society, endorsing his approval in his own hand. In a gesture of good will and gratitude, Kelley promptly sent to the seminary a subscription to *Extension Magazine,* and this so pleased Bonzano that he gracefully offered his future services to the society and archdiocese.[8]

Two years later Kelley met the rector in Rome, and his first impression, as he recalled later during the trouble with Archbishop Falconio, had been that Bonzano "would make a splendid Delegate for America."[9] In 1910 the acquaintance was renewed on Kelley's second trip to Rome, when he shared a meal with Bonzano. Kelley took the opportunity to invite the rector to the International Eucharistic Congress in Montreal, suggesting too that he should include Chicago in his tour. Bonzano was interested and reported the conversation to the auxiliary bishop in Brooklyn. Kelley had spoken highly of Bishop Mundelein, Bonzano commented, and wanted his best regards passed on to the young prelate. Hence, the announcement of Bonzano's assignment two years later as Apostolic Delegate in the United States had evoked almost as much satisfaction in Chicago as it had in Brooklyn. While handsome and trim, the new delegate was "not a strong looking man," Kelley conceded; but since its foundation this Roman exhibited the warmest feelings toward Extension, an attitude in stark contrast to that of his predecessor, Diomede Falconio.[10]

The third and last dimension in Mundelein which drew a response from Monsignor Kelley was a singular combination of intelligence and strength, a combination which fashioned a talented man into a man of decision. The biographical sketches which appeared in the Chicago press at the time of Mundelein's appointment had listed his early achievements in the East. But these standard pieces hardly impressed seasoned clerics, such as Kelley. A more striking display of talent soon followed when Mundelein inaugurated a firm and decisive regime in the archdiocese. Chicago's Catholic community was a notable mixture of nationalist and ethnic groups. Waves of immigrants had created its polyglot character, and successive nativist campaigns in the nineteenth century had failed to Americanize it. When Quigley arrived, 132 national parishes served twelve distinct colonies; and he had elected to follow a benign attitude of respecting their differences.[11] This policy had appealed to Kelley. The integration of ethnic groups, he wrote in 1911, "cannot be forced, nor should it be. . . . We cannot make Americans of [immigrants] by teaching them to hate either the language or the customs of the country from which they came."[12]

A national emergency, however, altered the complexion of American pluralism. In Quigley's last year, World War I divided the ethnic colonies in Chicago along belligerent lines. The most conspicuous reaction to the outbreak of the war was found among the Irish and Germans, the backbone of the archdiocese, who openly sympathized with the Central Powers.[13] Even Kelley's headquarters at Extension had not been spared the war's fragmentation of public opinion. A month after its outbreak, the "Boss" already noted split allegiances within his staff. "General [Simon A.] Baldus [managing editor of the magazine] is on the job," he teased Alfred E. Burke, a confirmed anglophile:

> Field Marshall Ledvina has mobilized; Ireland, represented by Father O'Brien, is preserving absolute neutrality. I myself am keeping the peace fairly well, except when I meet a Britisher. Then I fire a twenty-four inch krupp and run for dear life.

> This is a Dutch office with the exception of the girls. I strongly suspect they are for the French. You see, the French have such delightful mustaches.[14]

In a short time, however, the joking was ended as soon as Kelley perceived how dreadfully explosive the situation was. Early comments on the war which appeared in *Extensiion Magazine* had raised a torrent of criticism and forced Quigley to intervene. "I have had a conference with Baldus," Kelley told Joseph T. Roche, "and with someone bigger than Baldus. As a consequence we are not going to touch the war again. It is too delicate a subject. There is too much dynamite in everything we say about it. Frankly, we are afraid and that sums up the situation."[15] The Islander's spirit trembled as he composed these words. The war's impact on Extension's supporters was one of the few forces that silenced his pen.

When Mundelein followed Quigley in Chicago, a false note could have signaled a civil disturbance. At the hour of his succession, Kelley had said, the archidiocese needed a man of consummate tact. Instead of favoring nationalist groups, Mundelein's approach evolved into what he would call "assimilation." The basic problem of the big cities in the older parts of the country was, the archbishop believed, that "of the absorption of many racial elements, newcomers to our shores. . . ."[16] In the first years of World War I, Mundelein therefore heeded President Woodrow Wilson's call for the strictest neutrality in American history, an impartiality in thought as well as action. Without alienating his constituency, the archbishop devoted his early episcopate to strengthening the American consciousness of his foreign-born faithful. Though no one should forget his origins, insisted Mundelein, there was no need for hyphenated citizenship, such as German-Americanism or Irish-Americanism.

The entry of the United States into the war in 1917 served only to quicken the archbishop's program of Americanizing the ethnic groups in the archdiocese. There followed bond drives in church vestibules, clergy recruitment for the chaplain corps, and public statements in which Mundelein called for patriotic unity from his polygot community. After the war, this assimilationist policy continued. National parishes were discouraged in preference to territorial ones which blended any number of ethnic groups. The capstone of the grand strategy was Mundelein's seminary located on an extensive campus north of Chicago. The architectural style of Saint Mary of the Lake mirrored the churchman's abiding priority to weld together the diverse elements of his archdiocese. In the Illinois countryside rose some fourteen buildings in the splendid Georgian manner, a style associated with colonial America. In this environment mingled the sons of immigrant and native parents, all to be forged into an American clergy.[17] The policy of assimilation, however, stimulated its share of controversy. Some ethnic groups, as well as scholars who have studied them later, have never forgiven Mundelein's neglect of these heritages, but his contemporaries, like Francis Kelley, could not deny in him the essence of leadership. Though the priest had at first agreed with Quigley's tolerance of cultural pluralism, Kelley had been impatient with this archbishop's tendency toward inaction and ambiguity in most issues. In watching Mundelein reverse directions in the archdiocese, Kelley acknowledged the presence of a clearheaded and decisive churchman, and the Islander was quite willing to adapt himself to the new priority.

Not one for half measures, Kelley trumpeted his conversion to this new force in Chicago. Nine months after the installation, he prevailed upon Mundelein to publish his addresses. In 1918, these were collected in a volume entitled *Two Crowded Years* in which Kelley supplied a warm Irish welcome in a foreword touching on the issue of assimilation. Chicago was, the priest noted, a modern Babel, where the Sunday gospel was preached in no fewer than fourteen languages. The city needed what Mundelein represented—a poised ruler who, though cosmopolitan in his background, was thoroughly American in his heart. In him, proposed Kelley, the minorities—the Poles, Irish,

Slavs, and Germans—which had been cut adrift from each other, had at last found a common source of leadership. For "when he spoke it was always for the cause he had to champion—for the Country, for the State, for the City."[18]

The new archbishop was as complex as any human being, but contemporaries recognized the three focal points, if they might be put casually—Brooklyn, Bonzano, and brilliance. Though it is risky to give a final assessment regarding leadership, this much may be said of Mundelein. Coming to a see known everywhere to be "divided . . . into inevitable faction and . . . [a] linguistic Babel," he discouraged the ethnic pluralism of his faithful, a policy which has evoked a chorus of criticism. Nevertheless, this pressure brought some integration to Chicago Catholics who were known for their separatist tendencies, and, above all, it did not impede his spectacular success in multiplying the assets of the archdiocese. Under his leadership of twenty-five years, numerical progress was achieved in all categories—clergy, laity, real property, and so forth—with efficiency, intelligence, and little polarization. Resistance there was, but none could detour the inexorable will. His guiding rule was, as he confided to his intimates: "Don't let them wear you down." Perhaps Kelley sensed in the archbishop's person what Shane Leslie, the biographer of such a church luminary as Cardinal Henry Manning of Westminster, detected in Mundelein's writings: the quiet tenseness, the little sympathy for cranks or critics, the demand that things be done his way, the little waste of sentiment or emotion. In any case, this man from Brooklyn was a towering ecclesiastic who dealt always from a position of strength. Tagged early in clerical circles as "the Dutch cleanser," he would be Kelley's superior during the latter's final decade at Extension and in Chicago.[19]

* * * * * * * * *

Monsignor Kelley hoped for "a man of tact" in George Mundelein. This kind of leader was necessary not only for an archdiocese with its ethnic splinters but also for Extension, which was undergoing its first succession of chancellors. Furthermore, Kelley himself required a highly perceptive superior if his career was to continue. During the interregnum, the Islander had been associated with two controversial efforts that could have permanently alienated the new archbishop. First was Kelley's campaign in behalf of Bishop Muldoon, a campaign in which the priest had guilelessly sought an endorsement from Mundelein's own patron, Archbishop Bonzano. Even more questionable during the vacancy was the board's recommendation in August, 1915, that Kelley be given a titular bishopric, a bold move endorsed by Archbishop Messmer, the acting chancellor. Ten years of service at Extension, the board reasoned, had demonstrated the president's competency to fill higher positions in the church. Otherwise, when he retired from running the society, he could turn only to routine parish work which scarcely suited this accomplished executive. Kelley had not been a party to this recommendation, and it had been carried to Rome by Father Juan Navarrete, the Mexican priest who at the time served as his Spanish interpreter. Before its presentation to the consistorial congregation, Kelley intercepted it, fearing that such a request could jeopardize his other work; and the request returned with him to Chicago. In its meeting of December, 1915, the board unanimously insisted—against Kelley—that it be presented to Archbishop-designate Mundelein before the latter's arrival in Chicago.[20]

This unusual action on the part of Extension's board only complicated Mundelein's coming to Chicago. It was unprecedented and unfair. Unprecedented, because the event which had doubtless suggested this action had been the consecration in the previous year of Thomas J. Shahan, rector of The Catholic University of America. His promotion to the episcopate had originated with the university chancellor, Cardinal Gibbons, who had worked with Shahan for five years.[21] In Kelley's case, however, the chancellor of Extension had now been asked to sponsor an episcopal candidate with whom he had had no previous working experience and whose nomination had originated with the board. The action was also unfair, placing the archbishop-designate in an acutely delicate position. The request asked him to single out one of his priests, a controversial one, before he had set foot in his archdiocese. Even without Kelley's blessing, the action could have been a catastrophic mistake, making impossible a smooth transition between chancellors. To all appearances, however, Mundelein was unruffled, and Extension was given a first-hand lesson in tact. To his enormous credit, he and Kelley began a lengthy association with no evident reprisals from this episode. No doubt the "Boss" felt relieved when his titular see was quietly forgotten.

The Islander's early enthusiasm over Mundelein continued to grow during the opening months of the new administration. "He is on the job every minute," Kelley told Burke. "He thinks big and consequently acts big." His youth and optimism, added Kelley, had idealized working conditions, and thus far the young New Yorker manifested more interest in Extension than Quigley had. The clergy and laity had rallied to him. "There is no power behind the throne," Burke was assured. "He sees every man who can be of service to him and plays no favorites." Kelley was also impressed as to how the financial community had embraced this *Wunderkind.* Regarding this reception, the Islander's favorite story concerned two Protestant businessmen who wondered if the archbishop was a mason. He could not be, one declared, because he was Catholic. "Well," replied the other, "I thought he might be a Mason secretly because even the Masons of this town are swearing by him." The Brooklynite was no bumpkin; and with delight, Kelley sensed even a personal relationship evolving between the two. "I meet with him often and walk with him," he told his Roman friend, Monsignor Tiberghien; "in fact, I am more intimate with him than I was with Archbishop Quigley."[22]

So spectacular was Mundelein's entry into Chicago that Monsignor Kelley was forced to revise two pet ideas. The first one to go was his regret over the failure of his first choice for the see. "While I am sorry I lost Muldoon," he confided to Burke, "the sorrow was alleviated by what I got." Kelley had made a major concession when he acknowledged that Mundelein's selection was providential, and Tiberghien was urged to pass this on personally to the Holy Father. Kelley's second adjustment touched his deepest convictions, the bedrock of his spirit. He had long advocated the rights of the West until he studied this new force from Brooklyn. "If they have any more Germans like Mundelein in the East," he confessed early to Burke, "we will be glad to welcome them to the West. I have serious doubts if the East would produce another man like the present Archbishop of Chicago." The spell did not fade quickly. Two years after Mundelein's arrival, Kelley was struck by the success of the archbishop's Christmas appeal in the diocesan paper for the Holy Father, whose finances had been drained by the war. "The response of the people indicates the popularity of the Archbishop," he reported to Tampieri on the eve of Mundelein's second anniversary in Chicago; "they gave, probably, the largest offering from any Diocese in the world, $75,000."[23]

This extraordinary response from a published appeal demonstrated Mundelein's quiet efficiency usually behind the scenes, but what Kelley admired more was the New Yorker's public presence, an asset which, in the monsignor's view, was all too uncommon among American bishops. The young archbishop had unveiled this charism immediately upon his arrival. At the poisoned banquet given by Extension, Mundelein addressed the guests as soon as order was restored. In spite of the commotion, his self-possession and eloquence charmed the audience so much so that Kelley compared him to a triumphant Julius Caesar, parodying for Burke the Roman's famous remark: "I came, I talked, I got 'em.' " Cardinal Merry del Val was also given an appraisal of initial impressions in which Kelley described

Mundelein's first four addresses as nothing less than "masterpieces."[24] This early reaction led Kelley to suggest that Extension publish his talks in *Two Crowded Years.* In the years to follow, Mundelein's command of language never ceased to move the priest-editor, who delighted in an idea well-expressed. The archbishop, contemporaries noted, carefully rationed his appearances. The effect was that when he spoke, seldom as it was, his words were scrupulously pertinent and all the more heeded. Although Kelley seldom resorted to flattery, an invocation delivered by Mundelein in 1917 evoked from him an effusive but sincere response. The text, Kelley told the archbishop, was "beyond all praise," but even better was his presence. "I am proud of that prayer and the fact that you gave it yourself. . . ," he went on. "I was a gift worthwhile that God gave you, of knowing when to speak, where to speak and how to speak."[25]

Kelley's admiration lasted during his years in Chicago. A seasoned practitioner himself, he valued public speaking and did not offer idle commendations. Several of the best orators of his generation, including William Jennings Bryan, had stood before him; and he was not easily pleased. As a master of the spoken word, Mundelein met all of Kelley's demanding specifications. In Kelley's last year at Extension, the archbishop delivered what the Islander called "the best public utterance I have ever heard from a churchman. . . ." The voice carried, and it was graced with a musical quality which Kelley had never noticed before. The subject matter was well conceived; the expression well constructed. "It began," observed Kelley, "without any sparring for an opening. The river of thought and eloquence was just as wide at the beginning as it was in the middle and at the end"—all of it given without the assistance of a manuscript.[26] Mundelein had delivered a flawless performance.

To tighten his bond with his chancellor with more than words, Kelley was willing to volunteer special services. During the early stages of World War I, Mundelein had lost a shipment of expensive vestments from Germany. They were virtual art objects which had been purchased before the war, but the manufacturer had retained them for an exhibit. Shipped eventually by the way of Sweden, they never reached America, and the archbishop suspected that the British fleet had intercepted them. Kelley volunteered to ask Burke, soon to be commissioned a lieutenant-colonel in the Canadian chaplains' corps, to track down the missing, or confiscated, cargo; and Burke succeeded in recovering two of the three packages of vestments.[27] Kelley, moreover, catered to archiepiscopal hobbies. While Quigley's interest had lain in collecting maps, his successor favored autographs of distinguished persons, alive and deceased. Kelley gladly contributed to this collection those of Cardinal Merry del Val, ex-President William Howard Taft, and "Uncle Joe" Cannon, an "Old Guard" Republican, who had served as speaker of the House of Representatives under Theodore Roosevelt and Taft.[28] Kelley was, in addition, one of Mundelein's reliable occasional speakers, and the priest accepted these special invitations. These included the historic funeral of Mother Frances Xavier Cabrini, the Italian-born foundress of the Missionary Sisters of the Sacred Heart, who died in Chicago in 1917. Kelley was hardly the appropriate eulogist for her requiem. He had met her only once and acknowledged little interest in her work among Italian immigrants. Nevertheless, he delivered one of the most celebrated sermons of his career over her body on orders from Mundelein, who, along with his good friend, Archbishop Bonzano, had a personal devotion to her.[29]

Archbishop Mundelein had therefore become a singular force in Kelley's life. The two men would have their differences, and at times a coolness divided them. But this talented, poised easterner had touched Kelley uniquely. The priest was too old to be guilty of an adolescent hero-worship, but he clearly respected the abilities of this prelate. The value of reassurance for work well done was an obvious truth in those days. Kelley was quick to pass compliments and do favors when deserved, and he accepted them from others as reinforcements regarding the worth of his own work. In the lives of most people, however, a tribute from a special authority, no matter how slight, towers above the rest; and in Kelley's life, this authority was George Mundelein. Nothing could have pleased Extension's chief more than a reciprocal expression of satisfaction from the archbishop of Chicago. This was the man whom Kelley genuinely esteemed and to whom he looked, perhaps most of all, for acceptance and approval. Without knowing it, Mundelein had acquired a peculiar responsibility in Kelley's life: aside from being his superior, he was the one man before whom Francis Kelley was vulnerable. There is strong evidence of Mundelein's appreciation of this fact, but as the debts in the relationship piled up, the Islander giving more than receiving, this archbishop eluded the invitation to familiarity.

* * * * * * * * *

When Monsignor Kelley greeted the new chancellor in 1916, Extension was on the threshold of its second decade. The core of the program had been chapel-building; and during that period, 1,200 structures had been raised, averaging close to three a week. The program, Mundelein was told on his arrival, had briefly peaked at a chapel opening each day; and it was supplemented by other enterprises equally successful.[30] In this way, Kelley introduced the stranger to a young but enormously productive child of the West which had matured from infancy to a strong manhood; and the president, along which this board, looked forward to the new partnership with the easterner.

Three key projects set the direction of the society's next ten years. The first was *Extension Magazine.* Its importance stemmed not from profits but from its being the only organ that brought the society's message and appeals to the Catholic masses. In encouraging Catholic writers and illustrators, it also sought to emulate the literary and artistic features of the best secular magazines. Altogether, these aims required a large and skilled staff as well as substantial capital. Since its inception, the monthly had been financially unstable. For a decade, an outside publisher managed it and posted an annual deficit of about $12,000. These losses required a subsidy from the general fund, the reversal of what the board had expected. On May 1, 1916, the society recovered full control as publisher. With a staff of forty, it hoped to make the monthly as profitable a unit as the other departments.[31] Expenses were always a concern. After the entry of the United States into World War I, Congress came close to raising the rates on second-class mail in order to help finance the war. This would have taxed Extension another $37,000; and Kelley spent five days in Washington fighting the increase in rates. Later, postwar inflation, especially the rising cost of paper, caused new headaches. In 1920 Kelley estimated for Cardinal Dougherty that in one year the budget for the magazine would increase by $250,000. In an attempt to cut salaries, one member of the board suggested that a religious sisterhood be engaged to handle some details of the operation, a suggestion that went unheeded.[32]

Monsignor Kelley's approach to stabilizing the magazine was not merely to reduce expenses; it was more to broaden circulation and income. A variety of techniques were tested. Letters were mailed to clergy, explaining the rising costs of publishing and asking for long-term subscriptions. Kelley sought endorsements from bishops, and at length Mundelein yielded to a longstanding request for his recommendation. The archbishop's reluctance arose from the thought that his praise would be self-serving since the society was a Chicago institution. But, after getting favorable reports from the majority in the hierarchy, including Baltimore, New York, and Boston, Mundelein was encouraged to write "what has long been in my mind, that 'Extension' is the best Catholic monthly that has been published in this country." Though late in coming, the archbishop's comments were characteristically laconic but pointed. Not only, he continued, was the magazine professional in its layout, "from cover to cover . . . interesting, instructive, and thoroughly religious . . . ," but its revenue also supported America's home-missions. These two reasons, urged Mundelein, were sufficient to convince any literate Catholic to subscribe.[33]

Kelley's other effort in publishing was an attempt to bring some order to competition among Catholic periodicals. The Catholic community had been, in his view, plagued with the many magazines, mostly of poor quality, which had been aggressively promoted by local agents. Abuses forced some bishops to control periodical circulation in their dioceses, and occasionally barriers had been raised against *Extension Magazine.* One of the principal complaints came from Boston, where the archdiocese constituted a prime market area. There the competition had become so charged with fury, Kelley was told, that not only were agents violating the privileges granted to them but they actually threatened those who hesitated to subscribe. If this continued, Cardinal O'Connell promised to withdraw all permissions to solicit in Boston.[34]

This situation was, unfortunately, common in the major dioceses; to correct it was beyond the strength of one man. Nevertheless, it threatened Kelley's organ, along with the society itself, and this was sufficient to drive Kelley to find a *modus vivendi.* When Mundelein requested a list of magazines to be approved for Chicago, Kelley declined this opportunity to eliminate important competitors in the home archdiocese. A policy of excluding rivals would only stimulate resentment elsewhere. Besides, Kelley had confidence in the competitive strength of his magazine. "We have to live and let live," he explained. "That is my attitude."[35] His original approach centered rather on self-regulation. A new organization, the Catholic Publishers Protective Association, was therefore formed, located in Chicago. Its membership was open to those Catholic magazines that controlled their circulation departments, and its promise was that while the use of agents in the field was indispensable, their behavior had to be regulated. Religious periodicals did not sell on newsstands, and the cost of soliciting subscriptions through the mails was prohibitive. Kelley himself experimented with the latter method, discovering that out of 10,000 letters only one subscription was made. Hence, the agent was the most practical means of putting Catholic literature in homes, and *Extension Magazine* depended on 200 salesmen. The association was therefore formed in 1917 to supervise these local representatives, especially by means of having each of them bonded.[36] Unfortunately, this voluntary arrangement failed to correct the abuses. Only three periodicals joined the association—*The Missionary, The Queen's Work,* and *Extension Magazine.*

Next, Kelley appealed to national authority to temper criticism arising in the dioceses from the activity of these agents. In 1920 a pastor in Boston denounced *Extension Magazine* from the pulpit, reproaching Kelley by name and declaring that his agents "were nothing but frauds and grafters." This was libel, thought Kelley, who then appealed to the apostolic delegate. "If a Catholic publication is to be the victim of the whims and bad temper of a great number of priests in the United States," he told Archbishop Bonzano, "there is very little hope of having any national publications whatever." Instead of lawsuits, Kelley hoped that from Washington there would go forth the word that no individual priest had the right to exclude the magazine.[37]

The situation only worsened. Without interruption, complaints were heard in the dioceses; and worse yet, mission magazines continued to multiply, fifteen by the end of 1921.[38] No larger in size than cheap calendars, several publications charged high rates and, it appeared, suggested spiritual favors in direct return for cash subscriptions. This was accompanied by a more serious development. The vast majority of the magazines had given their circulation departments to independent agencies. Even one member of Kelley's protective association resorted to this and was forced to withdraw from that body. Not only were these agencies more aggressive but they also consumed the income of these periodicals, charging the mission societies as much as 75 percent of the subscription price. Besides reducing revenues for spiritual works, this formula dividing the income between the agency and the mission society violated postal regulations for nonprofit corporations and threatened a national scandal.[39] Within in five years, Kelley calculated, Catholic magazines would thus destroy themselves. With the failure of self-regulation, only a compulsory system, he concluded, could end the wild scramble. In edging his way to this extreme position, he acknowledged that within no diocese could a bishop interfere with the publication or circulation of a single magazine; otherwise he could be sued for restraint of trade. The solution would be a national plan of "approval" whereby the hierarchy's united endorsement of publications would drive others out of circulation.

In its annual meeting in 1921, Extension's board was sufficiently aroused as to authorize the president to prepare for the United States hierarchy a report on Catholic periodicals; and Mundelein and Bishop Michael J. Gallagher of Detroit offered to collaborate. After nearly a year, the bishops received a lengthy and impassioned document at their annual meeting in September, 1922. The problem was thoroughly reviewed, and there followed a plan to regulate the abuses. The chief recommendation recalled Kelley's earlier struggle over the national collection. Only two Catholic magazines, the bishops were told, should be given general approval, one representing the home-missions and the other the foreign-missions. In this way, both interests would be financially protected, as well as spared unnecessary competition between them.[40] The plan to end the proliferation of religious periodicals was, however, no more successful in Washington than had been the proposal for a national collection for home-missions.

Despite his failure to bring order to Catholic periodical publishing, Monsignor Kelley achieved the goals he had set as editor-in-chief of *Extension Magazine.* Its success in representing broad interests in its articles and stories was noted in mid-1916 when the subtitle was changed from introducing it merely as a "Catholic" national monthly to the proud claim that it was the "World's Greatest" one. At the same time, after the society acquired complete control of the publication, subscribers more than doubled in less than four years. In May, 1916, its patrons numbered 133,000, and by November, 1919, they had grown to 289,000. By the latter date, too, the magazine showed a profit of more than 10 percent of its assessed value and for the first time contributed $30,000 to the general fund. It soon fell back into a deficit as the price of materials rose abruptly, but by the end of 1921 Kelley cheerfully reported to Mundelein that it had returned to the break-even point. From that point on, the periodical continued to swing between profit and loss columns until Kelley's departure in 1924.[41]

Two additional programs were newly developed during Monsignor Kelley's last decade at Extension, programs which indicated that after years of chapel-building the society had entered a second stage of its history: missionary support and education. "What is the use of putting up chapels," the president asked, "if there were no priests to fill them?"[42] The old projects were not neglected. By the end of 1918, the number of chapels built by Extension approached 1,700. Nearly $500,000 had been distributed in Mass offerings, along with a vast assortment of church goods. Three chapel-cars rode the tracks assisted by two chapel-motorcars bouncing among Mexican communities on remote Texas ranches.[43] But the towns of the South and West had convinced Kelley that the chapel-providing era was near a close. The priorities had shifted and now became twofold: the maintenance of the home-missioner in the field and his preparation for this ministry.

In 1921 the society's attention turned to clergy support when Archbishop Mundelein urged some method of furnishing cash subsidies. Accepting this charge as a personal challenge, Kelley devised the "Dollar Club," a direct-mail solicitation the income from which would supplement a missionary priest's monthly salary.[44] The opening stages of direct-mail campaigns, it was known, brought almost no income. Within the first year, every dollar received had to be invested in materials, mailing lists, and postage. Mundelein virtually defied Kelley to do better than break even, and he set as the goal a return of no less than 15 percent net, an unprecedented target under these conditions. Toward the end of the first year, the president announced that the cost to Extension for each dollar collected would be only 75 cents; and already, he added, forty-seven priests in the field were selected to receive subsidies. Kelley's report stunned even the archbishop. Commenting in admiration, Mundelein acknowledged that "if Monsignor Kelley were given something impossible to do he would rise to the occasion." The "Dollar Club" was thus credited within the board as a "winner" in supplementing missionaries' salaries and in displaying the "Boss's" ingenuity.[45]

At the same time, the Islander turned to a final herculean task to ensure manpower for his chapels, the foundation of a home-missionary seminary. Here the results were less conclusive. The idea of educating a specialized clergy had long been ripening in Kelley's mind, and the key lay in training native Americans for the home-missions. Hence, Kelley deplored the tendency among missionary bishops to disdain recruitment among American lads in favor of importing priests, mostly from Europe. This policy, admitted Kelley, saved bishops the expenses of schooling local youngsters, many of whom never reached the priesthood. "But in the end," he argued, "the price was too high."[46] In this culture there was no substitute for the American-born priest. The problem, in Kelley's eye, was not a shortage of vocations but a squandering of available resources. To his horror, he had discovered further that candidates were turned away. In the mission areas this was due largely to finances—neither the diocese nor the student could afford the tuition, especially in the early stages in which the candidate was less committed to ordination. Even in large eastern dioceses, a surplus of clergy and crowded seminaries had discouraged recruitment, another gross waste of manpower. Perhaps, Kelley reasoned, Extension could provide the means whereby these youngsters from the city and country might reach the altar and strengthen the native clergy in the home-missions.[47]

Kelley's first attempt was to subsidize students from missionary dioceses who attended seminaries scattered across the country. Their room, board, and tuition were paid during college years; and this responsibility was passed onto the bishops when the lads advanced into their theology course. Generally the society supported about ten students, half of them persevering until graduation. This modest program was make-shift until, it was hoped, Extension could provide a separate seminary. One possibility was the Apostolic Mission House, run by the Paulist Fathers in Washington, D.C., which served as a training center for mission work in America, but Kelley envisioned a different sort of institution. His specifications included a location squarely in the home-mission territory, and the campus should be capable of accommodating 150 young men for specialized training.[48] At the Boston missionary congress in 1913, Kelley had announced this dream and a year later shared it with Cardinal Merry del Val. The sum of $200,000 had been drawn from the society's general fund and reserved as the cornerstone of the endowment, and in 1917 Kelley surveyed possible sites near Salt Lake City.[49]

In time, the contagion of Kelley's dream spread even to those board members who had thoroughly urban backgrounds. At the annual meeting of 1922, Monsignor Joseph H. McMahon of New York City was moved to declare openly that his "was probably the most provincial diocese in the country, for the reason that the New Yorker's world began and ended at the Hudson." This extraordinary confession was followed by his offer to bring the message to the eastern metropolis if only to save the vocations of those boys discouraged from serving at home. Chicago was not to be outdone. Archbishop Mundelein had recently journeyed westward across the continent, talking with several bishops and seeing first-hand a portion of the home-missions. As a result, he had proposed to the apostolic delegate, the board learned, that his archdiocese would establish a "protectorate" over Nevada, perhaps for ten years. Under this arrangement, he would virtually furnish a native clergy for this area. In an urban center, he explained, there inevitably were young men who have been forced to postpone seminary studies through family responsibilities. In Chicago, an appeal to these belated vocations would gather fifty men who, if trained, "would burn up the country." The archdiocese would provide the men, their education, and their support. At the start of Mundelein's administration in Chicago, Kelley had but suspected that he was a man of the broadest vision. This hunch was now confirmed with his proposal that Chicago would take up a "State" and stand behind it. Mundelein was deadly serious: the delegate already knew of it, and the archbishop was about to urge it again in Rome.[50]

Kelley could conjure dreams in most people, but he was unable to materialize that of a separate seminary. The staffing, programming, episcopal approval, administration, and institutional maintenance were practical aspects that defied quick solution. Instead, the society turned in 1922 to two seminaries already operating—Little Rock College in Arkansas and Saint Benedict's College in Atchison, Kansas. Both were situated amid the home-missions and were willing to adapt the training program to Kelley's specifications. In return, bishops were encouraged to enroll candidates whose tuition was subsidized by Extension. At first, these students were "belated vocations," that is, older men who were unable to join the clergy of large urban diocese and were adopted by missionary dioceses.[51]

During Kelley's last years in Chicago, Extension's momentum thus continued undiminished. As the society's annual receipts approached a million dollars, it continued to adjust to new needs and install innovative programs in response. Organizations tend to repeat early successes, and in so doing they run the risk of becoming overgrown or obsolete. Under its first president, however, the movement preserved its original spirit of adventure by remaining, above all, open to experimentation. It had not yet grown so experienced that new challenges were unwelcome, so hardened that fresh ideas were not tried. Of course, not everything worked. There was no home-mission seminary as there was at Maryknoll, New York, which trained Americans for the foreign-missions. The "Boss" did not pursue perfect records. Once the seminary project seemed beyond the resources of the society, he accepted the more feasible alternative of using established schools which wanted the business. Francis Kelley was more than Extension's founder: he was its greatest protector, preserving it from institutional sclerosis. Only his successor could appreciate this contribution. Within two years after Kelley's departure, Monsignor William D. O'Brien admitted that the foundations had been so well-built that "any priest can run the Extension Society successfully."[52]

* * * * * * * * *

Extension was more than an institution; it was also a network of human relationships built on the interaction of several strong individuals. The work had placed the officers in close quarters, and the result was a happy blending of personal and professional interests. There was never the suggestion of complete democracy, never a blurring of rank. "Led" Ledvina managed the office as general secretary, and "Willie" O'Brien worked several departments. Francis, however, remained the "Boss," and informal as office communications were, he was never forced to remind his collaborators that he was in charge. In 1919 Kelley received another dividend from his investment in Dennis Dougherty, who had been a stalwart advocate of Extension at the missionary congress in Boston and who now had been promoted from Buffalo to Philadelphia. The society's staff in that year welcomed from his diocesan Propagation office Eugene J. McGuinness, the last major addition during Kelley's presidency. Immediately, the 30-year-old priest plunged into the work, taking up stenography and typing, as well as studying Extension's programs.[53] Quickly dubbed "Mac" or "Gene," he rounded out a notable quartet who had tagged themselves as the "four horsemen" of Extension. Each would become a bishop, three administering missionary dioceses, and the fourth staying with the society that assisted them. After the closest of associations in Chicago, their assignments would scatter them into the South and Southwest; but the bond cultivated at Extension remained intact until their deaths.

Together their spirit mixed a sober professionalism with the warmth of friendship. An event that mirrored this combination was the joint celebration in 1918 of Kelley's and Ledvina's silver anniversaries in the priesthood. In the midst of a working session, the board of governors quietly arranged a luncheon at the "Boss's" favorite, the University Club, and invited over thirty persons. Toastmaster and fellow club member, the Reverend Thomas V. Shannon, called upon several dignitaries who recounted the milestones of both men and paid special thanks to the founder. The two jubilarians were next summoned to the podium. Kelley reminisced and thanked his clerical and lay friends, but Ledvina expressed particular delight that his anniversary coincided with Kelley's. As office manager, he also alluded to the splendid cooperation among the departments and their personnel. The luncheon therefore reflected the deep harmony within Extension on all levels, not the least of which was that among the priests in charge. But the high spirits at the club would not interrupt work. Once the tributes were paid, the board resumed its official business—right at the dining tables.[54]

Kelley's associates, furthermore, delighted in teasing each other. "You're always wrong," was McGuinness's constant retort to O'Brien's schemes, a taunt forgiven in later years but never to be forgotten in Willie's correspondence. The group, moreover, enjoyed their chief's harmless pretensions over appearances. They cherished the memory of the "Boss" exiting one day from his office and encountering a portrait of himself which he did not fancy. Raising his cane, he delivered a slashing blow against the canvas, ripping the offensive image, as Willie recalled it, "from crown to abdomen." As the remains were carted out, there was doubtless a round of chuckles poorly stifled in staff offices nearby.[55] These amusements, however, did not damage the loyalty and respect of each other, nor did they blind Kelley to the superior abilities of his three subordinates, abilities which suggested that each was made of episcopal timber. Their closeness and their competency allowed the president time away from his office. His staff's dedication, therefore, encouraged him to take on special assignments without a worry over Extension. In 1923, for example, he spent nearly two weeks in giving retreats in the Pacific Northwest, the first in a long series of such conferences for clergy. Effective speakers were always in demand, especially in such remote areas; and he candidly needed this chance for income. Besides, the retreats gave him an opportunity to live briefly among those in the field and to see the results of Extension's assistance.[56] All this would have been denied to Kelley unless he had a trusted team in Chicago.

Even more importantly, his dealings with this priestly staff were governed with neither personal ambition nor jealousy. Of this, there was no more striking proof than Kelley's attitude regarding the appointment of the second bishop of Corpus Christi. Nearly as large as Belgium and the Netherlands combined, this sprawling see in southern Texas had a notorious history of missionary difficulty. Ninety-five percent of the Catholic population in this territory consisted of Mexican settlers and migrants, and two of its first three ordinaries had resigned. In 1920, when it was again vacant, this opportunity to become a bishop did not interest Francis Kelley. Seven years earlier, he had feared that he would be named there and had taken steps against it. Though he evidenced no desire at this point to enter the episcopacy, this did not prevent him from sponsoring a colleague for promotion. When Bishop Paul J. Nussbaum resigned in

1920, Kelley began a campaign in favor of his right-hand man, Emmanuel B. Ledvina. The general secretary had a first-hand acquaintance with conditions in Corpus Christi, having made three tours through Texas and having befriended Henri A. Constantineau, O.M.I., a long time and influential missioner there.[57] Kelley's first appeals went directly to Ledvina's bishop, Joseph Chartrand of Indianapolis, and then to his friend, John J. Hennessy, bishop of Wichita, Kansas. An enthusiastic recommendation might draw suspicion that one was trying to discard an undesirable subordinate. But Kelley's endorsement of Ledvina's promotion was honest because, as the Islander told Chartrand, "I recommend him for a position much higher than my own." The same thought received even stronger language for Hennessy: "The fact that I am suggesting his elevation over my head, does not weigh with me for an instant. He is the man for the place."[58] These two letters would be, Kelley promised, his only interventions in the matter. The waiting now began.

In April, 1921, the appointment came to Ledvina in a manner that astonished him. First, he had no opportunity to decline as the official letter read: "Send your AFFIRMATIVE answer by wire." Then, as the word circulated, several episcopal comrades offered sympathy to his face for such an assignment, adding their hope of an early transfer. This was a poor introduction to a new career; it planted in Ledvina lifelong seeds of resentment over the way his assignment to Texas was executed by Rome and acknowledged by his colleagues. Concern deepened a bit more when some like Dougherty were "thunderstruck" at the news, no doubt because Kelley appeared to have been passed by.[59]

True, nevertheless, to his generous nature, Kelley spared nothing in trying to compensate for the disappointment of Ledvina and that of his own admirers. In becoming the first of the "four horsemen" to reach the episcopate, the general secretary had now become the "dean" of the group. When Bishop Chartrand first suggested Indiana, Ledvina's home state, as the site for the consecration, Kelley urged that it be shifted to Chicago. Not only would the event attract a greater crowd there but Extension would cover the major bills. Though Chartrand insisted upon Indiana, Kelley invited, at the society's expenses, the bishops of the South and West. And for a greater splash of color he even called upon Dennis Dougherty to attend, having just returned from Rome with the red hat, but the new cardinal was unable to come. A special appeal went out through Extension, and one week before the festivities Kelley reported to Tampieri that a handsome burse of $20,000 would be given to Corpus Christi. "This," he wrote with satisfaction, "will give the Bishop a good start." Throughout the preliminaries, however, a note of embarrassment hovered as rumors persisted that the secetary general's promotion constituted a rebuke for Kelley.[60] The ugly whispers notwithstanding, the ceremony was given as much flair and substance as the "Boss's" resources would allow for his friend and junior partner of fourteen years.

While Monsignor Kelley was able to fuse personal and professional interest with his priest-lieutenants, his relationship with Extension's chancellor was confined strictly to work. Archbishop Mundelein was an invaluable collaborator, imaginative and keen as well as wholly committed to the home-missions. He had notable friends and achievements, and Kelley ranked him with Dougherty as the two most authoritative American figures at the Holy See.[61] But Mundelein's sense of leadership did not allow friendship to complicate tasks. He was an alert and self-possessed executive, and Kelley learned to deal with him carefully, not taking the liberties which, as Extension's founder, he had taken with Archbishop Quigley. In projects that involved him, the new chancellor was in charge, operating with strong independence, and his determination led to clashes with subordinates. In these final years in Chicago, therefore, Kelley found himself frequently in the position of yielding, an unnatural situation to which he, reluctantly and with some pain, was forced to adjust.

The first skirmish centered on Kelley's living arrangements.

Thus far, quarters for the Extension officers had presented a frustrating dilemma. A separate home for all the priests proved too expensive when Kelley tried to open St. Philip Neri Parish, Chicago, and was forced to give it up. Yet, the dispersal of these priests to scattered rectories and apartments appeared awkward. On his arrival, Mundelein promised "a proper home." On July 10, 1916, Kelley was assigned as pastor of St. Francis Xavier Parish in Wilmette, which became the official home for the staff. This was a quiet suburb just north of Chicago where his predecessor, Thomas V. Shannon, had worked in the dual capacity as pastor and editor of the archdiocesan weekly. Given the Reverend John Lannon to assist him in parochial duties, Kelley expected to continue to give full attention to Extension, and under these conditions he welcomed the return to parish life. "This arrangement," he assured Burke, "is the result of Archbishop Mundelein's desire to see that I was not knocked from pillar to post. He has left me absolutely free for my Society work."[62]

The new appointment soon tempered his original enthusiasm. Shannon had bequeathed a debt of at least $15,000, along with announced plans for a new school building; and these were two major responsibilities which the pastor could not completely delegate. Complicated negotiations to build the school divided his time as pastor between the parishioners, who urged immediate construction, and the chancery which disapproved of the blueprints. The project was so expensive as to guarantee that under Kelley's tenure the parish would remain fixed in debt. Unless, however, the school received approval, the parishioners refused to support archdiocesan projects, even Mundelein's new seminary. In frustration, Kelley was forced in 1922 to suggest that the unpaid seminary assessment be added to the debt, and this humiliation was equivalent to parish bankruptcy.[63]

The archbishop soon offered relief but not freedom from parochial life. Kelley was next offered a downtown parish, Saint John's, which was closer to Extension's headquarters but which he firmly declined. "After the terrible noise and bustle of a day in the office," he told Mundelein, "that place would drive me crazy. I would have no rest at all and no opportunity for a bit of fresh air and sunshine in the country, which is doing so much for me now." If there was to be a move into Chicago, his preference was to a building that provided working and living quarters. In his place he recommended O'Brien, who eventually was given Saint John's and who remained there as pastor for thirty-eight years.[64] Eight years in a suburban parish thus handicapped Kelley. To one who managed a sizeable corporation downtown, it was a constant source of concern and embarrassment, its country "air and sunshine" notwithstanding. Yet, as a Chicago priest, he was in no position to question the archbishop's widsom in tying Extension's president to a parish. Only six years after Kelley's appointment to Wilmette did Mundelein give fleeting thought to providing a special building that would house the Extension priests, but, as it turned out, they continued to live in rectories during his episcopate.[65]

Two more circumstances disclosed to Kelley the new chancellor's increasing dominance in Extension. The first dealt with investing the society's capital in "Catholic Bishop of Chicago bonds." These long-term notes were obligations of the archbishop of Chicago and usually backed by some parish property as collateral. The board of governors discouraged this investment for two reasons. First, if Extension bought these securities, it would appear that Mundelein took advantage of his office as chancellor, and the society would compromise its national character. His predecessor, Archbishop Quigley, had been sensitive to the issue and during his term kept Extension from purchasing them. An even stronger note of opposition to the bonds came from the bankers on the board who felt, basically, that church investments were unsound because it was difficult to recover anything if there was a default. Though Kelley professed to Mundelein his indifference in the matter, he doubtless agreed with the board.[66]

Undaunted, the archbishop defended the notes as supremely

worthy of Extension. The fact, he insisted, that they were marketed at a return lower than competitive issues demonstrated the high rating of the archdiocese as a debtor. Mundelein's argument was shaped with consummate skill. The questions of the society's national character and the collectability of church debts were irrelevant. The priority for Extension's investments was safety, and no industrial or municipal bond was more secure than his. Only the federal government could compete, and its rate of return was no higher than his. The logic was irresistible: it was good business to invest in the archdiocese.[67]

Continued frustration over a cardinal protector further strained Kelley's relationship with Mundelein. The death of Cardinal Martinelli on July 4, 1918, freed Kelley to resume his campaign to have Merry del Val named his successor. Under Benedict XV, the cardinal had been moved from the secretariat of state to the Holy Office, a sign of his declining influence at the Vatican; but Kelley was determined to have him. The society's procurator, Monsignor Jules Tiberghien, offered to present the request personally to the Holy Father, but he warned Kelley that proper procedure required a letter from Archbishop Mundelein. Kelley's hints in behalf of the Spanish churchman, however, brought forth no such letter. The next year Kelley learned in Rome of a move to name Cardinal Aidan Gasquet, an English Benedictine who served as prefect of the Vatican Archives. To his relief, Kelley's friends blocked it, and again he appealed to Mundelein. "Card. M. del Val is in a changed position here," he wrote from Rome in a fruitless attempt to show the revival of the cardinal's prestige. "He is a *big man,* . . . and very highly held by the Pope. . . ." The archdiocese of Chicago was soon to commemorate its fortieth anniversary, and the cardinal, the son of a marquis, had lost none of his early glamour. Perhaps, Kelley suggested further to Mundelein, Merry del Val could be invited to participate in the jubilee as the newly appointed protector of Extension. The chancellor still declined to write a letter and, sensitive to the rhythms of Vatican power shifts, entrusted the matter to his friend, Archbishop Bonzano. This maneuver stalled any further action. The delegate did nothing; and as Tiberghien learned in Rome, Mundelein intended himself to settle the question of the society's protector during his next visit to Rome.[68]

The issue was actually suspended for another four years. Meanwhile, the Islander's annoyance at Mundelein was stirred briefly at Tiberghien's death in 1923, which left Extension without any representation at the Holy See. The chancellor, Kelley suspected by now, had no plans to name a protector. "Archbishop Mundelein says," he told Tampieri in anger, "that he wishes to attend to the matter and will do so 'when he goes to Rome.' In the meantime, instead of going to Rome he has gone to South America. I do not think he has any intention of going to Rome unless he is called there." As the hopes of a protector dimmed, Kelley named Merry del Val's confidant, Monsignor Sante Tampieri, as procurator to serve the society's interest in Rome.[69]

Mundelein's inaction continued to puzzle the president and new procurator. The archbishop was not a careless man; he was known to be deliberate about everything, including the veneer of ambiguity with which he coated his position on certain matters. Possibly, guessed Kelley, he planned to recommend his mentor Bonzano, now a cardinal who had been recalled to the Roman Curia in 1922 and who now served as protector of several institutes. But no cardinal ever received the call from Chicago, and Kelley was powerless to challenge the hidden reasons. No doubt, Mundelein was guided partly by the fact that Merry del Val's star had fallen during the pontificates of Benedict XV and his successor, Pius XI, and his service to Extension in the curia would have been quite limited. But this logic would not have applied to Bonzano, whose appointment to the curia occurred at the first consistory called by Pius XI and whose career seemed to have avoided the pitfalls of the rivalries within the Vatican. Mundelein's indifference to the president's pleas therefore was enigmatic, except for the possible reason that without a protector

Kelley would have no official line into the Vatican except through the chancellor himself. In any case, Mundelein continued to be the sole exception among Kelley's associates at Extension. Those below him—Ledvina, O'Brien, McGuinness—became lifelong friends who responded to the Boss's lead; but the one man above Kelley held himself firmly detached, setting his own course at all times.

* * * * * * * * * *

By 1922 Francis Kelley was in his fifty-second year, and his spirit ached. For four years he had engaged in tedious negotiations with Propaganda over the American Board of Catholic Missions, a story to be told later. He had also served on several diplomatic missions in Europe. The parish in Wilmette afforded a comfortable home, but its administration burdened him. Though the society continued to flourish—now with 200 employees in splendid downtown offices of the LeMoyne Building—the details of management had become a nuisance. The clutter of the workers and the racket of the typewriters kept him in the mornings at home where he worked with his secretary. "Little by little," he confessed to Tampieri, "I am throwing the responsibility on others." The Roman was, however, assured that his friend suffered no depression or emotional collapse; rather, he stood at a crossroad in his life. His contribution to Extension was almost completed. Since ordination he had undergone a "series of changes," and was ready now to settle down and make "the last change." Ambition did not color his motives. "I have tried to be His servant ever since the day of my ordination," he revealed to the procurator; "and I hope and pray that I will never be anything else. For fame I care nothing. That will not get me out of purgatory any quicker." Under his leadership, the society had been guided through the critical formative years. He was now, he felt, "a man . . . that has finished one thing and does not wish to stand in the way of younger men, while there are other things that he could do."[70] Indeed, this shift in his working routine, along with his willingness to give up the reins of command, were symptoms pointing to a man near exhaustion.

A cheerful distraction at this time was Kelley's preliminary work on Chicago's International Eucharistic Congress. Only once—at Montreal in 1910—had such a mammoth religious gathering been held in the western hemisphere, and Archbishop Mundelein was anxious to have the first one in the United States, possibly in 1926. Besides the devotional benefits, the congress would testify to the coming-of-age of the midwestern church and display his splendid new seminary to Catholics from every corner of the world.[71] Through Bishop Joseph Schrembs of Cleveland, Mundelein's request reached the Permanent Committee of the International Eucharistic Congresses, the body which selected sites and arranged the program. The chances for Chicago improved when in November, 1922, Kelley was elected to the committee, the only American to be given membership. This was arranged through the sponsorship of two English members, Cardinal Francis Bourne of Westminster and his financial secretary, Monsignor Maurice E. Carton de Wiart, whose friendship he had cultivated during diplomatic assignments after World War I.[72]

In this new capacity, almost a month before the official word was cabled, Kelley was able to tell Mundelein that his archdiocese had been awarded the privilege of hosting the twenty-eighth International Eucharistic Congress which was scheduled for 1926. The two men planned immediately to attend the 1924 congress in Amsterdam and to study its operation; and they began to correspond with the Count Henry d'Yanville, secretary of the Permanent Committee.[73] The archbishop soon learned of the gigantic effort required for the undertaking. "I managed two congresses that were only national in character. . . ," Kelley told him. "This is going to be bigger than both put together. . . ."

Nevertheless, Mundelein took personal direction of the early stages; but as a member of the Permanent Committee, Kelley was expected to help.

One early complication was that the correspondence between Europe and America would have to be in four languages and also that the exchanges between d'Yanville and Chicago required a fluency in French. Despite his early training in the province of Quebec, Kelley asked for the services of a priest skilled in French, Father Joseph Morrison, but Mundelein transferred the young scholar to the cathedral for his own use. This setback failed to dilute Kelley's fervor as he busied himself with the reports of the 1910 congress held in Montreal. To his trained eye, this material disclosed a few minor traps which he communicated to Mundelein. As the only priest member of the city's chamber of commerce, the Islander also helped arrange a speaking engagement for the archbishop. Not only would this important body be alerted regarding the impending congress but also, Kelley believed, an informed business community might assist with expenses for such an international event. After this, he attempted to organize a large tour from the archdiocese to the congress in Amsterdam; and this was to be his last service as a Chicago priest for Mundelein's pet project.[74]

Eighteen months of congress work had thereby placed heavy demands on Kelley's time, but he gave generously. The only return that would have satisfied his personal costs would have been the appointment of Cardinal Merry del Val as papal legate to the congress. Rumors circulated to the effect that the archbishop was interested, and nothing raised Kelley's morale more. "No one could make a finer impression on the American people . . . ," he told Tampieri. "His elegant English as well as his personality would be greatly in his favor, not only with our own people, but even with those outside the Church. . . . Indeed, I can picture the pleasurable astonishment of all America, on hearing a cardinal from Rome speak better English than we speak ourselves."[75] Despite the advantages of having Merry del

Val, Mundelein had his own man: Cardinal Bonzano, who was named legate to the Chicago congress. It was inconceivable that a veteran observer like Kelley would have seriously expected another. The Islander's only satisfaction from this project, therefore, was a timely distraction from the routines of the office and parish, along with having had a seminal role in the first International Eucharistic Congress in the United States, the colossal splendor of which would render Kelley and his contemporaries almost speechless.[76]

Other developments at this time, including those in the archdiocese, added to the unhealthy strain of Francis's nerves. Edward Hoban, the archdiocesan chancellor, was appointed in November, 1921, Mundelein's auxiliary bishop. Some months before, no one had applauded Ledvina's promotion more than Kelley, but he was indifferent even to attending what he tagged Hoban's "big consecration." "I may be there and then again I may not," he announced to his friend, Father Thomas V. Shannon, adding that a visit to New York City appealed to him more.[77] His absence from this ceremony, Kelley doubtless knew, would be unforgivably conspicuous and serve only to rekindle the old Chicago animosities against the society; but he was not enthusiastic over Hoban's promotion.

Far less tolerable, however, was the archbishop's apparent contempt of Extension's apostolic brief, *Qua Nuper,* especially in the matter of Kelley's reappointment as president. Since his arrival, Mundelein had seemed, in Kelley's view, to be supremely careless in this regard. Every five years, the society's chancellor was to send to the consistorial congregation the board's recommendations of officers. Kelley's reappointment by the Holy See had been due for the first time in 1915, but Quigley's death and Mundelein's succession had, to all appearances, so complicated the procedure that the transaction was not completed until mid-1917. The eighteen-month delay had flustered the Islander, who attributed it to hostile elements among the Chicago clergy and to indifference on the part of the new chancellor. Later, Kelley uncovered the details. An old enemy, Cardinal Falconio, then prefect of the congregation of religious, had led the opposition to Kelley's reappointment, and Mundelein had strengthened the cardinal's hand by remaining silent in the early stages. With Martinelli, the cardinal protector, terminally ill, it had been only through a fortunate combination of factors that saved Kelley. Falconio died in Feburary, 1917, and Merry del Val intervened at the curia, saying that Mundelein's behavior was due to the fact that he had not been consulted. Only when the endorsement finally came from Chicago did the consistorial congregation renew the appointment. In any case, the awkward suspension between terms, along with Mundelein's ambiguity, had driven Kelley into fits of depression. "I felt very much hurt over the matter," he had told Tiberghien.[78]

After five years, the agony began again—only with greater intensity. The *terna* of officer-candidates was due again in 1922, and at this stage Kelley was tensely anxious to have the question of his future settled. At fifty-two years, he was disposed for one more term, but, he reasoned further, if he was given another five years in the society, he would make provision to retire at fifty-seven, perhaps to a quiet chaplaincy whereby he would devote his last days to writing. But the Holy See was again silent. In the previous five years, the Islander had made new powerful enemies in the Roman Curia, notably Cardinal Willem van Rossum, prefect of Propaganda. Their conflict arose over the American Board of Catholic Missions, an episode to be discussed in a later chapter. In 1921 a veteran Vatican bureaucrat, Bishop George Calavassy, who then served as ordinary of the Uniate Catholics of Greece and Thrace, warned his friend in Chicago that Van Rossum was campaigning to have him replaced at Extension.[79] To make matters worse, Kelley suspected that Mundelein had sent no list, a strong hunch which again agitated the priest. At the annual board meeting in 1923, the archbishop simply announced that Kelley would remain in office until further notice; and for the second time the Islander was forced to carry on for months after his term as president had expired. "At any time in middle life . . . ," he confessed to Tampieri, "it is unfair and unjust to leave me in such an unsettled and uncertain condition. . . . I can only go on blindly, not understanding what it all means."[80]

It was natural for a man with a compulsion for order to blueprint the last third of his life. In his own calculations, however, Monsignor Kelley ignored one major factor: the possibility that his archbishop had plans for him, plans that included neither his reappointment to Extension nor a silver jubilee as the society's president nor a lengthy old age in Chicago. No doubt, there was some seriousness behind Mundelein's tease that Kelley might become a bishop of a remote insular diocese. In 1921 the Holy See had transferred the Hawaiian Islands to the jurisdiction of the Apostolic Delegate in the United States. In the following year, Archbishop Bonzano toured the archipelago accompanied by his friend from Chicago. On his return from the Pacific, Mundelein remarked, as Kelley recalled it, how appropriate it would be that "Dr. Kelley, who loves islands, might be sent there." Mundelein was much impressed with the flowers and fruits, the mountains and beaches of the tropical paradise, but the Islander politely but firmly discouraged the suggestion. Nevertheless, Kelley noted with interest that his demur over the Hawaiian Islands did not dissolve a mischievous "smile" which brightened Mundelein's face whenever the subject of Kelley's future arose.[81]

The commotion within Monsignor Kelley eased when his superior was created a cardinal on March 24, 1924. The Holy See had honored not only a productive churchman but also, in Kelley's eyes, a neglected part of the nation. No midwesterner took greater pride at this event than he, especially at Mundelein's own self-description as the first cardinal "west of the Allegheny Mountains." This climaxed a vision which had begun during the episcopate of Archbishop Quigley: the American heartland had come of age. Extension too had been included in this honor. Its chancellor was now a member of the College of Cardinals, just as the principal officers of two pontifical institutions of the East, the Propagation and The Catholic University of America, had at one time been. Kelley was not a member of the party that accompanied Mundelein to Rome, but he placed the society's procurator, Monsignor Tampieri, at the prelate's disposal. The new cardinal had many errands in the Eternal City, including, the Islander hoped, Kelley's reappointment as president of Extension; and in this matter, Tampieri would be a splendid aide-de-camp.[82]

Patrick Hayes of New York would receive the red hat at the same consistory as Mundelein and had discouraged public celebrations; but this austerity did not suit the eager Kelley. "New York has had three Cardinals," he explained to Tampieri, "and Cardinal Mundelein is the first for Chicago and the first in the West; so we expect to show our appreciation." Extension would again follow the archdiocese in arranging the receptions as it had eight years earlier when a young archbishop arrived from Brooklyn, except with one omission. The society, Kelley told the new cardinal, planned to provide another civic banquet—this time "minus the soup!" No precaution would be overlooked; even detectives would be stationed in the kitchen.[83]

When Mundelein returned home, he was given, as Kelley reported later to Tampieri, "the greatest welcome ever given in the City of Chicago to an individual. Fully a million people lined the streets as he passed from the station to the cathedral, for fifteen miles. I never expected to see anything like it."[84] On May 14, 1924, the society's banquet proceeded without a flaw at the Hotel Blackstone. The president's address gave an eloquent tribute from the impoverished but grateful Catholics in the South and West. The cardinal's work in the society, acknowledged Kelley generously, had made him "the protector of the Home Missions, the elder brother in the Episcopate of those . . . who keep lonely watch and ward over the scattered flock on mountain and prairie. . . ." All grievances between the two men were buried for the moment as Kelley's words pulsated with heartfelt pride in Mundelein's noble achievement for the West and Extension.[85] The red hat was thus a prize in which both chancellor and president could share. As a compensation for Mundelein's insensitivity regarding his future, it would buoy Kelley through his last month in Chicago before learning that plans for him had been carefully laid.

Monsignor Kelley abruptly learned that his fears for the future were groundless: on June 25, 1924, he was named bishop of Oklahoma. When the official word had arrived at his parish he had had almost no time to think, only a single hour to travel from Wilmette to Chicago, where he accepted the appointment. Though Extension had long helped the diocese, his acquaintance with the territory was at best superficial. Its first bishop was dead only four months, a circumstance suggesting that, aside from the consistory, Kelley's appointment might have been another of Mundelein's recent errands in Rome. The territory was economically promising, but, as one of the great strongholds of the Ku Klux Klan, it was riddled with anti-Catholic phobias. Less than 3 percent Catholic, the state had, according to his calculations, no more than half a dozen good parishes centered in the capital and the oil country. "I did not like the idea of going to Oklahoma," he confessed to Tampieri. "I was afraid that the change would be too radical after so many years of living in Chicago." But further reflection and inquiry revealed opportunities for him. The struggling nature of the diocese stimulated his sense of challenge. The new environment would allow him to test missionary strategies to non-Catholics, as well as provide the leisure to write books, "one of which in particular," he confided further, "is rather pretentious." Perhaps it was too early to announce his intention to publish an autobiography, but he already had an inclination. Furthermore, the state provided two solid bases of operation, a pair of cities of 100,000 apiece, and the seat of the diocese, Oklahoma City, had what he called a "good house" for its bishop.[86] The news of his appointment scarcely interrupted his hectic schedule. As soon as he accepted, he was off to Washington, to see the state department about Mexican affairs, and then to New York City, where he joined the cardinal's party traveling to the International Eucharistic Congress in Amsterdam.[87]

This breathless activity did not cease when he returned to Chicago in late August, 1924, six weeks before his consecration. Monsignor Gustave Depreitere, the diocesan administrator in Oklahoma, met Kelley at the ship, and both planned a secret trip to Oklahoma City, where Kelley would look over the episcopal residence and recommend changes. Next came the proper transition at Extension when the "Boss" resigned, effective September 30, and recommended O'Brien as his successor. The hierarchy also had invited its newest member to the annual meeting where he drew up the organizational plan for the American Board of Catholic Missions. Altogether, the bishop-elect was busier than ever, able to reserve but four days for his retreat.

On October 2, 1924, Cardinal Mundelein consecrated Francis Kelley at Holy Name Cathedral, Chicago. The ceremony drew forty-two bishops—probably, according to Kelley, the largest number ever assisting at a consecration. More remarkable was its international cast. With Mundelein serving as chief celebrant and Ledvina as preacher, Kelley selected as co-consecrators two representatives of neighboring countries, Leopoldo Ruiz y Flores, archbishop of Morelia (Michoacán) in Mexico, and Alfred A. Sinnott, an Islander who was now archbishop of Winnipeg, Canada. A minor bungle occurred during the sermon. Beforehand, Kelley had warned Ledvina to enunciate the syllables carefully; and the Texan's twenty-two minute talk lasted three-quarters of an hour. "He nearly articulated the Cardinal off his throne," Kelley recalled years later. This solemn ceremony merely triggered a whirlwind of engagements. There followed pontifical Masses at the parish in Wilmette and at the dedication of Father Shannon's new church, St. Thomas the Apostle, near the University of Chicago. Kelley's consecration had brought to Chicago a host of well-wishers who kept their friend in a continual round of parties. "There has been so much celebrating," he admitted, near exhaustion, "that I am longing to be in Oklahoma, and see the end of the last train move out, so that I can get a little sleep and then a little quiet."[88]

After a lengthy interregnum of nearly eight months, the second bishop of Oklahoma was ready to come to his diocese. As part of the province of New Orleans, Archbishop John W. Shaw would rightfully install Kelley in St. Joseph's Cathedral, but his absence in Rome allowed Mundelein to serve as his substitute and to give Oklahoma its first glimpse of a prince of the church. Two features highlighted Kelley's introduction to his new, and last, assignment. First, the new shepherd was immediately given a taste of the embattled condition of his flock in the state. The announcement of his coming had stirred up threats of violence at the hands of anti-Catholic bigots. Upon their arrival, both Mundelein and Kelley were placed under armed escort throughout the festivities, a precaution that would have been absurd in Chicago.[89]

The second notable feature regarding Kelley's reception was the cardinal's civic address to the people of Oklahoma on October 15. This performance, as stunning as any of his public appearances elsewhere, gave a rare glimpse into the inner core of this laconic churchman. Fundamental, of course, was Mundelein's well-known love of country, a theme which was repeated throughout his public life. Less familiar, however, was his admission that this throbbing patriotism had led to his interest in home-missions, the work of Extension. As a Catholic leader with such strong nationalism, his evangelical impulses had therefore sprung from the desire to reach "the scattered and isolated Catholics in our own land." The board members who attended these ceremonies knew that this was no hollow boast. The chancellor had offered to establish a religious protectorate over Nevada and was now sending one of his most gifted priests to another state where the church's presence was weak. The gospel must be preached everywhere but, according to the cardinal, in those areas "first where our own flag flies." Francis Kelley could not have better articulated the priorities of his own life's work.

Since neither Kelley nor Oklahoma was well-acquainted, citizen Mundelein arranged the introduction in patriarchal fashion. His interests extended to everything American; and though Oklahoma had joined the Union only fourteen years before, he confidently professed special insights into this newcomer, "the youngest portion of our country, . . . a State that has but recently arrived at its majority, where the climate is healthy, where the soil is fertile, and where the ground is rich in resources." The cardinal had studied Kelley's domain. Its new bishop, he declared, "comes to a people that is perhaps the most typically American in the land." They had been formed by native settlers, brought to the territory by the healthiest of motives—"ambition to better themselves, the spirit of adventure, the purpose to break new paths." Their natural sense of justice had made them, the churchman claimed further, inculpable of bigotry. Pockets of religious bitterness in this part of America were due more to "ignorance than viciousness," an ignorance that actually arose from the Catholic failure to instruct.

Lastly, Mundelein asked, who was this new frontier apostle? The speaker alluded first to Kelley's superficial attributes. The new shepherd had earned a reputation of being "essentially a promotor," and the cardinal acknowledged the Islander's success as a salesman and organizer. But, he added promptly, there was more: "The Lord has given him an attractive personality, a vast amount of patient perseverance, and more than a share of the milk of human kindness." His agenda in this sparse land was different from that in "the bigger cities" where many ethnic elements had to be transformed. "Yours is not a problem of assimulation," advised the cardinal, "rather one of co-ordination." For this task Kelley had had the best training possible. At Extension he served the missions like a staff general directing a campaign from headquarters. Now he had been given a field command, the diocese of Oklahoma, where his master strategies would be tested and where, too, he would share the raw life of those whom he had assisted earlier.[90]

Mundelein's talk stole everyone's attention. The thousand-word text would stir the reader today and in delivery must have spellbound the audience. Beforehand, the cardinal had wished not to take the spotlight from the new bishop, but his presence and eloquence had made this impossible. ". . . he delivered the greatest speech of his life," Kelley later told Chicago's chancellor, Bernard J. Sheil:

> His fear that he might "take the eyes of the people off their Bishop" was justified, but no one was more delighted that he did it than the Bishop. His coming was an epoch in the history of the Church in this Diocese and it did more to straighten out misunderstandings than would have been done had the eyes of the people been fixed on their Bishop for a year.[91]

Mundelein's address also pointed Kelley's life into a new direction. It was time for Kelley to move. At home he had fretted too much about his future. Though the staff had long admired his "equanimity" around the office, he had of late become edgy, too easily magnifying trifles into great offenses.[92] After nearly two decades he was becoming stale in Chicago, and Oklahoma offered a fresh start.

An undercurrent of this transition was the unavoidable question, why was this national figure awarded a relatively insignificant assignment? In a sense, Kelley had begun his "hidden life" at the height of his career, and even Oklahomans wondered. Mundelein's spoken words suggested that it was opportune for the theorist of the home-mission ministry to become the practitioner. Many perceived more in the cardinal's motives. Much later, Willie O'Brien, not perfectly reliable as an observer but one who knew the two churchmen, gave hints regarding how "the most prominent priest" in America could have become a nuisance in Chicago. Nearly twenty years after Kelley's departure, O'Brien recalled for his old Boss "the good old days when you were in the news and the big man here was getting uneasy over the situation."[93]

There had been the inevitable tension between these two mighty dynamos. Kelley's routes of access to Mundelein had been more limited than those he had had to Quigley, and working with the Brooklynite had grown progressively difficult. "The Cardinal is an excellent Chancellor," he once confided to Tampieri; "but he likes to have his own way."[94] With his absence from Chicago, Kelley suspected, the society would become as submissive to Mundelein's iron will as had the archdiocese.

With this mixture of fear and expectations, of isolation and joy, Francis Kelley managed the last move of his life.

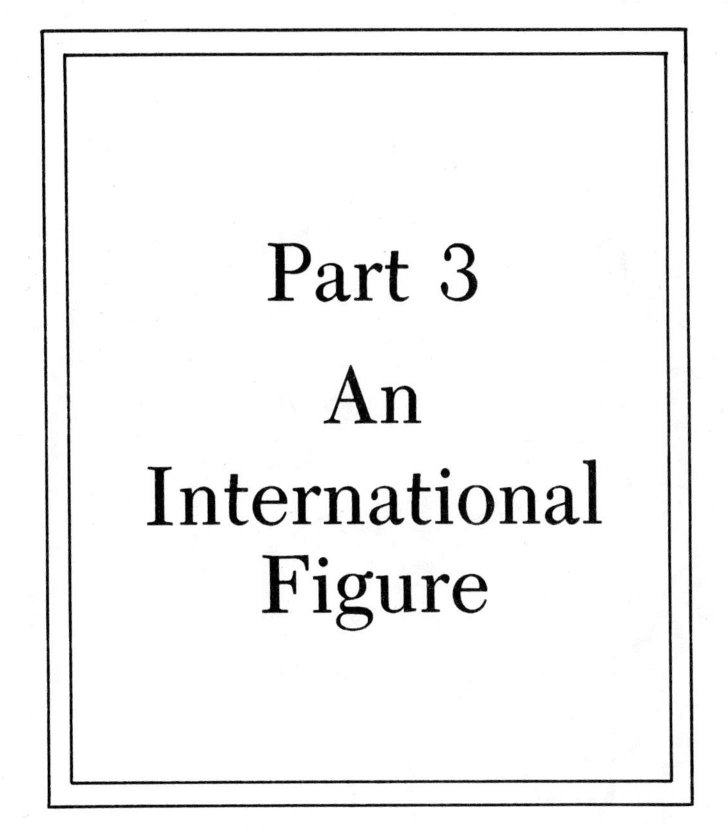

Part 3
An International Figure

(1914-1924)

KELLEY'S TOUR OF THE WESTERN FRONT

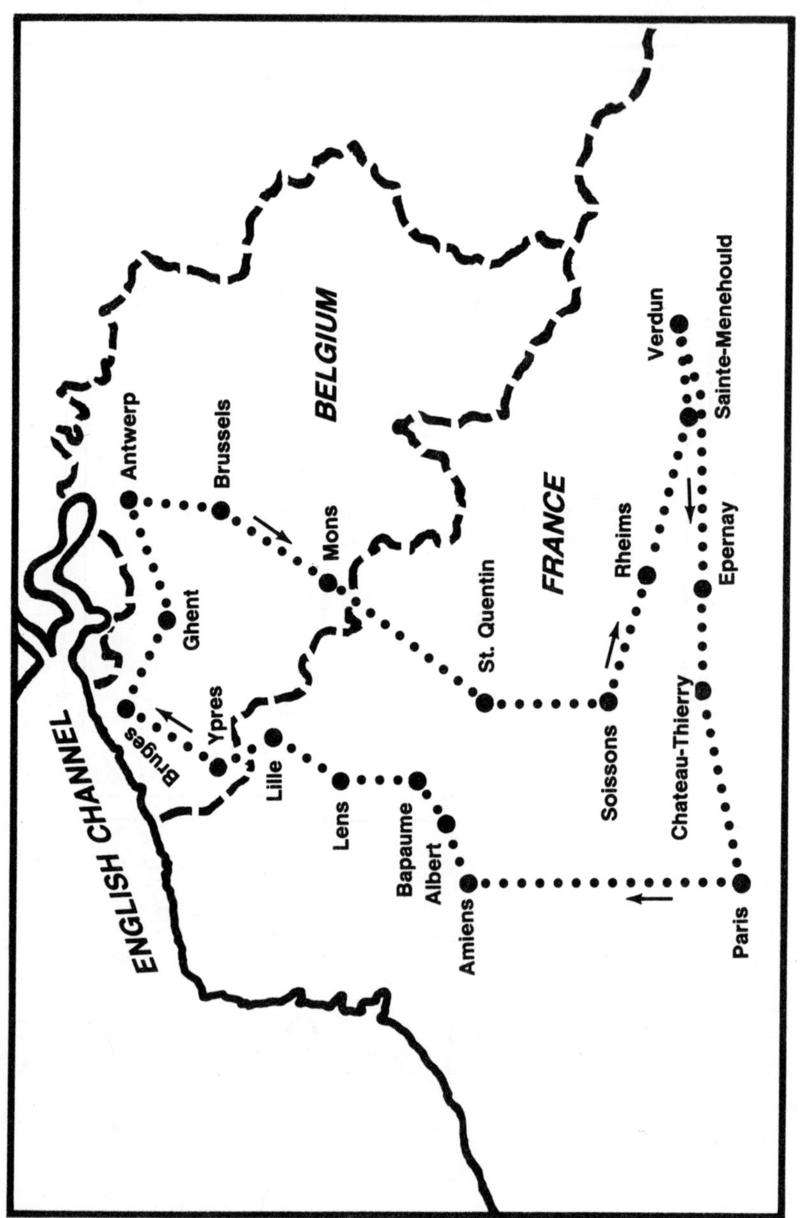

VI
The Great War

World War I marks the beginning of the contemporary era. It transformed societies, altered the boundaries of Europe, Africa, and Asia, and triggered global revolutions that shaped the twentieth century.

It was also the medium that fashioned Francis Kelley into an international figure of some importance. The full impact of this gigantic transition did not come suddenly to the Islander but progressed through three stages. During the preliminary interlude of American neutrality, he held himself aloof. He seemed not to sense that events across the Atlantic were molding the future, preferring to devote his energies to defending and comforting the church in revolutionary Mexico. This stage ended when the United States accepted a partnership in the making of world war and world peace. Though Kelley did not see combat first-hand, he was one of the first American civilians to visit the

Western Front. The rare opportunity to examine the steaming scars of war left a lifelong impression. "I saw the trenches," he wrote a decade later. "I touched the dead and saw them buried by the half-dead living. I saw the ruined homes and the demolished churches." This glimpse into a modern-day Inferno made him realize how close to self-destruction western civilization had come and how crucial the peace conference at Versailles was in preventing a recurrence.

The third stage arrived when he turned from fallen soldiers to the most defenseless adult victims of the war. His attention then centered on Austria, where he clothed and fed the clergy and religious in the old Hapsburg capital of Vienna. This remarkable relief work was, in the words of an eyewitness, Shane Leslie, "one of the many acts of American generosity for which sufficient gratitude has never been shown."[1] The war was therefore a powerful force in Kelley's life, changing him from a disinterested observer of geopolitics into a concerned world citizen and passionately involved humanitarian.

When the fighting erupted in Europe in August, 1914, Kelley was ready to comment on these events; but, as was noted earlier, the conflict was too volatile a dilemma for his editorial pen. Though, on the one hand, technically neutral from 1914 until the spring of 1917, the foreign policy of the Wilson administration appeared to be closer in spirit to the Allies, especially the British. Extension's support, on the other hand, depended largely on Catholics with German and Irish ties, whose sympathies lay with the Central Powers. It was an issue that bewildered the best observers of the age; and after a few sorties into the discussion, Kelley abandoned public comment on the war in favor of a series of predictable appeals for peace and moderation.

Had he been forced to take a stand, the pendulum would have swung toward the Central Powers. Not only was he known among his friends to be an anglophobe but he also feared that if the Allies were victorious, Czarist Russia—religiously Orthodox and politically autocratic—would emerge as the dominant authority on the continent, a prospect not agreeable to many western observers.[2] A safer topic, therefore, suited his energies as a commentator. This was the violent reforms of Venustiano Carranza, whose rise to power in Mexico coincided with the outbreak of war in Europe. When priests and religious fled into the American Southwest, Kelley rose to their defense, an important phase which will be treated later. The Mexican revolution thus provided a substitute for the greater struggle across the Atlantic, at least until American intervention; and Kelley's most notable public comments dealt with the Mexican issue.

During this interval of American neutrality, the tragedy of Europe seemed almost incidental in his private thoughts. As was seen, the "Boss" was amused at the divided allegiances everywhere in sight, even within the Extension staff. "It is a funny thing to live over here," he remarked, insensitively, nearly two years after the opening of hostilities, "and listen to the arguments on both sides. America is getting some of the fun out of the war anyhow, while others get the misery."[3] Kelley's superficial reaction to the war seldom extended beyond its being the source of an occasional chuckle. The bloody stalemate in Europe impressed many outsiders as little more than a terrible and sometimes deadly nuisance.

Movement and the mails encountered special problems. Kelley the traveler even had a brush with death soon after Italy's entry into the war on the Allied side. When Italy renounced its alliance with Germany and Austria, Germany was required to tighten U-boat patrols in the Mediterranean, and Kelley was given a direct encounter with this controversial weapon. He had spent much of the fall of 1915 in Rome on a variety of missions discussed earlier and had booked passage in November on the Italian liner *Ancona*. Meanwhile, a crisis over Mexican affairs had forced Father Shannon to telegraph from America that Kelley must return earlier for an interview at the department of state. In arranging to leave Italy a week ahead of schedule, he fortunately switched from the *Ancona,* which was torpedoed shortly thereafter, losing more than half of its passengers and crew at sea.[4] Instead, he boarded at Naples the French ship *Patria,* which was headed for New York City. Outside the harbor of Palermo, it was sighted by a submarine, probably the same—Kelley later thought—that would chase the *Ancona.* The *Patria* was forced to use evasive tactics, a maneuver which panicked the civilians and which Monsignor Kelley never forgot. The submarine missed its target in two attempts. "There is nothing like a little submarine and a zigzag course," he confided to his friend Burke, "to put the fear of the Lord in you."[5] The war also complicated transatlantic postal service. There was not only the increasing risk of losing letters at sea, but they were also subject to the scrutiny of military censors. To secure his correspondence with Monsignor Tampieri, Kelley used a Vatican address as a device to elude censorship; but he was soon told the only letters which were opened came from the war zones. Tampieri nevertheless cautioned his anxious friend to register his mail.[6]

Rallies for the belligerents likewise failed to melt his indifference toward the war. In early 1917, a mammoth bazaar for the Allies' hospital work in Chicago's Coliseum evoked thinly veiled sarcasm. "The whole fashionable world of Chicago is in it," he informed Burke, "and reports say they are making a tremendous amount of money." To equip the healing centers, the sponsors were exhibiting "war relics of all kinds, including a 'tank,' bits of zeppelins and other thrillers."[7] Kelley could scarcely miss the monstrous contradiction that only war could suggest; that is, a display of a lethal arsenal in order to stimulate support for life-saving facilities.

In November, 1916, President Wilson had managed to win an election so close that the outcome remained in dispute for several days. His victory, along with America's entry into the war six months later, sparked Kelley's first serious comments on Europe. *Extension Magazine* greeted Wilson's war message without enthusiasm and registered an early dissent. The editor-in-chief publicly sympathized with American soldiers of German blood who would now return to their Fatherland in the uniform of an enemy. He even questioned the integrity of the President whose campaign appeal to the electorate had centered on a pledge to keep American forces out of Europe, a pledge that had been broken, Kelley noted, within a month of the inauguration.[8] Soon, however, the nation's patriotic spirit, along with improvements in the spiritual care of the troops, mellowed the Chicagoan's mood. By January, 1918, he had visited several military camps where, as he told Tampieri, the young recruits appeared "cheerful about it and very much determined." As a veteran of the Spanish-American War, he was concerned over the chaplains' corps in which, he felt, the Catholic quota was usually too low and poorly managed. To his relief, he discovered that this situation had been remedied in two ways. First, the Wilson administration had reserved one-third of the commissions in the corps for Catholic clergymen, a very generous allotment; and, second, the American hierarchy had appointed Patrick J. Hayes, auxiliary bishop of New York, as chaplain-bishop with authority to coordinate these priests. Kelley was pleased, further, with the action of the Knights of Columbus, who had raised $3 million to provide facilities in the camps where soldiers could attend Mass and spend their leisure.[9]

In general, Kelley's role had been passive during World War I. Heedlessly, he had limited himself to little more than frivolous comments as Europe edged toward Armageddon. Other concerns—the growth of Extension, problems with the magazine, the adjustment to a new archbishop, his books, religious persecution in Mexico—kept him, in thought and in person, at the periphery of Europe's near collapse. His direct contact with events across the Atlantic amounted to no more than a hair-raising sea chase off the coast of Sicily. Aside from missing the monumental significance of these years, he did not share the secular idealism of the majority of his generation which held that America's partnership with the Allied would end all wars. His thoughts contradicted the impression of unanimity during this national emergency. They represented a heartfelt dissent from President Wilson's powerful war rhetoric, along with an abiding skepticism regarding his leadership. This interlude of aloof hesitation had thereby fashioned Francis Kelley into one of the few Americans prepared for the disillusionment to follow.

* * * * * * * * *

Kelley was uniquely fortunate to have spent early 1919 in Paris, representing the exiled Mexican bishops during the peace conference. The armistice had just ended military operations, and the city was a twilight zone of history. Its inhabitants, including the alert stranger from Chicago, were suspended between two worlds. One was dying, a proud and historic civilization whose lineage dated from the century of Johann Gutenberg and Christopher Columbus, of Martin Luther and Leonardo da Vinci. Its genius and energy had made Europe the center of the world. Another world was rising after four centuries, its features yet undistinguished and its future unplotted. But one truth had already unfolded from the war: the old culture had destroyed itself, and new competitors for the planet's wealth and power were arising on its margins. Kelley sensed this epochal transition. His letters from Europe stressed the new responsibilities given to postwar America, including the church there. He saw too the openings in the collapsed empires of the east—the Ottoman and Romanov—once forbidden territories where the church might now strike new roots. Kelley had dimly perceived the great lesson of the twentieth century: the world's power center was shifting—from Europe to its satellites—beyond the Atlantic and the Urals.[10]

Postwar Paris was thus suspended between the old and new; but it also teetered between death and life. Within its walls Kelley listened to the eloquent hopes of the peacemakers; but outside, a few miles away, there lay the ghastly accomplishments of the war-makers. Enthusiastic as Kelley was about the rise of a new civilization, he was a devoted product of the battered old one, and he did his share to save it. Europe had been crippled during the war, never to regain the absolute hegemony it once enjoyed on this planet. With his own eyes, the priest saw its destructive powers, walking through the scarred countryside and visiting its famished cities. Yet in this moment of supreme humiliation he never lost his faith in Europe, even in the defeated Austrians and Germans. With others who found little value in their extended punishment, Kelley looked rather to their enormous recuperative energies and contributed to their revival. The once elegant city of Vienna would be grateful for the prompt relief he organized. The Germans, stripped of their colonial empire, would have in this priest an advocate who would earnestly seek to salvage a part of their overseas interest, namely, their flourishing missions in Asia and Africa. Kelley was therefore on hand to see Europe's ruin; and he returned to help in its resurrection.

World War I was not his first exposure to the military. Two decades before the peace conference he had worn the uniform of the United States army, serving as chaplain to the 32d Regiment from Michigan in the Spanish-American War. His service, however, had been confined to training exercises in the southern states, and hostilities had been concluded before his unit could embark for the war zone in the Caribbean. Kelley's education in the horrors of war began rather with a ten-day tour of the battlegrounds of western Europe. In the lull between his work during the conference and the departure of his ship, he joined a party of Knights of Columbus led by Edward L. Hearn and William P. Larkin. To ease the strain of demobilization, the fraternal society maintained club houses for the troops, some of which were located near the fighting fronts. The plan was to visit by automobile these facilities and the battlefields nearby; the route selected was to motor directly to Belgium and then to circle back to Paris by way of northeastern France. Kelley welcomed the invitation as an opportunity to kill two idle weeks and perhaps to gather ideas for magazine articles.

On May 6, 1919, the congenial group left Paris. The first impression striking the priest was the proximity of the front to the capital. One year before, the Germans' last offensive had brought them within cannon shot of the city. A shell from a "Big Bertha" fifty-six miles away had struck a parish church on Good Friday of 1918, killing hundreds of worshippers. Just outside Paris, Kelley spotted rolls of barbed wire which had been recently removed from the battlefields. Old trenches, now filled in and surfaced with chalk, were easily visible to the eye, creating eerie traces running along the greening fields. Man and nature were already dismantling the instruments of war, but there remained deep scars marked in white. Heading due north, the travelers spent the first night in the old textile center of Amiens on the Sommes River. A town which had known many invaders, it had been taken by the Germans in 1914 and lost in the same year to the British. As an important Allied supply base, it had been heavily bombarded, especially in the last year of the war when the Germans had driven within twelve miles. On arrival, Kelley noted how the hotel still bore wounds from enemy fire. Bullet holes pitted the entire building, including the door of his room. A long visit was planned the next morning at the cathedral of Notre Dame, the largest and one of the finest in the French Gothic style. Some of the treasures were being returned to the 13th-century structure, but, as the Americans discovered, the stained glass windows were missing.

The tour continued northward through Albert, Bapaume, and Lens—scenes of heavy war damage which prompted Kelley's companions to take a great many moving pictures. There were frequent stops to inspect trenches and dugouts. Their car explored ruined streets of villages in which not a single house stood, and Kelley was moved at seeing a handful of refugees already returning, trying to rebuild their homes from the piles of stones that remained. In inflicting such incredible punishment, the war had not yet dealt a lethal blow to the sturdy Europeans. The day's journey was interrupted by an improvised lunch. Roadside restaurants had not yet reopened in the former war zone, and the travelers took their midday meal along the roadside.[11]

Nearing the Belgian border, the party drove in the direction of the city of Lille, once the brilliant residence of the 15th-century dukes of Burgundy. This northern center had been occupied by the Germans from 1914 through 1918. As the visitors approached, they found it unexpectedly intact. On the outskirts some houses had been shot up and others half destroyed; otherwise, noted Kelley, Lille appeared to have escaped with few scars. Lodgings were taken at the Hôtel Royale, which had been headquarters for the German officers during the occupation; and these, the priest observed, had badly mistreated the building. The city was blessed with undamaged historic sites, including its art museum, but Kelley's group elected to cross the border on the following morning and to tour the battlefields around Ypres (Ieper).

A visit to Ypres would cast a spell on most visitors. This town in west Flanders had long been a declining textile center, and its importance was due to its strategic proximity to the French frontier, an unhappy circumstance which had exposed its citizens to centuries of war. The war had made it one of the most hotly contested war zones, the scene of three gigantic battles. Here the Germans had used poison gas for the first time in 1915; and only eighteen months before Kelley's arrival the British Empire had sacrificed some 400,000 men in order to push their rain-drenched lines five miles to the east, a Pyrrhic victory of the first order. The town had been thoroughly devastated; and Kelley was brought close to tears as he viewed the ruins. The party moved through the combat areas of the British and Australians. Kelley found the silent remains impossible to describe, and he wondered how this ravaged earth could be coaxed back into civilization. The car halted, and the men walked solemnly among the shell holes, half hidden by lakes of spring water. Engines of destruction were much in evidence, tanks sunk in craters created by bombs. The incongruities of the battlefield compelled Kelley to see the strange humor of war, perhaps as a weak defense against the encompassing horror. In the face of such gloom, the Islander managed a smile when he saw one of the tanks christened "St. Patrick." With remarkable detachment, he admitted to an even broader smile when he spotted a half-buried tank with the inscription "Back Slider." "It had lived up to its name," he reflected, "for it had slid backwards into the hole."

This wholesale revelation of death soon sent Kelley into a bleak mood. His companions, he confessed, could have filled the car with war souvenirs—"shells exploded and unexploded, helmets, alas, even the bones of the dead." In this Belgian wasteland there occurred the most macabre moment of the trip. "I picked up a boot," recalled Kelley in staccato accents. "There was a rattle in it. I shook it and bones from some poor fellow's foot dropped out." In the distance the British had begun the gruesome task of gathering their dead. Thereafter the priest could no longer remain casual amid the sights and smells of death. The appearance of burial parties everywhere moved him to return to the car and quietly to compose verses on this encounter with "Flanders fields." His inspiration produced, he conceded, "not very good poetry but nonetheless a bit of consolation." The visitors departed from Ypres and completed the triangle of the great trading centers of medieval Flanders, proceeding by way of Bruges to Ghent. The historic Flemish capital had escaped serious damage during the war and accommodated the American visitors with a comfortable hotel, an unexpected stroke of good fortune at the end of an ugly day in the sanctuary of death nearby.[12]

The next stop was Antwerp, the second largest seaport of continental Europe. In the war the Germans had reduced its formidable defenses. As a major staging area for troops, the city had become one of the headquarters for the Knights of Columbus; and Hearn and Larkin took Kelley on a tour of their facilities. In this way he met many American doughboys, some of whom had been in Europe since they landed with General John J. Pershing in June, 1917. By evening the party had concluded its business and went south to Brussels.

The capital of Belgium had been graced, or cursed, with an extraordinary past. Repeatedly besieged since the Reformation, it had been the seat of rebellion against Spanish, Austrian, and Dutch rulers. A century before Kelley's arrival, it had served as headquarters for the duke of Wellington in his last Napoleonic campaign. During World War I, Brussels had had the mixed fortune of having been occupied by the Germans from 1914 until the armistice in 1918. During this lengthy interval its citizens had been cruelly oppressed, relieved only by the heroic stand of Cardinal Désiré Mercier. Physically, however, the capital had suffered no war damage. Its celebrated center—the *Grand' Place,* one of the choice monuments of medieval and Renaissance architecture—had survived. Kelley and his companions had reserved almost no time to tour this fine city, using it instead as a starting point of trips into the environs. After settling in their hotel, they spent the first full day in Malines, a small city north of the capital where they had a historic meeting with Cardinal Mercier, to be discussed later. On the day after, they moved directly south to the 19th-century battlefield of Waterloo and continued then to Mons, where, a century after Napoleon's encounter with Wellington, the British had engaged the Germans for the first time in World War I.[13]

By Sunday evening, on May 11, 1919, the car had reentered France and brought its passengers to Saint-Quentin on the Sommes River. This city of nearly 50,000 was another center of textile manufacture with a long history of assaults and captures. During the war it had been virtually demolished by the Germans, although it had been recovered in 1918 by the Allies after heavy fighting. Lodged in a battered hotel, the visitors were given their first living experience of the war. Nearby were pris-

Portfolio
1

Francis Clement Kelley's Mothe
Mary Ann

The Young Cleric

Jim Doyle's School in Summerville, Prince Edward Island

The Prince of Teachers — Alexander McAulay

Old St. Dunstan's School

Bishop James Rogers

Bishop John S. Foley

The Busy Army Chaplain

The "Yankee Volunteer" Mounted on "Teddy"

Francis Clement Kelley's Church in Lapeer, Michigan When It Was Dedicated in 1901

Francis Clement Kelley's Favorite Church, Christ the King, Tulsa, Oklahoma

Interior

Exterior

Bishop Dennis J. Dougherty at the Dedication of the First Motor Chapel

Cardinal Sebastiano Martinelli

Archbishop Diomede Falconio

Extension's Chapel Car "St. Anthony"

Archbishop James E. Quigley

ons filled with captured German soldiers, and the city hall had been turned into a surgical hospital. Kelley's quarters were practically in the open. The roof and walls half destroyed, he spent his first night under the stars and heard some shooting in the distance. Every church had been devastated, he observed; and only 10,000 were left in the city. Before retiring, he talked to some of the local priests about the conduct of the Germans. "Not one of them voiced any complaint," he recalled. "For days now I have begun to doubt a lot of the atrocity stories."

From there the party drove farther south to Soissons on the Aisne River, an ancient capital of the Frankish kings. The war had damaged the 13th-century cathedral, as well as the Abbey of Saint-Jean-des-Vignes, where Thomas Becket had lived for several years. Kelley met the cathedral rector walking among the ruins. "It was a discouraging sight," the Chicagoan lamented privately. "There was nothing left but the stone." From the debris Kelley rescued a book, evidently from the seminary library which had stood in the line of fire. It was a collection of the sermons of Jean-Baptiste Lacordaire, the idolized Dominican preacher. His preaching had been the sensation of mid-19th-century France, and Kelley kept the torn, ash-begrimed volume as his souvenir of the tour.

The priest and his companions next turned east into the champagne country, arriving at Rheims at midday and calling on Cardinal Louis-Henri Lucon. The 700-year-old cathedral had become a national institution as the customary site where the kings of France were crowned. Within its walls Joan of Arc had reached the pinnacle of her fortunes, standing next to the indolent Charles VII at his coronation 500 years before Kelley's visit. The magnificent Gothic building, unfortunately, had been shelled during the war. The interior, including most of the irreplaceable stained-glass windows, had been shattered. Though the cathedral would not be reopened for two decades, the cardinal insisted on conducting the Americans through the empty structure. The destruction, estimated Kelley, was not so complete as that in Soissons, and he hoped that the French government would restore the building. Before departure the cardinal showed his guests a unique relic of the war. His hands held a glass jar half full of drops of lead, about the size of human tears. They had been found on the cathedral floor and had fallen from the roof during the bombardment. The old man called them *les larmes de la Cathédrale*—"the tears of the cathedral."[14]

The visitors were anxious to view the war zones which had been held by the United States infantry, and they headed further eastward to Sainte-Menehould, the center of an uneven terrain known as the Argonne. Within this hilly and wooded area were located the *départments* of Meuse and Ardennes, where the party could find the battlefield of Verdun and a sector in the final victory drive that had been carried by the Americans. After weaving through squads of German prisoners at work, the group was stopped at a ruined village by a German prisoner acting as an interpreter. The travelers were asked to report at a nearby camp that the bodies of six American soldiers had been discovered in the woods. The entire area, Kelley observed, was full of corpses. "We found bones and saw several graves even along the roadside." An improvised burial site had a rosary tied around a little cross of wood and, in front, a New Testament lay open.

At one point Kelley stumbled across what he thought the most interesting sight thus far. Stopping the car on a side road, Hearn told the priest to explore the forest nearby, adding that he should shout if he discovered any surprises. In the woods Kelley located a hidden boardwalk and yelled to the others to assist him in the search. To his astonishment, it guided him to a camouflaged German stronghold. Aside from serving as a depot for matériel, this fortress—actually, a miniature city—provided conveniences unfamiliar to positions so close to the trenches, even a movie theatre. This, Kelley was told, served as a command post for Crown Prince Rupprecht, son of Bavaria's last king who commanded the German Sixth Army. Nothing fascinated Kelley more than this elaborate shelter, no doubt a welcome relief from viewing cemeteries and broken cathedrals.

But war was more than great campaigns and hidden bunkers. With an instinct for detail and humor, Kelley looked within this stronghold for the footnotes to the momentous history of this decade, those traces which touched the life of the foot soldier. War, he believed, was a great leveling experience, and sometimes the remnants, even the trash, from military occupation disclosed the irrepressible character of different peoples. "There was no mistaking the Germans," Kelley mused with a smile, "from the Rhine wine bottles that lay in heaps near what looked like miniature beer gardens. The Americans had contributed an innumerable number of wrappings from packages of cigarettes."

The next destination was the fortified town of Verdun, along the Meuse River. Its Catholic past was rich, its episcopal see dating from the fourth-century. In 1916 it had served as the focus of the longest and bloodiest battle of the war in which two million men fought and one million killed. Two years later American units, teaming with French ones, drove the enemy back, but by the war's end the city had been practically wasted. Its eleventh-century Romanesque cathedral was, judged Kelley, hopelessly ruined. "Part of the walls are standing," he noted, "but the inside just a heap of rubbish." The visitors motored out to the famed citadel and took in a panoramic view of the field of military operations. Kelley found the deepest trenches he had seen. "No shell could penetrate into some of the dugouts," he thought. "The stairway going down to one seemed interminable." Signs of Franco-American collaboration struck Kelley: in these historic ditches, he commented, "there were American relics everywhere."

From Verdun Kelley's friends began their return to Paris, turning westward to Épernay. This town of nearly 20,000 was, next to Rheims, the largest manufacturer of champagne, and the splendid vineyards suggested to the priest that he was returning to civilized life. Their lunch at the Grand Hotel was sumptuous, a faint reminder of the carefree luxuries in the French countryside before the war. The contented party celebrated their arrival in the champagne country with appropriate toasts. "It was an extravagance," admitted Kelley, "but after what we had to eat and drink since we left Brussels we felt like giving ourselves at least one good meal."

The meal was only a brief interruption in their grim journey. The group next followed the Marne River toward Paris and arrived at the last stop, Château-Thierry. A year earlier, this village had been a focal point of the last German offensive; and United States forces had helped the French check this onslaught. In a nearby forested area known as the Belleau Wood, American marines, with support from several infantry units, had taken the offensive, scouring the wood clear of enemy emplacements with such grit and losses that they earned special commendations. En route to this sanctuary, Kelley's car had a blowout, and the hasty repairs made touring more difficult. These battlefields impressed him; but despite greater American participation, they could not be compared to what he had seen in the north. Spring was already shrouding the horror. "The leaves are covering the damage to trees," he recorded, "and the grass is green in the fields." Ypres and Verdun had conditioned the traveler for what he surveyed closer to Paris. Like a seasoned field marshal, Kelley perceived the end of the stalemate tactic of the trenches. "You could see at once," he pondered, "that the military operations here were short and sudden and movements rapid." This was new and foreboding; and walking further into the new grass, he discovered that these new methods were as lethal as the old. "We picked up belts and cartridges," the neglected relics of the fallen.[15]

In less than two weeks, Kelley had relived the four years of the Western Front. A decade earlier he had made his first trip to Europe to be followed by many crossings. This time the wounds of a continent gaped before him, the final blow to an age which had touched his life. He had toured the sites of monumental clashes in a war devoid of all glory. In spite of the costs, no battle was decisive. None gave rise to a brilliant militarist, and none was the scene of old-fashioned gallantry. While Kelley stood in the fields, idealists like Woodrow Wilson were working to make it the last war on earth, and others were warning that if another was to follow, it would not be fought with trenches and barbed wire. Yet Kelley moved away from these scenes with remarkable detachment. He had carefully studied the data of war, and there were moments of pity without outrage. He had discovered, too, that Europe was no corpse. Amid the shambles, it possessed the signs of life—the spring grasses and foliage, the burial parties putting comrades to rest and ready to resume their own lives. Mutilated as it was, Europe was already reviving, and Francis Kelley would be back to assist.

* * * * * * * * * *

If the armistice in November, 1918, had ended hostilities in Europe, it had opened a floodgate of new problems. While the peace conference in Paris reordered national boundaries according to the principle of self-determination, the most pressing emergency was the physical condition of the defeated countries. The Allies had brought defeat to central Europe, but the specter of starvation and exposure threatened total collapse—or a take-over by the radicalism preached from Moscow. Wars have served as the most effective precondition to revolution, and the dislocation following World War I was about to confirm this lesson from the past. Wise counselors in the West saw that punishment in the form of continued economic deprivation led only to the complete disintegration of the continent. Relief programs for former enemies were therefore hastily arranged. In charge of American aid was Herbert C. Hoover, Wilson's capable food administrator, who had worked wonders in conserving food resources during the war. His survey of Europe in person after the armistice revealed conditions more deplorable than his original estimates. A year later, through Cardinal Gibbons, he asked Benedict XV to endorse his drive to relieve distress in central Europe. In a prompt response, the Holy Father commended the work and appealed to the generosity of all Americans regardless of creed or politics.[16]

Parallel developments were unfolding in Chicago. In July, 1919, Cardinal Gasparri, papal secretary of state, sent to Archbishop Mundelein a communiqué honoring the 63rd annual meeting of the Central Verein, a benevolent society of American Catholics of German birth and descent. It carried a special summons from the pope to help in postwar reconstruction, especially relief work in Germany. The archbishop read the letter at the convention in September, adding that the Holy Father had given this body an important assignment in the reconciliation of nations.[17] From this start the German parishes in Chicago soon took up collections in church and door-to-door campaigns. The response was heroic. By mid-November thousands of food and clothing parcels, as well as $25,000, had been gathered, all of which would be divided between the archbishops of Cologne and Vienna. Not only would life's necessities be provided but, as Mundelein explained to Richard H. Tierney, S.J., editor of *America,* the church's hand would be strengthened in troubled Germany and Austria as "the greatest agency for law and order." The prelate appreciated this remarkable generosity in his archdiocese. The cash contributions, he estimated, would reach $50,000, and each parcel destined for Europe would be "marked as coming from the German Catholics of Chicago." This solicitousness for the Fatherland, he told Tierney, needed no apology after their wartime record of patriotism at home.[18]

The tone had been clearly set for Monsignor Kelley regarding relief for the defeated. Earlier, however, he had been warned that relief programs for Europe would cripple Extension's fund-raising for the home-missions. A Canadian chaplain, A.

Bernard MacDonald of Calgary, had been stationed since the armistice in Belgium, where, he told Kelley, he saw swarms of clergy planning collection campaigns and "making for America and Canada to make their killing." The Belgians, he went on, intended to exploit sympathy already inflated by Allied propaganda and to "make a fortune out of the struggle which has not cost the country very much in money or life. . . ."[19] It is hard to assess the impact of this alarm; Kelley had been cyncial of war propaganda. In any case, the defeated countries like Germany and Austria had no opportunity to send advocates across the Atlantic to present their plight. Kelley was therefore willing to give the vanquished every assistance, no matter what the risk might be to the revenues of the society.

In May, 1920, he circulated among Extension members a circular entitled, "The Horror in Austria." While other appeals had centered on aid for children, Kelley's focused on perhaps the most helpless victims in that country, the priests and sisters. It is not clear exactly why Kelley singled out this country as the object of his concern. He had known the glittering prewar Vienna, having visited in 1910 his friend, Richard C. Kerens, who served as United States ambassador to the court of Emperor Franz Joseph. But this early association was hardly a factor for his interest in the clergy and religious a decade later. Disturbing newspaper accounts about Austrian children would have touched this priest, especially when an American relief team reported in January, 1920, that 97 percent of the children in Vienna were near starvation.[20] But children everywhere in Europe received the first priority in aid, and the Islander was confident that the relief organizations in Austria would attend promptly to their needs.

Kelley's interest was rooted probably in his conviction that postwar Austria represented the principal mistake of the Paris peace conference. The Austro-Hungarian monarchy had been dissolved into its many parts, among which was the new republic of Austria. To many, this tiny state was a geographic and economic nightmare. Its six million citizens were landlocked with no access to the sea, poor in natural resources and vulnerable on its eastern frontier. It had lost to Czechoslovakia the lion's share of the old monarchy's industries and minerals. Italy and Yugoslavia had taken its ports on the Adriatic, and to Hungary went the fertile plains that fed the capital. Its chief asset, Vienna, was actually a handicap to postwar recovery. Once a jewel in Europe's landscape, it was now swollen with one-third of the country's population, too large to be fed by the Austrian farmer. To survive, therefore, the republic would have to import both raw materials and food, a necessity that compromised any chance for self-sufficiency. Beyond this, the peacemakers in Paris had levied reparation payments for the sins of the Hapsburgs and prohibited Austria from uniting with Germany, the only course which offered hope to many and which, as some argued, was consistent with the governing principle of self-determination.

The new nation was, in Kelley's view, the pit of postwar Europe, a product of man's stupidity and vengeance. "How a city of two million inhabitants can exist in a country that has no coal and practically nothing but mountains," he wrote later in *Extension Magazine,* "is a puzzle that the Peace Conference must have worked out; but if it did work it out no one in Austria seems to have been given the secret." The new republic was condemned to permanent charity from the outside. "The country was shortchanged in Paris," he noted cynically. "That is the bald truth."[21] Among those who would suffer most, he perceived further, were the clergy and religious. They received no priorities from relief programs, and standing by their posts they could not escape the horror through emigration. Thus did Extension become a special patron for the stricken archdiocese of Vienna.

The society's appeal was a remarkable success, leading Father Ledvina to anticipate funds of over $50,000. The archbishop of Vienna, Cardinal Gustav Piffl, read Kelley's article and called it "a masterpiece of practical Christianity," telling the author too that his descriptive word "horror" did not exaggerate conditions.[22] Kelley was given the opportunity personally to supervise the distribution. In the summer of 1920, the British Foreign Office invited him to come to London at its expense to discuss the fate of German missionaries in the empire, a subject to be treated later. He was allowed to select a secretary, and the choice fell to another Chicago priest, Thomas V. Shannon. Kelley's travel plans mapped out a route in midsummer to London, Holland, and Germany, where he would gather information for the conversations with the Foreign Office in the fall. After these preliminaries, he would travel to Austria and personally survey the situation.[23]

In London, Monsignor Kelley encountered a disturbing first-hand description of Vienna, his ultimate destination. *The Times* of London published a lengthy letter from Herbert Kaufman, editor of *McClure's Magazine*, who gave his impressions from a recent tour of central Europe. The correspondent acknowledged hardships in Austria, alluding to instances of poverty and near famine; but he contended that the republic was viable and the solution to its problems minor. "Vienna," he explained, "is in far better shape than propaganda and uninformed sentimentality have taught us to believe . . . . Meat, butter, sugar, shoes, clothes, fabrics are expensive but plentiful." Hence the capital would revive, it was argued, once its citizens recover their will to work and the Allies cease pampering this elegant but spoiled lady.[24]

To Kelley, these reflections merited little attention, but the word of so noteworthy an American journalist might have an impact on English public opinion. In a prompt letter to *The Times*, the priest repeated his view that Austria was "the standing condemnation of and reproach to Versailles." The resolution of its problems required more than the simple redistribution of abundance, as Kaufman had recommended, along with the mere sparking of the people's resolve. A more radical answer was needed. The republic must be allowed to ally with a neighbor that supplied raw materials and markets—a thinly veiled suggestion that Kelley early favored the *Anschluss*, that is, union between Austria and Germany.[25] While this rejoinder opened no serious debate in the English press, it revealed his state of mind as he approached the Austrian capital in July, 1920. The letter throbbed with outrage against the wisdom of the Peace of Paris and at the same time showed the author's acquaintance with the economics and politics of postwar Europe.

In Vienna, Kelley and Shannon found the predicament of the priests and sisters deplorable. Even Kelley was at a loss for words. "Shannon is on the verge of tears all the time," he told Mundelein, "and I am not much better. No clothes for the winter, no coal, very little fats." Some of the sisters, he discovered, had already died of starvation; and others faced the cruelest hardships. The community of brothers who managed the largest Catholic hospital in Vienna, for instance, wore habits and patched shoes but had not a stitch of underclothing beneath. "What I have learned," he told Ledvina, "makes me want to cry at the awful blindness in America. It is just plain heart-rending—and no hope that I can see if Austria is left as it is. I have stories that will raise your hair."[26]

Nevertheless, the stunning effect of these sights did not immobilize Kelley, who made three decisions before this depature. He arranged first, with James Lockhart Dougan, head of the British Vienna Emergency Relief Fund, for 500 cases of condensed milk to be distributed through Caritas House, a social agency in Vienna. Next, while food was needed, the winter priority appeared to be clothing and leather for shoes; and Kelley elected to invest the bulk of funds in these commodities. Lastly, to take charge of his program, he set up a separate Catholic bureau which was associated with Dougan's operation; and the British generously supplied an office, stationery, and clerical help.[27] In searching for a director, his thoughts at first ran to Chicago priests such as Ledvina and Frederick Siedenburg, S.J., a well-known sociologist at Loyola University, but the need to be fluent in German led Kelley to choose an Englishwoman recommended by Dougan, Mrs. Charlotte Baynes. This enthusiastic lady met all the requirements—experience in relief work and good connections in the capital; in addition, she was willing to contribute her services. She was instructed to limit the range of assistance mainly to priests and religious in the archdiocese of Vienna and to keep meticulous records of all transactions. Extension had thus completed its relief plan for Vienna in less than a fortnight.

From this beginning there followed two simultaneous developments which, unfortunately, converged in a minor collision. The first was the work of Mrs. Baynes in Vienna, a heroic and resourceful woman who deeply involved herself in the suffering around her. At the start, a Quaker organization—the British Friends, who were collaborating with the American Friends Service Committee—impressed her as "definitely anti-Catholic," and, as she told Kelley, she raised "a great deal of noise." Her complaints were so effective in reversing these unfriendly sentiments that Quaker assistance was extended to several Catholic orphanages. Her protests next centered on a program of milk distribution. More than half of this consignment from Extension, she discovered, had not been delivered, as planned, to the convents and rectories. On visiting the cardinal's residence, she saw a large number of cases standing in the courtyard, open and unprotected. "It is obvious," she told Kelley, "that anyone can get milk by bribing the porter or taking it themselves when he is not looking!"[28] Very early Kelley learned that his agent in Vienna was a scrupulous and fearless worker who tolerated few obstacles in fulfilling her mission.

More critical than food shortages was the prospect that Vienna would have little fuel for heat during the winter of 1920-21. Hence, the heart of the Extension program was to buy and ship bolts of heavy cloth out of which the clergy and religious could make their outer wear. In order to expedite delivery, the purchase was to be made in England, and Monsignor Kelley enlisted an unlikely authority to investigate quality and price, Shane Leslie, the esteemed editor of the *Dublin Review,* who executed his task with admirable thoroughness. "The stuff I demanded," he told Kelley, "should last two winters." When Leslie located an attractive price, he had three experts examine the cloth sample, including an Irish weaver, and the unanimous verdict was that he had found a bargain. Once the purchase was made, the Leslie home was promptly transformed, as the editor recalled with pride, into an "exchange and mart for patterns and samples of every king of stuff." Extension eventually invested about $45,000 in this project, a sum which provided for two-thirds of the clergy and religious in Vienna. Kelley also approved of Mrs. Baynes's practice of accepting a token payment for the cloth. This spared the victims from a sense of pauperism and furnished the bureau with currency for a small emergency fund.[29]

In all, Kelley had enlisted two able and committed English assistants, and the details were executed quickly and humanely. No doubt the clothing saved the self-respect—and, perhaps the lives—of priests and sisters in postwar Vienna. There was no shortage in their expressions of appreciation. Frequently, too, the gifts evoked examples of extraordinary self-sacrifice, especially among the religious women. Mrs. Baynes reported difficulty in convincing a number of sisters that the cloth was for their personal use. Their first impulse was to pass it on to the poor around them. Once they understood, Kelley was told, that they were "to be given a little warmth," their gratitude was inexpressible.[30] The only difficulty in such a program as this one, however, was that it uncovered even greater suffering than expected. Humanitarians alternate between a sense of satisfaction and that of frustration; the call on their charity is never over. Kelley knew the importance of his limited program, but he was to learn that it was only a frail beginning in relieving the misery of Austria.

While Mrs. Baynes labored tirelessly in Europe, a related development unfolded in America—the establishment of a national program of Catholic relief which eventually replaced the efforts of Extension. Kelley's reports helped move Mundelein to envision a broader program that would include the general populations of central Europe, especially the children. In September, 1920, the archbishop proposed a national collection at the annual meeting of the American hierarchy. The bishops agreed to an appeal to be made voluntarily in the dioceses, and Cardinal Gibbons appointed Mundelein, along with Archbishop Messmer and Bishop Muldoon, to draft a circular letter. Curiously, Mundelein did not act promptly on the cardinal's charge, perhaps because his original proposal had been compromised when the collection was made only optional.

No action was taken until the press carried an interview between Gibbons and representatives of the Bonifatius Association, a home-missions organization in Germany. In the article the cardinal alluded to Mundelein's committee and the coming appeal. Moving with haste, the archbishop had Kelley draft a circular, and with slight changes in the text it was endorsed by Gibbons and distributed among the dioceses. Mundelein next appointed Monsignor Francis A. Rempe, a leader among the German-American priests of Chicago, as the special representative of the American hierarchy in directing the National Catholic Relief Fund.[31] This rapid sequence of events was supposed to have marked the end of Extension's modest effort. Giving his blessing to the new bishops' program, Kelley issued a second, and final, appeal to the society's patrons with the understanding that what was raised would go to Rempe.[32]

Unfortunately, these two developments—Extension's clothing of the clergy and religious of Vienna and the bishops' plan of general assistance for Germany and Austria—collided when the resolute Mrs. Baynes found it difficult to wind up her work. Kelley had notified her about Rempe's activity, but the continued distress around her compelled her to beg for more money from Extension. Dioceses outside Vienna were equally pressed for cloth, and within the city there was a desperate need for undergarments and shoe leather. Her persistence verged on annoyance, forcing Kelley at one point to exclaim that her plans would destroy Extension. "We have our choice," he told her firmly, "between becoming a spasmodic relief organization and doing the work for which we were established." But a man with Kelley's compassion for any victim was vulnerable to her earnest pleas: he agreed to pay her way from Vienna for a meeting in London.[33]

His interview with Mrs. Baynes occurred on January 6, 1921, an emotional experience that moved the priest against his better judgment. Her accounting of past work was meticulous, and her description of the work to be completed was irresistible. To clothe the remaining clergy and religious in Austria, she told Kelley, would cost only $31,000, and these unfortunates were as desperate as those in Vienna. Shortages in shoe leather especially frightened her. In many convents, Kelley learned, there were only two or three pair of boots; these were reserved for the sisters whose duties took them into the streets, the rest being forced to remain indoors and walk the stone floors in thin house slippers. This desperate account forced the priest to make further inquiries. Each of those whom he consulted in London, including Baron George Franckenstein, the Austrian minister to Great Britain, confirmed her report. Kelley's conscience had been touched. From these conversations, he came away with one firm idea: every cent of Extension's second appeal—which had amounted to $20,000—must, without delay, support not the bishops' program but this Englishwoman's work.[34]

Monsignor Rempe was due shortly in London, where Kelley planned to plea in person in behalf of Mrs. Baynes's program; but the two Chicagoans missed connections. Sensing a complication, Mundelein cabled a warning to Kelley against interfering with Rempe's instructions. Extension's second appeal, it was clear, was to be combined with the hierarchy's collection and given to their representative. Mrs. Baynes's tenacity, however, was contagious, and Kelley promised to carry her cause to the "stoney-hearted Archbishop of Chicago," as she characterized him. With no immediate word from America, she eventually encountered Rempe in Vienna and was stunned on discovering that he had no Extension funds to give her. When she learned further that the bishops' money would go toward general relief, she became bitter and reminded him, as she told Kelley,

> that the priests and religious would think always of others before themselves, & that they would continue to die of cold and hunger themselves and use the money for every kind of charitable purpose rather than their own needs—he replied, coldy, that he would be sorry to be the one to criticize them for so doing ! ![35]

This sharp and needless confrontation ended the Extension relief program. The embarrassed Kelley spent the following weeks explaining his maneuvers to Mundelein, while trying at the same time to calm his outraged volunteer in Vienna. "Of course, I regret that we did not finish the work for the clergy and sisters," he explained feebly to Mrs. Baynes, "but Archbishops are Archbishops, and the [Extension] money went for relief just the same."[36]

All in all, Extension sent more than $70,000 in relief to Europe without depriving the home-missions in America of their support.[37] Noble as it was, however, the program ended on a harsh note for which the president must be held largely responsible. His mistake consisted of having given in to the demands of such a spirited and relentless humanitarian as Mrs. Baynes, and thus trying to complicate the clear objectives of the bishops' relief program. But this fault had been committed in the service of humanity. It cannot obscure the vital importance of Extension's original appeal for Vienna, the first national Catholic response to the agonies of the conquered. This generous action moved the American hierarchy into accepting a major role in salvaging postwar Europe. This accomplishment should have merited for the magnanimous Islander a word of forgiveness from the disturbed parties in Vienna and Chicago.

World War I had worked its way into Francis Kelley step by step. At its start, he had drawn back from deep involvement in the issues that had brought it on, and he had failed at first to perceive the catastrophe that threatened Europe. Safe in America's heartland, he escaped direct contact with the war's devastation until his tour of the battlefields and cemeteries. These new landmarks, brutal and ugly, stirred his conscience. This plundered continent was not dead, and he became a factor in its recovery. In 1931 his role was recognized when the Federal Republic of Austria conferred on him the Great Golden Cross of Merit with Star.[38] The award was a decade late in coming, but it proclaimed that its proud recipient was truly a citizen of the world.

VII
Amateur Diplomacy and the Roman Question

Extension was a peculiarly American institution. Kelley's dream to evangelize everyone living on American soil materalized at a supremely delicate moment in the history of these people. After the turn of the century, industry and immigration were rapidly urbanizing the population. The growing metropolises of the East and North were spawning a new culture that sparked tensions between the cities and countryside. Popular literature suggested that twentieth-century Americans were separating into "city slickers" and "country hicks." Kelley's movement, however, challenged the erosion, seeking to bring together these elements into a joint enterprise. Through his coordination, the home-missions would find their opportunity in the countryside and their material support in the cities. This vision provided within the church a balanced relationship between rural and urban Americans, a relationship which the community at large found increasingly difficult to sustain.[1]

Yet, narrowly defined as it was, Kelley's leadership never succumbed to parochialism. Extension had strengthened his consciousness of the universal church. Its foundation had brought him into contact with the Vatican, especially with such international figures as Cardinal Merry del Val. His duties required repeated voyages across the Atlantic, and these soon fashioned him into a seasoned traveler who knew the major capitals of the Old World. Promotion of the society likewise forced him to develop an interest in affairs at home and abroad. From its earliest editions, the society's magazine had served as an occasional forum for contemporary issues troubling the church around the world. American as he was—champion of home-missions and of the ascendant West—Kelley's field of vision extended well beyond the territories which the Holy See had assigned to Extension. It was not surprising, therefore, that his life should be drawn into several of the most important international developments of his generation, the most significant of which was the Roman Question.

To be effective in this spacious terrain, Kelley developed over the years a diplomatic style that consisted of several personal qualities and skills. The essence of diplomacy, he later proposed in his autobiography, was humor; and he was generously endowed with the intelligence and charm to mellow most adversaries.[2] Though he was comfortable with strangers, his private thoughts point to other traits that characterize his style. Kelley's first principle was that no matter how heated an exchange became, the diplomat never lost self-control. Passionate causes placed enormous pressure on tempers, and Kelley was not immune from occasional outbursts. Nevertheless, firmness coupled with politeness was indispensable in presenting a position.

He attempted to teach this lesson to the volcanic Alfred E. Burke, who in 1915 asked his colleague to help draft for the Holy

See a letter explaining his resignation from Extension in Canada. The older priest erupted when Kelley softened the references to Archbishop Neil McNeil of Toronto, who had forced Burke's withdrawal. "He is your Archbishop," came the word from Chicago, "and every sign of respect should be shown in the letter which should be confined to the principles of the case only." In embarrassing his superior, the diplomat simply compromised himself. For Burke, however, Kelley's approach was too "mild and gracious." It served merely to inflame the Canadian into writing so rude a reply to Archbishop McNeil that Kelley returned it with the warning: "I have not been able myself to accomplish anything by the hammer and tong method. I do not believe that any of us can."[3]

Good manners were natural to Kelley, and equally so was the second quality in his diplomatic style, persistence. His interests abroad furnished only more work and expense for the busy priest, but he abandoned these adventures only when superiors called him off. After World War I, as will be seen in the following chapter, he chased minor clerks in London for concessions to restore the German missioners expelled from their posts in Africa and Asia. The cost to him included several months of work, two oceanic trips, and his personal fortune. But he remained in pursuit until the Holy See registered its willingness to accept the British postwar arrangement. Related to this trait was his conviction that governments should be blitzed with data. The Vatican, he told Archbishop Henry Moeller of Cincinnati, was itself a "glutton for information."[4] From him, accordingly, came letters, reports, personal visits, and the posting of alert pickets, such as Jules Tiberghien and Sante Tampieri, who kept the lines of communication clear. It was Kelley's unfaltering sincerity that fueled this perseverance. As the issues became increasingly complicated and confidants multiplied, his allies and adversaries could rely at least on a consistency of viewpoint. A steady advocate, he was guilty of no abrupt changes of position and no deliberate betrayals of trust. Added to this strong sense of integrity was the incurable tendency to moralize his causes. In facing war-toughened European diplomats or skeptical cardinals of the Roman Curia, he did not hesitate to present his case for the good of religion. Unfortunately, this tendency made the opposition more self-conscious, and compromise more difficult.

Less congenial to Kelley was what he acknowledged as the third requirement in international negotiations—patience. "Diplomacy in Europe," he mused late in life, "differs from diplomacy in America in the time consumed. . . . Time is nothing in European diplomacy. You can see an official today and wait a week to see the next."[5] This wisdom had ripened during days of idleness in Rome, Paris, and London. These capitals were not to be hurried, and Kelley's efforts to expedite decisions succeeded only in frustrating himself. An instance of his coping with this relaxed pace occurred during the peace conference in Paris. Having been forced to spend weeks in advocating religious freedom for Mexico, Kelley drew words of encouragement from his associate in Chicago, Monsignor Ledvina. "It must be very trying to do things in a slow way," the latter counseled; "however, it is the only way in which it can be done outside of America. We probably act too quickly anyway in some things; and the old world, with centuries of previous experience, can show us a thing or two."[6] This was a truth which Kelley found hard to accept. He likewise discovered that the Holy See did not match the quickness of action that characterized the Extension offices; and Monsignor Tampieri constantly reminded him to be patient with the lingering motions of curial officials. "We are going on very slowly . . . ," Tampieri cautioned in 1914 from the secretariat of state, adding gravely: "But believe me, we forget no one." The Roman sought to temper Kelley's anxiety over a document due from the Holy See, and he assured the Islander that it was at last en route. "It was not possible to work more rapidly," explained Tampieri casually, because *"Rome est toujours la ville éternelle!"*[7]

The final component to Monsignor Kelley's diplomatic style

was an adequacy in the Romance languages. He admired Merry del Val's ease in shifting easily among languages, but he never approached such a mastery himself. His student years had trained him in French, which he could read and use in conversation, but he declined to write in it. In time his skill was extended to reading Italian and Spanish, but he continued, when necessary, to find experts to write his thoughts in those languages.[8] More importantly, his experience had persuaded him into believing that he had developed a sure technique in language learning. Languages were not to be studied out of grammars. Kelley's French had been acquired by listening to others speaking it in the province of Quebec. On the commuter train between the rectory in Wilmette and the Extension office, he devoted his spare moments to Italian and Spanish. "The best way to learn a language I find," he told Tampieri with satisfaction, "is to listen to people speaking it, and then to see it constantly in print."[9]

These four elements—savoir-faire, tenacity of purpose, acceptance of a slower tempo of progress, and linguistic sufficiency—composed Kelley's diplomatic form. These did not constitute a revolution in international bargaining nor did they guarantee success. There were limitations to his style, such as the confinement of foreign languages to the familiar countries of the western Mediterranean. Nevertheless, he was adequately prepared to engage in several important missions of his time, including the Roman Question. A number of the most prestigious professionals in diplomacy took notice of this energetic, shrewd, and charming cleric from mid-America, admitting him to their confidences and, on occasion, entrusting to him weighty assignments. These four qualities thus allowed him a range beyond the clatter of the Extension office. They led him to a world of sophisticated and clever gentlemen who appreciated the polish of this Chicagoan—to arenas where the church's interests needed the protection of capable and motivated men, including an amateur like Francis Kelley.

* * * * * * * * *

The peacemaking after World War I brought Kelley to what he considered the summit of his life. In behalf of the exiled Mexican hierarchy, he went to Paris in 1919, where he served as an unofficial observer at the peace conference, advocating that the Treaty of Versailles sanction guarantees for religious liberty. Though persistent and sometimes heroic, his efforts were generally unsuccessful, but they accidentally introduced him into the "most interesting" adventure of his career, the negotiations over the Roman Question.

This complicated issue had arisen a half century before the peace conference when Italian nationalists completed the unification of modern Italy. Since the eighth century, Rome had been the center of a territorial state in which the pope was sovereign and which afforded him independence in conducting the business of the church world-wide. But his continued autonomy as a temporal ruler clashed with the objectives of Italian nationalists, who proclaimed the Eternal City in 1861 the capital of the new kingdom of Italy. Nine years later, after the withdrawal of the French garrison, royal troops had invaded the papal domain and, after a token skirmish, had taken the city. While nationalists and anticlericals cheered, the annexation of this territory to Italy ended the historic States of the Church and inaugurated what the Roman pontiffs termed the "occupation" of Rome.

After the seizure, regarded by devout Catholics as a *"peccato nazionale,"* the Italian government had sought to restore its relationship with the Holy See by legislating certain assurances for the dignity and spiritual independence of the pope.[10] In 1871 it passed the "Law of Guarantees," which provided a tax-exempt annuity and many rights of extraterritoriality. According to liberals and moderates, it was a generous solution, but in the eyes of the Holy See it was unacceptable for three reasons. First, the only effective guarantee against interference in spiritual matters was geographic sovereignty. According to Italy's proposal, however, the pope was denied this prerogative and remained technically a subject of the Italian state. Even the papal residence and gardens were not recognized as private property of the Holy See but were set aside simply for the pope's use and treated as the property of the Crown. Hence, mere "spiritual" sovereignty, that is, one without territoriality, was a concept too experimental for the bishops of Rome to accept; to them it was empty and dangerous. Not everyone understood the papal logic, even the most fervent of the faithful. The invitation of the Spanish king in 1915 to place the Escorial at the disposition of the pope did not supply the essential territoriality and was therefore declined.

Second, according to the Holy See, the Italian law was unilateral and contradictory. It had defined prerogatives of a sovereign with an authority not recognized by the same sovereign. Monarchs had agreed to constitutional limitations on their rule only when these were legislated by bodies whose jurisdiction these rulers had formally acknowledged. The pope, however, had made no concessions to the Italian parliament regarding its authority over him or in his states. Third, the right of the pope, listed in the law, were statutory, not constitutional, and thus not genuinely "sovereign." They were derived from the action of the legislature, and their continuance therefore depended upon the benevolence of that body, a risk which few rulers would chance. Hence, the pope's protests were more than the cries of a despoiled autocrat; they indeed pointed to serious juridical defects in the original solution proposed by the Italian government.

The last two popes of the nineteenth-century—Pius IX and Leo XIII—had been intransigent on this question, having secluded themselves within the Vatican and forbidding Catholics from political participation in the government. Again, these were not merely the acts of sulking monarchs. Their voluntary imprisonment and noncooperation allowed them to avoid any semblance of legitimating a regime which had usurped their patrimony and offered in its place a vulnerable position within the state. The pontificate of Pius X was, however, the first that appeared willing to explore conciliation. The proscriptions against Catholic participation in Italian politics were softened; and a conceptual breakthrough occurred through the efforts of Antonio A. Rossi, archbishop of Udine. In several public statements, he argued that the solution no longer lay in a simple return to the status quo before 1870. The Holy See, he implied, was disposed to negotiate its demands for territorial sovereignty and to accept something less than its former domain, perhaps even an alternative like a spiritual sovereignty guaranteed by several powers bound together by treaty.[11] In this way, the Roman Question, which had erupted in the year of Francis Kelley's birth, had, by the midpoint of his life, advanced to the stage whereby the Holy See was evidently anxious for a settlement.

Kelley's early years as president of Extension provided him with a more than ordinary interest in the cloistered papacy. Under his editorship, *Extension Magazine* advocated the restoration of papal independence and even took pains to acquaint its readers with the Roman Curia through a rare series of articles that described the major figures and departments. More importantly, he made remarkable efforts through photography to vivify the images of the popes. Not since 1870 did they make public appearances, not even imparting their blessing from an open balcony in the Vatican. This seclusion, Kelley feared, would obscure these spiritual leaders to the majority of the faithful who were unable to attend the audiences within the Vatican. A proposal to develop a motion picture on world missions in "Kinemacolor" interested him as a sponsor as long as it contained scenes with the Holy Father. The process had already filmed most of the heads of state, including George V of England, William II of Germany, Alfonso XIII of Spain, and President Wilson; and Kelley hoped that Pius X would join this illustrious cast. Complications arose, however, when it was discovered that an Italian company had bought the exclusive right to make such features at the Vatican. Kelley's associates seriously considered the purchase of this monopoly until it was further discovered that the pontiff had firmly declined to be filmed under any conditions. "He is a very humble man," explained Kelley to a saddened partner, "and probably his opposition is largely because of that fact. . . ."[12]

Kelley was forced to drop the project. World War I only worsened the isolation, but the idea to film the pontiff revived under Pius's successor, Benedict XV. Problems in wartime travel had drastically reduced the number of pilgrims to Rome who could catch a glimpse of the new pope. "I don't think," Kelley told the pope's confidant, Monsignor Tiberghien, "there are three people in Chicago who have seen him besides myself. We can see every emperor and king in Europe but not the Pope."[13] His efforts were not crowned with success, but they reflected a desire to use a tasteful and innovative medium in correcting bad effects of the pope's self-imposed seclusion. Isolation might have been the correct juridical response to the Law of Guarantees, but its price was to handicap the church's leadership. In days of enormous crisis, the Islander's project might have restored a measure of life and freshness to the figure of a pope whose impact on events was missed.

Kelley's fascination with the darkened papal image was in no way a preparation for what was to follow in 1919 at the Paris peace conference. It was a series of failures which then brought him briefly to the center of the Roman Question. The first disappointment consisted in the Holy See's inability to internationalize the issue. The deadlock between the papacy and Italy was approaching a half century, a long interval which had begun to take its toll on both parties. No doubt because of the recent overtures from the Vatican, the Italian government was determined to keep the issue strictly an internal affair between church and state. Thus, according to the Treaty of London of April, 1915, it won from France, Great Britain, and Russia the pledge that at the peace conference they would approve of Vatican representation *only* with Italy's consent, which was not forthcoming. In the early stages of World War I, therefore, this provision appeared adequate in keeping the major powers from interfering in the Roman Question.

This left the Holy See with two strategies. The first was to win the patronage of a late comer to the war, the United States, which was not a party to the Treaty of London. Cardinal Gibbons was contacted to enlist President Wilson. The American leader, it was hoped, might succeed in winning a seat at the peace conference for the Vatican, but a variety of circumstances thwarted this effort.[14] The second approach was to employ the prestige of one of the great heroes of the war, Désiré Mercier, cardinal primate of Belgium. For four years, when the exiled king of the Belgians and other leaders were separated from their people, this courageous churchman had become their spokesman. His resistance to German encroachment had been fearless, and his pastoral letters had helped sustain the independent spirit of the country. This record had won for him enormous respect in his own country and among the victors. Willing to do whatever possible, Mercier received soon after the armistice in November, 1918, a visitor from the Vatican, Archbishop Bonaventura Cerretti, Cardinal Gasparri's deputy in the secretariat of state. No known record has survived of this interview except Cerretti's notes which listed the three questions on the agenda: (1) How exactly had the loss of temporal sovereignty crippled the work of the papacy? (2) What modifications of the Law of Guarantees would be acceptable to the Holy See? (3) What interest would oppose an attempt to internationalize the question?[15]

Thoroughly briefed on the Roman Question, Mercier had no official credentials to attend the peace conference. Cardinal Gasparri had asked the Belgian government to name the cardinal as a delegate, but this was declined. The only hope lay in a special invitation. Gasparri therefore arranged that the cardinals of Brazil, Canada, and the United States—each representing a nation that would attend the peace conference—provide Mercier with written appeals that he be given a hearing on the Roman Question.[16] But these elaborate maneuvers evoked no summons from Paris. Mercier remained at his post in Malines, helplessly exploring other ways and means whereby he might reach the negotiators. Vatican diplomacy had been stalemated.

The second failure centered on Italy's attempt at territorial aggrandizement at the peace conference. On January 18, 1919, when the sessions formally began, the government of Vittorio Orlando was an acknowledged member of the Big Four. Italy was eventually awarded the northern boundaries promised by the Treaty of London, which included the whole of Trentino to the line of the Brenner Pass, as well as territory on the head and eastern shore of the Adriatic. In addition, however, Orlando claimed the port of Fiume, which would have given Italy a foothold in the Balkans. A party to no wartime treaties, Wilson would accept no argument in support of this demand and stood fast against the premier. During the struggle Wilson appealed directly to the Italian people to desert their leader in favor of a peace of justice. This unprecedented act strengthened Orlando's opposition at home, and his delegation was forced to quit the conference temporarily, only to return to Paris on May 6.[17]

In Kelley's judgment, these events had enormous political significance in the United States. Wilson's extraordinary behavior over Fiume was due partly to the fact that Orlando had no constituency in America to which he could appeal. Italy's appropriation of the States of the Church had alienated American Catholics, who, in the Chicagoan's view, applauded Wilson's harsh treatment of the government that continued to deny the pope his right to territorial sovereignty. The President's action had crippled Orlando's government. The latter's political opposition had been aroused in Italy, and, according to Kelley,

Americans were generally in favor of Wilson's bold interference in Italian affairs. The only way for Orlando's government to survive was to consolidate its position at home by settling the Roman Question.[18] Without knowing it, Orlando's defeat over Fiume had given the midwestern priest a golden opportunity to initiate negotiations which had thus far eluded Mercier and Gasparri.

The peace conference had thus far frustrated the two principals in the Roman Question, the Holy See and Italy; and the catalyst to bring them together was a third failure in Paris, Kelley's inability to bring relief to Catholics in Mexico. Kelley had not arrived in France until March 6, 1919, six weeks after the opening of the conference. A member of no official delegation, he served as a liaison in behalf of the exiled Mexican hierarchy. The American department of state had cautioned him against direct attacks on Carranza, and Kelley elected instead to lobby for a clause in the treaty which guaranteed religious liberty.[19] A series of disappointing interviews, however, revealed to him that religious liberty was not among the priorities of the peacemakers.

During these unsuccessful months in Paris, he did renew an old and important acquaintance. Though the Holy See had no official representative at the peace conference, Archbishop Cerretti had been sent to Paris in behalf of the German and Austrian foreign-missionary congregations. As ex-enemy aliens, they were threatened with explusion from the empires of the victor nations, as well as from the former colonies of Germany. Kelley had known the plain-spoken Vatican diplomat when he served as a staff member of the apostolic delegation in Washington, D.C., and in 1914 he had moved on to Australia as that country's first apostolic delegate. Three years later he had been recalled to Rome, succeeding Eugenio Pacelli, later Pope Pius XII, as secretary of the congregation for extraordinary ecclesiastical affairs. With the death of Cardinal Falconio that year, he was soon regarded as the curia's authority on America and other English-speaking countries. When he met Kelley in Paris on March 16,

1919, he had been entrusted with the task of defending the German missions in Africa and Asia. In time, his work as a diplomatic troubleshooter earned such confidence from Benedict XV and his advisers that he would be rumored to be the probable successor of Cardinal Gasparri in the secretariat of state.[20] Archbishop Cerretti possessed all the ingredients that would produce the most harmonious of partnerships with Monsignor Kelley.

* * * * * * * * * *

The peace conference in Paris formed an appropriate backdrop to Kelley's involvement in the Roman Question, the "high spot" of his life. It was a matchless season of international politics in which to form at first-hand views of the dominant personalities of the generation. Kelley's attention focused primarily on the leaders of the United States peace commission. President Wilson's performance did not impress the priest. On March 8, 1919, Kelley confided in his diary that America was the center of discussion and Wilson "the man of the hour," but, he added, the President's influence had already faded. "European diplomats are going to be too smart for him," he mused further; "I would not be surprised if we are getting into a mess."[21] Kelley was already sensing strong intuitions of the impending tragedy which would destroy Wilson's health and the chances of America's membership in the League. Within this official circle, however, Kelley grew to admire the President's best known confidant, Edward M. House. A private diplomatic adviser, he had served Wilson on several key assignments. Two interviews with him had been arranged for Kelley through Admiral William S. Benson, Chief of Naval Operations, a Catholic who accompanied the President to Paris. A native of Houston, House had been active in Southwestern politics, but he did not strike the priest as the stereotypical Texan. "He has become a complete diplomat," observed Kelley—"polished, slow in his talk and careful about his statement." The priest had found within the American delegation a reliable channel to the President, an asset which the Islander would unexpectedly need toward the end of the peace conference.[22]

Monsignor Kelley's involvement in the Roman Question resulted from a series of accidents. On May 6, 1919, the day before the final Treaty of Versailles was presented to the Germans, Monsignor Kelley left Paris with a group of Knights of Columbus for a tour of the battlefields of western Europe, where Kelley intended to gather material for magazine articles.[23] Four days later, the party arrived at Malines, the seat of the primate of Belgium. The exquisite medieval city betrayed the grim symptoms of invasion and military occupation. The archiepiscopal palace had been one of its notable buildings, but Kelley remarked how "pretty well shot up" it was. The 67-year-old Belgian patriot received his American guests in a reception room as unpretentious as it was historic. Within it walls, noted Kelley, the cardinal had "held the fort during the days of the occupation and conducted a battle of his own for Belgian independence." But Mercier directed the conversation away from his exploits and drew out the priest's opinion on subjects related to the home-missions. This invitation evoked such excitement that Kelley jumped to his feet and delivered in French an impassioned speech on the topic. His companions were surprised at this minor explosion. "You must speak fine French, Msgr.," one commented later. "I can't understand these Frenchmen when they talk but I understood you perfectly."[24]

Kelley was introduced into the Roman Question when, at the departure of the party, Mercier called him back for a private discussion. This time it was the priest who listened, and the cardinal who talked. The conversation centered on the latter's abortive attempt to have the Roman Question resolved at the Paris peace conference. The American priest left the disappointed cardinal with the promise to see Colonel House, who might arrange a conference between Wilson and Mercier. Little could come from this meeting, both men agreed, except that it would at least discharge the cardinal's obligation to the Vatican.[25]

The next stage consisted of Kelley's making contact with the Italian government, a second accident which was as unplanned as his talk with Mercier. A week after his visit in Belgium, the Islander won Colonel House's pledge to help arrange a discussion between President Wilson and the cardinal; and at this point Kelley expected to make his exit. En route from House's hotel, he ran into the Marquis Giuseppe Brambilla, counselor of the Italian peace commission, who spotted the American on the street and abruptly pulled him into the doorway of a closed shop. President Wilson's harsh treatment of Italy over Fiume, stormed Brambilla, would arouse protests in America, especially among Catholics. To the diplomat's surprise, Kelley replied that, as the "jailer of the Pope," Italy had lost the sympathy of the Catholic world.[26]

This animated exchange of views continued in the priest's hotel room, where Brambilla was persuaded that the solution of the Roman Question was a way to undercut Wilson's popularity in America, a prospect not unattractive to both men. Kelley followed up with assurances that the Vatican no longer demanded the restitution of the former States of the Church, which would cut out the heart of the kingdom of Italy. When Brambilla suggested an interview with Orlando himself, Kelley insisted that he did not represent the Holy See and that the publicity would only confuse his unofficial status. But the Italian pressed on, promising an innocent arrangement that would in no way compromise the priest. "What wrong would there be," Brambilla asked, "with one Catholic gentleman talking to another Catholic gentleman about a subject of interest to all Catholics?" On the next day, Kelley was expected at tea in Brambilla's apartment, where he would meet a "prominent person."[27]

The "social" contact between Vittorio Orlando and Monsignor Kelley was exquisitely choreographed. Once the priest entered Brambilla's suite in the elegant Ritz Hotel, he blended smoothly into the guests. When the premier arrived, Kelley found himself positioned last to shake his hand, and the two then took tea casually at the same table. After the gathering broke up, guests and hosts vanishing quietly, the pair were left alone in the room, engaged in lively conversation in French. Kelley was convinced of Orlando's sincerity. This was the first time, he learned, that a minister of Italy had consented to discuss the Roman Question with a Catholic cleric. Their chat ended with this agreement: since intermediaries like Mercier and Wilson would only internationalize the issue, the next step toward the solution of the Roman Question would be the arrangement of direct, but secret, negotiations between Italy and the Holy See. Even though Orlando anticipated some opposition in his parliament, he was prepared to take the risk. The question of the moment was but this: who was to alert the Holy See?[28]

Acting thus far without the Vatican's authority, Monsignor Kelley was reluctant to volunteer for this task, but a third accident entangled him further in this adventure. He had booked passage home on the *Rotterdam,* which was to leave for the continent soon; but, to his surprise, the ship had departed ahead of schedule, leaving him stranded in Paris. This odd twist of fate encouraged Brambilla to beg him to accept another errand, that of going to Rome in quest of a Vatican diplomat who would complete the work with Orlando. "The questions that were dwelt upon and the problems they involve," advised the marquis,

> are of such momentous and far reaching importance, the prospects of success, indeed, so hopeful, that nothing should be left to chance and [I] venture to suggest that you report what has been said in person.[29]

Once Kelley accepted this mission, Brambilla helped arrange the impromptu journey to Rome, providing the priest with an Italian passport, a tangible sign of the government's good intentions.

The drama continued in the Eternal City, where Kelley secluded himself in a hotel and quietly sought the counsel of the veteran curial bureaucrat, Monsignor Jules Tiberghien. The latter urged him to contact Cerretti immediately and even escorted the anxious American to the bronze doors of the Vatican, leaving him with the promise that he would pray before the tomb of St. Peter. Awakened from his afternoon rest, Cerretti was startled to see Kelley in Rome. As soon as the visitor explained his mission, both rushed to Cardinal Gasparri's apartments where an appointment with the pope was hastily arranged—from which Kelley was excused. When the two officials returned, he learned that Cerretti would go to Paris, a decision which suited the priest perfectly.[30]

In his unofficial status, Kelley had thus performed two key services in this complex development. He had delivered Mercier's proposal to the American and Italian peace commissions in Paris, and he had carried Orlando's private offer to the Vatican. At this stage he was given a third task: he would help camouflage Cerretti's departure from Rome. The Eternal City kept few secrets, and Gasparri was concerned over security. When the cardinal had learned of Tiberghien's part, he had to be assured that Kelley's friend was trustworthy and was the only one in Rome with whom the priest had spoken. Cerretti, it was decided, was to accompany Kelley back to Paris ostensibly for one reason—to negotiate with the peacemakers over the fate of the German missions; but this errand was intended also to screen a second one—to enter into secret conversations with Premier Orlando over the Roman Question.[31]

In Paris, the Chicagoan arranged the contact between Brambilla and Cerretti, neither having met each other beforehand; and this signaled the end to his work on the Roman Question. The archbishop was quickly consumed with the negotiations, but he managed a few visits with Kelley, commenting vaguely on the progress. When the latter expressed concern about his tardy return to Chicago, Cerretti notified Archbishop Mundelein that the priest had been on a special mission for the

Holy See; and this last favor signaled that nothing now prevented him from going home. On June 1, 1919, after an absence of nearly four months, the Islander left Cherbourg on the *Savoie.*[32]

The hectic shuttling between Belgium, France, and Italy had cost Monsignor Kelley no more physical trouble than an attack of sciatica, and he was able to return immediately to his duties at Extension, bringing with him a sense of extraordinary satisfaction. He had successfully executed several missions of supreme delicacy, and for the first time in nearly fifty years representatives of the Holy See and the kingdom of Italy were deep in serious conversations. "To tell you the truth," he told Ambrose Petry after his return home, "I had to work harder in Europe than I do here."[33] There was, however, one further demand which the Roman Question would make upon him—silence. It was as a journalist planning articles for *Extension Magazine* that Kelley had visited Cardinal Mercier and had been thrust suddenly into diplomacy. When he reached Chicago in mid-June, his diary contained the most important story he had ever covered. Yet neither would it reach print that year, nor would he ever have the pleasure of breaking it.

* * * * * * * * *

In Paris the Roman Question was left in the hands of the professionals, and Monsignor Kelley's contribution was to remain buried in state archives for another ten years, a curious postscript to his role in the deliberations. On June 1, 1919, the Orlando-Cerretti discussions began with great promise, leading quickly to a projected concordat. But domestic instability in Italy, along with the ongoing quarrel between Wilson and the Italian peace commission, forced Orlando to leave the peace conference ten days later. On July 19, his regime fell, succeeded by that of his minister of finance, Francesco Nitti. This change in leadership brought no relief to postwar Italy; conditions continued to deteriorate, giving rise to Fascism, and this forced the suspension of negotiations between the government and the Holy See.[34]

These developments brought alarm on both sides of the Atlantic. The Italian embassy in Washington remained interested in cultivating American-Catholic public opinion during the crisis. Within ten days after Orlando's fall, the embassy made contact with Kelley, a surprise to the priest but a welcome one.[35] Meanwhile, Cerretti remained two months in the French capital, defending the German missions in public and privately straining to salvage the agreement with Orlando over the Roman Question. On his return to Rome in August, he confided to Kelley that there was still hope, but curial officials in Rome noted that the archbishop was in desperate need of a vacation. By autumn, as the Chicagoan learned from a Vatican diplomat, Paschal Robinson, O.F.M., Cerretti had not recovered from the work which Kelley had "launched" in Paris. The only regret at the Holy See, the Franciscan added, was that "you had to leave before the real trouble began."[36]

The Vatican did not easily abandon Cerretti's efforts. In early 1920, it experimented with new strategies in helping to stabilize the threatened government with which it had begun negotiations. One approach enlisted Archbishop Mundelein, whose sponsorship of war-bond drives had earned him the gratitude of the Wilson administration. This led the apostolic delegate, Archbishop Bonzano, confidentially to ask his friend in Chicago to use any means possible to mellow Wilson's opposition to Italy over Fiume.[37] But it was already too late to save either Cerretti's groundwork with Orlando or what remained of Italian democracy.

The accession of Pius XI in 1922 renewed the church's eagerness to end the church-state feud. With the triumph of Benito Mussolini the same year, the state received through strong centralization the stability it had lacked since the war, and the political climate for resuming discussions returned. The Roman

Question was definitively settled on February 11, 1929, when Cardinal Gasparri and Mussolini signed the Lateran Pacts. Basically, these agreements created the Vatican City State, compensated the Holy See for the loss of the larger States of Church, and established Catholicism as the state religion. This agreement not only dissolved the obligation to keep the earlier negotiations secret, but it made public explanations necessary. The papacy might be accused of collaboration with Fascism, and doctrinaire liberals would charge that Mussolini's concession of the Vatican City State, along with a state religion, not only betrayed Italian nationalism but restored clericalism in the country.[38] Even before the signing of the pacts, the Vatican began quietly to assemble documentation, a prudent preparation to prove that its effort to solve the Roman Question preceded the Fascist revolution. Domestic politics in Italy thus reintroduced Francis Kelley for the last time into this issue.

In the interval between 1919 and 1929, radical changes had occurred in the lives of two clerics who had hastened to Cardinal Gasparri's apartments with the news that, for the first time in nearly fifty years, a premier of Italy awaited an emissary from the Holy See. A decade later, Francis Kelley was in his fifth year as bishop of Oklahoma, and Bonaventura Cerretti had graduated to a cardinal's hat and a position of importance in the Roman Curia. In January, 1929, Cerretti asked Kelley to prepare for the archives a memorandum of his role, adding that he had deposited his own statement. Once the bishop located his "cryptic notes" in his diary, he carefully reconstructed the events from these and memory. When he sent the memorandum, he was certain that the entire episode had been forgotten at the Holy See. "Cardinal Gasparri," he remarked moodily, "did not even remember me when I paid him a visit last year. I am afraid that the 'exile' in the land of the Red People has been completely forgotten. That fact helps me to make progress in the virtue of humility but it hurts."[39] With these testy words, Kelley destroyed his diary and expected the matter to end quietly.

On March 31, 1929, the Associated Press broke the story of his role in the Cerretti-Orlando conversations. "Closeted with a war time prime minister in Paris," the article began, "Bishop Kelley set in motion forces which ended a disagreement which had been troubling Europe since 1870." The dramatic account stressed the discussions between Brambrilla and Kelley, and the latter reasoned that the marquis's wife had given it out. Though it made the Oklahoman an instant celebrity, he was furious; he could now be accused of having planted the piece in the American press. A litany of inaccuracies also disturbed him, especially the statement that Mrs. Brambilla had invited him to a private tea where he was said to have had his conversation with Cardinal Mercier. Immediately, assurances were sent from Oklahoma to the Holy See regarding Kelley's innocence in this press release. "Frankly, I was worried," he explained to Monsignor Francis J. Spellman in the secretariat of state,

> because I feared people might misunderstand the reference to the lady and to meetings said to have been in her apartments. . . . I do not like the implication that Vatican diplomacy is done through "teas."[40]

In any case, this sensational revelation brought one important benefit: it was the first to establish the fact that the Vatican's campaign to resolve the Roman Question had orginated before the Fascist regime.

The Islander's role was further confirmed in an elaborate commentary published in the *Saturday Evening Post* of May 4, 1929. This was Orlando's narrative of his conversations with Kelley and Cerretti ten years earlier, a narrative written with obvious political motivation. A classic European liberal, the aroused Orlando stood as a champion of parliamentary processes and the secularized state, principles which he had not forsaken since his fall after World War I. Lately, he had become a notable critic of Mussolini, having resigned from parliament in 1925 and devoting himself to writing and teaching. Fundamentally, therefore, this article was a protest against Fascism, intended to argue the near success of his regime in ending the state's conflict with the church. *Il Duce* was not to have all the glory. Orlando's interpretation of the 1919 negotiations gave the Islander the most flattering tribute of his life. Writing for American readers, the ex-premier contrasted the role of two of their countrymen. Kelley was credited with the constructive contribution of having brought the diplomats together, and Woodrow Wilson was accused of having torn them apart with his stand on Fiume, which destroyed Orlando's ministry and crippled democracy in Italy.[41] Perhaps the contrast was merely a matter of Italian vengeance on the former President, but not many amateurs like Kelley have been measured seriously against a public figure thought to be one of the great statesmen of the twentieth century.

The Brambillas had their press release, the Italian liberals their magazine article; but neither was a party to the actual settlement. Hence, the final pronouncements on the Roman Question were yet forthcoming from the two signatories of the Lateran Pacts. Though the accord had been signed in February, 1929, final ratifications depended upon the approval of the Italian parliament, and not every deputy favored the agreement. "Old fears are still awake," observed the British ambassador in Italy, "and old resentments have not all died. . . . There is even talk of the eventual emergence of an opposition [to the Fascist party] that would be based on Anti-clericalism." On May 13, 1929, Mussolini delivered in the lower house a rollicking address, running over three hours, in which he underscored the fact that a liberal regime had attempted to do what the Lateran Pacts had achieved. Like the prior accounts of the Brambillas and Orlando, he detailed Kelley's contribution in bringing Cerretti and Orlando together. In this case, Mussolini was summoning parliamentary unity through a reminder that the reconciliation betwen church and state was not a partisan issue. This strategy succeeded in winning parliamentary approval, and on June 7, 1929, the Lateran Pacts were ratified. The political finesse of the Italian leader, which included a reference to Kelley's key part, inspired the British ambassador to send another comment to London: "So far Signor Mussolini continues to bestride, and skillfully control, his team of horses."[42]

Though far removed in the American Southwest, Bishop Kelley continued to play a featured role in the Roman Question. As the other party in the negotiations, the Holy See was determined not to leave the documentation of the Cerretti-Orlando conversations to the liberals and Fascists. Kelley's entire memorandum, along with Cardinal Cerretti's notes, was published in *Vita e Pensiero,* a bimonthly edited by the Catholic University of the Sacred Heart in Milan, a pontifical institution which was a personal favorite of Pope Pius XI. This completed the record, and, as Cerretti told Kelley, the publication had aroused "great excitement here, and everyone finds it very interesting"—kind words from a seasoned diplomat to a friend who appreciated the tardy recognition.[43]

* * * * * * * * *

One theme might conclude Kelley's lengthy association with the Roman Question: the chain of ironies in this historic affair. Stylish and pragmatic, Italians were notably successful practitioners of the diplomatic arts. Five centuries earlier, the papal court and the Renaissance city-states of northern Italy had created modern European diplomacy, creating the basic institutions and rules of conduct; and their countrymen continued to be peerless negotiators. Yet in spite of this rich experience, the Roman Question had frustrated them. These masters of statecraft had to await an outsider and amateur from the American Midwest before the first steps toward rapprochement could be taken.

There were also several accidents, those chance events that blocked Kelley's release from the issue. The novelist is allowed, it is said, only one coincidence in his story-telling, but Kelley's entanglement required at least three—the casual trip to Belgium, the encounter with a disgruntled Italian diplomat on the streets of Paris, the early departure of his ship for America. His future autobiography was to review these curious, uncalculated, authentic strokes of fortune in a narrative more compelling than any fiction he devised.

The final irony involved the recognition of Kelley's service. In 1930 the Italian government named him a Knight of the Order of St. Maurice and St. Lazarus, the highest honorary rank bestowed on commoners.[44] The bishop quietly accepted the title, conscious of this ultimate twist in the history of the Roman Question: his efforts to free the cloistered papacy had been duly rewarded not by the Vatican, but by the kingdom of Italy!

VIII
British Distress over Germany and Ireland

World War I fashioned Monsignor Kelley into a concerned world citizen. He had witnessed its destructive force when he toured the battlefields of Western Europe and the squalor of post-imperial Vienna. The Roman Question had also awakened in him a taste for diplomacy. "I think that I have one little talent," he wrote later to a Vatican official—"a diplomatic way of interesting important people outside the fold, and making them see the facts."[1] One more assignment in Europe yet awaited him, by far his most complicated international adventure to arise from the war. The British Crown had taken an interest in him as a molder of Catholic opinion in America through his writings and his monthly magazine. It was his success as an author and editor that drew him into two issues troubling London after the war: the disposition of the overseas missions of its former enemies and the future of the Irish people. This opportunity allowed Kelley to be among the first healers of the postbellum world as he strove to reconcile Great Britain with those who had fought her in the trenches or in rebellion.

The first issue—the "German missions"—arose over the right of Catholic missionaries to evangelize freely anywhere in the world.[2] These men and women represented the church as a universal and supranational institution whose base was the Holy See; their work was expected to be conducted independently of politics. In the field, however, there was an inescapable association with the state, especially during the burst of European expansion into Africa and Asia before the turn of the twentieth century. Many missionaries were then seen as agents of a colonial power, sent not only to preach the Gospel but also to assist in westernizing the natives through schools and clinics. Generally, missionaries received protection and some support from the state, a patronage which tended to make them overtly nationalistic. World War I contributed to the ambiguity which confused the missionary's obligations as a delegate of the church and as a subject of the state. It was the first "total" conflict in European history, one that made unprecedented demands upon noncombatants. At home or abroad, few citizens of belligerent nations could remain netural in thought and deed. Nor were they exempt from harassment in the war zones and, if they were Germans, from the penalties of defeat after the war.

Monsignor Kelley was introduced to the problem of the German missions through the Society of the Divine Word. Founded in 1875, this was the first German Catholic missionary congregation ever established, even though Bismarck's *Kulturkampf* had forced it to locate its headquarters at Steyl, Holland. An American branch had been established in 1897 at Techny, Illinois, a suburb of Chicago. In December, 1916, the local provincial alerted Kelley of wartime persecution in Mozambique, then a Portuguese colony in east Africa. Since 1910 Portugal had been governed by strident anticlericals who, once they joined the Allies in World War I, proceeded to imprison German missionaries in Africa on the pretext that they were enemy aliens. Allied propaganda censored reports of such actions; but, as Kelley learned in a rare breach of security, the internment camps inflicted senseless cruelties on these religious. The priests were deliberately kept from acting as chaplains to the brothers and sisters who were thus deprived of the sacraments.

Kelley appealed to Monsignor Alfred E. Burke, then in the Canadian chaplains' corps, telling him that British influence in Portugal could correct these abuses. Otherwise, he warned, stories leaked to the American press would create a bad impression regarding the Allies, a strong argument during these last weeks before America's entry into the war. Though Burke doubtless passed the word along, there is no evidence that it softened the oppression in Africa.[3] What was significant, however, was that Kelley had caught an early distress signal that the war would bring a crisis for the German missionaries.

The fate of the German missions in the British Empire was sealed in several stages beginning at the Paris peace conference, where Kelley was on hand to observe. First of all, the treaty established the legal basis to obliterate every German trace in the old Wilhelmine empire. According to article 119, Germany ceded its overseas colonies in Africa and in the Pacific, and it renounced in articles 156-158 its leasehold in China's province of Shandong (Shantung). Most of these territories were assigned to the trusteeship of the Allied and Associated powers, which administered them as "mandates." Two additional provisions touched directly upon the personnel and property of the German missions. Article 122 empowered authorities in the new mandates to banish, if appropriate, all ex-enemy nationals, including German and Austrian missionaries. In its original version, article 438 likewise ruled that title to mission holdings must be transferred from societies in Germany to local boards of trustees, regardless of faith.[4] These measures threatened the German missionaries with both repatriation and confiscation; their work of more than a generation in Africa and Asia appeared all but annihilated.

Once the general law was made in Paris, the policy to implement it in the British Empire was set soon afterward in London. The second stage, therefore, began when Cardinal Francis Bourne of Westminster notified the Holy See that, along with the French government, the British had decided to exclude German missionaries from all British possessions. Not only would missionaries be repatriated from the mandates but also from the whole British Empire, including India, where German religious congregations were still working. Just as the French were determined in vengeance to drive out all German nationals under their jurisdiction, so also, advised the cardinal grimly, were the British; and it was impossible to change the policy of his government. At the time of Bourne's letter to Rome, this policy was set for an indeterminate period, but the British cabinet later decided that it would be in effect for five years after the Treaty of Versailles, that is, until 1924, subject to renewal, or until Germany would be admitted as a member of the League of Nations. The news of this hopeless situation dismayed the Holy See. In reply, Cardinal Gasparri expressed the personal distress of the pope and acknowledged the inability of the church to replace the German and Austrian missionaries with those of an acceptable nationality.[5]

The next development appeared when the Holy See chose, against Bourne's recommendation, to press for a change of policy; and, in this, Francis Kelley might have played a greater role than he realized. The Chicagoan had arrived in Rome at the time of the Bourne-Gasparri correspondence—in late May of 1919. At this time, as was discussed, he revealed to the papal secretary of state and Archbishop Cerretti his conversation in Paris with

Premier Vittorio Orlando. The hope of settling the Roman Question might have persuaded Gasparri to reconsider diplomatic strategy regarding German missions. Since, according to Kelley, a Vatican emissary was expected in Paris, the cardinal dispatched Cerretti on a dual mission—to begin discussions with Orlando and to protest the repatriation of German missionaries at the peace conference. At any rate, during the journey to the French capital, Kelley examined the notes on the latter subject which had been prepared by Gasparri, and the priest drafted for Cerretti a brief on the subject which his companion used in the meetings ahead.[6] Kelley did not, of course, remain long in Paris; but from across the Atlantic he watched the Vatican diplomat's efforts with great interest.

The preliminary stages—the treaty provision, British policy, and the presence of a Vatican spokesman at the peace conference—were climaxed when Cerretti forced a review of law and policy regarding German mission personnel and properties. The papal diplomat succeeded in winning the following compromise on properties: although these would continue to be held in local trusteeship, the officers in control would be of the same denomination as had been the owners before the war. Catholic mission property, including that of the German societies, was thus acknowledged as belonging to the Holy See. While the pontiff expressed some satisfaction over this concession, his emissary was not so successful in the question of personnel. Before his departure, Cerretti reluctantly accepted the British right to repatriate ex-enemy missionaries.[7]

Cerretti's presence in Paris had also forced the British Foreign Office to make a secret reassessment of its policy of excluding the German missionaries from British possessions.[8] This review examined the evidence regarding whether or not the missionaries had actually collaborated with the enemy either through propaganda or through intrigue; and this crucial investigation merits our attention if we are to understand the issues. The first to report to London on the subject had been the British authorities in China, where German Franciscans and Divine Word Fathers had administered vicariates apostolic in Shandong. The British minister at Beijing (Peking), Sir John Newell Jordan, had long urged the expulsion of all German missionaries. He succeeded, according to the British count, in getting ten deported until the United States forced London to cease repatriation in China. In spite of his hostility toward the Germans, however, Jordan could produce no proof of their collaboration with the enemy; and the Foreign Office concluded: "No evidence has been received from China of enemy missionaries having carried on anti-British propaganda."[9]

In India, however, the British had greater control over the missionaries and considered the repatriation of three communities of German priests: the Jesuits in Bombay, the Savatorians in Assam, and the Capuchins in Bettiah. The viceroy, Baron Chelmsford, reported to London that intercepted correspondence had contained hostile sentiments among the German missionaries under his jurisdiction, but he could provide no proof of actual intrigue. If forthcoming, the expulsion of these German missionaries would therefore be based not on evidence of criminal offenses against the Crown. As he confessed, his grounds would be "largely a matter of probability of inference" since none of the deportees "could be accused of any overt act or known pronouncement of hostility." Seeing in Chelmsford's report no more than a vague indication of hostile feelings attributed to the missionaries, a clerk in the Foreign Office scribbled this comment in frustration: "There is not much in this."[10]

The most complicated report concerned Africa, where both Catholics and Protestants had worked in the former German colonies. The Catholic clergy had clustered in four separate centers. In the former German East Africa, Benedictines administered the vicariate apostolic of Dar-es-Salaam, capital of Tanganyika, where there had been almost continuous military action during World War I. In the west, the Divine Word Fathers worked in Togoland, and the Pallotines in the Cameroons; and both colonies had been occupied by Allied troops. German priests had even joined the Mariannhill missionaries in Natal, a province of the Union of South Africa and part of the British Empire. "The majority of the German Catholic Missions on the whole," began the general survey of African affairs compiled by the British Colonial Office, "have not used their influence among the natives in the direction of anti-Entente propaganda. . . ." Though there were instances to the contrary, these were regarded as minor and harmless. A large number of the members of the German congregations, it was noted further, were nationals of Allied or neutral countries, such as Belgium, Spain, South Africa, and the United States. The Colonial Office also reported that even among the German subjects there was not a unanimous sentiment favoring the enemies of Great Britain. Over forty Alsatians worked in German East Africa, most of whom were pro-Allies.

While the Catholic missionaries had thus remained generally free from politics, their Protestant counterparts were not similarly blameless. The majority of German missionaries in Africa belonged to two Protestant branches—a Lutheran branch, all German, with its center in Bremen; and a Calvinist one, Swiss-German, headquartered in Basel. Though they contributed noble service, British investigators accused them of active engagement in intrigues and anti-Entente propaganda. The evidence against the Basel Mission, though nominally a Swiss organization and therefore neutral, included specimens of German propaganda which the mission had distributed, intercepted letters which were to be forwarded to German agents in China, and statements that over 150 of its members were veterans of the German army. ". . . it is clear beyond all doubt," the British investigation concluded, "that the German missionaries of the Basel and Bremen breed will never be loyal subjects under the new Entente regime, and are thoroughly tarred with the Teutonic spirit, and are bound to work for the restoration of the German rule in Africa."[11]

This survey illustrates how complex the issue was. As of 1919, the evidence of anti-Entente propaganda and intrigue against Catholic missionaries was so thin as to be inadmissible in a court of law. In contrast to the more nationalistic Lutherans, this fact testifies to a general success among Catholics in having steered clear of politics during the war, no matter what pressures had been placed on their consciences. Nevertheless, this difference between the denominations, along with the paucity of proof, was not sufficient to convince the British to make exceptions in favor of missionaries who had given no trouble during the war. Instead, the government adhered to its comprehensive policy of repatriating ex-enemy missionaries, both Catholic and Protestant, even female as well as male, from all territories under British jurisdiction. There were reasons for this harsh reaction. It stemmed, in part, from the vindictive spirit which had grown among the victors after four years of savage combat and which had its most notable impact in the writing of the Treaty of Versailles. The blanket policy of repatriation also saved London from the burden of providing juridical proof of criminal behavior for individuals who were accused of intrigue and subject to expulsion, proof that was difficult to get. It likewise spared the government the charge that, in allowing some to stay and forcing others to leave, it discriminated among religious groups. Great Britain was therefore willing to repatriate all German missionaries and to throw on the church the responsibility of supplying substitutes for their field staffs, whether personnel was immediately available or not. The Crown's intransigence added a staggering burden to the postwar papacy by threatening it with the collapse of its missions in many parts of Africa and Asia.

* * * * * * * * * *

Monsignor Kelley's reentry into the issue originated from British concern over Catholic attitudes in America as they related to two matters. The first was Britain's postwar policy toward Ireland. Irish-Americans had been disappointed during World War I when the establishment of Irish self-government, known as Home Rule, had to be postponed. Their resentment was about to explode after the war, when the government of David Lloyd George attempted to suppress an uprising in Ireland through terror; and this policy led to what was called the Anglo-Irish War. A news specialist in the Foreign Office was alarmed at how the Irish policy had virtually turned the leadership of Catholic America into anglophobes. ". . . the Catholic Press Association is notoriously anti-British," he noted, "and has gone over absolutely to the Irish Republican propaganda in the United States. The entire Hierarchy is, with the exceptions of Cardinal Gibbons and the Bishop of Wheeling [Patrick J. Donahue], strongly anti-British."[12]

The second issue involving British concern over Catholic sentiment in America arose within a year of the Paris peace conference when numbers of German missionaries were repatriated from British and French territories. At first, London shared the criticism in America over this policy with Paris. In early 1920, two diocesan directors of mission-aid societies notified their superiors that no money would be sent to France unless the German missions were restored. At the same time, the Jesuit weekly, *America,* joined the chorus in a blistering editorial, "The Crime of the Powers." This article aroused another news specialist in the Foreign Office, who recommended to his superior: "In such an influential paper, I submit, this is dangerous and worth dealing with."[13] A final dimension was added to the protest in a booklet published by the Divine Word Fathers near Chicago and entitled, *An Appeal to the Catholics of the World to Save the German Foreign Missions.* In listing instances of internment, deportation, confiscation, and violations of international law, the unnamed author indicted the British, not the French, as the chief culprit for these crimes. This twist in the defense of the German missions was justified, he argued, because there were more ex-enemy missionaries under British authority—in Africa, Egypt, India, Sri Lanka, and the south Pacific islands—than under any of its Allies. The only name to appear in this anonymous booklet was that of Francis C. Kelley. He had added his imprimatur to the argument in a foreword which he later admitted was "nasty" and which caught the eye of a British expert on American attitudes, Robert Wilberforce.[14]

A Catholic careerist in the British foreign service, Wilberforce had met Kelley in Rome in April, 1919, while the former was serving in his first assignment as temporary secretary to the British minister to the Holy See. The Englishman's charm instantly touched Kelley, who also noted certain cultivated ploys of the professional diplomat, especially what the Islander labeled "a diplomatic deafness." At times, Wilberforce appeared hard-of-hearing, cleverly cupping his hands about an ear when he wanted to talk and not apologize for interrupting others. "I think his hearing, however," Kelley noted in a journal, "is rather good when he wants to hear." The young diplomat's specialty was public opinion. Soon after his meeting with Kelley, he was appointed to the British Library of Information in New York City from which, for thirty-two years, he reported on shifts in Catholic sentiment in America.[15]

In spite of this natural affinity between Wilberforce and Kelley, the latter's reputation was mixed in London. The Foreign Office credited him with authority as a writer and editor, and it was aware of his influence in the Republican Party. He was also known as anti-British because of a stream of editorials in which he had denounced British policy in Ireland. London noted, too, his friendship with the unpredictable Monsignor Alfred E. Burke, whose career as a Canadian chaplain had ended with a resignation so abrupt that Kelley had been forced in 1918 to give him a home in Chicago. Worse yet, Kelley was a man whose honesty had been questioned. En route to Paris in early 1919, he had introduced himself at the Foreign Office as the official liaison of the exiled Mexican hierarchy at the peace conference. Upon further inquiry in America, the department discovered that he had exceeded his instructions, a practice that was to be repeated later in his dealings with the British. Technically, the refugee bishops had delegated him to represent them only at the Holy See and not in Paris. According to the acting British chargé d-'affaires in Washington, good sources had thus described the monsignor as "unreliable and slippery."[16] Nevertheless, Kelley was too important to be ignored; his endorsement of the claim that the British were destroying Catholic missions in its empire could undermine American attitudes toward Britain, especially at a moment when its Irish policy already drew enormous criticism. At Wilberforce's suggestion, the priest was invited to London in March of 1920.

British strategy was not to reopen the question of the German missions but to silence the pen of a dangerous critic. No detail was spared in an effort to soften Monsignor Kelley's attitude. The genial Wilberforce was to escort him to England. At the government's expense, he was allowed to make any travel arrangements and to bring Father Thomas V. Shannon as his secretary. In the meantime, the Foreign Office prevailed upon Cardinal Bourne to offer hospitality to the visitor. The leader of the English hierarchy enjoyed the confidence of the government. A reliable British subject, he had steadfastly avoided an endorsement of Irish independence during the Anglo-Irish War, even at the risk of offending large numbers of faithful in his archdiocese. It was therefore expected that in the cardinal's household, Kelley would meet churchmen unabashedly loyal to the Crown. At first, Bourne strongly declined to be involved in this matter; but, much against his will, he consented to have the Chicagoan as a guest in his home.[17]

Despite the cordial preliminaries, however, the invitation

did not in itself define Kelley's exact role in London. When he discussed it with Archbishop Mundelein, the latter insisted upon direct authorization from the Holy See. Neither of them knew if the Vatican was exploring this question along regular diplomatic channels; neither knew if Rome had special instructions or objections to private, unofficial conversations between an American priest and members of the British government. Mundelein's intervention upset the travel preparations and irritated Wilberforce. In reporting to London, he described the prelate's action as an attempt to be a "persona grata at the Vatican at the present time." According to the Britisher, Mundelein was "afraid of [Cardinal] O'Connell, who has just sailed for Rome." In any case, it was wise counsel. Cardinal Gasparri consulted with the pope and cabled his approval. After further correspondence with Archbishop Cerretti, Kelley better understood his credentials: he did not represent the Holy See but went simply as a private consultant on Catholic public opinion in the United States as it related to the German missions and perhaps even to the Irish question.[18]

Extraordinary complications, in fact, offered little hope of relieving the German missions. First of all, they were located in a variety of jurisdictions in the British Empire—in traditional colonies where London had control, in self-governing dominions where local government prevailed, and in former German colonies and sensitive battle zones where British rule was being introduced. In addition, the war had fueled strong movements for independence, particularly in Ireland, Egypt, and India; these powerful forces would entangle themselves in any negotiations in London. Perhaps the greatest complication of all was Kelley's practice of interpreting his instructions liberally. Invited only as an expert on American attitudes, he perceived himself as more than a font of information; from the beginning, he planned to serve as an advocate for the missions. Armed thus with no more than Rome's quiet blessing, he left for England on June 26, 1920, with the view, as he confided to a friend, that as "diplomacy seems to have failed us this time, so I am going to try persuasion."[19]

Monsignor Kelley's initial contact with the British government extended over a harried two-month interval that took him all over Europe. His movements extended from early July through mid-September, 1920, and brought him to London, Holland, Germany, Vienna, and Rome—a hectic tour of duty that might be divided into four stages. The first consisted of conversations at the Foreign Office. As planned by the government, the briefing for this occurred during Kelley's sojourn with Cardinal Bourne. As his household guest, Kelley made two discoveries. First, the British had cultivated what he termed "a fear of everything Teutonic," which continued undiminished after the armistice. The postwar government of David Lloyd George had little control over these national jitters. The prime minister was forced to rule through a frail coalition of diverse factions; and, as Kelley ascertained further, this situation had made concessions to former war enemies politically impossible. Bourne's auxiliary bishop, Emmanuel Bidwell, admitted that the government was too sensitive to partisan tremors at home; but, he added, these domestic pressures were strong enough to make the cabinet extremely reluctant to relax its protective measures against exenemy nationals. Second, Kelley learned that an arrangement was evolving regarding the future of the German missions. The Vatican and London, it was hoped, would deputize the cardinal to work out a system whereby the departing Germans might be gradually replaced in the empire. Accordingly, English missionaries were to be allowed to go directly into the mission districts. Since their numbers were so small, Bourne was also to be allowed to give guarantees of good conduct for missionaries who were nationals of Allied, Associated, and neutral countries.[20] This arrangement would not resolve the crisis, but it offered relief to the stricken areas. These conversations within the cardinal's residence succeeded in disposing the visitor to approach the Foreign

Office in a conciliatory mood. The government's caution in revising its policy regarding the German missions had, Kelley discovered, won the sympathy of the Catholic leadership in England.

After this preparation, the Chicago priest proceeded to the Foreign Office, where he met with the assistant undersecretary, Sir William George Tyrrell, an Irish Catholic who was regarded, according to author Shane Leslie, as the "underground power" in the department. The meeting was notable on two counts. First, Tyrrell remarked that his government was sensitive to American sentiment, especially over its Irish policy. At this moment, it greatly feared a protest of the United States hierarchy against British expatriation of German missionaries, an action that would contribute to the anglophobia already growing in America over British policy toward Ireland. In uniting the two issues, Tyrrell led Kelley to see, astutely, that the attitude of the American bishops was the principal weapon in his arsenal for the German missions. Second, shortly after his visit with the undersecretary, the Foreign Office indicated a willingness to reopen the mission question—a willingness which was not necessarily shared by the departments actually governing the mission areas—when it asked Kelley to prepare a protocol that might serve as a basis for negotiations.[21] Though this surprise invitation revived his hopes, it did not entirely lessen his caution in dealing with professionals who were predictably cordial and cooperative. "These people are polite and nice speaking," he reported to Mundelein, "but that means nothing. They are always so." It was not justice, the priest sensed, but politics that had brought him to London. There was no chance to restore the German missions as they had been before World War I. Major obstacles loomed ahead, and his mission would lead him deeply into the labyrinth of British bureaucracy, notably to the Indian and Colonial Offices, which tripled the normal work.[22]

In a week his protocol was ready, an unofficial ten-page document which displayed Kelley's considerable skills in bargaining. Its nucleus was a practical proposal as to how Great Britain could relax the provisions of the Treaty of Versailles without endangering security in the empire. The new American Board of Catholic Missions, or ABCM, would act as a guarantor of the German missions under British authority. This body would take the responsibility of assigning missionaries of any nationality as individuals and guaranteeing their conduct in the field. No German missionary, it would be understood, could be named superior; and ex-enemy nationals would be replaced as soon as Great Britain and America could supply the manpower. This formula, argued Kelley, would save the missions and furnish the government with assurances that a competent authority would safeguard British interests. No doubt, too, public opinion on both sides of the Atlantic would hail such a generous concession from London.[23]

Monsignor Kelley could have cited two more advantages in his proposal. It paralleled the system of trusteeship by which the Paris peace conference had divided the German and Turkish empires among the victors. In a sense, the German missions would become a "mandate" of the ABCM, which would be accountable to the British Crown, in much the same way as the ex-enemy territories had been "mandated" to Allied and Associated powers in the name of the League of Nations. Kelley's idea also offered to the British a leverage whereby it could influence American Catholic attitudes through the ABCM, a precious dividend during the days of Irish agitation. In any case, the protocol was a stunning performance. Not only was the Foreign Office satisfied, but it volunteered to urge Kelley's formula at the India and Colonial Offices. There was an unexpected final touch to this success. Colonel House, Wilson's long-time adviser, was visiting London at this time and invited Kelley for a chat. His many years as a private diplomat and on the peace commission in Paris had acquainted him with all of Lloyd George's cabinet, and he promised, if necessary, to press this issue at the ministerial level.[24]

After the ice had melted in the Foreign Office, Kelley next left London for a tour on the continent to gather data on the missions, and he discovered an emergency in India. A strong nationalist movement was growing there since the turn of the century. After the war had temporarily united all factions behind the Crown, an irrepressible champion of anticolonialism arose, Mohandas Gandhi, who in 1919 had led the first of many passive-resistance campaigns against British rule. The Government of India was forced to control carefully the foreign population of this seething subcontinent, including missionaries. By January, 1920, it therefore ruled that former enemy aliens would be expelled permanently or for a period of five years after the Versailles Treaty.[25] This was sufficient to efface German religious personnel in India; but, as Kelley learned even before his arrival in London, other less visible political actions had prevented their replacement with acceptable nationals. Several Jesuits in New York, who had been assigned to succeed their German colleagues in Bombay, had been awaiting their visas since July, 1919. For more than a year, their travel permits were not forthcoming from London, a sign that, according to Kelley, these Americans too were unwelcome.[26]

His tour in the summer of 1920 brought him to Steyl in Holland, as well as to Bonn, Germany, where a number of deportees had gathered. The two most resourceful authorities were Frederick Schwager, S.V.D., secretary general of the Conference of the Superiors of Germany, who was known to be the leading expert on the question; and Christopher Becker, S.D.S., the exiled prefect apostolic of Assam in northeast India. Kelley's protocol with the Foreign Office was scrupulously examined, and Becker suggested minor modifications. The latter also supplied rich notes on his tenure in Assam, emphasizing uninterrupted service in behalf of the British Crown. In his district, he was responsible for English schools for Europeans and natives; and several provincial reports had lauded his contribution as an educator. At the beginning of the war, the German-born prefect had also ordered his missionaries not to discuss politics with the natives, an action which, Becker argued, proved his loyalty. But India was not the only part of the British Empire expatriating German religious. Later, when Kelley arrived back in England, Becker notified him further that Bishop Thomas Spreiter, O.S.B., vicar apostolic of Dar-es-Salaam in former German East Africa, was under final orders to leave the mission, along with his entire staff.[27] Kelley's experts had not spared the feelings of their American advocate, having schooled him thoroughly in their crises throughout the British Empire and having prepared him as their only hope in London. "You are the very man to speak to the Lords of England," Becker's religious superior told Kelley, "and we hope it will not be in vanum."[28]

The Germans provided only a fraction of what Kelley required; he needed directions from the Holy See. The next phase of his tour therefore began in August, 1920, when he reported his progress in the Vatican.[29] The highest levels in the curia—Benedict XV, Gasparri, and Cerretti—were pleased with the Islander's work in London, especially with the protocol drafted for the Foreign Office. His rounds in the Eternal City also included a meeting with Monsignor Camillo Laurenti, secretary of Propaganda, who added his approval. Finally, the visitor was given—for the first time—a diplomatic rank, when he was told to return to London with the authority to represent the Holy See. While Cardinal Bourne remained the official Vatican liaison with the British government, the priest was deputized to work as his associate on this question to pursue the lines of the protocol. The ABCM was thereby approved as the guarantor of the German missionaries working in British territory, and the Holy See was willing to give the additional pledge of assigning only British or American administrators to these missions.[30]

The papal secretary of state thus made extraordinary concessions regarding missionary appointments, and Kelley's new rank indicated Rome's hope of stopping the repatriation of German missionaries. The rest of August was then spent in shaping this loose protocol with the Foreign Office into a precise "Memorandum," which would serve as the basis of discussion with the India and Colonial Offices. Even the British minister to the Holy See, Count John de Salis, was "enthusiastic" over the prospects, Kelley whimsically reported to Mundelein, "as far as an Englishman can work himself into that condition." But the priest's soaring morale was tempered by thoughts of the twists and turns to come within the British bureaucracy. "I am half sorry that they are making the Mission official," he told the archbishop; "it makes it harder to fall. I prefer to drop on the cushion of nonentity, rather than on the sword of officialdom."[31] With this mixture of trust and fear, the visitor returned to London at the beginning of September, 1920, the cycle of his first diplomatic tour almost completed.

The last stage consisted of lengthy discussions with the India Office, the department which reviewed legislation and policy for the subcontinent. The first important meeting took place on September 7, lasting over an hour, in which lower officials yielded tentatively to Kelley's three demands. India would first stop expulsions, particularly those of 150 Loretto Sisters who, it was reported, were stationed in Ahmednagar, near Bombay. Next, the American Jesuits assigned to Bombay would receive their visas. Finally, the ABCM would have the right to give guarantees for German missionaries working in India. This formal interview, however, introduced to Kelley the two trials that accompany serious diplomatic negotiations. First, he was compelled to wait patiently for results. While he had won concessions at this level, they had yet to go to the secretary of state for India, who had the right to reject them; and, after him, to the viceroy in India, who also could veto them. Secondly, he was forced to make a significant trade. In return for his meagre success thus far, the priest agreed to leave for home and to notify the American bishops of his progress. In the most reluctant decision of his life, Kelley also promised to dissuade the hierarchy from issuing at their annual meeting a resolution of sympathy for Irish or Indian nationalism. As a sign of good faith, the India Office approved visas for the American Jesuits and temporarily suspended the expatriation of the Loretto sisters until January 1, 1921, when Kelley would be back in London to resume discussions. The Colonial Office followed this lead, notifying the colonies and protectorates under its jurisdiction—with the exception of the former German colonies—that the further expatriation of Catholic nuns would be suspended for the rest of the year.[32]

This understanding climaxed Kelley's first diplomatic tour. His skill and persistence had won several advantages. He had been accepted in London—and eventually at the Vatican—as an emissary. He had succeeded, further, in reopening the question of the German missions and had awakened the possibilities of concessions toward the defeated enemy only a year after the peace conference had branded them as criminally responsible for the war. His proposals would have led to the first truly "postwar" act of the twentieth century, a pioneering move toward international reconciliation after the bloodshed. The basis of the plan was the return of the missionaries as individuals, not in full communities. Each would have to secure a guarantee from Cardinal Bourne or the ABCM, and agree to be subject to British or American superiors.[33] The mechanism was awkward but, if approved in London and Delhi, it would have salvaged these flourishing stations abroad. It demonstrated, too, that the papal secretariat of state would cooperate, if not lead, in the restoration of Europe. If the victors would soften some harsh clauses of the Treaty of Versailles, the papacy would relax its historic claim of the right to send evangelists anywhere in the world without secular interference. The Vatican was quite familiar with the dangers of setting a precedent—that is, of permanently weakening that claim through conceding certain guarantees. But, as Kelley was to learn, compromises that the secretariat was willing to make were not always acceptable to other congregations in the Roman Curia, especially Propaganda, when the matter concerned the foreign-missions.

His progress notwithstanding, Kelley sparred with an adroit officialdom in London. To begin with, his success was far from complete. Concessions thus far were temporary and narrow. Expatriation ceased only for four months; and while this accommodation covered German sisters in India and some colonies, it applied neither to male religious nor in the ex-enemy territories where the largest numbers of German missionaries had concentrated. When, moreover, the American Jesuits were, after a lengthy delay, offered their visas to Bombay, they had decided instead to accept a commitment in the Philippine Islands. The price for these damaged goods was exorbitant. It was Kelley's promise to discourage the American hierarchy from openly endorsing freedom for Ireland or India, a supremely risky obligation. But the greatest payment exacted in London consisted of the one which he had completely failed to notice: the subtle transformation of Kelley's values, engineered by the British team, ecclesiastical and civic. The Foreign Office noted a different man, a convert, returning to America. "He was a most bitter anti-British [critic]," observed a clerk;

> but thanks to his reception here, to Cardinal Bourne's handling of him and to the concessions made by the India Office, he has gone back to America much changed in his outlook, and we ought to get the benefit in Catholic episcopal discouragement of extreme Irish and Indian propaganda in the U.S., where these two are at present in alliance. He has promised to do his best in these directions.[34]

This was the balance sheet, when Monsignor Kelley sailed for home in September of 1920—"returning . . . ," observed another clerk in the Foreign Office, "in a very good frame of mind." The cabin on the ship homeward bound was splendid, the voyage pleasant, except for the fact that his genial companion Wilberforce was sick for three days. The British had been astute traders, and perhaps they posted a slight net gain in Kelley's admission that he had fallen into a bit of their culture, the "tea habit."[35]

* * * * * * * * * *

Francis Kelley returned to America faced with two herculean tasks: he had to mute Catholic criticism of Great Britain and to strengthen sympathy for the German missions from within the British Empire. First, he promptly set about to fulfill his pledge to meet with the bishops at their annual meeting on September 22, 1920. Cerretti requested Cardinal Gibbons to invite the Chicagoan to address the assembly on his work in London; but, at Kelley's suggestion, both prelates agreed that a letter would do. In either case, it was irregular for a priest to make recommendations to the hierarchy in a speech or writing. As he explained his goal to Cerretti, Kelley would not discourage the bishops from passing a resolution censuring the British repatriation of German missionaries but would simply ask them not to publish it until his work in London was concluded.[36] The Islander's letter was drafted in a great hurry, finished only a few minutes before Mundelein took it with him to Washington, where the old cardinal of Baltimore read it to the hierarchy.

At the bishops' meeting, Kelley engaged in a strategy that bordered on deception—all in behalf of the German missions; and his behavior would perhaps confirm the judgment of those who had seen him as "unreliable and slippery." First, in the letter he exceeded his original intention when he urged that any resolution condemning British policy on the missions should be "tabled."[37] This request broke his promise to Cerretti; the priest, it had been understood, was to ask that the publication of such a resolution be merely postponed. Next, his activity in the nation's capital was instrumental in killing the resolution for Irish independence, an accomplishment which betrayed his known sentiments on this issue and one which he disavowed for the rest of his life.

His vigilant companion, Robert Wilberforce, tracked his movements during the critical hours before the meeting. The champion for the anti-British resolution, it was learned, was Bishop Michael J. Gallagher of Detroit, who served as president of the Irish Self-Determination League. Though he had the majority of bishops behind him, his opposition numbered such influential leaders as Cardinal Gibbons and Archbishop Dennis Dougherty, both of whom insisted that political questions be excluded from the bishops' deliberations. "Then Kelley arrived on the spot," Wilberforce reported to the Foreign Office, "and, himself a Celt, leaped into the breach, mobilising the German bishops to the slogan of the Foreign Missions and the success of his work in London, and routed the massed forces of Gallagher."[38] In the end, the Gibbons-Dougherty team was joined by Archbishops Mundelein, Henry Moeller of Cincinnati, and Patrick J. Hayes of New York; and the resolution was defeated.[39]

Kelley's antics had actually amused Wilberforce, who some days later prepared for William Tyrrell a more detailed narrative of the Islander's contribution. "I was determined not to let him out of my sight until the work had been done," Wilberforce began:

> . . . I accompanied him to the Apostolic Delegate, brought him back to luncheon at the Embassy and motored up to [Catholic] University with him afterwards. There we remained until after dark, meeting a great many of the bishops. I then went back to dinner at the Embassy arranging to meet Kelley at the Shoreham Hotel after dinner. He did not arrive until nearly 11 o'clock, sank into a chair in a great state of depression and informed me in a tragic tone that he had lost all his friends and after all there was no chance of stopping the Irish resolution. I wished that I

> had brought some whiskey from the Embassy to revive his spirits. We had to content ourselves with iced water and after a time when he was calmer I told him that the work for the missions which he had done in London would be futile if an Irish resolution was passed. Gallagher had been canvassing Bishops wildly, followed closely by Kelley canvassing them also, in the course of which some rather uncomplimentary things were said. I told Kelley it was essential he should win, otherwise people in London would argue, "Kelley is not the man we took him for." The result was the next morning he again joined the fray and won his point.
>
> Last time I saw him he was really very cheerful again although he informed me he had lost two of his greatest friends as a result. It didn't seem to affect him much.[40]

Wilberforce's humor notwithstanding, Monsignor Kelley had kept faith with the bureaucrats across the Atlantic. Reports from the United States had made it "evident," according to the Foreign Office, "that he carried out his side of the bargain at any rate to an important extent."[41] Nevertheless, he had earned the enmity of Irish nationalists and was told that he had been put under surveillance by their most notable leader, Eamon de Valera, who at this time was collecting funds in America. Until his death, Kelley described his behavior as no more than a few innocent conversations prior to the bishops' meeting. When he was repeatedly accused of having been a leading factor in preventing the Irish resolution, he resigned himself to serving as a life-time "goat" for Gibbons and his allies.[42]

Hushing anglophobia within the hierarchy was but a part of Kelley's general strategy: he sought also to temper public remarks of leading Irish-Americans. This phase evoked tactics that were as questionable as those he had used with the bishops. One spokesman was Daniel F. Cohalan, as associate justice of the New York Supreme Court, who headed a fund-raising organization known as the Friends of Irish Freedom. The British suspected that, although an American citizen, he had conspired with Germany during World War I in the cause of Irish independence; and the Crown was assembling a White Paper that would accuse him of treason. Though carefully watched from London, his postwar movements puzzled the Foreign Office, especially when he had broken openly with de Valera and in several public talks had prophesied that war was inevitable between the United States and Great Britain.[43]

On October 19, 1920, Kelley arranged an interview with the justice. Not only did the priest try to mellow this Irish patriot but, more importantly, he also supplied the British with intelligence regarding Cohalan's strategy. First, Kelley detailed for Wilberforce the reasoning behind the prediction of an Atlantic war. Cohalan "cited history showing how England was dependent upon sea power for her life," Wilberforce reported to London,

> how one by one she had destroyed the countries who had arisen to challenge this power, Spain, Holland, France and lastly Germany. The United States, said Cohalan bitterly, helped England to destroy this last rival. Before long, the time of the United States must come and she must fight to win the freedom of the seas.

Kelley also furnished Wilberforce two reasons for Cohalan's desertion of de Valera. The first concerned the management of fund-raising in the United States. ". . . de Valera wanted Americans to be guided by [an] Irishman as to how they conduct the Irish campaign here," Wilberforce learned; "[Cohalan] wanted to act as an American not as a colonial Irishman." Second, the New Yorker questioned the commitment of the two leading Sinn Feiners to an Irish republic. According to Cohalan, both de Valera and his lieutenant, Arthur Griffith, "would compromise with the British Government for autonomy within the Empire." Finally, Kelley provided the reason why nothing less than total separation suited Cohalan:

> . . . in the event of this [Anglo-American] war, of which he is sure, he would have to fight as an American against England and he hoped there would be an independent Ireland, which could remain neutral, so that he would not have to fight against his kith and kin.

Before their meeting ended, the justice was critical of Kelley's behavior before the meeting of the bishops a month earlier. "Incidentally," Wilberforce's commentary concluded, "Cohalan accused him of stopping the Irish resolution [in Washington], which K. denied by evasions."[44]

Kelley's first objective during the recess had been negative, to gag a condemnation of British policy in Ireland; but his second was the positive task of gathering endorsements for the German missions from notable subjects of the British Crown. This project began by enlisting the support of the hierarchy of Britain's premier dominion, Canada. While London might discount American views, he confided to Archbishop Cerretti, "it is very difficult for them to ignore the opinion in their most important colony."[45]

Archbishop Neil McNeil of Toronto responded with exceptional energy. His own war record included personal contributions exceeding $6,000, along with his purchase of bonds, work on recruiting committees, and patriotic statements in speeches and writings. One Toronto parish had sent nearly 700 men to the front, the vast majority having volunteered. As a proven loyal subject, he could not see the justification of this policy of repatriation in peacetime. If London should not adjust its attitude, as he warned in his response to Kelley, then "I shall consider myself free to work as hard in defence of our Catholic Missions as I did in defence of the British Empire during the war." The archbishop expected some twenty bishops to attend his silver jubilee and invited Kelley to address his guests in the hope of getting a signed petition from the Canadian hierarchy. In addition, McNeil offered a unique theory regarding British mulishness over the German missions. London, he suspected, wanted to demonstrate what harm it could inflict upon the church if the latter did not cooperate in the Irish question, a comment that once again tied the two issues together.[46] The German missions had thus become hostages of the Crown—perhaps an unfair judgment but a tempting one. The Islander arrived too late to participate in the jubilee, but he attended a dinner at the seminary where he met a few bishops. The Canadian hierarchy had already decided to have McNeil write a joint protest in their name. Individual episcopal statements, meanwhile, continued to come into Chicago, all eighteen signatories making the basic demand that the Crown restore the prewar liberties of German missionaries.[47]

The solicitations did not stop with the Canadians. Kelley called on another British notable, the ambassador in Washington, Sir Auckland Geddes, who seemed an easy convert to Kelley's mission. In mid-October, 1920, after a relaxed two-hour conversation with the priest, the diplomat committed himself to a strong letter. Generous concessions to the German missionaries, he agreed, would mellow American thinking in the general interests of the British government; and Kelley offered to send suggestions for the text of the ambassador's letter. The main difficulty, the priest suggested, was the inability of missionary congregations in the victor nations to replace the Germans. None had the manpower, including France with its long tradition in the overseas missions; and Kelley cited an example. When the war-weary French occupied Togoland in west Africa, they could supply no more than five priests to replace the forty Germans who were expelled. This lack of personnel continued to cripple missions not only in Africa but also in India.[48]

The interview at the embassy was instrumental in securing more than the ambassador's recommendation. Evidently, Geddes encouraged his visitor to devise a formula to be presented on his return to London. One reason for the hesitancy in the India Office, Kelley had been told, was that, while it had little complaint regarding Catholic missionaries, it did not welcome a return of German Moravians and Lutherans, whose wartime behavior had disturbed the government. Delhi, however, felt compelled to exclude all ex-enemy missionaries because the reinstatement of only Catholics would raise charges in England of religious discrimination.[49]

In this situation, Kelley developed a scheme based on the capacity of personnel replacement. His premise was that Protestant congregations could more readily substitute British and Americans for their German colleagues, whereas at this stage it was virtually impossible for Catholics to do so. He thus evolved a statement of exceptions to the government's policy—a complicated but clever formula which applied to all Christian bodies but one which also assured the return of German Catholics as individuals. Accordingly, German missionaries were to work only in British territory where they could not be replaced—provided that the superior would be British or American, that the religious congregations had a residence in the British Empire or America, and that the missionaries obtained guarantees from authorities recognized by the British government. As intricate as it was, Kelley's formula ingeniously served his and the government's ends. "It applies," he told a friend at the Foreign Office, "only in those cases where missionaries cannot be found to save a mission from grave injury or destruction. Everyone understands that it is far more important to save the missions than to keep out enemy nationals."[50] Without overt discrimination, it would virtually exclude the unwelcome German Protestants, who had a history of political partisanship and who could be more easily replaced by Anglo-Saxons than their Catholic counterparts could be. Likewise, the German Catholics would retain their missions as long as there was no British or American personnel to staff them.

Monsignor Kelley had used the recess fully. Partly through his efforts, the American bishops had not embarrassed the British government with condemnations of its policy on the German missions or on Ireland. Moreover, impeccable Britishers in North America had endorsed his cause. He had himself fashioned a formula that would save the German missions and calm British fears of readmitting undesirables to the politically volcanic areas in the empire. That winter, the noble *Aquitania* carried the tired priest back to England, taking him close to London around December 20, 1920. While the corridors of power would be deserted in the capital until after New Year's Day, he saw in this lull one advantage: "It won't hurt me to get a glimpse of an English Christmas."[51]

* * * * * * * * *

Francis Kelley's diplomatic fortunes had peaked in America. What remained were wintry visits to two European capitals where the professionals were to frustrate his early gains.

London was the first stop, where he planned final meetings at the India and Colonial Offices. The objective remained twofold: to prevent further deportations and to readmit the banished Germans into the empire. As expected, the Foreign Office was very supportive, offering to hold members of Lloyd George's cabinet in reserve. It first arranged an interview at the India Office with permanent undersecretary Sir Frederick William Duke, a veteran of the Indian civil service. Duke's absence from London, however, compelled Kelley to deal with two top assistants, Sir Malcolm Seton and Sir Arthur Hirtzel.[52] Though these were willing to extend the moratorium on expulsions only into the spring, Kelley succeeded in getting an agreement to an indefinite suspension of the deportations, provided that the viceroy and his executive council, known as the "Government of India," approved.

Telegrams were dispatched to the winter capital at Delhi, the first of a series of local consultations that would idle the

American priest. These delays complicated his plans to leave next for Rome, and the inactivity was unbearable. ". . . I should like to see the sun again," he confided to Cerretti, "for the weather is beastly in London, and very depressing when one has nothing to do but sit around and wait." In Chicago, Father Ledvina received much the same message of impatience. "I cannot move out of London," wrote Kelley,

> waiting for telegrams from India, and the principal one is ten days overdue. I cannot get at the bottom of the reasons for these delays. Everybody here seems perfectly willing, but there are so many governments within the Government that it is almost hopeless to get things done in anything like decent time.

The waiting eased a bit when Kelley was given an interview with the secretary of state for India. Edwin Samuel Montagu was more than cordial: he endorsed the visitor's ideas, adding that if Delhi objected, he would stand by Kelley and work to smooth out the problems.[53] On January 14, 1921, the Government of India cabled its agreement to stop all expatriations. When Kelley was called to the India Office to receive the offical word, Cardinal Bourne happily notified the missionary leaders of this victory, commenting further: "this is the first fortress captured."[54] It would also be Kelley's last.

The second objective—the readmission of the German missionaries—was far more problematic than the simple stopping of the deportations. Monsignor Kelley's formula received warm approval in London, According to Bourne, it served the interests of both empire and missions. Hirtzel personally redrafted it as an "addendum" to the policy governing the admission of former enemy aliens into India, and mailed it to Delhi. In the interest of time, Kelley had urged that it be cabled, but the assistant undersecretary declined firmly, explaining that the formula could not be properly compressed into a telegram. The Government of

India would have to study the complete text and would no doubt consult local authorities—all of which would take time, from six weeks to three months.[55]

Once London was won, Kelley did what he could to encourage a favorable reception in India. The Vatican, he told Cerretti, should instruct Catholic leaders there to pressure officials, and Kelley himself wrote to the archbishop of Bombay. The visitor was then given a special opportunity to promote his cause. The viceroy, Baron Chelmsford, was known to be a difficult man, having been once described to Kelley as an "old woman." Since his term was about to expire, there was little chance that he would bind his successor to a new policy, such as the readmission of German missionaries. The former Lord Chief Justice, Lord Reading, was about to replace Chelmsford in India; and Kelley had met him when he had served as ambassador in Washington. With Tyrrell's help, the Chicagoan had two meetings with Reading, one at the latter's home and the other at the India Office, where Kelley managed to win a major convert to his formula. Everything would be done, Reading promised, to promote its adoption because the work of the missions must go on unfettered. The viceroy-designate expected to take up residence first in the summer capital at Simla, where, he added, he would be pleased to receive the local Catholic archbishop.[56]

No more could be accomplished in behalf of the German missions located in India. Monsignor Kelley had won sympathy and commitments in both England and on the subcontinent, but there remained the question of the British colonies, a much more taxing issue. The Colonial Office had adamantly avoided an interview with the visitor until the India Office had settled upon a policy. On the day that Kelley's formula was posted to Delhi, he was given his first—and only—conference with Sir Herbert J. Read, assistant undersecretary at the Colonial Office, who was joined by officials in charge of the East African and American desks. Here, the resistance to Kelley's proposal was far more pronounced, and the bargaining tougher. To begin with, the office exercised no jurisdiction in several major territories overseas. Kelley made this discovery, when he presented complaints of deportations in the former Bismarck Archipelago, a group of islands in the southwest Pacific which had been mandated to Australia. Since, he was told, Australia had self-government since 1901, the Colonial Office disavowed any authority over its policy of repatriation.[57]

Furthermore, in those possessions where the Colonial Office had authority, the clerks were reluctant to give worthwhile concessions. Their agreement to end expulsions in the colonies was an empty gesture because the German missionaries had already been driven away. Therefore, the key issue was the readmission of these exiles. The Colonial Office accepted Kelley's formula—except in those areas of Africa where combat had taken place. Catholic missionaries, the Colonial Office charged without offering proof, had collaborated in these war zones, stirring up the natives and promising that they "would be back." Though, according to Read, they had done no more than what British missionaries would have under similar circumstances, he and his associates remained fixed in their opposition to the opening of the mandated colonies. German missionaries were thus barred from the principal African colonies of the Wilhelmine empire: Togoland and Cameroons on the Gulf of Guinea in the west, and Tanganyika along the Indian Ocean in the east. These areas, the British explained, were extremely vulnerable, with several million natives supervised by only a handful of British garrisons. When Kelley brought this news to the Foreign Office, his friends there were astonished, but, as he was told, the final decision rested not with the clerks but with the colonial secretary, Viscount Milner. This little comfort was short-lived, however, because Milner shortly adopted the position of his subordinates.[58]

This frustrating interview at the Colonial Office ended Monsignor Kelley's work in London. Insofar as word was yet to come from India and the Colonial Office remained determined to bar Germans from recent combat zones in Africa, he promptly departed for Rome, the second European capital in this final diplomatic shuttle, where he reported the latest results. To his astonishment, he discovered that not everyone was pleased with his performance—the least of all, the officials of Propaganda. This department, which supervised the church's missions, not only faulted his work in London but shortly had him defending it. The ecclesiastic who confronted him with the congregation's disappointment was its secretary, Monsignor Camillo Laurenti. Soon after his arrival in the Eternal City, Kelley was told that he had earned too little for the missions and too much credit for himself. The only certain results from his lengthy presence in England consisted in saving 150 Loretto Sisters from being deported from Ahmednagar and in producing a complicated formula of readmitting those who had been exiled. "Monsignor Laurenti painfully told me that I had gotten practically nothing," he reported to Cardinal Bourne. "He rather swept aside all idea that I had been a profitable servant, though he did it rather graciously. But he, or someone else at Propaganda, had complained even to the Pope that there was too much publicity."

Since his gains were so meagre, Kelley added, the congregation was about to adopt another arrangement. The Germans would be assigned to other fields and be asked to yield their missions to nationals acceptable to the victor powers that controlled the mandated territories. "It is bad enough wringing concessions out of the English," he commented tartly to Archbishops under Mundelein and Moeller of Cincinnati,

> but it is terribly distressing to find that in some quarters there is no desire to take advantage of them, and there is serious danger that the Germans will lose all that they have built up after years of sacrifice and men and money. The missions were so well built up that I am afraid others covet them.[59]

In Kelley's tired eyes, Propaganda's solution was foolish and would destroy three decades of work and investment.

The German missions had brought Kelley to two capitals of Europe. In London he had groped his way through the blind alleys of British bureaucracy and hammered out a formula that might have saved a portion of the German missions. In Rome new and greater frustrations had awaited him. His compromises were regarded as inadequate. His behavior had triggered byzantine suspicions of ambition. The constant motion of a half year had cast him into the blackest gloom. "I am running on my third week in Rome," he confided to Mundelein, with yet a month to spend in the Eternal city, "and am dead tired, anxious to get back to London to finish up there and to get home. Next time anyone suggests diplomacy to me there will be trouble on the spot."[60]

* * * * * * * * *

Despite the blows received at Rome over the German missions, Monsignor Kelley's lengthy presence in Europe soon registered a major diplomatic gain on the Irish issue, a gain that was wholly unexpected. As Cardinal Bourne and his household had succeeded in softening their guest's anglophobia, as was discussed earlier, so Kelley mellowed the English churchman's attitude on Ireland, a change of sentiment which contributed to the agreement between London and Dublin. During his negotiations over the missions, Kelley had the good fortune of knowing, from three parties, about the secret preliminary discussions that led to the establishment of the Irish Free State in 1921. The first source was Herbert A. L. Fisher, president of the Board of Education and a member of the Irish committee of Lloyd George's cabinet. The Foreign Office had recruited Fisher to brief Kelley on its Irish policy; this had been done, as a clerk noted, "at great length and with good effect."[61] Another key person was a Belfast-born newspaperman, John Scott Steele. Chief of the London bureau of the Chicago *Tribune,* he was an old friend of Kelley, and his professionalism was fast gaining for him the reputation of being the dean of American correspondents in England. It was Steele who introduced to Fisher the third figure, an inscrutable grocer from Galway, Patrick Moylett. In his brushes with Kelley, Moylett never verified his credentials as representing the Sinn Fein, but he did not hesitate to enlist the priest in the service of Irish freedom. Together, the English minister and his two Irish-born associates helped convince the Prime Minister that his long-time adversary, Eamon de Valera, was ready to negotiate.[62] It was this trio—Fisher, Steele, and Moylett—who have been credited with thus paving the way to the Anglo-Irish settlement; and Kelley knew them all intimately.

Not only was the Islander one of the few Americans informed of these secret discussions but he assisted them by bringing the English hierarchy into open sympathy with a negotiated settlement over the Irish question, a formidable task which the priest had undertaken with gusto. Intolerant of brutality and loyal to the government, Cardinal Bourne was regarded as a relentless foe of the Irish insurrection. In February, 1921, while Kelley sojourned in Rome, he had issued a pastoral letter which denounced the outrages committed by the revolutionaries and which recalled Cardinal Manning's denunciation, a half century earlier, of conspiracies against the Crown. In the eyes of Irish nationalists, Bourne had switched from a cool indifference to the problems of their island to active hostility against its freedom. There followed a torrent of verbal abuse against the cardinal, who was then described in one impassioned article as a "dyed-in-the-wool Tory, a self-confessed militarist, and an imperialist of the Rhodes-Chamberlain school."[63]

This outburst, along with the continued deadlock over Ireland and the threat of greater bloodshed, made Bourne more conciliatory, a position which Kelley encouraged when he returned to London after his brief visit in America. A change in the cardinal's sentiment, reasoned the priest, would not only quiet the resentment among Irish nationalists but it would also assist the Fisher-Steele-Moylett team in eroding intransigence within the British government. In two strokes, the American visitor was instrumental in revising Bourne's public position. First, the general public learned of this shift in a friendly interview which Kelley arranged between the cardinal and correspondent Steele. Appearing in the Chicago *Tribune* and released to the London and Dublin press, the article revealed a breakthrough in the churchman's thinking, whereby he denied that he had ever denounced the Sinn Fein. His condemnations had extended only to the "violence" on the part of Irish terrorists and to the "reprisals" inflicted by the British police and irregular units known as the Black and Tans, or "Tudor's Toughs." Steele then guided the prelate into a discussion of Ireland's legitimate aspirations. Conceding a degree of independence, Bourne admitted that he favored "Dominion" status, like Canada, which would give to Ireland autonomy in its domestic matters. But, he insisted strongly, before this issue could be settled, the two parties must enter into negotiations. ". . . let us first stop killing one another," ran his eloquent appeal: "Let us then try to be less suspicious of one another. Let us get around a table, with a prayer for peace in all our hearts, and talk to one another."[64]

After the general public was informed on Bourne's new viewpoint. Kelley next urged the churchman to notify the government. The Islander was the cardinal's house guest, when the English hierarchy held its annual meeting after Easter, 1921. While the bishops were in favor of passing a resolution expressing concern over conditions in Ireland, Kelley addressed the body at Bourne's invitation and suggested, instead, that a joint letter be sent directly to the Prime Minister. As a result, Lloyd George received an unexpected appeal from Bourne sent in the name of English bishops. Recent "terrible happenings," it charged, especially the acts of retaliation against innocent persons, had made it "impossible to explain or justify" the government's Irish policy. The bishops next demanded the withdrawal of the Black and Tans and other auxiliary forces, the restoration of civil order, and serious steps to be taken immediately toward "permanent reconciliation."[65] It is impossible to measure the impact of this powerful statement on the course of events. The government now had evidence that one of its chief and most important supporters regarding Ireland, the Catholic hierarchy in England, had broken ranks. This sudden alienation reinforced the atmosphere of crisis already created by such pressure as King George V's earlier appeals for peace, the steady deterioration of a weak coalition ministry, and the erosion of the diehards in the cabinet. A host of factors—among them the bishops' letter—led Lloyd George on June 24, 1921, to invite de Valera to a conference in London, the first step toward peace.

Whether or not Bourne's letter expedited a truce between London and Dublin, it certainly shifted the leadership of Catholic England to an enlightened position on the issue before the government itself arrived there. The English church was thus saved from future charges that it had totally abandoned their Celtic cousins in their most desperate hour. Though ancillary, Kelley's part was sufficiently crucial as to merit this cryptic tribute from Moylett: "You will never know how much you have done for Ireland." Later, when planning to publish a chronicle of his role in the negotiations, the Irishman wanted to include Kelley's participation. Such a reference in print by a Sinn Fein leader would have rehabilitated the priest's reputation among Irish nationalists. Unfortunately, however, Kelley had been so thoroughly scorched by the Vatican over the German missions that he adamantly refused to have his named linked with the peace in Ireland. Had his role been acknowledged, Irish leaders might have forgiven his success in having blocked an expression of sympathy from the American bishops; but, as it turned out, Kelley never fully recovered the trust of the Irish nationalists—to his everlasting regret. Afterwards, when the Islander recounted the episode at private gatherings, his intention was less self-serving than to show how Cardinal Bourne had been misjudged as an enemy of the Irish. On one occasion at Louvain, he told the story in the presence of Bourne and Cardinal Patrick O'Donnell of Armagh. "The Irish," he noted with evident pleasure, "were so astounded that they were knocked speechless."[66]

* * * * * * * * * *

The fate of Kelley's formula regarding the German missions still hung in the balance. On March 19, 1921, he was relieved of his diplomatic duties, and further negotiations were to be handled in London and Rome.[67] There followed an aftermath in which he observed, at a distance, the total dismantling of his work. This consequence inflicted one of the greatest agonies of his life, and his unofficial status allowed him to be freer than before in expressing his pain, especially in criticizing both Vatican and British officialdom.

At first, all signs pointed to a prompt implementation of Kelley's formula, when the Salvatorian Fathers volunteered to accept its provisions. As Austrians, they had been excluded from their mission in Assam in northeastern India and with some reluctance agreed to place themselves under an English bishop. Propaganda likewise appeared cooperative, appointing as head of the Assam mission a superior whose loyalty could not be questioned in London—Bishop Felix Courturier, O.P., a French-born British subject whose heroism as a chaplain during World War I had earned him the Order of the British Empire.[68]

As events unfolded, however, the Vatican was playing a delicate game with the British. Though the secretariat of state was willing to use Kelley's device, Propaganda would not give it formal approval, fearing that this would set a precedent that would handicap the free assignment of missionary personnel outside the British Empire. When the Vatican thus deferred a statement on the formula, the British mission at the Holy See made an inquiry regarding its status, and this forced Rome to repudiate Kelley's work on two counts. First, as Cerretti explained, the Holy See could not accept the principle that only British subjects qualified as superiors in mandated territories in the empire. "To do so," the British were told, "would involve restrictions on the liberty of the Church to fulfill her mission in spreading the Gospel." Second, there was a practical factor which handicapped the formula. According to Cerretti, there was not available a sufficient number of British subjects willing and able to serve as superiors of ex-enemy congregations.

As a result, Couturier was in June, 1921, reassigned to a diocese in Canada, and the Salvatorians yielded their mission in Assam to Salesians from Italy in exchange for a post in China. "There seems to be no doubt," the Foreign Office was told further, "that Mgr. Kelley went too far in the negotiations with the India Office and had no authority forming the proposed arrangement which resulted." This disclosure of Kelley and the Vatican going in opposite directions so puzzled Earl Curzon of Kedleston, the British foreign secretary, that he summed up the confusion as a "dense ecclesiastical fog."[69] In one stroke, six months of Kelley's hardest effort were wasted. The news evoked from the priest genuine regret not so much for himself as for the exiles. The German missions were thus forever taken from those who had founded and developed them. The empire suffered, too. "This is a great loss to India," the disappointed Kelley told Wilberforce, "for these Germans were the best possible missionaries."[70]

The Treaty of Versailles had stripped the Germans of their political empire, but Francis Kelley had tried to save their spiritual one. Postwar Germany had been reduced to a continental power with no ties overseas. Kelley's fear was that a rich source of evangelism would dry up if German Catholics became discouraged over their losses abroad. To champion these missionaries was a noble cause for which he sacrificed time, health, and a personal fortune of $5,000. His tactics often blundered, but his motive—"to save the missions"—extenuated the offense.

In the end, his only reward was a sense of hopeless futility. Work never troubled him, but unproductive work plunged him into dark moods of pessimism. A year after this diplomatic adventure, he calculated the net results in terms of bankruptcy and abandonment. "Not only have I wasted my money," he confided to Wilberforce—

> though for that I have no regrets—but I left myself open to charges that pained me exceedingly. Some said that I was a paid British propagandist. The German papers reported that my mission was a failure. There were important people in Rome who said the same thing. The French put me down as a pro-German. The Irish complained that I was at least indirectly hurting their cause by dealing with the British Government at all. And today one of the top officials of the Society, returning from a trip South, tells me he met an English priest there who called me a Sinn Feiner.[71]

Self-pity is seldom excused, but these words, intended to remain private, were among the most poignant he ever wrote.

He cared—profoundly.

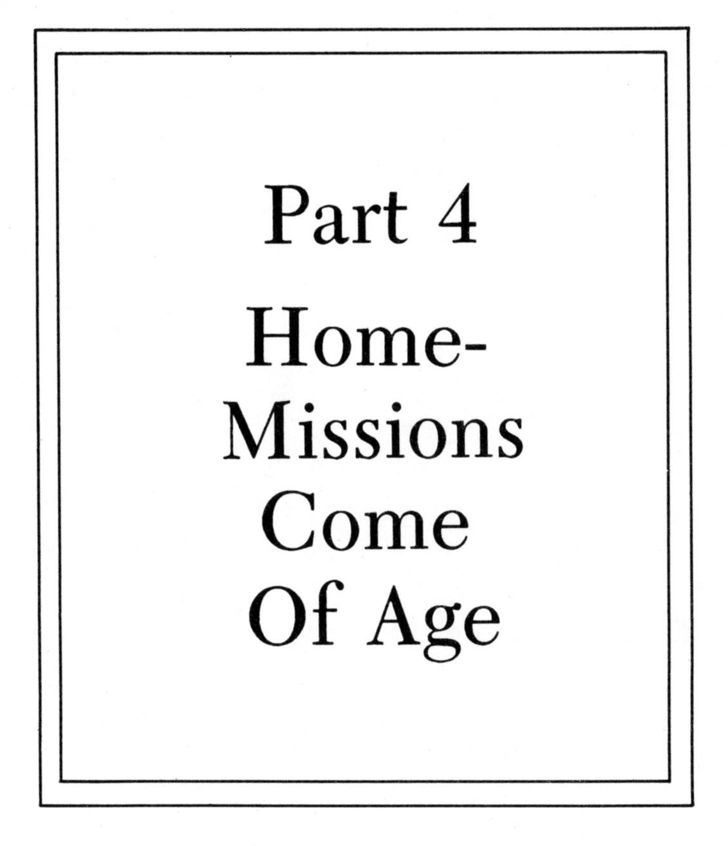

Part 4
Home-Missions Come Of Age

(1916-1947)

IX
A Catholic Vision for America

In January, 1923, Bishop Thomas J. Shahan, rector of The Catholic University of America, touched the pulse of Monsignor Kelley, when he tagged him a "man of vision and daring."[1] The president of Extension, one could argue, was a master of administrative detail, a realist with ability. His shuttling across the Atlantic and through Europe in behalf of the Vatican or German missionaries had likewise demonstrated that he could be a good foot-soldier. Later, as a bishop, he was invited to serve on important national bodies, further proof that this Canadian-born cleric was respected as a man of experience and common sense. But Shahan's comment pointed to a dimension beyond competence and energy; namely, the exquisite realm of imagination.

Francis Kelley was obsessed by a compelling vision that

governed his life in Chicago and Oklahoma. It consisted of two convictions, one looking at the church in its timeless essence and the other focusing on what he judged to be its key shortcoming in the world of his day. First, the church was, at its roots, an evangelical movement. At no time and in no place could it dispense itself of the responsibility to share its faith with mankind. The word "missionary" had been generally limited to efforts in non-western civilizations; churchmen spoke of "missions" in Africa and Asia. But, according to Kelley, a more accurate indicator of whether a territory was "missionary" or not was the church's strength, not a cultural description of the environment. With its Catholic minority, America was as much "missionary" as the developing areas overseas. Its home-missions were therefore no less important than the foreign ones. This was not a novel idea. In the mid-nineteenth century, the Bonifatius Association had been founded in central Germany with the idea of recovering the Catholic diaspora, which had been scattered by the Reformation. If Catholic Germany could thus view itself as "missionary," so could their coreligionists in the United States, where they were outnumbered by their Protestant neighbors.

Kelley's second conviction centered on the current need for coordination. The church's high officers and programs tended, according to him, to be wasteful and inefficient. In Catholic America there were no shortages in manpower, wealth, and natural leadership, but these elements had to be brought into a unity of effort. This desire for consolidation had inspired much of his early work. Extension had sought to blend the interest of the American church in the city and countryside. His proposal for a national collection had been intended to bring together support for foreign- and home-missions. In this way, he was applying to the church the principle of synergism. As in physics, these institutional components, he hoped, would be so engaged in cooperative action that their total effect would be greater than the sum of these parts taken individually.

This analysis, or vision—a missionary church in search of

modernity, a movement with such enormous but wasted energies that it was achieving only a fraction of efficiency—shaped Kelley's many fantasies about the future of American Catholicism. An early one was prompted in 1916, when the archbishops of the United States were alarmed over a flurry of anti-Catholic propaganda. Since there existed no vehicle that could organize a national response, the hierarchy was forced to consider the creation of new agencies representing them as a body. One possibility was a weekly newspaper modeled along the lines of *Our Sunday Visitor* and published in several centers. Another was an official home-mission society that would aim at building a Catholic church in every town of 2,000 or more.

This development sparked Kelley to compose a playful letter to "Bishop Roe," who ruled the imaginary diocese of "Podunk." Extension was prepared, the Islander explained, to take on the hierarchy's home-mission program, and the *Visitor* would be a perfect campanion. Only in its fourth year, this Indiana weekly had become a notable success as the only national Catholic newspaper. Its subscriptions already approached half a million, and it was giving the home-missions a monthly subsidy of $1,000. A third unit was needed, added Kelley; namely, "The International Catholic Truth Society." This Brooklyn-based organ responded to charges appearing in the secular press and provided elaborate anti-defamation copy for the *Visitor.*

Kelley's recommendations bore little originality until he came to his suggestion regarding a new coordinating agency known as the "American Catholic Board of Home Missions," which would supervise these units. This arrangement would require adjustments from existing organizations, but for the sake of coordination Kelley was willing to make any sacrifice, including the demotion of Extension to a "secondary position." It was a luxurious fancy to confide in the benevolent bishop of "Podunk," but these musings were not without importance in determining Kelley's fundamental values. The hierarchy's new interest in sponsoring national departments had stimulated his first recorded thoughts on a mission board that would supervise not merely the church's defense against bigotry but also the conversion of America. He did not share the protective instincts that were normal in founders of institutions like Extension. The evangelization of America was his ultimate goal, and everything else, including his home-mission society, was expendable, "To make [Extension] part of a bigger and greater movement," he reflected, "would only be to make it bigger and greater anyhow."[2] This view remained fixed throughout his life; it was his dream.

This vision lay in incubation for the next three years, awaiting the opportunity for refinement, which came after World War I. His visit to Paris during the peace conference had brought him to a busy crossroad in which a host of issues and personalities had intersected. In behalf of the Mexican hierarchy, he had tracked down every diplomat who would listen to his views on religious freedom. The horrors of modern war loomed before him as he visited the soft fields of military glory, a diversion which had accidentally entangled him in the Roman Question. The plight of the German missionaries next crossed his path, as he helped prepare Archbishop Cerretti's presentation to the peacemakers. These questions would have been sufficient to exhaust the energies of an ordinary visitor to postwar Europe; but Kelley had the capacity for another adventure during this busy interlude when he was given the opportunity to unveil his vision to the two most powerful ecclesiastics in the missionary church.

His recess in Rome in 1919 brought him first to Propaganda, where he met the perfect, Cardinal Willem Van Rossum. The Dutch-born Redemptorist was a veteran in the Roman Curia, having served in the Holy Office and the Pontifical Biblical Commission. A forceful leader who had been appointed to the congregation only the year before, Van Rossum was beginning a fourteen-year term that would significantly reorient Propaganda's policy. His earlier years had been spent in seminaries and the curia, but this domestic service had not blinded him to the truth that the war had crippled Europe as the traditional source of missionary personnel and money. Hence two corresponding trends were to unfold during his years. The first was the drive to strengthen local clergies with new seminaries and the ordination of native bishops. This would relieve dependence on European personnel. The second consisted of centralized supervision through new apostolic delegations in mission areas and through the relocation of mission-aid societies in Rome.[3] As these ideas were ripening, Francis Kelley entered the new prefect's life and remained a focus of Propaganda's attention for a difficult half decade.

In Rome, the Dutch churchman was respected as a leading expert in Vatican administration and was even thought to be the leading non-Italian candidate for the papacy, ahead of such international notables as Cardinals Merry del Val and Mercier. In spite of this reputation, however, he was also known to be, in the view of the British minister to the Holy See, "ascetic, [and] unpopular as being strict and unyielding. . . ." The first meeting between Van Rossum and Kelley stenciled a deep impression on the visitor. "Here's one man," the latter noted in his journal, "who sticks to the point. He must eat and drink mission questions at every meal. I never met a man so completely absorbed in his own special work." Nevertheless, the Chicagoan's views on coordination reinforced the cardinal's tendencies, and Kelley departed with a promise to draft a synopsis of his views in the form of a memorandum which Van Rossum would present to the Holy Father.[4]

A papal audience followed this interview at Propaganda. As the hour to see Benedict XV approached, the priest sensed that major decisions on the missions were pending and that his opinion would be important. During the audience the pope repeated the request regarding the memorandum. "The Holy Father," Kelley reflected soon after, "is more interested in Missions than anything else." The next five days were given almost entirely to the document. When he delivered it at Propaganda, the prefect expressed enormous pleasure. "I would not be surprised," Kelley confided to himself, "if that accidental acquaintance with Cardinal Van Rossum does not turn out to be the most important event of this whole trip."[5]

The memorandum notably advanced the views that had been entrusted earlier to the bishop of "Podunk." This careful analysis presented a disturbing overview of conditions in the United States, followed by a trinity of recommendations. American Catholics, he explained first, had not matched the Protestant success in mission support, and the secret in this difference lay in organization. In the promoting of their creeds, Protestant denominations had made enormous gains through cooperation, while Catholic programs had stumbled and fallen because they duplicate and compete with each other. The memorandum pointed to one factor that would not fail to catch the prefect's attention The Society for the Propagation of the Faith was still administered in France, a historical curiosity which, according to the American priest, had handicapped support of foreign-missions in America, where it had a dismal record of cooperation with the home-mission movement.[6] Since its appearance in 1905, Extension had quintupled its revenues—not through devices that excluded support for foreign-missions but through the effective promotion of the overall missionary spirit, proof that the two movements could co-exist. Though grateful for past generosity from the Propagation in France, the American hierarchy, noted Kelley, was dissatisfied with an alien clearing house of mission funds, and it preferred to work through an organization based at home.

This candid analysis next introduced three recommendations. Postwar conditions, first of all, had made opportune the publication of an encyclical on the missions. New territories had opened up to Catholic preaching, such as the Ottoman Empire; and, in the Islander's view, World War I and its aftermath had stimulated a new interest in Christianity. His suggestions then touched on the structures of the congregation itself. As Propaganda proceeded toward greater centralization, it should form advisory international commissions composed of representatives from the field. At this point, Kelley might have overstepped the boundaries of prudence regarding how the Roman Curia should seek advice, but his most important and controversial recommendation was his last: Propaganda should deputize national bodies the world over. Acting in the congregation's name, these would enjoy extensive powers of coordination, such as eliminating "unauthorized societies" and seeing to it that the mission-aid societies were organized down to the parish level.[7] The priest's ideas were as yet embryonic, not fully practical, but they must have struck several familiar chords in the prefect. Later that year *Maximum illud* would be issued, an apostolic letter on the missions, no doubt inspired by Propaganda; and Van Rossum was about to undertake the gigantic task of transferring the Propagation from its century-old headquarters in France to the Eternal City.

The conversations and memorandum had meanwhile penetrated deeply into Kelley's mind, perhaps more than he knew. A month after his second meeting with Van Rossum, he was in the presence of another cardinal, Désiré Mercier, in Malines. As the Belgian primate drew out the priest's view on missions, Kelley returned to the theme of coordination, speaking passionately in French and at one point jumping to his feet. It was an impromptu display of such feeling that it startled his American companions. They could not follow the words, one admitted later, but they could understand the message.[8]

Kelley's dream was thus a powerfully organic force, evolving almost without notice through stages of psychological possession. In three years it had progressed from innocent written musings for the eye of a phantom bishop to serious exchanges with a pontiff and prefect. It had settled so firmly within its author that he once found himself lecturing on it to the heroic Belgian cardinal. It was not long after his return home in summer of 1919 that it stirred up the bitterest controversy of his life and dominated his last years at Extension.

* * * * * * * * * *

The opportunity to pursue Monsignor Kelley's dream materialized in 1919, when the American hierarchy decided to transform the temporary National Catholic War Council into a permanent secretariat. The preliminary phase began with Cardinal Gibbons's appointment of a committee on Catholic affairs, which was to conduct three regional meetings and report recommendations regarding the future organization. The vice-chairman, Bishop Peter J. Muldoon of Rockford, was, in Kelley's mind, the committee's "ruling spirit." A meeting was arranged at the University of Notre Dame on July 22-24, 1919, to which the bishop invited experts on missions, education, social questions, the press, and other special ministries. Before the sessions, Muldoon had approached his friend at Extension, looking for a preview of the priest's position. At one level, the bishop was told, the organization of mission work must reach down into the heart of the parishes; but, at the other level, no plan could omit the overall supervision of Propaganda, an early jab at the French-based Propagation which operated independently of the Roman congregation. "I told the Bishop," Kelley reported later to Van Rossum, "that, even if the Catholic Church Extension Society should be swallowed up in a greater unity, there would be no opposition from me; for I consider that it is the life of the Church and the life of souls that is to be thought of, and not the life of any one organization."[9]

At Notre Dame, seventeen directors of mission societies met with a member of Muldoon's committee, Bishop Joseph Schrembs of Toledo, and reviewed practical ways of cooperation in collecting funds. After three days of study, the experts unanimously adopted a report which called for a mission department in the new secretariat and endorsed Kelley's vision of coordination. Details of the plan are not important at this stage, except for two features. The committee first recommended the formation of a board composed of directors of mission societies and headed by a bishop. This prelate was to function like the rector of The Catholic University of America, having no residential see but enjoying membership in the hierarchy. This notion of having a bishop in charge had been a favorite of Extension's board of governors; a half decade earlier, they had urged that Kelley receive a mitre as the society's director. Second, the Propagation in America appeared willing to end its affiliation with its international headquarters in France. Sickness had prevented Monsignor Joseph Fréri, the society's national director, from attending the meeting at Notre Dame, but three local directors endorsed the separation from their superiors in Europe. This would virtually complete the Americanization of mission-aid programs in this country, as well as their direct subordination to Propaganda. Kelley's delight with the results was not concealed in his swaggering account to Van Rossum. ". . . the plan is suspiciously like the one I suggested to you in Rome," he remarked confidently. "As a matter of fact, the plan is almost all mine."[10] This harmless lapse into self-commendation was not lost on the prefect; it triggered unfortunate suspicions of consuming ambition in the Chicago priest.

Nevertheless, the plan proceeded through the two stages of episcopal approval, beginning with the committee on Catholic activities. It was next submitted to the hierarchy for its meeting on September 24, 1919. The assembled bishops welcomed it with only two significant adjustments. They first appointed a standing committee, consisting entirely of bishops, to supervise mission programs. Archbishop Henry Moeller of Cincinnati, was named chairman, and memberships were given to Archbishops Mundelein, Hayes, and Jeremiah J. Harty of Omaha, and to Bishop J. F. Regis Canevin of Pittsburgh. The bishops' committee then appropriated from the plan its own title, "American Board of Catholic Missions." The second change to the original proposal also confirmed the paramount importance of this body. The ABCM was to be subject directly to the hierarchy. Since the bishops' authorization of this board preceded the formation of the permanent secretariat, the ABCM was from its beginning "senior" to the new National Catholic Welfare Council.[11]

Endowed from the start with strong leadership, the ABCM was quick to recruit an executive committee of nine priests, who met the next month and polished the constitution. The concept was simple. The bishops' board was to regulate all collecting activities, and two departments—one for foreign-missions and the other for home-missions—were to supervise the distribution. Kelley was elected "director general" and would serve as chief executive officer with offices in New York City. The coolness between the Propagation and Extension, which had been a factor in keeping the latter out of the eastern dioceses, appeared to have been resolved in a congenial fusion of interest. Monsignor Fréri accepted second place on the committee, and the revenues of the ABCM were to be divided between the foreign- and home-missions. Francis Kelley had thus reached the summit of an extraordinary campaign. By mid-November, it seemed, the ABCM would adopt a constitution that would coordinate every mission program in the United States; and Rome was expected to give a routine ratification.[12]

Events in Europe, however, complicated the orderly execution of the new plan. In a confidential letter from Van Rossum, Monsignor Kelley first learned of the stubborn resistance that the French were prepared to offer in the face of any changes involving the Propagation. The prefect's early attempts to integrate the society within the congregation had brought to the Holy See a committee from France which pleaded for continued independence. Kelley was then asked to supply data—statistics, testimonials, and such—that would strengthen Van Rossum's effort to bring the society to Rome. The cardinal's decision to confide in him and to confront the Propagation gratified Kelley, who sent to Archbishops Mundelein and Dougherty copies of Van Rossum's "strictly personal" letter, an evident breach of trust.[13]

The Chicago priest complied with the prefect's request with a lengthy brief in which he defended the evolving plan to unify American mission activities. The most provocative portion alluded to the Propagation. It was intolerable, Kelley argued, to have the bulk of mission funds in the hands of foreign laymen over which neither the Holy See nor the French bishops had any control. Futhermore, this society had little appeal for German-Americans. This generous group was sensitive to the reprisals which the French government had engaged in against the Fatherland since the close of the war, a sentiment that was bound to discourage an interest in foreign-mission support.

Next came the argument that the Propagation's preference for French overseas missions had silenced legitimate requests for funds to be used in America. Kelley recounted the sobering experience of his early patron, Bishop John J. Hennessy. When the latter had been first appointed to Wichita in 1888, he took possession of an impoverished rural diocese and went to France in a personal appeal to the Propagation. On his arrival in Paris, he was told blankly: "Monseigneur, the greater part of the money of the Society for the Propagation of the Faith comes from France, and it will be spent in the French missions."[14] Kelley's argument was hardly fair; the society had given abundantly to America and no doubt did not view Hennessy's diocese as sufficiently desperate to merit special consideration. But casual statements like the one spoken to the Kansas bishop created resentment among Americans, a reaction that the Islander did not hesitate to point out in his effort to unify the societies.

But the ABCM was far from assured. The struggle in Europe unfolded itself only gradually to those across the Atlantic. Kelley was aware of the tension mounting between Propaganda and the Propagation, but he assumed that his bond with Van Rossum eliminated the danger that Rome and France would join hands in crippling the ABCM. Unfortunately, the priest's hope was not realized; together, Propaganda and the Propagation paralyzed the ABCM for half a decade. The Propagation delivered the first blow. Though he had been absent from the meeting at Notre Dame, Monsignor Fréri had apparently given cautious assent to Kelley's plan, unaware of any activity in France.[15] In early November, 1919, however, while the final approval of the constitution was arranged to take place in Chicago, Kelley received Fréri's abrupt resignation from the executive. committee. The Propagation, the Islander was told, did not want to surrender its independent status in the United States and therefore refused to join the ABCM.

Fréri action did not deter the ABCM from meeting as planned. Despite the confusion, the five prelates on the board sent to the apostolic delegate, Archbishop Bonzano, a two-fisted unanimous protest against this apparent defiance of the American hierarchy. The Holy See was therefore asked to clarify whether the Propagation was to continue undisturbed and sovereign in this country or whether the ABCM was to fulfill its mandate to coordinate all mission programs. The bishops kept their request secret, but Kelley knew enough of their show of strength to understand that the constitution had been sent to Rome, unchanged in spite of the Propagation's withdrawal. Resentment was spreading against the French-based society. Archbishop Dougherty, Kelley confided to Van Rossum, had vowed that no matter what Rome decided, no foreign-mission collection in Philadelphia would ever go to France.[16]

Formidable as it was, the Propagation's opposition was not nearly so serious as the second blow against the ABCM plan. A month after Fréri's resignation, Kelley received word that Propaganda had rejected the ABCM constitution, contending that it was not opportune to fuse foreign- and home-mission societies. Van Rossum had interpreted the plan as an effort to combine the Propagation with Extension under Kelley. His frequent communications to the prefect, the Chicagoan reluctantly noted, had led the cardinal to suspect that the ABCM was a one-man conspiracy to enlarge Kelley's authority in America. The Propagation's defenders in Rome may well have contributed to a nasty impression of unbridled ambition. His immediate retaliation consisted of a flurry of explanations from Chicago, all in the assurance that the ABCM was the product of many churchmen and that under it Extension was no less expendable than any other society.[17]

The reform of mission societies in the United States, Kelley realized, would encounter difficulties, and thus far he had managed several obstacles successfully. But he had underestimated the impediments in Rome, especially on the part of Cardinal Van Rossum, who had given him his first taste of hardened opposition.

* * * * * * * * *

The prefect's letter had given only the ruling on the congregation. Since the pope had not acted on the question, it was technically open for further discussion. Hence there followed a long siege of rumors, warnings, apologies, complaints, compromises, threats—all bringing Kelley to the Eternal City, where he spent the most trying four months of his life. He first encountered the counsel of Roman friends who hoped to temper his zeal. The issue, Archbishop Cerretti reminded him, was enormously complicated, involving strong national conflicts. Also sensitive to the Propagation's influence was Monsignor Sante Tampieri, who had studied the plan. ". . . allow me to tell you in all sincerity," he remarked to Kelley frankly, "that I cannot grasp all your ideas. My dear friend, it seems to me, the great Work of Lyons [the Propagation] could hardly be grateful to you." The confidant of Benedict XV, Monsignor Jules Tiberghien, warned him, too, that the Holy Father was reluctant to modify the Propagation's work simply because of its record of success. ". . . you will do better in asking for only a portion of the changes which you want. . . ."[18] His three sentinels in Rome had sounded out the climate at the Holy See. The ABCM had struck at a respected institution of the modern church, and the only way to save the plan was through compromise.

Before negotiations could resume, Monsignor Kelley had to determine the response of the American bishops to Propaganda's action. This search for re-endorsement was the second stage in this phase of Kelley's life. Two factors helped prevent the bishops from abandoning the ABCM. The first was the report that Propaganda had severed several countries from the Propagation's jurisdiction, including Germany, Holland, Italy, Spain, and the United States. This loss brought to Rome a distinguished delegation from France, headed by Cardinal Louis-Joseph Maurin of Lyons. But, as Kelley learned, Van Rossum resisted all pressures, agreeing only to postpone the actual transfer of authority. Indeed, the Dutch cardinal was not satisfied with limiting the Propagation's jurisdiction; he was intent even to bring its French headquarters to Rome. In a short time, the prefect's relentless drive to centralize the mission world in Rome earned him a reputation of being consummately autocratic. "No Card.," commented an anonymous newspaperman in Rome, "dares now say what Card. Van Rossum does." Even Count John de Salis, the British minister to the Holy See, admitted that "he always felt ashamed when he had to deal with the Propaganda."[19] This discouraging news about Van Rossum's abrupt manner did not distract Kelley from the welcome report that the French monopoly of the Propagation in America was about to be broken. He had feared that it was France's influence that stalled the papal approval of the ABCM, but the Propagation's failure to budge the prefect suggested that it had ceased to be a factor and that the ABCM stood an excellent chance for ratification. When Kelley circulated this information among the bishops on the ABCM, they agreed to pursue the new advantage. "We are," commented Archbishop Harty, "at the First Vespers of a distinct development in the mission field."[20]

The ABCM's continued sponsorship of the plan of coordination was an indispensable preliminary to its re-endorsement by the entire hierarchy. There also entered a second and wholly unexpectant factor that contributed to this renewal of support—the intervention of the Sacred Congregation for the Oriental Churches. The affairs of Oriental-rite Catholics had been handled by a bureau in Propaganda until 1917, when Benedict XV created a separate congregation for them, reserving for himself the post of prefect. The new department in the Roman Curia had complete jurisdiction over Catholic bodies in the Middle East, as well as Oriental-rite faithful elsewhere. The fall of the Ottoman Empire after World War I had opened up new missionary prospects in the Middle East, and the Vatican desperately searched for patrons who would help support the work of the new congregation.

Kelley's trip to Rome in 1919 had introduced him to its work and its poverty. The Oriental offered him a post as consultor, and he assured the pope that Extension would help. Other officers in the society, however, including Mundelein and Monsignor Ledvina, had opposed the additional responsibility. If the new congregation could not look to Extension for help, Kelley found an alternative arrangement in the ABCM. If approved by Rome, the board would assume support of the Oriental's work as one of its foreign-mission responsibilities. This plan was ingenious but risky: it would inevitably provoke a clash between two departments in the curia.[21] While Propaganda remained unyielding in its opposition to the ABCM, the Oriental, having the ear of the pope as its perfect, became a key advocate of the American plan to coordinate mission support.

A year later, the infant congregation associated itself directly with the ABCM. In August, 1920, Kelley arrived in the Eternal City, after having set up the Extension relief program in Vienna. Since Van Rossum's rejection of the ABCM had threatened the Oriental's interests, the latter congregation warned the pope through George Calavassy, the newly consecrated ordinary for

Uniate Catholics in Thrace and Greece. During the audience, the young prelate was told to bear this papal message to the United States hierarchy: "The Bishops of America are free to do what they think best." Though no more than a verbal concession, it represented to Kelley, along with the staff at the Oriental, a signal that the Vatican would not support Propaganda in its opposition to the ABCM. With only a summary of the ABCM plan at hand, Cardinal Niccolò Marini, the Oriental's secretary, dispatched to Kelley a letter addressed to the hierarchy which expressed the pope's warm approval of the plan to coordinate mission activities in America. This sealed, it was thought, the support of the most powerful forces at the Holy See. "The Vatican does not want to actually come to an issue with the Propaganda," Kelley explained to Mundelein, "but it will uphold the bishops."[22]

The meeting of the hierarchy opened on September 22, 1920. When Archbishop Moeller reported to the bishops on the progress of the ABCM, not everyone wished to sponsor the plan as orginally conceived. Cardinal O'Connell of Boston alluded to a conversation with Van Rossum in Rome, in which the New Englander had found the prefect determined to keep the work of the foreign- and home-missions entirely apart, and this conversation had weakened O'Connell's support of the plan. As confidence in the ABCM rapidly waned, Moeller broke the spell with the announcement that the Oriental had communicated the Holy Father's approval of the plan. The sixty-three prelates in attendance were thus faced with conflicting positions within the Roman Curia, a dilemma which doubtless rattled the assembly. They eventually chose to side with the reportedly express wishes of the pontiff, each one rising to his feet in a unanimous endorsement of the ABCM for an unprecedented second time. Their only qualification centered on a minority's wish for a clearer endorsement from Rome, especially regarding spiritual favors such as indulgences; and the board agreed to submit the plan again to the Holy See, a fatal mistake that Kelley soon regretted.[23]

Though Monsignor Kelley remained in the shadows, his had been almost a virtuoso performance. While fully engaged in Austrian relief and a defense of the German missions, he had also averted the scrapping of the ABCM and had won a repeated vote of confidence from the American bishops, drawing the most prominent objectors into line. His board had not broken ranks. The episcopal chairman from Cincinnati trusted the Chicago priest and appeared fearless in the face of any resistance, whether it be a tough prefect in Rome or the cardinal in Boston who would soon succeed to the nominal leadership of the American hierarchy. To those seasoned in the ways of the Vatican, the Oriental's word regarding papal approval was sufficient for the bishops to implement the ABCM. The Islander had thus passed the first two phases—he had listened to good counsel, and the bishops had stood firm; now he was about to enter the third one, that of negotiation with Propaganda, which constituted the most demanding stage in the cycle and ended his string of successes.

The ABCM followed up this victory at the bishops' meeting. On December 1, 1920, Archbishop Moeller summoned the board and executive committee to Cincinnati, where the final touches were applied to the plan. No detail was neglected, and several were of paramount importance. First, a new member had joined the ABCM, Kelley's friend in Philadelphia, Archbishop Dougherty, who had already expressed strong commitment to the plan. Second, diocesan organization of missionary support was mandated "whatever possible." This provision amounted to a curious contradiction. Diocesan participation in the ABCM program was, technically, voluntary, but national cooperation was expected without exception. Third, the disbursement of funds no longer provided for equal parts between foreign- and home-missions but was to be discretionary according to needs reported to the

ABCM. Fourth, the board controlled the allotments for the home-missions and would send those for the foreign-missions to Rome, mostly to the "*Congregations* for Foreign Missions." The phrase acknowledged the Oriental as a missionary congregation that would share the allotment with Propaganda.

This edition of the plan therefore presented a stronger challenge to Cardinal Van Rossum than the previous one he had rejected. It reflected the confidence that the Holy Father would restrain this freewheeling Dutchman in favor of the promises of American aid for the Oriental. At home, even the most stalwart opponents of the ABCM conceded defeat. Astonished at the bishops' endorsement of the board despite Propaganda's official attitude, Monsignor Fréri judged that at this stage it would take "at least a miracle" to save the Propagation in the United States. His private comments sharply criticized not only the resourceful Kelley who, he felt, had engineered this victory, but also the American bishops, especially their venerable leader, the 86-year-old Cardinal Gibbons. "It is infinitely regrettable," Fréri confided to a friend,

> that we are governed by a hierarchy composed largely of intriguers and incompetents, and especially regrettable that at their head is a man of such great age that he is incapable of following an idea or of having an opinion. a condition that makes him vulnerable to [clerical] politicians.

In any case, the New York *Times,* along with the Catholic press, announced the completion of a permanent organization. This step, it was reported, practically climaxed the unification of missionary activities in America.[24] Meanwhile, Kelley was about to return to Europe to finish his work in behalf of the German missions. Determined to be at the center of events, like the intrepid moth circling a flame, he also planned to be on hand when the new ABCM plan arrived at the Vatican.

There had been storm warnings that the ABCM and Francis

Kelley were about to enter upon the battle of their lives. Kelley had suspected treachery even within his executive committee. The archdiocesan director of the Propagation in Boston, Father Joseph F. McGlinchey, had not resigned from this body, but Kelley regarded him as a spy for his superiors in France, as well as for Van Rossum. At any rate, the Boston priest had tried to dissuade Kelley from pursuing the ABCM plan. In spite of the endorsement of the Oriental, he advised, the American proposal had been irrevocably rejected with Van Rossum's veto, and Propaganda was determined to keep foreign- and home-missions separate. Moreover, Father Edward I. Galvin, S.S.C., founder of the Columban Fathers, who favored the ABCM plan, alarmed Archbishop Mundelein regarding the Propagation's activities in New York. The bishops and vicars apostolic in China, he reported secretly, had received from Fréri a circular asking them to protest to Rome the formation of the ABCM. This was no doubt part of a world-wide campaign. Furthermore, Kelley had long been aware of a conspiracy to discredit him personally. This campaign, which he attributed to the Propagation, consisted of anonymous letters circulating out of New York and typewritten on Propagation paper stock.[25]

A frontal attack erupted in February, 1921, when Monsignor Alfred Baudrillart, rector of the Catholic Institute of Paris, published a blistering critique of the ABCM in *Echo de Paris.* World War I had made the United States the wealthiest nation in the world, a development that had an important impact on the church. According to Baudrillart, the ABCM, with its enormous treasury, was the vehicle whereby the church's overseas missions were to pass exclusively into American hands. The board had thus become, in this author's eyes, not merely a religious issue but also a political, national, and commercial one—a partner in postwar American imperialism. Disturbed over this charge that the ABCM intended to monopolize the missionary world, Kelley composed a lengthy rejoinder but declined to publish it out of a fear that a public debate would only hurt the missions abroad.[26]

At the end of January, 1921, when Monsignor Kelley arrived in Rome to discuss his negotiations in London over the German missions, the ABCM constitution reached the secretariat of state. As expected, the plan triggered a sharp division within the curia. Reflecting the agreement between the pope and the Oriental, Archbishop Cerretti immediately endorsed it, but Cardinal Van Rossum's opposition at Propaganda was fixed. The latter's tactics had already suggested total war. American bishops visiting his congregation had been encouraged to renounce the ABCM, a maneuver designed to erode the unanimity within the hierarchy. Bishop Joseph Schrembs, now of Cleveland, blunted this campaign with a forceful representation at the Holy See, even in the pope's presence. Next, Kelley found himself the target of serious charges circulating in Rome and alleging his indifference to authority. Propaganda accused him of having intruded at the last meeting of the American hierarchy—forcing the ABCM upon the American bishops; and the congregation complained further that he had deliberately ignored it during the formative stages of the board and that his promises to help the Oriental infringed upon the rights of the foreign-missions.[27] Unfair as these charges were, Van Rossum eventually succeeded in postponing the implementation of the ABCM. The controversial American plan, the curia decided, was to be re-submitted to the Holy Father for approval. In this way, the Dutch cardinal was given a second opportunity to cripple and perhaps destroy Kelley's dream. "I greatly respect the fighting ability of His Eminence," the Islander admitted to Moeller. "He is certainly giving us a fine battle, God bless him! I think he is perfectly honest in his stand."[28]

The weary priest was forced to leave Europe without the satisfaction of witnessing the final approval of the ABCM. His lengthy stay away from Chicago had placed a heavy strain on him. Perhaps the darkest moment was the stern reception, which he had encountered at Propaganda, where, as he recalled, Van Rossum "was almost brutal in his coldness to me. . . . I never met a man so bent on the destruction of anything as he is on this. . . ."[29] By and large, however, the American bishops had stood firm, and the congregation, Kelley heard later, was forced to consider a compromise. This rumor was confirmed in his final hours in Rome, when he received a special message from Archbishop Camillo Laurenti, the secretary of Propaganda. The congregation had given its general approval, Laurenti notified Kelley, and its qualifications of the plan were trivial, merely a device to save the honor of his opponents. This mellowing signaled to the priest, as he told Cardinal Hayes, that the "white flag was raised" over the Piazza di Spagna, the historic site where Van Rossum conducted his business.

Departing the Eternal City on March 21, 1921, the Islander ended what he described as the "hardest four months" of his life, and on his arrival home he contacted two of his strongest allies. "I have come back in pretty fair shape," he assured Moeller. "Considering what happened I ought to be in my grave." The same sentiments were sent to New York City. "I got back safely . . . ," he told Hayes, "and with my scalp still on. . . . ."[30] Once safe across the Atlantic, he was far from the front where he had fought hard for his dream. Unfortunately, "white flag" or not, the war had only begun.

* * * * * * * * *

The death struggle between Propaganda and the ABCM began on March 31, 1921, when Cardinal Van Rossum announced the reservations under which the congregation would approve the American plan. Despite Laurenti's assurances that these would be unimportant, the prefect required two conditions, both of which Kelley and his associates found unacceptable. First, the foreign-mission section of the new organization was still to be known and function as the "Society for the Propagation of the Faith," a shrewd maneuver that eliminated any claims of the Oriental congregation on foreign-mission revenues. Second, the income of the two mission sections—foreign and home—was to be kept separate, a requirement that clearly destroyed the unity of the plan. Such a division would require for each section separate fund-raising drives, separate accounting, and perhaps even a separate team of officers. The Dutch cardinal, however, made one concession: he invited the bishops to react in writing to this formula before implementation.[31] The announcement, however, came as a complete surprise. Two unanimous endorsements of the ABCM by the American hierarchy had had no impact on Propaganda, and Van Rossum's requirement for a written response betrayed his stubborn conviction that the plan did not represent the episcopal will—just that of a troublesome priest in Chicago.

The new crisis plunged Kelley into long moments of despair. "It looks," he confided to Cardinal Dougherty, "as though my fate in life is to be constantly struggling toward an ideal and never seeing the end." This sentiment sounded the keynote. Those who did not admire the priest were quick to claim a personal loss for him, some even linking Propaganda's decision with Monsignor Ledvina's appointment to the episcopate. On May 31, 1921, two months after Van Rossum's announcement regarding the ABCM, Extension's vice president was named bishop of Corpus Christi, a promotion of a junior officer which, according to the Islander's critics, had sealed his defeat. A more serious threat to his future was unfolding outside of public view. His five-year term as the society's president was due to expire in 1922. Determined to eliminate Kelley's influence, Van Rossum exploited this opportunity and, as Kelley learned later, even asked Dougherty to block his reappointment, branding the priest as an enemy of Propaganda and the Catholic missions.[32]

The ABCM, however, pivoted on Archbishop Moeller, whose readiness to confront Propaganda never faltered. Accepting Van Rossum's invitation to reply in writing, he sketched a rough text of a letter which was to represent the mind of the board and in which he requested the prompt approval of the plan without the congregation's conditions. The bishops, Moeller explained carefully, had already registered their preference for the original plan; and these delays in its ratification served only to handicap the work of mission support. When the chairman circulated his draft among the board members, he encountered two unexpected reactions, both reflecting opposite extremes. Instead of endorsing Moeller's position, Archbishop Mundelein submitted an alternate draft that capitulated to the will of Propaganda, while at the other end of the spectrum stood the newest American cardinal, who was impatient with this stalemate. Until, proposed Dennis Dougherty, the ABCM heard differently from the Holy Father himself, it should immediately begin its operations as originally planned and without Propaganda's conditions. This radical solution, the Philadelphian had confided to Kelley, had been recommended by reliable authorities in Rome. At any rate, the majority on the board favored the chairman's middle course, vetoing both Mundelein's virtual surrender and the hasty implementation of the ABCM urged by Dougherty, and approved Moeller's reply to Propaganda.[33] While the Cincinnatian had decisively sealed leaks in the ABCM, his letter to Rome gave Van Rossum another chance to cripple the plan before the next annual meeting of the American hierarchy.

The deadlock soon evolved into a war of attrition. The ABCM's written response had so heartened Kelley that he foresaw no major hazards ahead. When Mundelein offered him a new parochial assignment in Chicago itself, closer to his office at Extension, he declined, partly because he expected the approval of the ABCM within a year. Already elected as its director general, he would then be required to resign the parish and move to New York City. While his life seemed at this point temporarily suspended in Chicago, he nonetheless dreaded Van Rossum's grinding tactics. "The only thing we fear," he reflected, "is that Propaganda will delay the matter, through interminable letter-writing, until the bishops decide to drop it. . . ." A long and inconclusive correspondence appeared to be most effective weapon in the prefect's arsenal; Mundelein had nearly fallen for it, and others might follow. The stalemate had evidently taken its toll in Rome, too. Sounding the emotional climate within the Vatican, Monsignor Tampieri noted faint symptoms of impatience with the American bishops. There were reports, he warned Kelley, that "ill-humor was spreading in America, but who wants these sobs?" Meanwhile, the struggle over the ABCM had not enhanced the health of the sturdy Dutchman. While his tactics had displayed tenacity and extraordinary energy, the 67-year-old Van Rossum had become so seriously ill that Merry del Val was concerned over his condition, shortly before the prefect's departure for a brief holiday in Switzerland. ". . . he appeared," remarked Tampieri grimly, "to be a finished man."[34]

But the frazzled prefect was not disposed to yield easily. The approach of the annual meeting of the American hierarchy offered him an opportunity to recover the offensive. After thirty-five years the episcopal leadership had changed: In March, 1921, Cardinal Gibbons died, to be succeeded by Cardinal O'Connell, whose support of the ABCM was questionable. In his last effort to dissolve the bishops' solidarity over this issue, especially since the new dean of the hierarchy was the mercurial O'Connell, Van Rossum sent to each bishop a special appeal which urged the veto of the original plan and which arrived only a fortnight before the meeting. In a separate communiqué, Moeller was directed to have the bishops vote again on the issue.[35] Supremely confident of victory, the prefect had thus reduced the issue to a simple choice between Propaganda and the ABCM. "His Eminence," Moeller wryly commented, "is certainly very active and adheres tenaciously to his views." But the humor shortly faded, as he next acknowledged to Kelley that the bishops on the ABCM board had angrily interpreted Propaganda's action as an appeal "over our heads." "I fear," he added, "that inimicus homo has been doing underhand work." The reaction in Rome was one of equal astonishment. The prefect's mulishness, Tampieri confessed, was "sad and deplorable! And, as I say, inexplicable." Even the pope was known to be displeased.[36]

Complying with the Dutch cardinal's order, the board presented the bishops on September 21, 1921, a choice between it and the congregation. In another unprecedented action, the hierarchy approved the original ABCM plan—for the third time, in unanimity. Van Rossum's dramatic maneuver had completely backfired. As Kelley viewed it, the special message from Propaganda had compelled each bishop to study the issue carefully and come to the meeting better prepared. Furthermore, as Archbishop Edward J. Hanna of San Francisco later confided to the Islander, the bishops shared the board's indignation at the appeal to each diocese.[37]

The ABCM appeared to have passed its last hurdle. Propaganda had its answer and could no longer evade approval. On December 5, 1921, the congregation sanctioned the ABCM without Van Rossum's conditions, and a week later the pope gave his approval. Its enactment had passed so smoothly, Tampieri remarked, that the triumph would lead to a bishop's mitre for Kelley. On January 5, 1922, Moeller received word from Van Rossum. The congregation's only qualification was that, before the apostolic brief would be sent, the ABCM should fix a percentage of revenues to be given to the foreign-missions. Since this seemed a sensible request, the board willingly conceded its discretionary authority over allotments and authorized an equal division between the two sections.[38]

Cardinal Van Rossum's promise of the apostolic brief represented the summit of Kelley's attempt to implement his vision of national coordination of mission programs. After two and a half years, no peril appeared in view that could snatch this victory from the ABCM. Success had depended upon a multitude of factors—three endorsements of the American hierarchy, a sufficient steadiness within the board, a battery of active Vatican associates, subtle pressure from the pope, and Kelley's own capacity not to yield under the blows of a resourceful opponent. By January, 1922, the effort had reached its peak but not its climax. The ABCM had covered every contingency—except one, which was beyond any man's control.

On January 22, Benedict XV died at the age of sixty-seven after a sudden attack of influenza.

The accession of Pius XI introduced the final stage of the ABCM's formative years, a stage bringing a series of minor tremors which, together, destroyed the original plan. The drafting of the apostolic brief for the ABCM was suspended during the conclave and papal coronation, a crucial interruption that created some concern. Little was known about the man who now occupied the see of Peter. The steps to this prominence had been too sudden to have merited much notice across the Atlantic—years of hidden service in the Ambrosian library of Milan, a difficult term as nuncio to Poland, and less than a year as archbishop of Milan. Kelley was calmed a bit by Cerretti's claim of close friendship. "Perhaps you know," the archbishop told him, "that I was responsible in a great measure of [*sic*] his appointment to Poland."[39] In any event, the death of Benedict had created a measure of disturbance in Rome—and Chicago.

A second shock followed. On February 25, 1922, the Vatican suppressed the National Catholic Welfare Council because it seemed to impinge upon the authority of individual bishops. This unexpected action confused the status of the ABCM. The latter had been authorized at the 1919 meeting of the hierarchy, the same one which had established the NCWC; but some bishops had forgotten that the two bodies were independent, thinking that the mission board was but one of the council's many departments. Hence, the suppression of the NCWC raised in their minds the possibility that the ABCM had suffered the same fate. These early days of the new pontificate had thus confounded no less a churchman than Cardinal Dougherty, who, as he cautioned Kelley secretly, planned to seek clarification from the Vatican in person. In this limbo, the Islander's thoughts turned to retirement after seventeen years of mission work. "Cardinal Van Rossum seemed to think that my whole effort was one of personal ambition," he told Cerretti. "The only answer I can make to that is to show him that I know pretty well how to die gracefully."[40]

It was Propaganda that shortly defined the ABCM's status, the third blow. Since the death of Benedict, the congregation had given no clues regarding its thinking. When Dougherty had delivered to Rome the ABCM's generous decision to split revenues evenly between foreign- and home-missions, Van Rossum had accepted it without comment. Another visitor at the congregation was Archbishop Moeller, whose request to see the prefect failed to produce him. But the veils were dropped when Moeller returned to Cincinnati, where he received the awaited apostolic brief dated May 2, 1922, and signed by Pope Pius XI. The document exceeded the worst of Kelley's fears: the congregation won its case without rescinding the deceased pontiff's approval of the original ABCM.

The decree featured three directives, each of which Kelley deplored as ruinous. First, the board was given approval for only seven years. This, Kelley judged, was the length of time that Van Rossum calculated as sufficient to satisfy home-mission needs in America, needs which, according to the priest, would last another half century. This limited term would further strangle the work of the home-missions by inhibiting long-range planning and by discouraging large contributions and legacies. Next, Propaganda's decree confirmed the right of each bishop to set up in his diocese foreign-mission programs independent of the ABCM. This provision destroyed Kelley's vision of coordination and reopened the possibility of the helter-skelter proliferation of programs. Thirdly, the decree not only sanctioned the division of the ABCM's revenues as proposed but added this coda. Programs in the territorial dependencies of the United States were to be administered as foreign-missions under Propaganda, and they were to be funded out of the allotment for the home-missions. This division of jurisdiction, observed Kelley, deprived Extension of its rights in the Philippine Islands, Puerto Rico, and Alaska, rights which had been granted a decade earlier when it had been made a pontifical institute. The funding formula, he noted further, would impoverish the home-mission program, reducing its share of the ABCM revenues from half to a mere 12 percent.[41]

The ABCM bishops agreed with Kelley's criticisms, but they had lost their wind. The first draft of their reply to the pope contained a frank expression of disappointment at Propaganda's decree. On September 27, 1922, after the hierarchy debated the letter, it unanimously adopted a three-part resolution proposed by the new archbishop of Baltimore, Michael J. Curley. First, the board's strong message of regret at Rome's decision was to be sent unchanged. Each bishop was next urged to establish the Propagation in his diocese. Lastly, the ABCM would continue with the same officers and restrict itself to the home-missions.[42] While the resolution offered peace terms, Moeller viewed these more as a polite protest than as a complete capitulation. The Propagation was not made mandatory in each diocese, and his board had received a strong vote of confidence. Indeed, the lengthy dispute between the ABCM and Propaganda had been settled, but some embers of temper and wounded pride still flickered in this intrepid chairman who, most of all, shared the Islander's dream.

The fourth jolt, which in Kelley's eyes sealed his defeat, was the assignment of a new apostolic delegate, Archbishop Pietro Fumasoni-Biondi, who, on December 14, 1922, succeeded Archbishop Bonzano. Kelley acknowledged certain advantages in this change. His acquaintance with the 50-year-old prelate dated to early years in Rome when he had served as secretary to Cardinal Martinelli, Extension's protector. The appointment had aroused the enthusiasm of Monsignor Tampieri, who told the Chicagoan: "He has traveled and visited broadly, and for that reason he knows more than the European world." The manner of a new delegate, moreover, was receptive and responsible. "I found in him," Kelley assured James A. Walsh of Maryknoll, "an excellent listener who had an honest desire to get at the facts." In conducting any inquiry, this Roman's intention "is not a matter of mere curiosity. He has a reason for wanting to know everything."[43] Aside from these expressions of respect, several other factors raised dark suspicions in Kelley. Fumasoni-Biondi's service in the Roman Curia had been confined virtually to Propaganda. In 1919 he had been named the first apostolic delegate in Japan, where he had implemented Van Rossum's policy of developing local clergy in mission territories. His success abroad had earned him a higher post in Rome as secretary of Propaganda, a promotion that made him the prefect's first lieutenant. These connections suggested not only that the Dutch churchman had the ear of Pius XI but also that the new delegate came with instructions to smother any pockets of resistance to Propaganda's decree, a suspicion which Tampieri later confirmed for Kelley as fact.[44]

The selection of Archbishop Fumasoni-Biondi was therefore due, in part, to the fact that the ABCM chairman had not surrendered entirely to the Propaganda. After the meeting of the hierarchy, Moeller addressed to Pius XI the bishops' three-part resolution along with a clear statement of his own objections to Propaganda's decree. Instead of an alert response from the Holy Father, the archbishop received in return a routine acknowledgement from the secretariat of state, coupled with Van Rossum's urgent behest to establish the Propagation in each diocese. This reply led Moeller to suspect, along with Kelley, that the new pontiff was not fully informed on the dispute between the congregation and the American bishops. At the priest's prompting, the Cincinnatian dispatched another complaint regarding the decree, in the hope that it would reach the pope's personal attention. While Moeller this time expected a reply from the pope, it came instead from the new delegate. The Holy Father, Fumasoni-Biondi pointed out firmly, had studied the documents himself and had consulted the experts regarding the ABCM; and it was the papal will that the decree be carried out without further changes or delays. The delegate then circulated among the bishops printed copies of his reply to Moeller, confirming that the dispute over the ABCM had been settled and that under the new pontificate there was perfect harmony of spirit between the pope and the prefect at Propaganda.[45]

This was Rome's last word. "Causa finita" was Kelley's greeting to the news, the end of a cause and a dream. He had guided it as close to success as possible, only to see it dissolved by an unforeseen circumstance, the death of a pope. "For the last year," the Islander confided to a friend, "I had been like a man afraid to win a fight because he knew that another was awaiting him."[46] In settling the lingering dispute over the ABCM, the delegate's letter had thus excised a malignancy developing in the bond between the Holy See and the American bishops, a growth that defied almost all control and could have led to further complications on both sides of the Atlantic.

In the aftermath, Monsignor Kelley alternated between a willingness and a reluctance to accept the verdict. Though the ABCM had been crippled at the end, he was grateful for the other dividends which he had earned from the time, money, and energy invested in this campaign. The work of four years since the inaugural meeting at Notre Dame had, for one thing, impressed the hierarchy with the importance of the home-missions. Several prelates—notably Archbishop Moeller and Cardinal Dougherty—had likewise gained his respect as faithful allies who had taken extraordinary risks when others, perhaps more prudent, had given up. Failure too had had a cleansing effect on him. "My discouragement is past," he assured Tampieri, "and I recognize the spiritual value of a little personal opposition. Instead of complaining about it, I have learned to thank God for it."[47] But no matter how magnanimously he rallied, he could not subdue the sadness and anger within. In his judgment, Propaganda's indifference to the home-missions had scuttled the opportunity to transform America from coast to coast into a Catholic nation. "In the meantime," he commented dryly to Bishop Ledvina,

> we have over twelve million negroes, intelligent and able to read and write, a finer mission field than anything Africa possesses, and we are letting it go. We have half a million Mexicans headed straight for Atheism through absolute ignorance of their religion, and we have no Catholic churches in nine out of ten small centers of white population. Our leaders seem blind to the facts.[49]

As he confided these thoughts to an old Extension comrade, they appeared to be an epitaph to his dream.

Chapter X
An Elder Statesman

The failure of the original ABCM marked Francis Kelley's graduation to the rank of elder statesman in the home-mission ministry. By 1922 his age numbered more than fifty years, a third of which had been devoted to this movement. His experience at Extension had been placed on the line throughout the struggle with Cardinal Van Rossum, and the defeat had cut deeply into his reputation as an authority on missions. These factors led naturally to the thought of withdrawal. What years remained for an active life would accommodate no more than one new assignment. "Now," he confided to Monsignor Tampieri, "I should make the last change and settle down. . . ." Another close associate was told the same. Propaganda's decree, he professed to Bishop Ledvina, had not discouraged him, but, he added, ". . . I am getting on in years. I cannot be on this job forever. I am feeling the lonliness [*sic*], and my limbs will soon be shaking."[1]

In spite of these inclinations, the action of the Holy See did not drive him into a new field of interest. For the remainder of the decade, he retained a central role in nuturing the home-missions. Not only would he help set up the ABCM within the confines laid down by Propaganda, but he would be a guiding parent during its infancy. Through these years, too, he piloted Extension through the delicate process of succession when the presidency passed from him to Monsignor William D. O'Brien. But difficulties appeared by the end of the decade, climaxing in a tragic misunderstanding that deprived both institutions of their founder's wisdom and spirit.

The first task after Propaganda's decree was to clarify responsiblity in the territorial dependencies of the United States. While the congregation had assigned these to the Propagation, Extension had been long active in Alaska, Puerto Rico, American Samoa, and the Philippine Islands. Since the beginning, the society's assistance to these possessions surpassed $300,000. This figure pointed to a significant interest beyond the continental United States, which Kelley was reluctant to yield. At Tampieri's suggestion, he asked for a clarification through the apostolic delegate, and the ruling came shortly.[2] Home-missions were confined to the actual limits of the continental mainland, including Alaska. The other areas were considered as overseas missions under the Propagation. As Kelley reported the decision to Bishop George Calavassy, only the Hawaiian Islands remained in some doubt, and the priest was not prepared to risk another inquiry over them.[3]

Once the sphere of the home-missions was defined, the next step was to structure the ABCM according to Propaganda's guidelines. A related experience that occurred at this time once again reminded Kelley of the difficulties in fusing the missionary societies into an effective union. The congregation sponsored the Vatican Missionary Exposition as part of the Holy Year celebration in Rome for 1925. Pilgrims were expected to receive at the

Eternal City a capsule view of the progress of the foreign-missions around the world. Home-missions should be represented at the jubilee, reasoned Kelley, and the preparation of special exhibit would strengthen the working relationship among the societies. When Propaganda granted his request, Kelley took the leadership in the arrangements, urging each mission-society director to join in behalf of "the honor of the Church in America." His manner of recruitment was earnest proof of the importance that he attached to the project. "Do not say that you have no time," he insisted. "You can work with every finger on both hands and still not have enough to do."[4]

Very shortly the enthusiastic priest discovered that achieving coordination among the home-mission societies was a goal that exceeded even his ability and fervor. The complicated arrangements broke up when the governing board of the Bureau of Catholic Indian Missions declined not only to participate in the exhibit but even to recognize the ABCM. The reasoning of the bureau, reported its director, the Reverend William Hughes, was that it had been established by the Third Plenary Council of Baltimore in 1884 and should remain independent. His governing board had already directed him to develop a separate exhibit, and Hughes excused himself with the refrain: ". . . I am a man subject to authority."[5] This reply was a severe blow, throwing Kelley into a mild tantrum because two members of the bureau's board—Dougherty and Hayes—belonged to the ABCM. Kelley could not fathom their apparent refusal to cooperate in the joint project, a complete reversal of their previous support of the ABCM. "So far as I am concerned," he lamented in sheer exasperation,

> I have taken one of St. Ignatius' teachings to heart: "I am indifferent." I have strong opinions on the subject, but they will not count very much. Let the bishops settle the matter themselves as they please. At any rate, I am getting too old to bother about it.[6]

The bureau's withdrawal left Kelley with no alternative but to have Extension provide its own display in Rome—and to nurse doubts about the episcopal leadership on the ABCM.[7]

The home-mission movement had thus taken two jolts. America's insular possessions had been taken from it, and effective collaboration seemed to baffle the societies. As the annual meeting of the hierarchy approached in September, 1923, there naturally arose the fear that the ABCM would be allowed to die. This prospect alarmed Bishop Ledvina, who raised his pen in an effort to salvage the remaining fragments of interest among his colleagues. Since circumstances prevented his attendance at the bishops' meeting, he circulated a letter that richly detailed his work in the diocese of Corpus Christi. Conditions in southern Texas, he explained, had forced him to travel extensively to eastern dioceses and to take up collections as a "beggar bishop." Though his reception had been generous, these lengthy absences handicapped his diocese. His fellow bishops were therefore asked to reorganize programs of assistance that would permit missionary bishops to remain at home to govern. The letter from Texas was warmly received by two old associates in Chicago. Monsignor Kelley followed immediately with a 6,400-word treatise elaborating Ledvina's themes and at one point defending himself as a misunderstood visionary. "These things have been burning the heart out of me for the last ten years," he wrote in a temper. "I suppose I am a fool to say them. . . . I have been God's fool for a long time now and I might as well stay classed where circumstances placed me." Ledvina's appeal had touched another midwesterner, Archbishop Mundelein, who brought to the bishops' meeting in Washington a briefer and more sober commentary from Kelley.[8]

These three men helped keep alive an interest in a coordinating board. In implementing Propaganda's decree, the hierarchy revised the ABCM according to the guidelines. Each parish was to have two mission organizations, the Propagation and a home-mission society. The former would receive 60 percent of the income from memberships, the remainder going to the ABCM. In structuring itself, the board was directed to consult with the home-mission authorities and perhaps even to adopt Extension's machinery as serving them all.[9] After this action, however, Kelley found it difficult to sustain the momentum. He arranged a follow-up meeting with the directors of home-mission societies in which they reflected a halting timidity in collaborating with each other. They wanted, as he reported to Archbishop Moeller, more assurances of episcopal commitment, along with a firm understanding that the ABCM would begin operation in slow, careful stages.[10] There followed a temporary breakdown. Meetings that were to gather busy bishops and directors were impossible to schedule. In March, 1924, moreover, the elevation of Archbishops Mundelein and Hayes to the cardinalate occupied the attention of two ABCM members. Then came Kelley's appointment to Oklahoma and a trip to the International Eucharistic Congress in Amsterdam. Meanwhile, on his next birthday in January, 1925, the doughty Moeller would reach his eightieth birthday, a factor that hardly expedited his effectiveness as board chairman.[11]

When, therefore, the bishops reconvened on September 24 and 25, 1924, the ABCM had no progress to report, but it had in attendance a new voice in Bishop-elect Kelley, who had been invited to the meeting before his episcopal ordination because, as he told Tampieri proudly, the agenda featured items upon which he had "what we Americans call 'inside information.' "[12] Nevertheless, as he reported later to his Roman friend, he went to his first episcopal gathering with the "resolution to sit down, listen and say nothing." After a warm welcome the discussion shifted eventually to the home-missions. Within ten minutes the newcomer was recruited to write a proposal and submit it to the assembly in the morning, and he had to work well into the night. On the following day, his plan "was adopted unanimously without a change in even a word or a syllable."[13]

The essence of this revised plan was, in Kelley's judgment,

close to the original ABCM. Each diocese was urged to have a *single* organization with two responsibilities. It would collect mission revenues both through membership in the indulgence-rich Propagation and through an annual collection in each parish. It would next divide this money, 60 percent to the Propagation and 40 percent to the ABCM. Kelley's revised plan incorporated a subtle compromise. The single mission office, on the one hand, protected home-mission support in the wealthy dioceses in the East, where the Propagation dominated and could have suffocated the formation of a separate unit for home-missions. On the other hand, the official motion at the bishops' meeting did not mandate the establishment of this diocesan agency but strongly "urged" it, a provision which in a technical sense kept home-mission support entirely voluntary. When the proposal reached Rome, Cardinal Van Rossum had no objections, and on November 7, 1924, Pius XI sanctioned it.[14]

For Kelley this action concluded five years of controversy, an acceptable settlement that was reached in a moment of exquisite irony. "It is strange," he mused soon after, "that, after all the trouble I had over it and all the criticisms that I received, I should have been called on at the end to make the final plans."[15] Papal approval had thus ended more than half a decade of struggle and suffering over his dream of coordination. It also climaxed another, even older, dream. After nearly twenty years at Extension, Kelley's compromise had achieved, for the first time, a guaranteed income for the home-missions. No longer would these be treated like stepchildren within the mission family, relying on the unsteady successes of private groups like Extension. They were finally given their birthright when the American hierarchy opened its teeming parishes and pledged almost half of their mission gifts.

* * * * * * * * *

The approval of the revised ABCM plan led to a second task: the American bishops were expected within the first year to make this new vehicle into a success. One interested observer was Archbishop Fumasoni-Biondi, who set the tone with this stern warning to the bishops. "The H. Father is closely watching the development of the mission situation in the U.S.," as Mundelein recalled the delegate's words. "After all the plan under which they are working is that proposed by the Bps. themselves. The Holy Father agreed to it and ratified it, and he is anxious to see how it is going to work out."[16] But the watchful presence of the delegate was hardly necessary to add much to the hierarchy's wish to translate the blueprint of the ABCM into a productive agency. Three internal factors were sufficient to spark the new board into the promising start looked for in Rome.

The first was its initial leadership. At their annual meeting of 1925, the bishops chose a new six-man board with staggered terms. Both Mundelein and Kelley received full terms of three years; Bishops Hugh C. Boyle of Pittsburgh and John F. Noll of Fort Wayne were given two years; and two archbishops completed the roster with one-year terms, Michael J. Curley of Baltimore and Albert T. Daeger, O.F.M. of Sante Fé. At Boyle's suggestion, the new body withdrew momentarily and soon reported the election of officers. Mundelein was named president, Kelley secretary, and Noll treasurer.[17] The board's direction was thus assigned to veterans in the home-mission ministry, all of them on Extension's own board. Kelley's credentials were uncontestable, and Noll's newspaper, *Our Sunday Visitor,* had regularly subsidized the work.

Perhaps less known was the contribution of the first chairman. Cardinal Mundelein was the ideal choice, bringing to the ABCM several advantages. His rank as cardinal endowed the board with enormous prestige. His heartland archdiocese commanded such vast resources that it alone could challenge the authority of the older sees of the East. His sophisticated yet scrupulous habits in administering funds had earned him respect among managers of the money markets. An inborn drive to be first had likewise transformed him into a vigorous executive, whether building the largest diocese in the country, arranging the first International Eucharistic Congress in the United States, designing the most elaborate seminary of his generation, or advocating the canonization of the first American citizen.[18]

In addition to these attributes, the cardinal was genuinely dedicated to the work of the home-missions. To Kelley, however, this interest appeared at times to be ambiguous and superficial. Under Propaganda's pressure, the cardinal had been the first, and perhaps the only, member of the ABCM to buckle, willing even to see it dissolved. This turn had compelled the Islander to look to Cincinnati, Philadelphia, and New York to carry the fight. But Kelley's criticism of Mundelein was unfair. While the latter openly despaired of the board's success, his interest in the home-missions had never weakened. During the darkest hours of the ABCM struggle, he looked for other means whereby Catholic presence might be strengthened in rural America. One substitute was the idea that the great dioceses might establish individual protectorates in areas where the church could not sustain itself. In early 1922, when Mundelein had given up on the ABCM, his thoughts had turned to the state of Nevada, where his archdiocese could take a special responsibility in sending clergy and funds. At one point, he confided to Father O'Brien his intention of installing there "a 'rough-neck' Bishop." Mundelein "went on to explain," O'Brien later recalled for Ledvina, "that he meant by 'rough-neck' rather one who was able to rough it and if necessary live in a Ford."[19] This plan failed to materialize, no doubt, because the ABCM received approval and he was appointed its first president. In a word, therefore, the ABCM had in the cardinal an able and resourceful devotee of the home-missions. Yet his views followed a spirit of independence and authority which Kelley had encountered during the ABCM struggle earlier and which he would continue to confront in the years to come.

After the selection of three energetic, nationally respected officers—Mundelein, Kelley, and Noll—the ABCM next produced a series of policies that anchored the new agency. First, its headquarters were located permanently in Chicago.[20] This decision revived Kelley's abiding views regarding sectionalism in the American church. Aside from its being Mundelein's home, the city would keep the ABCM independent of what he regarded the Boston-New York-Baltimore axis, where there were located such supra-diocesan institutions as The Catholic University of America, the Propagation's central offices, and the National Catholic Welfare Conference. Experience had converted Mundelein to the same view. In 1924 he had tried to make his new seminary, Saint Mary of the Lake, a pontifical university, even suggesting the transfer of the Catholic University in Washington to his Illinois campus; but easteners like Cardinal Dougherty had succeeded in blocking this, an action which Mundelein never forgave.[21] But the ABCM had broken this near monopoly of responsibility and prestige. In Chicago the West now had not only its first cardinal but also in the board its first national agency of importance.

The second policy consisted of an intensive program to keep before the hierarchy its pledge to fund home-missions. The board announced its firm intention to control all monies that were collected by diocesan officers, though it might occasionally enlist the services of private societies. One such use would be to offer a corps of skilled organizers at Extension to any diocese which found it difficult to organize its mission office. In any case, the board expected each bishop to forward no less than 40 percent of the sum gathered through regular membership in the Propagation and through parish collections on Mission Sunday.

Thirdly, the board gradually enlarged its scope of responsibility and accepted, to Kelley's delight, jurisdiction over the island dependencies from which Extension had been lately excluded. At the annual meeting of 1925, two bishops from the Philippine Islands were admitted as members of the NCWC —Archbishop Michael O'Doherty of Manila and Bishop Sofronio Hacbang y Gaborni of Colbayog. This action raised the question of whether they qualified for ABCM assistance. This possibility was strengthened further when the bishops were reminded that Propaganda no longer governed the islands from Rome as foreign-mission territory. After cautious study of the added obligation, the board was by 1928 giving full shares of support, not only to the Philippine Islands but also to another Extension's former wards, Puerto Rico.[22]

The final course of action of the early board was to negotiate successfully with the major mission societies. No problems loomed at Extension, which had offered its entire organization. The Propagation's new national director, Monsignor William Quinn, spared no effort in cooperating, pledging to send to the ABCM the expected 40 percent from dues for ordinary memberships.[23] More sensitive probings were needed with the Commission for Catholic Missions among the Colored People and the Indians, with headquarters in Washington, D.C. The Third Plenary Council of Baltimore had authorized the commission in 1884 and endowed it generously with authority and money. Its governing board consisted *ex officio* of the archbishops of New York, Philadelphia, and Baltimore; and the commission's work was supported through an annual collection. At the 1925 meeting, Mundelein urged that the ABCM control all home-mission funds, including those of the commission. In return, the board guaranteed an allotment at least equal to the commission's annual income, averaged over the last five years. In this way, home-mission planning and financing would be centralized in Chicago, and the commission would lose nothing in receipts.

The offer, however, was declined through the remarkable teamwork of the commission's board. Only another plenary council, contended Cardinal Hayes strongly, could alter the commission's constitution. Cardinal Dougherty likewise consulted the consistorial congregation, which discouraged a change. And, as Archbishop Curley reported, the commission annually grossed more than $200,000 a sum that the fledgling ABCM could not match.[24] It was therefore decided that the commission would keep its programs and traditional sources of income. Certainly the independence of this eastern body was a disappointment to Mundelein and his colleagues; but, more significantly, the ABCM was willing to tolerate it in an effort to keep the missions from again dividing the hierarchy. A quarrel at this stage would destroy the board. Though Kelley wanted to bring the commission to heel, Mundelein visited Hayes in New York in the spirit of conciliation. The conference between the two cardinals, Mundelein told Curley later, had been intended simply "to remove every danger of friction between the two Boards, which at this time would only entail untold damage to the missions, and accomplish no good as far as I can see."[25] The cardinal's wisdom prevailed over his hot-blooded associate in Oklahoma, who would risk the alienation of three major centers in the East.

The ABCM foundation had been laid securely during its first year, at the end of which the chairman composed a brutally candid report. By the next meeting of the hierarchy in September, 1926, the balance sheet did not post an overwhelming response. Receipts had not reached $100,000, a disappointing return, of which Chicago had given nearly half. Perhaps, Mundelein suggested to his peers, some dioceses had encountered snags in their organization; but, in a stage whisper, he added his suspicions that, perhaps through a misunderstanding, a number of bishops kept a portion of the ABCM percentage for diocesan work. Passing from this less than promising financial report, Mundelein announced tentative guidelines for distribution. Until the bishops indicated otherwise, disbursements would not be lavish, and the board intended to keep a balance on hand for emergencies. The chairman then tried to personalize the need for more support by pointing to the diocese of Amarillo as a model home-mission. Erected only a month before, Kelley's new neighbor in the Texas Panhandle covered some 72,000 square miles—"all along the Mexican border," the cardinal added, in a grievous slip in geography—"no paradise just now." Its founding bishop, Rudolph A. Gerken, had nothing with which to inaugurate an episcopal see. "Now while we have no intention of pensioning him for life," Mundelein explained, "yet we ought to give him enough to keep body and soul together until he can get his organization started. . . ."

One topic remained in the report whereby Mundelein teased Bishop Kelley, who had evidently pressed for the assistance of an executive secretary. The meagre receipts had perhaps made such an addition in personnel an extravagance at this time, but, continued the chairman, there were advantages to a staff worker. An industrious executive secretary could raise the income beyond $500,000. His colleague from Oklahoma, Mundelein added wryly, had stressed that "the man should be a handsome chap with winning ways to attract the Bps. right from the start and enlist their cooperation." The decision was then left to the hierarchy. "If you take no action," Mundelein challenged, "it means you want us all to continue as dollar a year men in your service." The first-year report was thus a gentle but firm scolding. The hierarchy was advised that its responsibility did not end with the mere appointment of a board. Prompt and continuous support were indispensable; otherwise, the ABCM would stagnate—to the scrutiny of the apostolic delegate and the irreparable loss to the church in America. Mundelein's parting word was a stunning appeal to episcopal consciences: "There are as many souls waiting to be saved right here in our own land as in China, and, what is more, have a greater claim on our charity."[26]

This first year of the ABCM had left Bishop Kelley with three inescapable conclusions. First, the results were a disappointment. By December, 1926, only twenty-eight out of 105 dioceses had contributed $115,000, of which Chicago's share alone amounted to $50,000.[27] Second, this poorest of starts raised the issue of the board's authority. Technically, the ABCM was not a compulsory program. The hierarchy's final proposal to Rome in 1924, drafted by Kelley, merely "urged" diocesan affiliation. Propaganda's approval did not require its establishment in each diocese but only encouraged it by granting spiritual favors to those cooperating. As chairman, Mundelein had scrupulously respected this voluntary arrangement, but the dismal results had convinced Kelley of the need for a more direct approach. The board should apply as much pressure on the wealthy dioceses as they could bear, in living up to their promises. This change of strategy led him to the third conclusion. Thus far he had played a subordinate role. With Mundelein's blessing, however, he now took the lead in conducting the field operations which would hopefully boost revenues in the board's second year.

Since the missionary dioceses formed a sizeable group at the meetings of the hierarchy, the first step consisted of organizing them. On January 3 and 4, 1927, bishops of the South and Southwest met with the ABCM in Chicago. The discussion produced a published set of minutes that detailed conditions in the home-missions, along with a joint petition to the whole hierarchy; and both documents were sent to every bishop in the country. "I thank God," commented John J. Mitty, bishop of Salt Lake, "that something is being done to call the attention of the East to the needs of the West."[28] As Mitty reflected the enthusiasm of the missionary bishops, he touched upon a weakness in this approach. In organizing its clients, the ABCM was developing a bloc of partisans and suggesting a sectional division within the hierarchy, the South and Southwest against the North and East. The strategy therefore ran the risk of alienating the wealthy dioceses which it sought to interest.

A showdown in some form was inevitable at the annual bishops' meeting of 1927. As Mundelein planned to make a special appeal in the board's behalf, Kelley encouraged the missionary bishops to be present and even helped a few with suggestions regarding what might be said from the floor. "If we do not succeed this time," he told Bishop Ledvina, "I am going to give it up."[29] On September 14, 1927, Mundelein's second report signaled a vast improvement in revenues, nearly doubling the results of the previous year. Participation had expanded to forty-five dioceses, which contributed a total of $192,000.[30]

Thereupon the missionary bishops opened an acutely intensive discussion. Trembling with emotion, Kelley spoke first in the name of the bishops of the South, urging the absolute need of national action in support of the hierarchy's "China at home." His topic evoked frequent interruptions, including this protest by Archbishop Austin Dowling of St. Paul: "I don't think you are taking the right line."[31] The theme was nevertheless pursued relentlessly when Bishop William J. Hafey of Raleigh announced that in proportion to the general population, Catholics of North Carolina were less numerous than those in China. Mitty soon followed with a moving description of his diocese in Utah and Nevada, which he claimed to be the largest in the world and in which Catholics numbered only 2 percent. Along with Bishop Patrick A. McGovern of Cheyenne, Kelley recommended that a committee of bishops be appointed to visit some dioceses in the West. His friend from Pittsburgh, Bishop Boyle, confessed his apathy as an easterner until his appointment to the ABCM. His recent experience on the board, he added, had verified the criticism directed against dioceses that had failed to support this program.

The unfolding indictment eventually triggered a response from the eastern prelates led by Bishop Joseph Schrembs of Cleveland, who retorted that his diocese was organized and his check for the ABCM was ready. Others joined him in saying further that the East had mission problems of its own and that a tardiness to assist the West did not mean a lack of interest. These strong exchanges ended the morning session, and the afternoon one reflected the mixed reception which the East had given to the discussion. Hints of a negative reaction could be seen in the absence of the presiding officer. Cardinal O'Connell of Boston failed to return to the afternoon session, reportedly too ill but perhaps suffering then from the annoyance that he would in time communicate to Kelley. Positively, however, Schrembs introduced a series of eight resolutions which reinforced the bishops' immediate obligations of honor to the ABCM. Several provisions even strengthened the board's authority, one allowing it to appoint the executive secretary whom Mundelein had requested the year earlier, and another empowering it to circulate public notices of receipts from each diocese.

The meeting had set the ABCM on a true course, but it was not a total triumph. A month later O'Connell sent to Kelley a stinging complaint regarding his thought and behavior. As an old friend, the New Englander suggested that the Oklahoman's zeal might ultimately weaken his effectiveness for the ABCM. To separate bishops along geographical lines "would be absolutely fatal and deplorable." Problems abounded everywhere, including the East, where "the richest sees in the country are burdened with staggering debts. . . ." Nevertheless, the cardinal continued, these dioceses had long assisted the home-missions by giving to their bishops the chance to take up collections in large parishes. O'Connell was particularly critical of Kelley's emotional performance. ". . . at the last meeting in Washington," he wrote, "when you said that you trembled when you reflected on the great needs of the Missions, I thought your emotions were carrying you far afield." Not only were some of Kelley's statements exaggerations but, he added, any plan that even appeared to "arouse a local or factional sentiment among the Bishops of America would be nothing short of disastrous. . . ."[32]

The dean of the hierarchy did not succeed in persuading Kelley that he had misbehaved; instead, it only triggered a strong defense of his actions and motive. The generally poor response to the ABCM in the East, the Islander argued, had inspired his "plain speaking," which might have appeared insolent because of so many interruptions from the floor. He next challenged O-'Connell's charge that he had misrepresented the missionary difficulties. Three years in Oklahoma had educated him first-hand as to the church's losses in the American countryside; and his presentation to the bishops had not distorted the emergency. "Your Eminence may think," he explained firmly,

> that I am a wild, if sincere, enthusiast crying for the impossible. I am not. I am merely one who has seen and studied the sad situation and has not been afraid to speak out. Someone had to do that. From the day I was ordained, I have had nothing but the hard tasks, and today, with the best of my life behind me, Your Eminence knows that my prospects are to continue to be a working horse to the day I die. I do not complain of that. It is my place and I am glad to be in it.[33]

The first exchange of views led only to another, which further refined the ideological differences between them. The ABCM, O'Connell explained in reply, would succeed only if it was based on *"sympathetic cooperation."* No diocese had even been compelled to support another, and no bishop had ever been given the right to demand outside assistance. The cardinal then alluded to several bishops who had communicated to him their regrets over what was described as the "performance staged at the last meeting." The manner of the missionary bishops had been "such an offense to them that they would stay away in the future." O'Connell admired Kelley's energy but reminded him of Talleyrand's classical principle that, in dealing with men, one should not display *"too much zeal."*[34]

The final word, as might be expected, came from Oklahoma. The ABCM, Kelley conceded, could not force compliance among the bishops, but, he added, neither could the Propagation, which in his view had been only recommended, not mandated, by the Holy See. The ABCM enjoyed no less an endorsement from Rome and therefore deserved the same generous response which the bishops had given to the Propagation. But Kelley's second letter to Boston was more than an idle tit for tat. He was indignant at O'Connell's attempt, albeit paternal, to mute him at future meetings; and for this reason he elaborated his views on sectional favoritism in the American church, a risky topic with the nominal head of the hierarchy.

In words suggestive of the Marxist principle of class warfare, Kelley coldly pointed to "the fact that there are two classes of dioceses and two classes of bishops in these United States, the rich and the poor." The wealthy dioceses were in the East, where easteners succeeded each other. "How then," he asked, "shall the bishops of the prosperous dioceses know conditions in the poor ones, since they never were in them?" As long as westerners appeared barred from appointments in the East, the truth could come "only . . . from us who know it to our sorrow. Why should any bishop resent our telling that truth frankly when we meet?" The bishops of the South and West have come of age, he warned, and they "shall be heard."[35] The exchange between Massachusetts and Oklahoma achieved little in persuasion; both men remained rooted in their positions. But Kelley had once more demonstrated a nearly reckless commitment to the home-missions as a priority that bowed to no other, including the foreign-missions. The opportunity to communicate privately with an important friend allowed his ideas to reach a clarity and force which were seldom seen in his cautious public statements.

The three-year terms of Cardinal Mundelein and Bishop Kelley expired at the annual bishops' meeting of 1928, an appropriate point to conclude this discussion on the ABCM. By that time, the board and Extension had combined some operations through the appointment in the previous year of Eugene McGuinness, a priest of the archdiocese of Philadelphia, who served in the dual capacity of ABCM executive secretary and Extension's vice president and general secretary.[36] The two bodies remained distinct, however, each with its own governing board. The union consisted simply in the coordination of ABCM and Extension allotments to missionary bishops in order to avoid duplication and inequities. When the hierarchy assembled on November 14, 1928, the ABCM reported that in the past year seventy-nine dioceses out of 106 had contributed $324,279. Its support had more than tripled in two years. In spite of this remarkable beginning, both Mundelein and Kelley submitted their resignations. The board, the cardinal contended, had received only half of what should have been given; his archdiocese alone accounted for the bulk of the revenues, a full quarter of them.

Bishop Kelley's own criticism regarding these initial years focused on two different problems. First, he had secretly complained of certain aspects of the cardinal's management, particularly his natural dominance on the board. When several missionary bishops had appealed to him privately, Mundelein had, on his own authority, advanced money to them, frequently in subsidies greater than the usual allotment. "Cardinal Mundelein," Kelley had confided earlier to Ledvina, "has been our best friend and gives the largest amount. He has a kind heart and does not like to refuse." But, the bishop added, he ought to be protected by a regulation that "no money should be given out during the year except at meetings."[37] At the 1928 meeting of the bishops, therefore, Kelley had in mind the cardinal's casual style of administration when the Oklahoman recommended that the board be reconstituted without cardinals or archbishops. In this way, there would be no senior prelate whom missionary bishops would approach separately and to whom board members now tended to defer. The next organizational weakness, according to Kelley, lay in his own appointment to the board. Of the six members, he was the only missionary bishop and was expected to represent his impoverished colleagues in rural America. Unfortunately, criticism had been heard regarding allotments to Oklahoma, suggesting that he had used his position to assist himself. His second recommendation, therefore, was that the board derive its membership from dioceses in need of no outside support.

Neither Mundelein's nor Kelley's comments, however, moved the bishops to change the personnel or constitution. Their resignations were declined in an overwhelming display of confidence.[38] The cardinal remained chairman until his death in 1939, and Kelley kept on as secretary until Bishop William D. O'Brien of Extension succeeded him a year later. By the time of his departure in 1940, the ABCM had become a fixture in the American church. The depression had interrupted a steady climb in revenues, but by that year the annual income from 112 dioceses resumed its strong upward course and passed the $400,000 mark. More significantly, in its first fifteen years the board had dispensed to the home-missions over $12 million in undesignated gifts.[39] Bishop Kelley gladly shared in this singular accomplishment with his colleagues in the hierarchy, but no one could deny his unique role. He had been the principal force in providing this mechanism whereby Catholic America could extend itself to the needs at home which it had long neglected.

* * * * * * * * * *

Francis Kelley's work for the ABCM did not weaken his interest in his other creation, the Catholic Church Extension Society. His appointment to Oklahoma in 1924 had forced the retirement of the founder from the presidency after nineteen years of enlightened leadership, but to his former associates in Chicago he was still esteemed as the "Boss." Kelley remained on the board of governors. His successor, Monsignor 'Willie" O'Brien, maintained a lifelong friendship, corresponding with him intimately about the society's affairs. In these years Kelley welcomed reminders of the secure foundations which he had bequeathed to Extension. The transition had brought no symptoms of collapse or stagnation. In 1926 O'Brien proudly announced that receipts had for the first time passed $1 million. In the same year, when O'Brien returned from a visit to Europe, he discovered that the office was virtually self-operating. ". . . it was run so well in my absence," he told his predecessor, "that the realization was brought home to me again that you have builded [*sic*] so well that any priest can run the Extension Society successfully."[40] O'Brien could be careless with his compliments, but this rambling sentiment hardly exaggerated the founder's achievement.

Eugene McGuinness was the other priest whom Kelley had left behind. On loan from Cardinal Dougherty, "Mac" enjoyed an even warmer relationship with the "Boss," who, both in Chicago and later in Oklahoma, advocated greater responsibility and honors for the Philadelphian. In 1923 a vacancy in the diocese of Tucson had led Kelley to articulate his respect for the young priest. "What the Church needs in Arizona," he reflected, "is a young, energetic, American bishop with a missionary spirit in him and a desire to do hard work"—demanding specifications which, in Kelley's judgment, McGuinness met admirably.[41] Though Kelley had failed in Chicago to place him in a diocese, he succeeded from Oklahoma in engineering a doctorate for him, a lesser accomplishment certainly but one testifying to the older man's continued interest. In 1927, when McGuinness was to tour the Philippines, Kelley arranged through the apostolic delegate, Archbishop William Piani, that the University of San Tomás grant him a degree in theology. The university was cooperative, requiring only that the candidate produce a thesis and deliver it in a public lecture. On tour, McGuinness was scarcely disposed to fulfill these requirements, racing through the capital in what the delegate described as "a chicagoan rush." This compelled Kelley to settle for an honorary degree, and "Mac" was elevated to "Doctor McGuinness," a somewhat contrived dignity that delighted his Extension comrades.[42]

Bishop Kelley had therefore been a successful parent not only at birth of his creation but also when it reached maturity. The favored child of his years in Chicago, Extension had not evolved into a personal possession to be smothered and monopolized by its founder. He gracefully cut the ties of origin, leaving it in charge of two others whom he trusted and in whose successes he rejoiced. But parents are frequently disposed to worry afar about their offspring, even the sturdiest of them; and Francis Kelley was no exception. His last two decades with Extension were not altogether happy. His departure to the American Southwest signaled the start of an association that troubled him for practically the rest of his active life. It centered on two throbbing and contradictory concerns. The first was fueled by charges made by outsiders that he had retained too much influence, and the second was due to internal developments which suggested the subtle elimination of what influence of his remained within Extension.

The source of Kelley's first worry, therefore, was criticism that Extension played favorites. If allowed to stand, this accusation would destroy the society's credibility. For this reason, Kelley had resolved never to take advantage of his special relationship with the officers. This vow was not easy to keep. Not only was Oklahoma an indigent diocese, but Monsignor O'Brien had himself promised to be especially attentive to its needs, pledging that no request from Kelley would ever be denied. "Anything the boss wants [in] any way that he wants it," ran O'Brien's guiding principle, "will be taken care of."[43] The bishop, however, faithfully resisted the temptation and kept his requests reasonable. "You know," he explained to O'Brien, "that I do not want the Diocese of Oklahoma to be considered, or thought of, [as] a favored client. That's for the sake of the Society, not myself. Rather than have criticism directed at the Society I would prefer to give the money to another."[44] The constant threat of this criticism was but one factor that tempered his applications for Extension money. He was also convinced that missionaries must not condition themselves as permanent dependents. Kelley once commended Ledvina for having discouraged his clergy from "rushing to Extension instead of trying to help themselves." Extension, he said, "was founded to help little places get on their feet. When they managed to do that, they ought to make the effort to walk alone. It is good for the place and good for the priests."[45]

Though it bothered him throughout his episcopal career, only once did the danger of charges regarding favoritism become acute. This occurred through the ill-mannered goading of Timothy Corbett, first bishop of Crookston. His diocese extended broadly in western Minnesota and was supported in large measure by his active solicitation of outside funds, including Extension. A respected administrator, he had also earned a reputation of being an eccentric—"somewhat insane" and "violent," as one neighboring bishop profiled him.[46] During Kelley's last years at Extension, Corbett's appeals had become virtual ultimata, perhaps because of the pressures of managing a poor and isolated diocese. Unfortunately, however, his requests often concerned routine diocesan obligations, such as parish indebtedness and building repairs—only to be turned down by Extension and the ABCM. These rejections served only to inflame the hardpressed prelate. A man conscious of his authority, he could not understand such denials to the word of one "whom the Holy ghost placed to rule . . ."; and he blamed Kelley for deliberately discriminating against his diocese.[47]

Bishop Corbett's carping was tolerable until 1924 when Kelley was appointed to Oklahoma, and Extension listed a subsidy of $25,000 for the latter's diocese, an allotment larger than usual. This disclosure opened a flood of accusations from Corbett, pointing to a sinister collusion between Kelley and Extension, and the Minnesotan threatened to appeal to the Holy See. That sum, Kelley pointed out, had come not from Extension revenues but from gifts received at his episcopal ordination.[48] The money had simply passed through the society's ledgers as a "designated gift" from him to his new see. This bookkeeping device had been occasionally used to give Extension extra credit in reporting its annual receipts. Though Corbett was beyond reason, nothing resulted from his charges, except that Kelley became extremely cautious regarding the society's funds. In his view, Corbett had injured his southwestern diocese because, as he told Ledvina, he had "trumpeted . . . from one end of the country to the other that I took twenty-five thousand for myself before I left." Without question, the Minnesotan had intimidated him. From the beginning of his episcopal administration, Oklahoma was forced to be modest in its requests to Chicago because, as Ledvina learned further, antagonists like Corbett had "turned the guns on me."[49]

Kelley's special connection with Extension had therefore handicapped it as a source of help for Oklahoma. Nevertheless, this irony had two positive effects. Kelley's prudence propelled the diocese toward self-sufficiency and strengthened outside confidence in the society's fairness in helping bishops in need. At his death, his two successors—O'Brien at Extension and McGuinness in Oklahoma—acknowledged this little known contribution to the home-missions. "As a Missionary Bishop," recalled O'Brien, "he was most considerate of Extension and taught his clergy to ask for help only in the most needy cases."[50]

His second lingering concern pivoted on the transition of Extension's command. William D. O'Brien was his picked successor, having served the society in a variety of capacities for seventeen years until his appointment as its second president.[51] At first there was every indication that the years to follow would bring an untroubled association between the pair. Once relieved of the presidency, Kelley immediately promoted a step upward in Monsignor O'Brien's rank by recommending that his title be raised from that of papal chamberlain to that of domestic prelate.[52] In return, O'Brien was eager to complete a number of his predecessor's pet projects. Without doubt the Boss had long wanted to enlarge and improve *Extension Magazine,* and a cash legacy left to the society in 1926 enabled O'Brien to expand the format for a year. Beginning with the October issue, the monthly featured four to six short stories by such distinguished writers as Frank H. Spearman and Gene Markey, along with articles on Catholic doctrine, sports, humor, and current political topics —illustrated lavishly and laid out in a plump edition of fifty-six pages. The new makeup, it was hoped, would increase revenues through increased circulation and advertising.[53] Few ventures could have pleased Kelley more.

Inevitably, however, Bishop Kelley's departure from Chicago brought changes that were unwelcome to him. The key, of course, lay in the relationship between his successor and the chancellor. As founder, Kelley had preceded Cardinal Mundelein into home-mission work by a decade. This might have been the factor that allowed him as president some indpendence of thought and action. His successor had neither these credentials nor the temperament to stand up to an insistent superior. Almost from the start Kelley perceived this difference. His first trip to Chicago after his installation in Oklahoma revealed that Mundelein was now determining the direction of the society and was tying it too closely to Chicago interests. "Extension is a national institution," Kelley confided to Tampieri, "and the tendency of Monsignor O'Brien is to make it too local. Naturally that is the tendency of the Cardinal, and Monsignor O'Brien is completely subservient to him."

O'Brien's docility suggested to Kelley that as a rule no Chicago priest should be named president. If the chief officer was automatically a lifelong subject of the chancellor, the society would lose its national character and become an archdiocesan institution. In addition, there would follow an unhealthy professional relationship which would destroy the checks and balances essential to any organization. "I left Chicago feeling very uneasy . . . ," he told a friend, "for I saw the tendency to concentrate power in the hands of the Chancellor through Monsignor O'Brien." So disturbed was Kelley by these early developments that he now opposed O'Brien's permanent appointment until he had been given a longer trial. In conscience, the founder was thus torn between his fears for Extension's future and his wishes for O'Brien's success. "If it is a question between the interests of the Society and my friendship for Monsignor O'Brien," he concluded grimly, "the latter will have to take a second place." In spite of Kelley's fears for Extension, O'Brien won Mundelein's confidence. Unlike the previous nightmares over the Islander's reappointment as president, O'Brien's terms were renewed without difficulty, and he retained his post for nearly forty years, twice as long as his predecessor.[54]

The society continued its basic work of subsidizing the home missions, dispensing even greater amounts of assistance than had been possible during Kelley's regime. There occurred, however, the dismantling of one minor feature that was particularly dear to him, a preview of a greater difficulty to come. As a pontifical institute, Extension had been entitled to a liaison at the Holy See, normally through a cardinal "protector." Since the death of Cardinal Martinelli in 1918, Mundelein had procrastinated in securing a successor. Convinced of the importance of personal representation in Rome, Kelley was induced to improvise the office of "procurator," which in 1923 had fallen to Monsignor Sante Tampieri, a veteran insider of the curia and confidant of Cardinal Merry del Val. Trouble arose soon after this appointment when Kelley nominated the Italian churchman to take charge of Extension's exhibit at the Vatican Missionary Exposition scheduled in Rome for 1925, an action which Mundelein was expected to confirm. The nominee was known to the chancellor, having introduced himself at a reception in Rome in honor of Mundelein's elevation to the cardinalate.[55] Regarding representatives at the Holy See, however, Mundelein steered an independent course. He steadfastly ignored each communication from Tampieri and decided in the meantime to handle local details for the exhibit through a sister whom he knew in Rome. This slight stung Tampieri, to whom Kelley could offer only limp excuses. "He likes to do things his own way . . . ," explained Kelley. "When the Cardinal has something on his mind he rushes at it and makes arrangements without consulting anybody."[56]

Mundelein's ambiguity had left Tampieri's connection with Extension in doubt. When Kelley broached the subject with O'Brien, the latter anticipated no change in policy unless, he said, the cardinal would order the appointment; and his intervention in this matter was unlikely. In transmitting this message to the puzzled Roman, Kelley added this observation: "The Cardinal is an excellent Chancellor, but he likes to have his own way."[57] The matter was not, however, entirely insignificant for Mundelein, who soon instructed O'Brien to conduct his Roman business through a priest at the Urban College of Propaganda, Torquato Dini. This news embarrassed Kelley, who was conscious of Tampieri's unique service to Extension. It had begun fifteen years earlier in Merry del Val's secretariat of state, where he had written the apostolic brief making the society a pontifical institute. Mundelein's behavior displayed such insensitivity as to prompt Kelley's waspish comment: "I hate to think of even a faithful dog getting a kick."[58] The cardinal's cold indifference was in the Oklahoman's view not only an unworthy reward for many personal favors to the society; but it also ended decisively Kelley's tradition of Extension's special representative at the Holy See.

Tampieri's disengagement as procurator served as a prelude to a greater jolt when the founder himself was passed over. Upon the death of Archbishop Sebastian Messmer of Milwaukee in 1930, the position of the vice-chancellor was vacant for the first time since the beginning of Extension. Bishop Kelley fully expected to be named to the second place on the board. It was basically a title of respect—not an active office that could complicate the chancellor's function. In twenty-five years, Messmer had presided at only one meeting, the one held in the interregnum immediately after Archbishop Quigley's death. Business corporations, the Islander reasoned further, honored their retiring chief executives by awarding to them special positions on their boards. As founder and first president, he saw himself the only one deserving and qualified to succeed to the vice-chancellorship. It was, besides, the year of the society's silver jubilee, another circumstance that made his appointment logical.

Having taken the vice-chancellorship for granted, Kelley was astonished to learn that Mundelein had other plans. As the board meeting in November approached, Mundelein expressed his intention to nominate Messmer's successor in Milwaukee, Archbishop Samuel A. Stritch. Three times O'Brien carried to the cardinal Kelley's strong wish for the position, along with serving notice that the Oklahoman would resign from Extension's board if someone else was named. Mundelein was adamant. He ignored the ultimatum and injected a personal taunt when he confided to O'Brien his grievance at Kelley's practice of coming to Chicago without calling on him. The cardinal's reaction dumbfounded Kelley. The constitution did not provide an *ex-officio* position for the archbishop of Milwaukee; Stritch had himself never even served on the board of governors. And Kelley had declined to call upon Mundelein only in the fear that these visits would intrude upon his time.[59]

Events surrounding the board meeting of November 20, 1930, were among the darkest in Kelley's life. Mundelein's decision had left him with two alternatives: either to oppose the cardinal's candidate or to withdraw formally from the executive committee; and he chose the latter. "The night before the meeting," he told Bishop Edward F. Hoban, now of Rockford, "was a night of torture for me. I had no choice but to get out of the Society after so many years of successful services. It was like tearing out a piece of my heart. I did not sleep at all." He next went to the society's offices and handed Mundelein a letter of resignation. "I need not tell you how I felt," he confessed to Hoban further. "For a little while I tried to barricade myself in one of the rooms until I was fit to go on the street." Before he left Chicago, Bishop James A. Griffin of Springfield, Illinois, confided to him as to how the board meeting had been engineered. Griffin had been instructed to nominate Stritch as vice-chancellor, and O'Brien had been told to present Griffin as Kelley's successor on the executive committee. These maneuvers confirmed the cardinal's readiness to eliminate Kelley entirely from the society. The momentum had been halted, Griffin continued, only when another of Mundelein's suffragans, Bishop Hoban, had risen to the Islander's defense and countered the move to accept his resignation. The founder was thus retained on the executive committee. "Out of that whole miserable picture," Kelley admitted to Hoban gratefully, "the bright touch for me is what you did. Nothing but a sense of justice and fairness on your part could have brought such a thing about."[60]

This shock forced two long-term adjustments in Bishop Kelley's relationship with the society he had established and brought to maturity. First, he became more openly critical of the partnership between Mundelein and O'Brien. The cardinal's conduct had added to Kelley's abiding confusion regarding him: ". . . I don't understand him."[61] More importantly, he noted a dangerous twofold trend under the new regime. Authority was increasingly concentrated in the hands of the president. The executive committee, observed Kelley, no longer checked his activity as before, a lapse that virtually left O'Brien accountable to the chancellor alone. This freedom, moreover, allowed his successor to accumulate vast "reserves," perhaps as much as $5 million. In Kelley's mind, this new policy to bank money, mostly for endowments, needlessly diverted immediate assistance from desperate missionary dioceses.[62]

Until his resignation, Kelley had kept these objections secret, but Mundelein's insensitive behavior over the vice-chancellorship shifted his sense of loyalty from discreet silence to well-placed complaints. The disgruntled Islander promptly shared these concerns with Archbishop Fumasoni-Biondi and narrated for him the details of his withdrawal from Extension. "I feel," he charged angrily, "that His Eminence took advantage of the situation to force me out of the work I founded and made."[63] At this time, another who was allowed into Kelley's thoughts was Edmund A. Walsh, S.J., president of the Catholic Near East Welfare Association. Father Walsh was engaged in developing a plan of coordination between his office and the Propagation, and solicited comments from Kelley. The response included a withering passage on Extension. The accumulation of large treasuries or endowment funds, Walsh was counseled, not only denied to missionaries necessary aid but also made the society practically a hostage to the government. "Great sums of invested money become a danger," reflected Kelley, because they merely tempted politicians to tax or confiscate them.[64] This harsh truth was, accordingly, the principal lesson that Extension had now to offer to Walsh's new agency, a devastating reflection on O'Brien's administration.

The gulf between Kelley and Extension was widened further by his voluntary boycott which lasted a decade. While his diocese continued to receive the society's assistance, the founder made his intention as an *ex-officio* board member clear to the apostolic delegate. "I shall never enter a meeting of the Society again except as its Vice Chancellor," he vowed firmly on the last day of 1930:

> Evidently His Eminence had decided that this proper recognition of the one who brought "Extension" into existence shall not be accorded. My permanent retirement from the Society is then assured.[65]

This angry pledge included a virtual withdrawal from the ABCM as well. The board's meetings were held regularly at the Extension office, where as long as Mundelein presided and the "Boss" never appeared.[66]

Meanwhile, O'Brien's correspondence with Kelley not only continued to enclose subsidies for Oklahoma; it also kept him in close touch with events in Chicago. As the president repeatedly besought Kelley to return, he discovered how fixed was his predecessor's decision to stay away. First, the Oklahoman was informed that the bishops, including the cardinal, had missed him at board meetings, and his absence had forced O'Brien and McGuinness to contrive excuses.[67] There followed an appeal to Kelley's generosity. ". . . I have been wondering lately," wrote O'Brien, "if you would not be big enough to practice some of the things you have preached so well to the priests of the country. . . . If you walk into the next meeting, you know just as well as I that everybody from the Cardinal down to myself would receive you with open arms." But Kelley would not come back as a prodigal; the conditions for his presence were made clear. Since Mundelein had made no overture, the Islander's return might arouse more of the cardinal's displeasure. "I don't believe in fighting," he told McGuinness, "and I have a soul to save."[68]

Kelley and Mundelein were never reconciled, the two men rooted in their positions until the latter's death on October 2, 1939, which was, coincidentally, the fifteenth anniversary of Kelley's episcopal ordination by the cardinal. The founder's return to Extension was soon made possible when Archbishop Stritch succeeded to Chicago. This appointment gave the society a new chancellor, and the vice-chancellorship was again vacant. Kelley's friends at Extension immediately conspired to end his boycott. With Stritch's blessing, he reappeared at the board meeting of November 13, 1940, his first in ten years, and was elected vice-chancellor. The title remained with him, even through illness, until 1947, when, within the last year of his life, the board gracefully added "emertius."[69] Thus was healed a long festering wound that had grieved both parent and child.

Bishop Kelley's later connection with the home-mission movement was tragic. He had given to it two major institutions—the Extension Society and the ABCM; and he had been the key instrument in securing their financial foundations. But they were unfinished vehicles which continued to need his guidance as an active missionary bishop who was the virtual patriarch of the movement. His experience in Oklahoma therefore allowed him to see the flaws more vividly than most bishops. The ABCM, he told a confidant, dispensed its aid in a haphazard and casual fashion—without a serious study of national priorities. Extension seemed bent on ensuring its institutional future by building assets to the neglect of some urgent needs in the field. Neither institution had halted the leakage from the church in rural areas where Catholic adults still drifted into indifferentism and their children into Protestantism. "I have seen them by the thousands in Oklahoma as sad examples," he observed grimly. "I still know what I am talking about, for I have been over this country from end to end, not as a tourist, but as a student of its missionary problems." Moreover, neither bishops nor seminaries in this country supplied effective missionaries for newly arrived Catholics, notably immigrants from Mexico. "In my Diocese," he reflected further, "I have not one priest who has learned enough Spanish to preach in that language."[70]

The years in the American Southwest had thus taught him a basic lesson: the ABCM and Extension had evolved into mere financial clearing-houses. Their concentration on collecting and distributing funds had, he felt, prevented a thorough analysis of the home-mission crisis whereby the church's resources would be channeled according to careful priorities. "Giving money here and there to poor places is only putting salve on the wounds," he concluded after thirty-five years in the movement:

> They will break out again. The thing to do is to get at the root of the thing. But somehow we never understood that and a lot of money that could have done good has been wasted.[71]

An unfortunate misunderstanding between two unyielding men, however, eliminated Kelley's influence at a critical stage of these two institutions. His perspective as elder statesman would have been a major asset in the Chicago meetings in the 1930s. But a clash of personalities had produced a lengthy self-imposed exile, much to Kelley's own grief and to the loss of the rural church he had championed so well.

Key to Abbreviations Used In References

AAC	Archives of the archdiocese of Chicago
AAOC	Archives of the archdiocese of Oklahoma City
AAW	Archives of the archdiocese of Westminster, London
ASBA	Archives of Saint Benedict's Abbey, Atchison, Kansas
ASC	Archives of the Séminaire de Chicoutimi
ASN	Archives of the Séminaire de Nicolet
ASPF	Archives of the Society for the Propagation of the Faith, New York City
CCL	Confederation Centre Library, Charlottetown, Prince Edward Island, Canada
CUA	Department of Archives and Manuscripts, The Catholic University of America
EP	Papers of the Catholic Church Extension Society of the United States of America
FO	Papers of the British Foreign Office, Public Record Office, London
Jots	Francis Clement Kelley, *The Bishop Jots It Down: An Autobiographical Strain on Memories* (New York, 1939)
MP	Papers of H. L. Mencken, The New York Public Library
NA	National Archives, Washington, D.C.
NCWC	Archives of the National Catholic Welfare Conference, Washington, D.C.
n.d.	no date
n.p.	no place
PA	Public Archives, Government of Prince Edward Island, Canada
PRO	Public Record Office, London
WP	Papers of Woodrow Wilson, Library of Congress, Washington, D.C.

VOLUME 1
References

PROLOGUE

1. Mencken Papers (hereafter cited as MP), Dudek to Mencken, Oklahoma City, November 6, 1925; memorandum written by Mencken, n.p., September 9, 1941, copy. Oklahoma City *Times,* November 3, 1936, p. 1. Wilson Papers (hereafter cited as WP), Wilson to Joseph P. Tumulty, n.p. [*ca.* February 22, 1918].

2. Interviews with Leo J. and Marie Starry, Oklahoma City, October 17, 1975; with Albert L. Fletcher, Oklahoma City, April 14, 1977; and with Sister Alicia Blick, A.S.C., Oklahoma City, February 6, 1978. Archives of the archdiocese of Oklahoma City (hereafter cited as AAOC), FCK to Alexander McAulay, n.p., December 2, 1922, copy. Louis Arand, S.S., to the writer, Baltimore, December 19, 1978.

3. AAOC, FCK to Christopher E. Byrne, n.p., April 4, 1942; February 13, 1943; and February 28, 1944, copies.

4. AAOC, FCK to Emmanuel B. Ledvina, n.p., January 7, 1929; FCK to

Dennis Dougherty, n.p., February 22, 1929, copies.

5. AAOC, "The Bishop's Salad"; FCK to Boyle, Cliff Haven, New York, August 14, 1938, copy. Interview with Joseph F. Murphy, O.S.B., Oklahoma City, October 18, 1975.

6. Interview with Raymond F. Harkin, Oklahoma City, October 20, 1975. AAOC, FCK to Cyril D. Day, n.p., September 5, 1931; James W. O'Keefe to Ray O. Wyland, n.p., December 29, 1934; FCK to Charles Breitung, n.p., March 21, 1944, copies.

7. AAOC, Michael G. Shean, C.R.I.C., to FCK, Taulignan (Drôme), France, October 4, 1936; and January 17, 1937; FCK to Shean, n.p., January 2, 1937, copy; FCK to William D. O'Brien, n.p., March 20, 1937, copy.

8. AAOC, FCK to John A. O'Brien, n.p., March 29, 1938, copy; Matthew F. Brady to FCK, Burlington, Vermont, January 25, 1939; FCK to Brady, n.p., January 30, 1939, copy; WIlliam D. O'Brien to FCK, Chicago, October 6, 1941; Eileen Duggan to FCK, Wellington, New Zealand, n.d. Extension Papers (hereafter cited as EP). Lucey to William D. O'Brien, San Antonio, October 3, 1941. Interview with Joseph T. McGucken, Menlo Park, California, July 4, 1978. Joseph F. Murphy, O.S.B., to the writer, Shawnee, Oklahoma, December 30, 1978.

9. AAOC, FCK to Harold H. Nevanas, n.p., December 20, 1924; and June 4, 1928; FCK to John F. Golden, M.D., n.p., May 6, 1933; FCK to Matthew Schumacher, C.S.C., December 27, 1937; and April 15, 1938, copies.

10. AAOC, FCK to Maurice Schexnayder, n.p., May 14 and 18, 1934, copies.

11. FCK, *Dominus Vobiscum* (Chicago, 1922), 260. Interview with Mrs. Frank Martin, Oklahoma City, October 19, 1975.

12. AAOC, FCK to Richard R. St. John, n.p., December 13, 1943, copy. Hal Hudson to the writer, Palo Alto, California, January 12, 1979.

13. EP, FCK to William D. O'Brien, Oklahoma City, July 15, 1943.

14. AAOC, Duggan to Dudek, Wellington, New Zealand, n.d.; Drossaerts to FCK, San Antonio, July 7, 1929.

15. FCK, *Dominus Vobiscum,* 193.

16. AAOC, FCK to William C. Bruce, n.p., February 13, 1935, copy.

17. AAOC, FCK to Joseph A. O'Sullivan, n.p., July 27, 1943, copy.

18. AAOC, FCK to Charles L. O'Donnell, C.S.C., n.p., September 27, 1930; and April 16, 1931, copies; O'Donnell to FCK, Notre Dame, Indiana, April 14, 1931; Wilson to FCK, Oklahoma City, April 17, 1931. For details related to Oklahoma's "bone-dry" law, see Thomas Elton Brown, *Bible Belt Catholicism: A History of the Roman Catholic Church in Oklahoma, 1905-1945* (New York, 1977), 65-87.

19. AAOC, FCK to Urban de Hasque, n.p., July 8, 1926, copy.

20. FCK, *Dominus Vobiscum,* 51.

21. AAOC, Joseph P. Lynch to FCK, Dallas, August 12, 1944.

22. AAOC, FCK to Joseph J. Quinn, n.p., October 7, 1924, copy.

23. AAOC, FCK to G. Paul Butler, n.p., March 28, 1944, copy.

24. AAOC, FCK to Francis Borgia Steck, O.F.M., n.p., October 3, 1929, copy.

25. FCK, *Letters to Jack: Written by a Priest to His Nephew* (Chicago, 1917), 165.

26. FCK, *Sacerdos et Pontifex: Letters to a Bishop-Elect* (Paterson, New Jersey, 1940), 10, 101-2.

27. AAOC, FCK to Orozco, n.p., February 18 and October 2, 1925, copies.

28. AAOC, FCK to Orozco, n.p., August 27, 1926, copy; Orozco to FCK, Guadalajara, September 7, 1926.

29. AAOC, FCK to Orozco, n.p., July 15, 1929, copy.

30. AAOC, Spearman to FCK, n.p., June 3, 1937.

31. AAOC, FCK to Brother Leo, F.S.C., n.p., March 5, 1937; FCK to John J. Mitty, n.p., December 23, 1937; FCK to Francis Meehan, n.p., December 19, 1941; and June 23, 1942, copies; Meehan to FCK, East Orange, New Jersey, December 10, 1941, and January 3, 1942.

32. Francis Barry Byrne's views on design may be found in "Towards a New Architecture of Worship," *Architectural Record,* CII (September, 1947), 93-96; and in scattered articles in *Liturgical Arts* (Concord, New Hampshire), the most representative of which are "Plan for a Church," X (May, 1942), 58-60; "On Training for Architecture," XIII (May, 1945), 56, 61-62; and "In Search of a Client: On the Cardinal Lercaro Award Competition," XXIX (Feburary, 1961), 51-53. Some years after these articles appeared, Byrne's ideas seem to have won the full endorsement

of the American hierarchy. See Bishops' Committee on the Liturgy, *Environment and Art in Catholic Worship* (Washington, D.C.: National Conference of Catholic Bishops, 1978), 24-25.

33. AAOC, Byrne to FCK, New York City [*ca.* July 1, 1934]; FCK to Allan T. Pendleton, n.p., March 11, 1939, copy. Charles D. Maginnis, "A Survey and a Hope," *Liturgical Arts,* X (November, 1941), 3-4. The interior plan of the Church of Christ the King, dated 1941, is given in the *New Catholic Encyclopedia* (New York, 1967), III, 829, 835. FCK's singular fondness for this church is evident from the fact that it was the only building in Oklahoma in which he placed one of the most precious relics of Christianity, viz., an authenticated remnant from the table used by Jesus at the Last Supper. The remaining fragments in FCK's possession went to two other special places—the Edward J. Doheny family and FCK's former parish in Wilmette, Illinois. AAOC, FCK to Martin McNamara, n.p., December 20, 1940, and February 1, 1941, copies.

34. AAOC, FCK to William D. O'Brien, n.p., April 9, 1938; FCK to William Thomas Walsh, n.p., December 31, 1938, copies.

35. FCK, "A Visit, Not Ad Limina, to Number One Glencoe Street," *America,* LXI (May 20, 1939), 138-39. *Jots,* 320. FCK, *Sacerdos et Pontifex,* 22-23. AAOC, Duggan to FCK, Wellington, n.d., ms.; FCK to H. L. Binesse, n.p., April 14, 1943, copy.

36. AAOC, FCK to Phillips, n.p., June 6, 1929, and September 28, 1939; FCK to W.C. ("Clay") Smoot, n.p., July 31, 1942, copies.

37. AAOC, Dougherty to FCK, Philadelphia, June 3, 1937.

38. AAOC, Spellman to FCK, New York City [*ca.* May 26, 1940.].

39. AAOC, Phillips to FCK, Bartlesville, Oklahoma, June 1, 1937.

40. AAOC, FCK to Phillips, n.p., December 18, 1943, copy; Phillips to FCK, Bartlesville, December 22, 1943.

41. AAOC, FCK to Phillips, n.p., October 24, 1940, copy. See also AAOC, Smoot to FCK, Bartlesville, August 10, 1942.

42. *Jots,* 229, 232. A brief study of the controversy over the leasing of oil reserves is Burl Noggle, *Teapot Dome: Oil and Politics in the 1920's* (Baton Rouge, Louisiana, 1962).

43. AAOC, FCK to Edward L. Doheny, n.p., May 17, 1926; FCK to Estelle Doheny, n.p., November 25, 1926, copies.

44. *The Acolyte* (Huntington, Indiana), II (April 24, 1926), 15. AAOC, FCK to John F. Noll, n.p., May 1, 1926, copy.

45. AAOC, FCK to Estelle Doheny, n.p., February 20, 1929, copy.

46. AAOC, FCK to Estelle Dohney, n.p., March 11, 1937, copy.

47. AAOC, FCK to Bruce R. Baster, n.p., September 16, 1940, copy.

48. AAOC, FCK to Edward D. Kelly, n.p., December 2, 1915, FCK to Raphael Merry del Val, n.p., November 21, 1929, copies; Thomas Carey to FCK, Lapeer, Michigan, April 26, 1927.

49. AAOC, FCK to John M. Doyle, n.p., May 29, 1929; and April 17, 1930; FCK to Merry del Val, n.p., January 30, 1930; FCK to Michael J. Gallagher, Tulsa, June 9, 1930, copies. A partial explanation of Hallissey's trouble, which is unconfirmed, is that the charges originated with another Detroit clergyman, Charles E. Coughlin, the future "radio priest" and virulent critic of the administration of Franklin D. Roosevelt. Interview with a priest of the archdiocese of Detroit who wished to remain anonymous, Oklahoma City, December 15, 1977.

50. AAOC, FCK to Frank Phillips, n.p., July 2, 1936; FCK to Joseph F. Thorning, n.p., April 19, 1938, copies.

51. AAOC, FCK to Mooney, n.p., February 12 and March 8, 1943, copies; Mooney to FCK, Detroit, March 3, 1943.

52. *Extension Magazine* (Chicago), XI (June, 1916), 3-4; XIII (June, 1918), 4.

53. AAOC, MacNeil to FCK, New York City, January 8 and August 11, 1942; FCK to MacNeil, n.p., August 3, 1942, copy.

54. AAOC, FCK to Joseph A. O'Sullivan, n.p., September 8, 1942, copy. New York *Times*, September 20, 1942, I-20; September 21, 1942, p. 4.

55. AAOC, MacNeil to FCK, New York City, September 20, 1942; Exman to FCK, New York City, September 22, 1942; Hugh C. Boyle to FCK, Pittsburgh, November 12 and 30, 1942.

56. FCK, *Letters to Jack*, 84.

57. Hal Hudson to the writer, Palo Alto, January 12, 1979.

58. *The Times* (London), June 10, 1921, p. 9. AAOC, FCK to Thomas V. Shannon, n.p., December 1, 1921, copy. FCK, *The Epistles of Father Timothy to His Parishioners* (Chicago, 1924), 137-38.

59. AAOC, James M. Reardon to FCK, Minneapolis, February 4, 1925; FCK to Estelle Dohney, n.p., May 6, 1938, copy.

60. AAOC, FCK to Mr. and Mrs. C. G. Burnham, n.p., November 28, 1922; FCK to William Thomas Walsh, n.p., December 31, 1938, copies.

61. AAOC, Philip Burnham to FCK, New York City, September 28 and October 9, 1939; FCK to Burnham, n.p., October 17, 1939, copy. Interview with Hal Hudson, Menlo Park, California, January 12, 1979.

62. AAOC, FCK to Rummel, n.p., March 29, 1935, copy.

63. AAOC, FCK to Andrew N. DeMuth, n.p., March 24, 1943, copy.

64. AAOC, FCK to Edward Mallen, n.p., March 26, 1928, copy.

65. FCK, *Letters to Jack,* 101. AAOC, Dudek to Maurice O. Dannis, n.p., September 22, 1938, copy. See also AAOC, FCK to Arnold N. LaRoque, n.p., June 1, 1931, copy.

66. FCK, *Sacerdos et Pontifex,* 133.

67. AAOC, Dudek to Dannis, n.p., September 22, 1938, copy. See also AAOC, FCK to Joseph H. Conroy, n.p. [*ca.* September 1, 1932], copy.

68. FCK, *Dominus Vobiscum,* 159.

69. AAOC, FCK to William T. Hall, n.p., February 14, 1941, and July 18, 1942; FCK to Charles Breitung, n.p., February 19, 1943, copies.

70. AAOC, FCK to Major Bart A. Murtaugh, U.S.A., January 25, 1943, copy.

71. AAOC, FCK to Henry Carr, C.S.B., n.p., September 7, 1933; FCK to Peter De Strycker, n.p., October 30, 1934; FCK to Wilfrid Parsons, S.J., n.p., April 27, 1936, copies; Leven to FCK, Louvain, February 7, April 15, and June 6, 1936, and May 6, 1938. Leven, "If Catholics Really Believe," *America,* LV (May 23, 1936), 154-55. In 1928 FCK ordained the first native priests of the diocese, Leven and John T. Murray. The former joined the Texas hierarchy in 1955 when he became an auxiliary bishop in the archdiocese of San Antonio, and fourteen years later he was named the third bishop of San Angelo, where he served until his retirement in 1979. *The Texas Concho Register* (San Angelo, Texas), XVI, (May 26, 1978), 28.

72. AAOC, Leven to FCK, Louvain, June 21, 1937; FCK to Leven, n.p., June 30, 1937, copy; FCK to A. F. Monnot, n.p., May 30, 1941, copy.

73. AAOC, minutes of the meeting of the Administrative Board, NCWC,

Washington, D.C., November 14, 1935, pp. 1, 3. Archives of the National Catholic Welfare Conference (hereafter cited as NCWC), Treasurer's Report, 1935. The NCWC was restructured in 1966 and is known today as the United States Catholic Conference.

74. AAOC, Boyle to FCK, Pittsburgh, May 20, 1935.

75. AAOC, FCK to the American bishops, Oklahoma City, April 28, 1936; Michael J. Ready to FCK, Washington, D.C., January 6, 1936; Mitty to FCK, San Francisco, January 13, 1936.

76. AAOC, FCK to Francis W. Howard, n.p., August 24, 1936, copy; Mundelein to FCK, Chicago, November 2, 1936; FCK to Mundelein, n.p., November 3, 1936, copy.

77. NCWC, Treasurer's Report, 1941. AAOC, FCK to Stritch, n.p., December 4, 1941, copy; Stritch to FCK, Chicago, December 1, 1941.

78. AAOC, FCK to Thomas J. Toolen, n.p., March 30, 1931, copy.

79. AAOC, FCK to Victor F. Kidder, n.p., September 22, 1932, copy; FCK to the American bishops, Oklahoma City, March 24, 1933; news release for April 8, 1933; report of the secretary of the Catholic Committee on Scouting, October 17, 1933.

80. AAOC, Robert F. Keegan to FCK, New York City, January 23, 1934; minutes of the Catholic Committee on Scouting, Washington, D.C., November 18, 1937; FCK's report to the Catholic Committee on Scouting [*ca.* November, 1939].

81. AAOC, minutes of the meetings of the Administrative Board, NCWC, Washington, D.C., October 11, 1933, p. 9; and November 15, 1940, pp. 2, 3. *The Awards of the Silver Buffalo and the Silver Beaver,* Twenty-ninth Annual Meeting of the National Council, BSA, New York City, June 28 and 29, 1939, p. 5. *Catholic Action* (Washington, D.C.), XIV (August, 1939), 14. *The Tablet* (Brooklyn), January 12, 1942, p. 6.

82. AAOC, FCK to John A. Duffy, n.p., April 4, 1941, copy.

83. AAOC, original indult for the "portable altar," Rome, December 31, 1913, in the Merry del Val file; Sante Tampieri to FCK, Rome, January 8, 1914; FCK to Pietro Pisani, n.p., March 6, 1941, copy; Pisani to FCK, Rome, March 21, 1914; indult signed by Cardinal Michele Lega, Rome, April 18, 1932; FCK to Charles J. Callan, O.P., n.p., September 17, 1935; copy; FCK to Major Brown, U.S.A., n.p., September 18, 1934, copy. Bernard Botte, O.S.B., one of the leading liturgists of FCK's time, has surveyed the church's reform of its worship in *Le*

mouvement liturgique; témoignage et souvenirs (Tournai, Belgium, 1973).

84. FCK, *Letters to Jack,* 51-52; *Sacerdos et Pontifex,* 66.

85. FCK, *Dominus Vobiscum,* 82-83.

86. MP, memorandum of Mencken, n.p., September 9, 1941. AAOC, FCK to Guilday, n.p., May 1, 1933. copy.

87. FCK, *Dominus Vobiscum,* 170.

CHAPTER 1

1. General surveys on Canada include Ramsay Cook, John C. Ricker, and John T. Saywell, *Canada: A Modern Study* (Toronto and Vancouver, 1963); and Donald Creighton, *Canada's First Century, 1867-1967* (Toronto, 1970). An indispensable reference for Prince Edward Island is Andrew Hill Clark, *Three Centuries and the Island: A Historical Geography of Settlement and Agriculture in Prince Edward Island, Canada* (Toronto and Buffalo, 1959). The Island commemorated its centennial as a member of the Dominion of Canada with a splendid series of studies in Francis W. P. Bolger, ed., *Canada's Smallest Province: A History of the Prince Edward Island* (n.p., 1973). A helpful monograph on the farming community around the time of FCK's birth is Dorothy Cullen, "Rural Life in Prince Edward in 1864," unpublished paper, University of Prince Edward Island, 7 pp. Catholic developments on the Island are chronicled in James Morrison, "Roman Catholic Church . . . till 1860," in D.A. MacKinnon and A. B. Warburton, eds., *Past and Present of Prince Edward Island* (Charlottetown, n.d.), 227-95; John C. Macmillan, *The History of the Catholic Church, 1721-1891* (2 vols., Quebec 1905 and 1913); and James Donahoe, *Prince Edward Island Priests* (2nd edition, n.p., *ca.* 1936).

2. Clark, *op. cit.,* 207-13.

3. Public Archives, Government of Prince Edward Island, Charlottetown (hereafter cited as PA, PEI); D. J. Lake, *Topographical Map of Prince Edward Island in the Gulf of St. Lawrence from Actual Surveys and the Late Coast Survey of Capt. H. W. Bayfield* (St. John, New Brunswick, 1863), 17.

4. AAOC, FCK to Alice Forristat, n.p., November 24, 1926; FCK to George Barnard, n.p., April 22, 1931, copies. A search of parish records in Ireland was inconclusive regarding FCK's paternal grandparents. Gabriel Loughry to the writer, Inistioge, County Kilkenny, Ireland, July 25, 1977.

5. Sister Patricia Kelly, C.S.M., "The Intertwining of the Families of James Kenny and Anne Whelan, James Kelly and Catherine Kavanaugh, John Whelan and Jane Carmichael, Anthony O'Donnell and Anne O'Keefe," unpublished genealogical compilation, University of Prince Edward Island, Charlottetown, 1973, p. 26. 1973, p. 26.

6. Confederation Centre Library, Charlottetown, Prince Edward Island (hereafter cited as CCL), census data, 1841 and 1861. One should note the extreme caution with which family tradition may be used in reconstructing the past because five-year discrepancies occur between it and the census data. First, for example, tradition dates the birth of the first child, Walter, at 1830. The census data, however, record the oldest male child as aged between sixteen and forty-five years. If he is counted as a sixteen-year-old—and this is likely—this would push his birthdate back to 1825. Another difference centers on John Kelly, FCK's father, whom tradition lists as the eighth child. The census of 1841 lists only seven children, therefore requiring tradition to date John's birth after this year. John Kelly's obituaries, on the other hand, noted that at his death in 1892 he was fifty-six years old, fixing John's birthdate around 1836. A record of his birthdate would, of course, clear this puzzle up. The Bureau of Vital Statistics, Department of Health, Prince Edward Island, has collected baptismal data from around the Island, and these usually reported birthdates. Unfortunately, the bureau has no record of a John Kelly who would likely be FCK's father.

7. CCL, Queens County Courthouse, Probate Office, Province of Prince Edward Island, VIII, 453-54, will of Patrick Kelly of the Georgetown Road Lot or Township 51, filed on February 25, 1874. FCK, *The Bishop Jots It Down: An Autobiographical Strain on Memories* (New York, 1939), 8, hereafter cited as *Jots*. *Illustrated Historical Atlas of the Province of Prince Edward Island* (Philadelphia, 1880), 107.

8. CCL, census, 1841. *Jots,* 297.

9. PA, PEI, Register of Deeds, Kings Country, Conveyances, XI, 237-43, Agreement between Andrew Murphy and Alexander Murphy, dated May 2, 1873, registered on May 4, 1885; *Illustrated Historical Atlas* . . . , 107-8.

10. Interview with Mrs. Cathrine Praught, Vernon River, Prince Edward Island, July 6, 1977. AAOC, FCK to Joseph P. Murphy, O.M.I., n.p., January 3, 1930, copy. *Jots,* 8, 46.

11. The baptismal register, St. Joachim's Parish, Vernon River, records the baptism of Lawrence Murphy of February 23, 1855, son of Lawrence Murphy and Catherine Fitzgerald. The parish marriage register also records the marriage be-

tween John Kelly and Mary Ann Murphy on February 13, 1865. Curiously, the bride's father is listed as "Patrick" Murphy. The best man, registered as "Edmond Kelley," might have been the groom's brother Edward. Mary Ann's sister Margaret served as maid of honor.

12. CCL, censuses of 1841 and 1861, "General Remarks"; *Frederick's Prince Edward Island Directory and Book of Useful Information for 1889-90* (Charlottetown, 1889), 597-98. Clark, *op. cit.*, 207-8.

13. PA, PEI, Register of Deeds, Kings County, Conveyances, XI, 589, Lawrence Murphy to John Kelly, March 10, 1868, assignment of lease on Lot 51; LXXXIX, 554-55, Patrick Kelly, Sr., to John Kelly, April 27, 1868, release of a plot (85 yards by 55 yards) in Lots 51 and 66.

14. Baptismal register, St. Joachim's Parish, Vernon River, lists the birthdays of the Kelly's first three children: Catherine Mary on May 10, 1867; Francis Clement on October 23, 1870; and Joseph Augustine on February 10, 1873. See also [Parnell Wood] *The History of Vernon River Parish, 1877-1977* (n.p., 1977), 41-44.

15. AAOC, Raymond F. Harkin to M. L. Karch, n.p., November 30, 1944, copy.

16. Clark, *op. cit.*, 140, 144. PA, PEI, Register of Deeds, Kings County, Conveyances, XCI, 662-63, John McRae and wife to John Kelly, January 20, 1869, purchase of a plot in Lot 52.

17. PA, PEI, Register of Deeds, Kings County, Conveyances, II, 774-76, John and Mary Ann Kelly to Malcolm Lamont, July 23, 1873, purchase of plot (60 feet by 30 feet) in Lot 52; II, 749-51, Michael Sanphy to John Kelly, September 24, 1874, purchase of a town lot in Georgetown. Clark, *op. cit.*, 62.

18. PA, PEI, Register of Deeds, Kings County, Conveyances, XCV, 417-19, Andrew and Jane Murphy to John Kelly, "Merchant," March 15, 1871, purchase of fifty acres in Lot 51; II, 698-700, John and Mary Ann Kelly to James Doyle, July 14, 1871, purchase of a parcel in Lots 51 and 66. CCL, Census of 1861, "General Remarks." Interview with Bernard H. Hughes, Charlottetown, July 7, 1977. *Jots*, 28-29.

19. CCL, *Lovell's Canadian Dominion Directory of 1871* (Montreal [1871]), 2198. Clark, *op. cit.*, 61-62, 117.

20. PA, PEI, Register of Deeds, Queens County, Conveyances, IV, 690-92, James and Ann Trainor to John Kelly, August 21, 1875, purchase of a town lot in Charlottetown. Bureau of Land Titles and Registry, Register of Deeds, Queens

County, Conveyances, XLIII, 29-31, Mary A. Kelly to Bridget Ellen Kernan (?) and Annie Kernan, May 12, 1899, purchase of the same lot.

21. PA, PEI, Register of Deeds, Queens County, Conveyances, VII, 23-26, Robert and Margaret Lucy Longworth to John Kelly, August 1, 1876, purchase of a parcel in Charlottetown; VI, 854-55, James Paton to John Kelly, May 4, 1877, deed of exchange of property; X, 860-62, John Kelly, "Esq.," to Patrick C. Kelly, February 16, 1879, deed of right-of-way over land in Charlottetown; X, 862-65, John and Mary Ann Kelly to Alexander Ryland, March 17, 1879, purchase of property. CCL, *PEI Directory, 1880-81,* p. 135. There is no record of birth for Lucy Gertrude, but she was baptized on November 3, 1876. Arthur Ambrose was born on November 28, 1878, and Ursula Ann Kelly on December 20, 1880. Baptismal records of St. Dunstan's Basilica, Charlottetown.

22. PA, PEI, *Journal of the House of Assembly of Prince Edward Island* (1876), Appendix AA. *Jots,* 18. Records in Charlottetown disclosed at least three variant spellings of Miss Fennessey's name, and the one appearing in the provincial directory is used. CCL, *Teare's Directory and Handbook of the Province, 1880-1881,* 107.

23. James M. Reardon, "The Boyhood of Bishop Kelley," *Southwest Courier* (Oklahoma City), Golden Jubilee Number, October 23, 1943, p. 19.

24. PA, PEI, *Journal of the House of Assembly of Prince Edward Island* (1879), Appendix A. John C. Macmillan, *The History of the Catholic Church in Prince Edward Island* (Quebec, 1913), II, 277, 292, 386-92. *Jots,* 20. AAOC, FCK to Emmett J. Mullally, n.p., May 16, 1940, copy.

25. CCL, *Chappelle's Prince Edward Island Almanac* (Charlottetown, 1883), 153 and 161; *The Daily Examiner* (Charlottetown), January 28, 1886, p. 2.

26. The highlights of a City-Council meeting published in *The Daily Examiner,* March 22, 1887, p. 2, show John Kelly as among the most vocal members of that body.

27. The construction of water works under a separate board of commissioners was recommended to the City Council at a public meeting on January 21, 1887. A series of articles describing the problem appears in *The Daily Examiner,* March 5 and 8-10, 1887.

28. *The Daily Examiner,* June 7, 1887, p. 2.

29. CCL, O. H. Manuel, "History of Malpeque Rd. Water Pumping Station Operated by Commissioners of Sewers and Water Supply, City of Charlottetown, Prince Edward Island, Canada," unpublished manuscript (3 pp.) based on the

minutes of the Water Commissioners, city annual reports, and other primary sources; dated August 6, 1976.

30. PA, PEI, Register of Deeds, Kings County, Conveyances, V, 620-22, John Kelly to John McDonald, February 3, 1880, purchase of fifty acres in Lot 52. Interview with Bernard H. Hughes, Charlottetown, July 7, 1977.

31. PA, PEI, Register of Deeds, Kings County, Conveyances, John and Mary Ann Kelly to Alan McDonald, March 27, 1885, purchase of six tracts in Lot 52; XII, 854-57, John and Mary Ann Kelly to Edmund Kelly, November 13, 1886, purchase of fifty acres in Lot 51; XIV, 166-68, John and Mary Ann Kelly to Jedidiah Mason Carvell, February 15, 1888, purchase of a lot near Cardigan. See also Clark, *op. cit.*, 210-11. *Jots,* 33-34.

32. Reardon, *loc. cit.* "Rev. James M. Reardon," in James Donahoe, *Prince Edward Island Priests* (2nd ed., n.p., *ca.* 1936), 165-77.

33. Macmillan, *op. cit.,* II, 228-35, 426-27.

34. Archives of the University of Prince Edward Island, Student Registers for 1885-1888. AAOC, FCK to Waite Phillips, n.p., September 11, 1943, copy.

35. Interview with J. P. Emmet O'Hanley, Charlottetown, July 9, 1977. *The Collegium* (St. Dunstan's College, Charlottetown), I (July-August, 1888), 12, in the possession of Bernard H. Hughes. Oklahoma City *Times,* October 25, 1943, p. 6. FCK's published tribute to McAulay and others at the college appears in *Jots,* 20-23.

36. Oklahoma City *Times,* October 25, 1943, p. 6.

37. AAOC, FCK to Joseph A. O'Sullivan, n.p., July 27, 1943, copy.

38. *Jots,* 34.

39. Archives of the Séminaire de Nicolet (hereafter cited as ASN), file of Joseph A. Ir. Douville, II, 44, FCK to [Douville], Chatham, New Brunswick, November 18, 1889.

40. Frank C. Kelly, "How the Athenian Philosopher Found True Happiness," *The Collegium,* I (July-August, 1888), 9-10. AAOC, FCK to Walter Romig, n.p. [*ca.* 1940], copy.

41. FCK, "The Great Conviction," in *Anniversary Essays* (n.p., *ca.* 1934), 14-15.

42. *The Collegium* I (July-August, 1888) 3-4. ASN, Douville file, II, 44, FCK

to [Douville], Chatham, November 18, 1889.

43. A splendid account of Chicoutimi's foundation is given on the occasion of its centennial in Jean-Claude Drolet, "Un collège-séminaire á Chicoutimi en 1873,"*Saguenayensia: Revue de la Sociètè Historique du Saguenay* (Chicoutimi), XIV (September-October, 1972), 118-34.

44. Archives of the Séminaire de Chicoutimi (hereafter cited as ASC), *Annuaire 1888-89,* pp. 402-3; financial statement for John Kelley from September, 1888, to June, 1889.

45. Ramsay Cook, John T. Saywell, and John C. Richer, *Canada: A Modern Study,* 104-5, 123-35; Donald Creighton, *Canada's First Century,* 18-19, 53-61, 143.

46. Charlottetown *Herald,* February 5, 1890, in the scrapbook of Bernard H. Hughes.

47. Macmillan, *History of the Catholic Church in Prince Edward Island,* II, 250, 301, 409-10, 414.

48. ASC, *L'Alma Mater: Une Revue du Saguenay* (Chicoutimi), Series IV, Volume I (January-February, 1948), 67.

49. AAOC, FCK to Emmanuel B. Ledvina, n.p., September 16, 1942, copy. FCK's published account of his year with Rogers appears in *Jots,* 38-44.

50. ASN, Douville file, II, 44, FCK to [Douville], Chatham, November 18, 1889; II, 50, FCK, to Douville, Chatham, March 4, 1890.

51. ASN, file entitled "Examens des Ecclésiastiques du Séminaire de Nicolet," from 1873 to 1941; Joseph A. Ir. Douville, *Histoire de Collège-Séminaire de Nicolet, 1803-1903* (Montreal, 1903), II, 110-12. In this centennial history, FCK does not appear on the student-body lists but is listed among the faculty during 1890-91 and 1891-92. The correspondence suggests that his new bishop, John S. Foley of Detroit, might have preferred another seminary for FCK's last year, and this might have delayed his request to serve on the faculty in 1892-93. In any case, he returned to Nicolet for his third year and ordination but, for whatever reason, did not teach. ASN, file of Moïse-Georges Proulx, V, 6, FCK to Proulx, Charlottetown, July 3, 1892.

52. Invitation to "the celebration of 'St. Patrick's Day' at Nicolet," dated March 14, 1891, in the scrapbook of Bernard H. Hughes. Robert Charland, "Son Excellence, Mgr. Francis Clement Kelley, D.D., L.L.D., Ph.D., Litt.D., Eveque d'Oklahoma City-Tulsa (1870-1948)," *La Vie Nicolétaine* (Nicolet), number 106

(March, 1948), 4. FCK, "About Preaching," *Homiletic and Pastoral Review,* XXX (October, 1929), 9. FCK's description of St. Patrick's Day in the Nicolet cathedral is found in *Jots,* 58-59. Unfortunately, he dated the episode in 1890 instead of 1891.

53. ASN, Proulx file, V, 5, FCK to Proulx, Boston, July 11, 1891. The two recruits that ended up going to Nicolet were James M. Doran and James Nulty. Douville, *Histoire de Collège-Séminaire de Nicolet, 1803-1903,* II, 272-73.

54. ASN, Proulx file, V, 6, FCK to Proulx, Charlottetown, July 3, 1892.

55. The account in FCK's autobiography (*Jots,* 48-50) clearly identifies Chicoutimi (1888-89) as the site of Broderick's visit and proposal that the younger man transfer to Baltimore, but this appears to be another slip of the author's memory. It would have been more logical for FCK to have had thoughts about his health *after* the year with Bishop Rogers in which he had contracted catarrh (1889-90). Futhermore, it would have been out of FCK's character to have spent a full year in Rogers's household while seeking a different diocese. Moreover, the autobiography itself suggests a discrepancy of dates. In one place, FCK firmly dates the original exchange between him and Broderick as having occurred in 1888; and in another he dates the application to Baltimore as the year *before* Gibbons's visit to the Island, which took place in 1892. In submitting FCK's name, Broderick would hardly have delayed the follow-up to his proposal for three years. Hence, it is more likely that FCK's contact with American dioceses began as a student at Nicolet. It may be noted, lastly, that on the Island the name of FCK's patron in Baltimore was spelled "Broyderick." ASN, Proulx file, V, 6, FCK to Proulx, Charlottetown on July 3, 1892. Notice of "Broyderick's" arrival in Charlottetown on July 7, 1892, in the scrapbook of Bernard H. Hughes. See also "Rt. Rev Thomas J. Broderick," in James Donahoe, ed., *Prince Edward Island Priests,* 81-86.

56. The scrapbook of Bernard H. Hughes contains an undated press notice that FCK received "minor orders" for the "diocese of Detroit, Mich." This would have preceded the summer of 1892 during which he expected to receive the subdiaconate. ASN, Proulx file, V, 6, FCK to Proulx, Charlottetown, July 3, 1892.

57. ASN, Proulx file, V, 6, FCK to Proulx, Charlottetown, July 3, 1892. AAOC, petition for the subdiaconate, Nicolet, September 10, 1892, co-signed by FCK and Bishop Elphége Gravel of Nicolet.

58. ASN, Proulx file, V, 6, FCK to Proulx, Charlottetown, July 3, 1892; Charland, *art. cit.,* 4.

59. Obituaries in the Charlottetown *Herald* and *Patriot,* December 17, 1892, in the scrapbook of Bernard H. Hughes. PA, PEI, Register of Deeds, Queens County, Conveyances, XXXV, 102-5, Katie A. Brothers of Boston to John Kelly,

October 8, 1892, conferral of the power of attorney. CCL, Queens County Courthouse, Probate Office, Province of Prince Edward Island, XIII, 286, last will and testament of John Kelly [dated on December 14, 1892], filed on December 24, 1892.

60. *The Daily Examiner* (Charlottetown), December 17, 1892, p. 2.

61. PA, PEI, Register of Deeds, Queens County, Conveyances, IV, 690-92, James and Ann Trainor to John Kelly, August 21, 1875, purchase of a town lot in Charlottetown; Bureau of Land Titles and Registry, Charlottetown, Register of Deeds, Queens County, Conveyances, XLIII, 29-31, Mary A. Kelly to Bridget Ellen Kernan (?) and Annie Kernan, May 12, 1899, purchase of the same town lot. This property had failed not only to appreciate in value but in twenty-five years lost nearly forty percent of its market price. When John Kelly bought it in 1875, he paid $1,865.55; but in 1899 his wife was able to get only $1,100.

62. *Jots,* 297.

63. AAOC, FCK to Sante Tampieri, n.p., January 9, 1923, copy.

64. AAOC, FCK's resumé attached to FCK to James Edward Quigley, n.p., October 25, 1910, copy.

65. Scrapbook of Bernard H. Hughes. AAOC, Joseph A. O'Sullivan to FCK, Charlottetown, August 31, 1943. Macmillan, *History of the Catholic Church in Prince Edward Island,* II, 468.

CHAPTER II

1. AAOC, press clipping, "The Young Priest . . . ," dated November 22 [1893].

2. AAOC, FCK to Alfred E. Burke, n.p., February 12, 1912; FCK to Donald Gordon, n.p., March 7, 1933; FCK to Bertin Roll, O.F.M. Cap., n.p., April 30, 1942, copies. The New York Public Library (hereafter cited as NYPL), John B. Dudek to Henry L. Mencken, Oklahoma City, April 20, 1942. Some confusion may yet arise over the spelling of FCK's surname because no abrupt change occurred. The diocese of Detroit continued to address him as "Kelly" through 1907. AAOC, Frid. J. Baumgartner to FCK, Detroit, February 8, 1907. The only known instance where in his father's name had the second "e" appeared in a memorial card dedicated to "John Kelley Esq." Internal evidence suggests that FCK arranged the text to commemorate his father's death in 1892. Scrapbook of Bernard H. Hughes. The

earliest evidence that FCK applied the longer spelling to himself is a press notice of his assignment to Lapeer, Michigan, dated November 22, 1893. AAOC, press clipping, "The Youngest Priest: The Unique Distinction Enjoyed by Fr. Kelley, of Lapeer," dated November 22 [1893]. His mother, brother Joseph, and sister "Cecilia" continued to use "Kelly," but another sister, Lucy Gertrude, followed FCK in adopting the longer version. *McAlpine's Prince Edward Island Directory, 1914-1915* (Halifax, Nova Scotia, 1915), 278; two poems by Lucy Gertrude Kelley in the scrapbook of Bernard H. Hughes.

3. *Michigan Catholic* (Detroit), "October, 1893," in the scrapbook of Bernard H. Hughes; and *ibid.*, February 5, 1948, p. 1. AAOC, Foley to FCK, Detroit, October 26, 1893.

4. Statement of Patrick R. Dunigan, fourth pastor of Lapeer [*ca.* 1907], signed.

5. AAOC, press clipping, "The Youngest Priest . . . . ," dated November 22 [1893]. FCK baptized Francis Clement Lynch on December 3, 1893. Charles J. Goentges to the writer, Lapeer, August 26, 1977.

6. AAOC, FCK to Burke, n.p., March 18, 1912, copy.

7. Archives of the University of Prince Edward Island, *The Collegium,* IV (October, 1894), 6 and 7.

8. AAOC, FCK to John J. Burke, C.S.P., n.p., May 24, 1923, copy. FCK, *The Story of Extension,* 15-20.

9. Bernard X. O'Reilly, "An Appreciation of Bishop Kelley," *Southwest Courier,* February 21, 1948, p. 6.

10. AAOC, statement of Foley's assignment of FCK to the 32d Regiment of Michigan Volunteers, Detroit, May 17, 1898; FCK to Thomas R. Carey, n.p., January 3, 1924, copy. *Michigan Catholic,* May 12, 1898, p. 5; and June 9, 1898, p. 4. FCK's published account of his experience during the Spanish-American War appears in *Jots,* 96-105, 289.

11. AAOC, FCK to Lewis J. O'Hern, C.S.P., n.p., June 10, 1913, copy.

12. AAOC, FCK to John F. O'Hara, C.S.C., n.p., February 28, 1942, copy. *Jots,* 102-3.

13. FCK, "Dropping the Pilot," *Extension Magazine,* XV (October, 1920), 3-4.

14. AAOC, FCK to Joseph T. Roche, n.p., February 28, 1913, copy. *Michigan*

Catholic, September 29, 1898, p. 8.

15. AAOC, O'Hara to FCK, New York City, June 20, 1941; FCK to Franklin Delano Roosevelt, n.p., December 9, 1941, copy.

16. AAOC, FCK, "The Maid of Orleans: A Lecture," March 1898. FCK, *The Story of Extension,* 22. *Jots,* 106-12. Anonymous, "God Is Unto Me a Strong Fortress," *Extension Magazine,* XLII (March 1948), 28a-28b. Another favorite lecture was "The Last Battle of the Gods," which analyzed the life-and-death duel between Christianity and paganism. The text may be found in *Extension Magazine,* II (July, 1907), 3-4, 21. A splendid history of the Lyceum movement may be found in Carl Bode, *The American Lyceum: Town Meeting of the Mind* (Carbondale, Illinois, 1968).

17. AAOC, FCK to John S. Foley, Lapeer, January 14, 1907, copy; Dunigan's statement [*ca.* 1907], signed. Anonymous, "God Is Unto Me a Strong Fortress," *Extension Magazine,* XLII (March, 1948), 28a.

18. FCK, *The Story of Extension,* 23-24. *Jots,* 115.

19. FCK, *The Story of Extension,* 29-39. *Jots,* 115-17.

20. FCK, "Church Extension," *Ecclesiastical Review,* XXXII (June, 1905), 573-85.

21. FCK, *The Story of Extension,* 40-45. *Jots,* 117-19.

22. FCK, *The Story of Extension,* 45-47; and "Reminiscences of the First Meeting," *Extension Magazine,* XXV (October, 1930), 102, 155.

23. Board of Governors, Record of Minutes (hereafter cited as Board Minutes), I (December 12, 1905), 8-17. FCK, "Church Extension and Convert Making," *Extension Magazine,* I (July, 1906), 14.

24. AAOC, Noll to FCK, New Haven, Indiana, January 8, 1906.

25. AAOC, FCK to Quigley, n.p., February 4, 1910, copy. *President's Report to the Board of Governors, 1905-1910* (hereafter cited as *Report, 1910*), p. 43. Board Minutes, I, 19, 24, 27, and 28.

26. AAOC, FCK to Camillus P. Maes, Monroe, Michigan, December 13, 1906. FCK to Amleto G. Cicognani, n.p., December 7, 1939, copies. EP, FCK to Quigley, Lapeer, December 17, 1906; the letter of FCK's change of dioceses is EP, rescript with protocol number 07/75963, April 3, 1907. See also *Jots,* p. 123. Foley's negative feeling is reported in AAOC, FCK to Burke, n.p., February 2, 1910; and FCK to Michael J. Gallagher, n.p., October 14, 1918, copies.

27. EP, copy of "Certificate for Corporation Not for Pecuniary Profits," May 3, 1912. Board Minutes, I, 176, 185, 194.

28. Board Minutes, I (December 12, 1906), 28. EP, copy of the Apostolic Letter of Pope Pius X (the original is missing). Quigley to Pius X, Chicago, July 18, 1907, copy.

29. AAOC, FCK to Philip J. O'Donnell, n.p., November 3, 1911, copy. This profile of Quigley is drawn from a variety of Kelley's comments in AAOC, FCK to Alfred E. Burke, n.p., December 17, 1909; February 18 and July 28, 1910; FCK to Quigley, n.p., February 6, 1914, copies. FCK, "Archbishop Quigley—A Personal Tribute to Our First Chancellor," *Extension Mazazine,* X (August, 1915), 3-6. One should also consult Andrew M. Greeley's views in "Catholicism in America: Two Hundred Years and Counting—A Personal Interpretation," *The Critic,* XXXIV (Summer, 1976), 28ff.

30. AAOC, Joseph T. Roche to FCK, Toronto, January 3, 1912.

31. Board Minutes, I (December 12, 1906), 30, 31; (December 13, 1906), 44. AAOC, FCK to Mr. Heath, n.p., April 6, 1908, copy; Emmanuel B. Ledvina to FCK, Chicago, April 23, 1909.

32. EP, FCK to Quigley, Chicago, March 23, 1910. AAOC, FCK to Petry, n.p., October 22, 1917, copy.

33. AAOC, FCK to Marshall O. Straight, n.p., July 29, 1914; FCK to Petry, n.p., October 5, 1912; January 30 and February 19, 1914; May 26, 1920, copies.

34. AAOC, FCK to Merry del Val, n.p., November 12, 1910; May 8, 1911, copies. Pam's professional credits included leading roles in the formation of United States Steel and International Harvester, two mammoth corporations at the turn of the twentieth century; and he was also associated with the interests of railroad tycoon Edward Henry Harriman. New York *Times,* September 15, 1925, p. 25.

35. AAOC, FCK to Joseph Chartrand, n.p., May 17, 1920, copy.

36. AAOC, Ledvina to FCK, Chicago, May 23, 1919; Alfred A. Sinnott to FCK, Winnipeg, April 28, 1917.

37. EP, Quigley to FCK, Chicago, November 25, 1907; O'Brien to FCK, n.p., December 2, 1941, copy. Board Minutes, I (May 18, 1909), 116-17; (April 19, 1911), 187. AAOC, FCK to Sante Tampieri, n.p., July 29, 1914, copy. An idea of O'Brien's early career may be found in Eugene J. McGuinness, "Msgr. W. D. O'Brien's Extension Jubilee," *Extension Magazine,* XXVII (December, 1932), 20-21.

38. AAOC, Roe to FCK, Chicago, August 10, 1911.

39. AAOC, FCK to Quigley, n.p., October 25, 1907, copy.

40. AAOC, FCK to Quigley, n.p., July 14, 1910; FCK to Ledvina, August, 3, 24, and 29, 1911; FCK to Petry, n.p., November 29, 1911; FCK to Muldoon, n.p., January 30, 1914; FCK to Ledvina, n.p., August 12, 1914, all copies; document granting the "portable altar" privileges, in the Merry del Val file, dated December 31, 1913. EP, letter of agreement between the board of governors, n.p., n.d., copy; FCK to Quigley, Chicago, February 6, 1914; executive-committee minute book (hereafter cited as Committee Minutes), pp. 42 and 43-44, meeting of December 10, 1910. Interview with Francis A. Cimarrusti, Chicago, October 2, 1976.

41. AAOC, FCK to Tampieri, n.p., December 15, 1924, copy.

42. AAOC, FCK to George W. Mundelein, Chicago, May 25, 1922, copy.

43. AAOC, Ledvina to FCK, Boston, February 2, 1923.

44. Board Minutes, I (November 8, 1911), 203.

45. Board Minutes, I (August 28, 1906), 25-26.

46. Board Minutes, I (May 18, 1909), 120; (October 18, 1910), 163. EP, FCK to O'Brien, Oklahoma City, April 15, 1939. For remarks on the luxurious offices of Extension, see *Jots,* 132f.

47. Board Minutes, I (April 22, 1908), 68-69; (October 18, 1910), 164; (November 13, 1912), 211-12, 215-16. AAOC, FCK to Petry, n.p., November 14, 1912, copy.

48. AAOC, FCK to Tampieri, n.p., April 1, 1911, copy. EP, O'Brien to Eugene J. McGuinness, n.p., February 9, 1948, copy. Board Minutes, I (May 18, 1909), 113-14.

49. Board Minutes, I (November 8, 1911), 201.

50. EP, *Sixth Annual Report* (1911), p. 23. AAOC, FCK to Quigley, n.p., *ca.* 1913, copy.

51. Board Minutes, I (December 12, 1906), 30, 33; (June 17, 1907), 49; (May 18, 1909), 119-20; FCK to John Barton Payne, n.p., October 23, 1918, copy. EP, O'Brien to Ledvina, n.p., March 4, 1938, copy. The Catholic University of America, Department of Archives and Manuscripts (hereafter cited as CUA), papers of Simon A. Baldus, Ledvina to Baldus, New Orleans, October 3, 1916. One may add that the chapel-car also led FCK to a minor compromise in his integrity.

The railroads were willing to give free passes to chaplains, but laymen were charged. The chapel-car superintendent, George Hennessey, was thus encouraged to identify himself as "reverend." This deception did not deter FCK from requesting a medal "Pro Ecclesia et Pontifice" for the "reverend" Mr. Hennessey. AAOC, Roe's report, August 14, 1912.

52. AAOC, J.A.J. McKenna to FCK, Winnipeg, November 22, 1907; Fallon to FCK, Harrisburg, Pennsylvania, January 16, 1908.

53. Burke was an extraordinary civic leader on the Island. Before embarking on Extension work, he had presided over several local agricultural and political bodies; and one of his most notable efforts was to promote a tunnel from the Island to the mainland. D.A. MacKinnon and A. B. Warburton, eds., *Past and Present of Prince Edward Island,* 241, 576-77. Andrew Hill Clark, *Three Centuries and the Island,* 142.

54. AAOC, FCK to Sbarretti, n.p., March 13, 1908, copy; Burke to FCK, Ottawa, March 17 and 18, 1908; same to same, Alberton, Prince Edward Island, March 23, April 14 and 18, 1908; FCK to Burke, n.p., January 5, 1909, copy. Board Minutes, I, 125. For a charming description of McEvay's enlistment, see FCK, *The Story of Extension,* 162.

55. Archives of the archdiocese of Chicago (hereafter cited as ACC), 1-1906-A-1, minutes of the annual meeting of the American archbishops, Washington, D.C., April 26, 1906.

56. Board Minutes, I (December 12, 1906), 29; (April 22, 1908), 60; (May 18, 1909), 117; (October 23, 1909), 139. AAOC, Ledvina to FCK, Chicago, February 27, 1908.

57. Board Minutes, I (May 18, 1909), 124-25. The papers have been published in FCK, ed., *The First American Catholic Missionary Congress* (Chicago, 1909); hereafter cited as *First Congress.*

58. *First Congress,* 310-11.

59. *Ibid.,* 95-110.

60. Board Minutes, I (November 17, 1908), 72-101; see especially, pp. 97-99.

61. EP, Fréri, to Quigley, New York City, April 23, 1906. Joseph Fréri (1864-1927) was one of the towering figures in Catholic missionary work in the United States. Born in France, he first served as a missionary in Arizona and then taught at St. John's Seminary, Boston. In 1903 he was appointed national director of the Society for the Propagation of the Faith, a post which he held for twenty-one

years. His accomplishments were monumental. During this period he raised the SFPF's annual revenue to more than twenty-five times the amount collected by his predecessor; and he moved his headquarters from Baltimore to New York City, where the society still maintains its offices. In 1907 he was made a domestic prelate, and when he retired from his duties at the SFPF, he was named a titular bishop and returned to his native country. *The Arizona Observer* (Phoenix), November 12, 1927, p. 1.

62. Falconio to FCK, Washington, D.C., February 25, 1908. Board Minutes, I (May 18, 1909), 114-15; (November 8, 1911), 200-1.

63. AAOC, FCK to Pam, n.p., June 23, 1909, copy; *Western Watchman* (St. Louis), dated December 10, 1908, in Petry files. *True Voice* (Omaha), October 24, 1913, p. 4.

64. AAOC, FCK to Quigley, n.p., December 29, 1908, copy. See also AAOC, FCK to Peter C. Gannon, n.p., January 23, 1909, copy.

65. AAOC, FCK to Burke, n.p., January 5, 11, and 20, 1909, copies; Burke to FCK, Toronto, January 9 and 10, 1909. Board Minutes, I (May 18, 1909), 123. Joseph J. Quinn in *Jots* (Memorial Edition, 1948), ix.

66. Helpful comments on the Roman Curia under Pius X may be found in John de Salis, "Report on Mission to the Holy See," London, October 25, 1922, in Thomas E. Hachey, ed., *Anglo-Vatican Relations, 1914-1939: Confidential Annual Reports of the British Ministers to the Holy See* (Boston, 1972) (hereafter cited as Hachey, *Anglo-Vatican Relations*), 15; Walter H. Peters, *The Life of Benedict XV* (Milwaukee, 1959), 32-39; Henri Daniel-Rops, *A Fight for God: 1870-1939* (London, 1966), 234-36; and, from the viewpoint of the suppressed intellectuals, Lorenzo Bedeschi, *La Curia Romana Durante la Crisi Modernista* (Parma, 1968), passim.

67. AAOC, FCK to Quigley, Rome, March 20, 1909, copy.

68. AAOC, FCK to Burke, n.p., May 7, 1909, copy.

69. AAOC, FCK to Burke, n.p., August 10, 17, and 24, 1909, copies.

CHAPTER III

1. AAOC, FCK to Burke, n.p., January 21 and 28 and February 3 and 11, 1910, copies; Joseph T. Roche to FCK, Toronto, January 19, 1910.

2. AAOC, Ledvina to FCK, Chicago, September 11, 1909; FCK to Burke, n.p., February 7, 1910, copy. Board Minutes, I (October 23, 1909), 139.

3. AAOC, FCK to William O'Connell, n.p., n.d., a first draft perhaps scribbled on a train returning to Chicago from the East.

4. AAOC, FCK to Burke, n.p., January 18, 1910, copy.

5. AAOC, FCK to Burke, n.p., February 2, 1910, *personal,* copy.

6. *Idem;* Kelley to Quigley, February 4, 1910, copy; Kelley to Burke, n.p., February 7, 1910, copy. Board Minutes, I (February 15, 1910), 145-55.

7. AAOC, FCK to Burke, n.p., February 16, 21, and 28, 1910, copies.

8. AAOC, FCK to Burke, n.p., November 27, 1914, copy.

9. EP, *Qua Nuper,* granted by Pope Pius X, Rome, June 9, 1910. Curiously, the briefs for the American and Canadian societies have minor differences, and a comparison may be found in AAOC, Sante Tampieri to FCK, Rome, May 19, 1910.

10. AAOC, FCK to Merry del Val, n.p., July 23, 1910; FCK to Ambrose Petry, n.p., October 24, 1910, copies.

11. AAOC, FCK to Quigley, n.p., October 25, 1910; FCK to Petry, n.p., October 31, 1910, copies.

12. AAOC, Ledvina to Austin Fleming, n.p., September 28, 1910, copy.

13. AAOC, FCK to Petry, n.p., October 31, 1910, copy. On Tampieri's role in drafting *Qua Nuper,* see AAOC, FCK to O'Brien, n.p., October 12, 1925, copy.

14. Quigley's responsibility is suggested in AAOC, Roe to FCK, New York City, January 27, 1911.

15. Board Minutes, I (May 18, 1909), 126.

16. Board Minutes, I (November 17, 1908), 100-1; (November 13, 1913), 211-12, 216.

17. AAOC, Ledvina to FCK, Chicago, March 16 and April 23, 1906.

18. Board Minutes, I (October 18, 1910), 169-72. EP contains a printed and slightly abbreviated form of the petition, as well as the *Report of the Board of Governors of The Catholic Church Extension . . . 1905 to 1910.* The national collections already approved were those for the Holy See, The Catholic University of America, the Indian and Negro Missions, the Holy Land, and the Society for the

Propagation of the Faith.

19. AAOC, FCK to Quigley, n.p., October 15, 1910, copy.

20. AAOC, Patrick J. Hayes to FCK, New York City, January 9, 1911.

21. AAOC, Roe to FCK, New York, January 27, 1911, *personal;* FCK to Burke, n.p., February 1, 1911, copy. Soon after the report of his conversation with Kennedy, Roe recorded a kindly reception by Gibbons. AAOC, Roe to FCK, Philadelphia, February 4, 1911. A full account of the cardinal's views is found in John Tracy Ellis, *The Life of James Cardinal Gibbons* (Milwaukee, 1952), II, 405-7.

22. EP, Martinelli to Quigley, Rome, February 14, 1911. AAOC, FCK to Martinelli, n.p., March 2, 1911; draft of a set of instructions regarding the petition, n.p., n.d., in FCK's script, in the Merry del Val file; FCK to P. O'Kelly, n.p., March 14, 1911, copy; Martinelli to Quigley, Rome, April 12, 1911; "Receipts of the Catholic Church Extension Society of the United States of America," 1905-17.

23. ACC, 1-1911-A-1, minutes of the meeting of the archbishops, Washington, D.C., April 27, 1911, p. 6.

24. AAOC, FCK to Martinelli, n.p., May 15, 1911, copy.

25. AAOC, FCK to Burke, n.p., May 6, 1911, copy.

26. AAOC, FCK to Shahan, n.p., July 27 (two letters) and August 4, 1911, copies.

27. EP, FCK to Quigley, Rome, August 25, 1911. An idea of his interview with Cardinal Merry del Val is found in AAOC, FCK to Merry del Val, London, September 21 and 22, 1911, *official* and *personal* copies.

28. CUA, minutes of the meetings of the board of trustees, Volume I (April 26, 1911), 195; I (October 12, 1911), 198. AAOC, Quigley to Martinelli, Chicago, October 25, 1911, copy. Gibbons's role in supporting Shahan's mission is discussed in Ellis, *Gibbons,* II, 192-93.

29. Both Farley and O'Connell were native Americans, and Falconio, though born in Italy, was a naturalized United States citizen. See the Chicago *Tribune,* August 3, 1911, p. 1.

30. AAOC, FCK to Philip J. O'Donnell, Chicago, November 3, 1911. EP, O'Connell to FCK, Boston, November 2, 1911. See also AAOC, Roe to FCK, Chicago, August 19, 1911; FCK to Burke, n.p., August 3, 1911, copy.

31. AAOC, Petry to FCK, New York City, October 31, 1911.

32. EP, Merry del Val to Quigley, Rome, October 2 and November 21, 1911; Quigley to Merry del Val, Chicago, November 3 and 22, 1911, copies. See also AAOC, FCK to Martinelli, n.p., November 29, 1911, and January 2, 1912, copies.

33. EP, Burke to FCK, Rome, December 8, 1911. AAOC, Roche to FCK, Toronto, January 3, 1912.

34. AAOC, FCK to Roche, n.p., December 26, 1911, copy, EP, Kennedy to Quigley, Rome, January 7, 1912. See also EP, Merry del Val to Quigley, Rome, January 20, 1912.

35. AAOC, FCK to Tampieri, n.p., February 29 and January 22, 1912, copies.

36. AAOC, FCK to Shahan, n.p., April 13, 1912, copy.

37. AAOC, Roche to FCK, Toronto, March 12 and 18, 1912.

38. AAOC, Gibbons to FCK, March 1, 1912.

39. AAOC, Pam to Gibbons, New York, June 1, 1912, copy. As it turned out, FCK selected the first two student priests who received the Pam scholarships, and both belonged to "western" dioceses—Dallas and Wichita. AAOC, FCK to James M. Reardon, n.p., September 12, 1914, copy. The importance of the Pam scholarships to The Catholic University of America is covered in Ellis, *Gibbons,* II, 193-94.

40. Board Minutes, I (May 18, 1909), 130; I (November 13, 1912), 217-18. Committee Minutes (February 28, 1911), 46. AAOC, Charles J. Sullivan to FCK, Boston, November 15, 1912, telegram; FCK to Tampieri, n.p., February 29, 1912, copy.

41. AAOC, FCK to Quigley, Rome, March 20, 1909, copy.

42. EP, Burke to FCK, Rome, December 8, 1911.

43. AAOC, FCK to Philip J. O'Donnell, Chicago, November 3, 1911; FCK to O'Connell, n.p., October 31, 1911, copies.

44. AAOC, McGlinchey to FCK, Boston, November 8, 1920. Ledvina to FCK, Boston, February 3, 1923. EP, O'Brien to FCK, n.p., August 29, 1927, copy.

45. FCK, *The Story of Extension,* 54. AAOC, FCK to Tampieri, n.p., April 16, 1913, copy; Roe to FCK, Philadelphia, June 30, 1913; Dougherty to FCK, Philadelphia, July 4, 1913. Board Minutes, I (April 23, 1913), 129. A touching tribute to

Dougherty appears in *Jots,* 223.

46. AAOC, FCK to Martinelli, n.p., March 8 and May 3 and 13, 1913; Roe to FCK, Philadelphia, July 4 and 5, 1913, telegram; FCK to Roe, n.p., July 7, 1913, copy; Roe to FCK, Philadelphia, July 9 and 10, 1913. See also FCK to Tampieri, n.p., June 16, 1913, copy.

47. AAOC, FCK to Burke, n.p., August 9, 1913; FCK to O'Connell, n.p., November 15, 1913; FCK to Pisani, n.p., January 24, 1913, copies; Roche to FCK, Rome, April 2, 1913.

48. EP, FCK to Quigley, Chicago, September 18 and 26, 1913. AAOC, to Burke, June 29, 1909, and May 20 and November 15, 1913; FCK to Jules Tiberghien, n.p., February 10, 1913; FCK to Tampieri, n.p., June 16, 1913, copies.

49. FCK, ed., *The Two Great American Catholic Missionary Congresses* (Chicago, 1914), 194, 197-98.

50. AAOC, FCK to Gaetano De Lai, Chicago, January 30, 1913; FCK to Merry del Val, n.p., March 14, 1914; FCK to Martinelli, Chicago, March 31, 1914; FCK to John J. Wynne, S.J., n.p., August 31, 1931, copies.

51. Board Minutes, I (November 13, 1912), 214, 215; I (November 12, 1913), 222. Committee Minutes (March 10, 1914), 79-85. AAOC, FCK to Quigley, n.p. [1912 ?], fragmented letter; FCK to Merry del Val, n.p., March 14, 1914; FCK to Tampieri, n.p., March 14, 1914, copies, EP, Merry del Val to FCK, Rome, May 15, 1914.

52. AAOC, FCK to Roche, n.p., August 30 and December 17, 1909, copies.

53. EP, O'Brien to Eugene J. McGuinnes, n.p., April 15, 1941, copy. Charles Shanabruch to the writer, Chicago, March 27, 1977.

54. EP, Edmund M. Dunne to Dougherty, Peoria, November 3, 1913. In this letter, Bishop Dunne's grievance against the priests at Extension reflected a strong trend among the Chicago clergy. He had been chancellor in the archdiocese and in 1915 would be the clergy's choice to succeed Quigley.

55. AAOC, FCK to Burke, n.p., March 3, 1911, copy. See also AAOC, Tampieri to Burke, Rome, May 23, 1910; FCK to Merry del Val, n.p., July 23, 1910; FCK to Burke, n.p., July 28, August 4, December 14, 1910, and February 1, 1911, copies. EP, Burke to FCK, Rome, December 8, 1911; FCK to Quigley, Chicago, December 23, 1911.

56. AAOC, Burke to Tiberghien [Chicago], June 4, 1915; FCK to Tiberghien,

n.p., September 2, 1915; FCK to Camillo Laurenti, n.p., March 5, 1921; John B. Dudek to Joseph B. Code, n.p., November 3, 1951, copies.

57. AAOC, FCK to Muldoon, n.p., December 4 and 10, 1915, copies.

58. "Bishop Kelley, By One Who Knows," *Extension Magazine,* XIX (November, 1924), 7.

CHAPTER IV

1. AAOC, FCK to Burke, n.p., November 5, 1910; August 3 and November 3, 1911; April 12, 1912; September 12, 1916; FCK to Ledvina, n.p., August 1, 1911; June 12, 1912; FCK to Quigley, n.p., June 10, 1911, all copies; Burke to FCK, Toronto, January 17, 1911.

2. AAOC, FCK to Burke, n.p., September 23, 1910; and January 10, 1911, copies.

3. AAOC, Kelley to Burke, n.p., July 28, 1910, copy.

4. AAOC, FCK to Merry del Val, London, September 22, 1911, copy corrected in FCK's hand.

5. AAOC, FCK to Tampieri, n.p., February 29, 1912, copy.

6. AAOC, Tampieri to FCK, Rome, July 16 and August 15, 1912; FCK to Tampieri, n.p., September 17, 1912, copy.

7. AAOC, McNeil to FCK, Toronto, January 31, 1913; FCK to McNeil, n.p., February 4, 1913, copy.

8. AAOC, Burke to FCK, Toronto, November 9, 1913; Alfred A. Sinnott to FCK, Ottawa, November 12, 1913, *confidential;* FCK to McNeil, n.p., February 5, 1914, copy; FCK to Quigley, n.p., July 15, 1915, with attachment, copies.

9. AAOC, Roche to FCK, Toronto, November 11, 1914.

10. AAOC, FCK to Roche, n.p., November 21, 1914; FCK to Burke, n.p., November 27 and December 1, 1914, copies; Burke to FCK, Toronto, April 2, 1915.

11. AAOC, FCK to Peregrine Stagni, O.S.M., n.p., April 16, 1915; FCK to Burke, n.p., June 2, 1915; Burke to Gaetano De Lai, n.p., n.d., copies.

12. AAOC, FCK to Martinelli, n.p., March 8 and May 8 and 13, 1913; FCK to Tampieri, n.p., June 16, 1913, copies.

13. AAOC, FCK to Tampieri, n.p., September 11, 1914, copy; Tampieri to FCK, Cotignola in Ravenna, October 2, 1914; FCK to Merry del Val, n.p., December 2, 1914, copy.

14. AAOC, Burke to FCK, Toronto, May 25, 1915; Tampieri to FCK, Rome, August 9, 1915; Tiberghien to FCK, Rome, January 8, 1916.

15. AAOC, FCK to Quigley, n.p., February 6, 1914, copy.

16. AAOC, FCK to Burke, n.p., May 14 and 27 and June 1, 1915, copies.

17. AAOC, Burke to Tiberghien, n.p., June 4, 1915, copy.

18. AAOC, Burke to FCK, Toronto, [July 1] 1915; FCK to Burke, n.p., July 2, 1915, copy.

19. FCK, "Archbishop Quigley: A Personal Tribute to Our First Chancellor," *Extension Magazine,* X (August, 1915), 3-6.

20. AAOC, Tampieri to FCK, Rome, August 9, 1915.

21. AAOC, FCK to Tampieri, n.p., September 17, 1912, copy.

22. AAOC, Tampieri to FCK, Rome, August 9, 1915.

23. Board Minutes, I (August 19, 1915), 257-58.

24. AAOC, FCK to Tiberghien, n.p., June 4, 1915, copy.

25. AAOC, FCK to Burke, n.p., May 26 and 27, 1915; FCK to McNeil, n.p., May 26, 1915; FCK to Stagni, n.p., May 26, 1915; FCK to John Bonzano, Rome, *ca.* October, 1915, copies.

26. AAOC, Ledvina to Tiberghien, n.p., September 2, 1915; Board of Governors to George W. Mundelein, n.p., December 23, 1915; FCK to Mundelein, July 26, 1916, copies.

27. AAOC, FCK to Pietro Pisani, n.p., July 6, 1915; FCK to John Bonzano, Rome, October 13, 1915, copies. Also FCK to Ambrose Petry, n.p., June 29, 1915, copy; Burke to FCK, Toronto, July 12, 1915; FCK to Tampieri, n.p., July 20, 1915, copy.

28. AAOC, FCK to Muldoon, n.p., December 31, 1908; Ledvina to Tiberghien, n.p., September 2, 1915, copies. Actually Muldoon did not command the

majority sentiment. He appeared only in second place on consultors' list of candidates to succeed Quigley, and he failed to be named by the bishops of the province. Ellis, *Gibbons,* II, 418, n. 137.

29. AAOC, FCK to Quigley, n.p., May 13, 1909, and February 4, 1910, copies.

30. AAOC, original indult for the portable altar, Rome, December 31, 1913, in Merry del Val file; Tampieri to FCK, Rome, January 8, 1914; FCK to Pisani, n.p., March 6, 1914, copy; Pisani to FCK, Rome, March 21, 1914.

31. AAOC, Roche to FCK, Rome, December 12 [1910].

32. EP, O'Brien to Rudolph A. Gerken, n.p., August 8, 1938, copy.

33. AAOC, [Tiberghien to] Tampieri, Rome, September 30, 1915, copy.

34. AAOC, Tiberghien to FCK, Rome, January 8, 1916.

35. AAOC, [Tiberghien to] Tampieri, Rome, September 30, 1915, copy. These materials offer an intriguing problem regarding how much did FCK know of the charges. The defense by Tiberghien and Tampieri, dated approximately September 30, 1915, contains details which were supplied only by FCK at Rome. But Tiberghien's letter of January 8, 1916, describes the interview with Benedict XV. In this, Tiberghien sought not to upset FCK and told him vaguely: "I am led to believe that your arrival in Rome after the death of your Archbishop excited those who do not agree with you and who have written against you." This statement suggests that FCK did not have full knowledge of the charges until after his return to Chicago.

36. AAOC, FCK to Tiberghien [Chicago], November 29, 1915, copy.

37. AAOC, FCK to Burke, n.p., August 30, 1909; FCK to Bonzano, Rome, October 13, 1915, copies; Tampieri to FCK, Rome, February 26, 1923. Board Minutes, I (December 1, 1915), 267-68.

38. AAOC, FCK to Burke, n.p., July 20, 1915; Ledvina to Charles Warren Currier, n.p., July 24, 1915; FCK to Bonzano, Rome, October 13, 1915, copies. Interview with Edward J. Slattery, Chicago, September 7, 1976.

39. AAOC, FCK to Tiberghien, n.p., November 29, 1915, copy. AAC, 2-1915-M-83, Bonzano to Mundelein, Washington, D.C., November 29, 1915, telegram clocked at 8:28 p.m.

40. Chicago *Daily News,* November 30, 1915, p. 3.

41. AAOC, FCK to Edward D. Kelly, n.p., December 2, 1915; FCK to Burke, n.p., December 10, 1915; FCK to Merry del Val, n.p., December 21, 1915, copies.

42. AAOC, Muldoon to FCK, Rockford, December 3, 1915. For Gibbons' position, see Ellis, *Gibbons,* II, 418-20.

43. AAOC, FCK to Edward D. Kelly, n.p., December 2, 1915; FCK to Burke, n.p., n.d., December 10, 1915, copies; Tiberghien to FCK, Rome, December 15, 1915. Four years after Mundelein's appointment to Chicago, FCK received a qualified confirmation regarding the rumor that Dougherty and Mundelein had been originally intended for Chicago and Buffalo respectively. After the success of these two prelates in their first American dioceses, the Holy See seemed to FCK to be intent in taking more credit for exchanging their sees in 1915. AAC, 5-1919-M-137, FCK to Mundelein, Paris, April 25, 1919. Mundelein himself verified it frequently in conversation. Interview with Harry C. Koenig, Mundelein, Illinois, September 15, 1976.

44. AAOC, FCK to Burke, n.p., December 10, 1915, copy.

45. AAOC, FCK to Tiberghien, n.p., December 7, 1915, January 7, 1916; FCK to Burke, n.p., December 10, 1915, and January 5, 1916; FCK to Muldoon, n.p., December 10, 1915; FCK to Bonzano, n.p., December 20, 1915; FCK to Merry del Val, n.p., December 21, 1915; FCK to Petry, n.p., January 27, 1916, copies.

46. AAC, 3-1916-M-267, Fitzsimmons to Mundelein, Chicago, January 13, 1916; 3-1916-J-13, Mundelein to Henry Pratt Judson, Chicago, February 15, 1916, copy.

47. AAOC, FCK to Tiberghien, n.p., May 16, 1916, copy. AAC, 3-1916-M-140, Lewis Drummond to Mundelein [New York], February 13, 1916. FCK's lengthy account may be found in "The Poisoned Banquet," *Sign,* XVIII (February, 1939), 423-24; and *Jots,* 207-13. See also Mundelein, *Letters of a Bishop to His Flock* (New York, 1927), 263; and the Chicago *Tribune,* February 11, 1916, p. 1; and October 3, 1939, p. 10.

CHAPTER V

1. AAC, 1-1909-M-21, McDonnell to Mundelein, Rome, July 1, 1909. For Mundelein's life, one may consult Paul R. Martin, *The First Cardinal of the West* (Chicago, 1934) and Harry C. Koenig, "Mundelein, George William," in the *New*

Catholic Encyclopedia (New York, 1967), X, 70-71. Also helpful are the obituaries in the Chicago *Daily News,* October 2, 1939, pp. 1, 6; and the Chicago *Tribune,* October 3, 1939, pp. 1, 10.

2. Board Minutes, I (August 28, 1906), 23; I (November 17, 1908), 73, 90, 92-93. AAC, 1-1907-M-34, Joseph McNamee to McDonnell, Chicago, January 29, 1907; 1-1907-M-9, McDonnell [to Mundelein], n.p., January 30, 1907, *confidential.*

3. AAOC, FCK to Merry del Val, n.p., December 21, 1915, copy.

4. Interview with John J. Fahey, Chicago, October 3, 1976.

5. AAC, 1-1894-B-1, Joseph S. Mechler to Bonzano, New York, October 26, 1894.

6. AAC, 1-1909-M-21, McDonnell to Mundelein, Rome, July 1, 1909; 1-1909-M-23, same to same, Rome, July 2, 1909; 1-1906-M-16, Bonzano to Mundelein, Rome, April 18, 1906; 1-1909-M-7; same to same, Rome, July 4, 1909; 1-1912-M-5, same to same, Rome, March 12, 1912; 1-1913-M-6, same to same, Washington, D.C., July 6, 1913; 1-1913-M-4, same to same, Washington, D.C., July 15, 1913; 1-1913-M-42, same to same, Washington, D.C. [mid-October, 1913].

7. AAOC, FCK to Tampieri, n.p., October 25, 1912, copy.

8. EP, Bonzano to Quigley, Rome, May 23 and June 21, 1907.

9. AAOC, FCK to Tampieri, n.p., February 29, 1912, copy.

10. AAC, 1-1910-M-59, Bonzano to Mundelein, Rome, May 14, 1910. AAOC, FCK to Alfred E. Burke, n.p., May 31, 1912, copy.

11. Charles Shanabruch, "The Catholic Church's Role in the Americanization of Chicago Immigrants: 1833-1928," unpublished doctoral dissertation, University of Chicago, 1975, p. 85, table 5. Andrew M. Greeley, "Catholicism in America: 200 Years and Counting," *The Critic,* XXXIV (Summer, 1976), 14ff.

12. FCK, "The Question of Assimilation," *Extension Magazine,* VI (September, 1911), 3.

13. AAOC, FCK to Tampieri, n.p., February 20, 1920, copy.

14. AAOC, FCK to Burke, n.p., September 17, 1914, copy.

15. AAOC, FCK to Roche, n.p., November 13, 1914, copy.

16. "George Cardinal Mundelein to the People of Oklahoma," *Extension Magazine,* XIX (December, 1924), 1. Mundelein's administrative style is surveyed

in Edward R. Kantowicz, "Cardinal Mundelein of Chicago: A 'Consolidating Bishop,' " a paper read at a conference on American Catholicism, St. Mary's College of California, Moraga, California, July 28, 1978.

17. Shanabruch, chs. X-XII. Joseph B. Lux, "Area's Woods Turn to Mundelein," *Extension Magazine,* XXIX (November, 1934), 6-7, 36-37. AAC, 5-1918-M-274, Thomas V. Shannon to Mundelein, Chicago, April 17, 1918; and Wenceslaus J. Madaj, "Fifty Fruitful Years, Jubilee History of St. Mary of the Lake Seminary, 1922-1972," unpublished manuscript.

18. FCK's foreword in Mundelein, *Two Crowded Years* (Chicago, 1918), iii-xv. See also AAC, 6-1920-L-21, a draft of Shane Leslie's review which was to appear in the *Dublin Review* (London) but which was revised before publication in CLXIV (1920), 143.

19. AAC, 6-1920-L-21, Shane Leslie in his review of *Two Crowded Years.* EP, O'Brien to McGuinness, n.p., September 4, 1946, copy. Interview with John J. Fahey, Chicago, September 2, 1976. A convenient summary of Mundelein's accomplishments may be found in Harry C. Koenig, "Chicago, Archdiocese of (Chicagiensis)," *New Catholic Encyclopedia* (New York, 1967), III, 561-62.

20. AAOC, board of governors to Mundelein, n.p., December 23, 1915, copy.

21. Ellis, *Gibbons,* II, 194.

22. AAOC, FCK to Burke, n.p., April 17 and 26, and July 26, 1916; FCK to Tiberghien, n.p., May 17, 1916, copies.

23. AAOC, FCK to Burke, n.p., April 26, 1916; FCK to Tiberghien, n.p., April 1 and May 17, 1916; FCK to Tampieri, n.p., January 4, 1918, copies; John T. McNicholas, O.P., to FCK, Rome, February 28, 1918. *New World* (Chicago), November 16, 1917, p. 1; December 28, 1917, p. 1.

24. AAOC, FCK to Burke, n.p., February 14, 1916; FCK to Merry del Val, n.p., February 15, 1916, copies.

25. AAOC, FCK to Mundelein, n.p., October 22, 1917, copy. Mundelein's prayer is found in the Chicago *Tribune,* October 22, 1917, p. 2.

26. AAC, 8-1924-M-47, FCK to Mundelein, Chicago, May 15, 1924. The occasion of Mundelein's address was Chicago's civic reception in honor of his elevation as a cardinal. For FCK's published comments on Bryan and other orators, see *Jots,* 88.

27. AAOC, FCK to Burke, n.p., June 22 and September 22, 1916; FCK to

Mundelein, n.p., November 6, 1916, and February 14, 1917, copies; Burke to FCK, London, January 16, 1917.

28. AAC, 7-1922-M-54, FCK to Mundelein, Chicago, December 19, 1922. AAOC, FCK to Tampieri, n.p., June 18, 1922; FCK to Edward F. Hoban, n.p., February 10, 1923, copies.

29. FCK's eulogy delivered at the Columbus Hospital chapel, Chicago, December 27, 1917; the text was generously provided by Sister Mary Louis Sullivan, M.S.C., president of Cabrini College, Radnor, Pennsylvania. See also the *New World,* December 28, 1917, p. 1. Bonzano's health prevented his coming to Chicago to attend the funeral; but after Mother Cabrini's body was transported to New York City, he delivered a eulogy there on December 31, 1917. AAC, 5-1918-M-253, Bonzano to Mundelein, Washington, D.C., January 11, 1918. Bonzano was the first to undertake the espousal of her canonization, and after his death, his role was assumed by Mundelein. The latter presided at her beatification in 1938, and was pleased that he had been the "first" to preside at both the funeral and beatification of a saint. Interview with John J. Fahey, Chicago, October 14, 1976. Father Fahey had been a graduate student in Rome during the beatification and had had lengthy conversations with Mundelein. In 1946 she was canonized, the first United States citizen to be enrolled in the list of saints. Though at the end of his life FCK had become one of her enthusiasts, his original indifference to her work is reported in AAOC, FCK to Christopher E. Byrne, n.p., February 28, 1944, copy.

30. AAOC, FCK, welcome to Mundelein [1916], typed ms. corrected in FCK's hand. Board Minutes, I (August 18, 1915), 260.

31. AAOC, FCK to Tiberghien, n.p., May 17, 1916; FCK to Burke, n.p., July 5, 1916, copies.

32. AAOC, FCK to Alfred A. Sinnott, n.p., May 21, 1917; FCK to Dougherty, May 24, 1920, copies. Board Minutes, II (November 10, 1920), 62.

33. AAC, 4-1917-M-359, FCK to Mundelein, Chicago, December 22, 1917; 4-1917-K-20, Mundelein to FCK, Chicago, January 3, 1917, handwritten draft.

34. AAOC, Richard J. Haberlin to FCK, June 6, 1919; FCK to Haberlin, n.p., July 2, 1919, copy.

35. AAC, 2-1916-H-120, FCK to Hoban, Chicago, March 31, 1916.

36. AAC, 4-1917-O-5, FCK to Peter J. O'Callaghan, C.S.P., Chicago, March 17, 1917; 4-1917-M-332, FCK to Mundelein, Chicago, March 20, 1917. AAOC, FCK to Donulus Evers, O.F.M., n.p., January 4, 1918, copy.

37. Board Minutes, II (November 20, 1920), 56. AAOC, FCK to Bonzano, n.p., January 3 [1921], copy.

38. AAOC, FCK to Timothy Corbett, n.p., December 6, 1921, copy.

39. The alleged violation of postal regulations consisted of the requirement that under second-class mailing privileges, the publication was to receive in return no less than 50 percent of the subscription price.

40. Board Minutes, II (November 9, 1921), 70. AAC, 7-1922-M-75, [Mundelein and Gallagher to the] United States hierarchy meeting in Washington, D.C., September 27 and 28, 1922.

41. Board Minutes, II (November 13, 1918), 24; (November 12, 1919), 37; (November 10, 1920), 63. AAC, 7-1922-M-76, FCK to Mundelein, Chicago, February 25, 1922; 8-1924-M-46, FCK to Mundelein, Chicago, May 26, 1924. AAOC, FCK to Dougherty, n.p., November 11, 1922, copy. CUA, papers of Simon A. Baldus, Brother Leo, F.S.C. (Francis Meehan) to Baldus, Oakland, California, March 23, 1912. *Extension Magazine,* XI (August, 1916), front cover.

42. EP, annual meeting of the board of governors, November 8, 1922, summary of proceedings from the shorthand notes of FCK's secretary, George Barnard (hereafter cited as Barnard's notes), p. 9.

43. AAC, 4-1918-C-62, FCK to Benedict XV, Chicago, October 18, 1918, copy corrected in FCK's hand.

44. "Monsignor Kelley's Dollar Club," *Extension Magazine,* XVI (January, 1922), 1, 14. Board Minutes, II (November 8, 1922), 87. FCK, *The Story of Extension,* 263-75.

45. Barnard's notes, pp. 5-9, 18. EP, William D. O'Brien to Emmanuel B. Ledvina, n.p., April 17, 1922, copy. Board Minutes, II (November 8, 1922), 87.

46. AAOC, FCK to Charles M. Driscoll, O.S.A., n.p., May 15, 1923, copy.

47. AAC, 4-1918-K-7, FCK to the board of directors, Knights of Columbus, n.p., n.d.

48. AAC, 4-1918-C-62, FCK to Benedict XV, Chicago, October 18, 1918.

49. FCK, ed., *The Two Great American Catholic Missionary Congresses* (Chicago [1914]), 103-4. EP, FCK to Merry del Val, n.p., June 17, 1914. AAOC, FCK to Mundelein, n.p., August 1, 1917; June 14, 1920, copies. Board Minutes, II (November 12, 1919), 37, 50; (November 14, 1917), 11; (November 13, 1918), 21.

50. Barnard's notes, pp. 15-16, 18-19. See also AAOC, FCK to Alfred E. Burke, n.p., April 26, 1916, copy.

51. Board Minutes, II (November 8, 1922), 88; (November 14, 1923), 97. AAOC, FCK to Walter Elliott, C.S.P., n.p., January 19, 1924, copy. John B. Morris, "A Seminary for the Missions," *Extension Magazine,* XVII (April, 1923), 23-24; Eugene J. McGuinness, "Extension's Students," *ibid.,* XIX (January, 1925), 20. Little Rock College was designated as the "official" preparatory seminary for the South, whereas St. Benedict's College trained students representing dioceses mostly of the upper Midwest and Pacific Northwest. EP, FCK to Martin Veth, O.S.B., n.p., February 9, 1924; and related materials in the St. Benedict's College file. See also William D. O'Brien, "Between Friends," *Extension Magazine,* XIX (January, 1925), 5ff.

52. EP, O'Brien to FCK, n.p., October 15, 1925, copy.

53. AAOC, FCK to Dougherty, n.p., October 9, 1919; FCK to Patrick J. Hayes, n.p., May 18, 1923, copies. O'Brien in *Extension Magazine,* XXXII (December, 1937), 3-4.

54. Board Minutes, II (November 13, 1918), 26-28.

55. EP, O'Brien to McGuinness, n.p., April 1, 1943; O'Brien to Ledvina, n.p., July 16, 1941, and May 1, 1943. AAOC, FCK to Dougherty, n.p., October 22, 1925, copies.

56. EP, O'Brien to Albert T. Daeger, August 15, 1923, FCK to O'Brien, Oklahoma City, January 31, 1942. AAOC, FCK to Francisco Orozco y Jiménez, n.p., July 7, 1923; FCK to Tampieri, n.p., September 11, 1923, copies.

57. AAOC, Ledvina to FCK, San Antonio, January 19, 1911; same to same, Hidalgo County, Texas, January 28, 1911; and same to same, Victoria, Texas, February 5, 1911; Ledvina to Tampieri, n.p., July 25, 1912, copy; FCK to Joseph T. Roche, n.p., April 4, 1913, copy.

58. AAOC, FCK to Chartrand, n.p., May 17, 1920; FCK to Hennessy, n.p., May 18, 1920, copies.

59. EP, Ledvina to O'Brien, Corpus Christi, December, 1929 [*sic*]; February 4, 1940; and April 7, 1943. AAOC, Dougherty to FCK, Philadelphia, April 30, 1921. New York *Times,* April 28, 1921, p. 12.

60. AAOC, FCK to Chartrand, n.p., April 20, 1921; FCK to Dougherty, n.p., May 3, 1921; FCK to Tampieri, n.p., June 8, 1921; FCK to Merry del Val, n.p., May 10, 1921, *confidential;* FCK to Bonaventura Cerretti, n.p., May 24, 1921, copies.

FCK, "Our Heartiest Congratulations," *Extension Magazine,* XVI (June, 1921), 1.

61. AAC, 5-1919-M-272, FCK to Mundelein, Rome, April 12, 1919.

62. AAOC, FCK to Tiberghien, n.p., April 1, 1916; FCK to Burke, n.p., July 5, 1916, copies.

63. AAC, 3-1916-K-61, Hoban to FCK, Chicago, July 10, 1916, copy; *ibid.*, FCK to Hoban, Chicago, July 11, 1911; 6-1921-K-12, Mundelein to FCK, Chicago, October 15, 1921. AAOC, FCK to Mundelein, n.p., November 13, 1922, copy; Dennis J. Dunne to FCK, Chicago, December 22, 1922. See also "Solemn Dedication," a parish history of St. Francis Xavier Church, published on May 14, 1939. FCK's embarrassment regarding the parish's poor support for Mundelein's seminary was partly offset when a local family, who were FCK's closest lay friends in the area, made the largest single contribution to the project. In 1920 Mr. and Mrs. Edward A. Hines pledged $500,000 for the Hines Memorial Chapel, which today dominates the entire group of buildings on the campus and in which Mundelein himself lies buried. AAOC, FCK to Estelle Doheny, n.p., May 6, 1938, copy. Paul R. Martin, *The First Cardinal of the West,* 81-85.

64. AAC, 6-1921-M-200, FCK to Mundelein, Chicago, May 28, 1921; 8-1924-M-143, O'Brien to Mundelein, Chicago, July 15, 1924. O'Brien was given the assignment in 1924 when FCK was named to Oklahoma, and St. John's became the official residence for Extension priests.

65. Board Minutes, II (November 8, 1922), 88-89; (November 14, 1923), 96-97; (November 13, 1924), 107. AAOC, FCK to Amedee V. Reyburn, n.p., November 10, 1922, copy.

66. AAOC, FCK to Mundelein, n.p., May 25, 1922, copy.

67. AAC, 3-1916-M-314, Ledvina to Mundelein, Chicago, December 7, 1916; 6-1920-L-6, Mundelein to Ledvina, Chicago, February 10, 1920, copy; 7-1922-H-3, Dennis J. Dunne to L. P. Hurkmans, Chicago, June 6, 1922, copy, with attachments.

68. AAOC, Tiberghien to FCK, Rome, July 20, 1918; FCK to Bonzano, n.p., June 19, 1919, copy; Tiberghien to FCK, Rome, August 10, 1919; FCK to Tampieri, n.p., November 17, 1919, copy. AAC, 4-1918-C-62, FCK to Benedict XV, Chicago, October 18, 1919, copy; 5-1919-M-123, FCK to Mundelein, Rome, March 31, 1919.

69. AAOC, FCK to Tampieri, n.p., January 29, 1923, copy; Tampieri to FCK, Rome, February 26, 1923.

70. AAOC, FCK to Tampieri, n.p., June 23 and July 12, 1922; January 4, 1923; copies.

71. AAC, 7-1923-D-24. Mundelein to Henry d'Yanville, Chicago, July 28, 1923, copy; 7-1923-M-180, FCK to Mundelein, Chicago, October 11, 1923, with attached reply of d'Yanville, n.p., dated September 27, 1923.

72. AAC, 7-1922-M-66, J. Alfred Pauzé, S.S.S., to Schrembs, New York City, November 8, 1922. AAOC, Carton de Wiart to FCK, London, December 4, 1922, in the Mundelein file; FCK to Bonaventura Cerretti, n.p., January 4, 1923, copy.

73. AAOC, FCK to Tampieri, n.p., April 18, 1923, copy. AAC, 7-1923-M-20, Schrembs to Mundelein, Cleveland, April 29, 1923; 7-1923-M-18, same to same, Cleveland, May 12, 1923, with the attached telegram from d'Yanville; 7-1923-M-169, FCK to Mundelein, Chicago, May 1, 1923.

74. AAOC, FCK to Mundelein, n.p., April 27 and May 29, 1923; FCK to Schrembs, n.p., June 3, 1924, copy. EP, O'Brien to FCK, n.p., September 22, 1943; FCK to Tampieri, n.p., December 6, 1923, copies. AAC, 7-1923-M-178, FCK to Mundelein, Chicago. December 1, 1923; 7-1923-M-179, same to same, Chicago, December 6, 1923; 8-1924-M-57, FCK to Mundelein, Chicago, June 30, 1924.

75. AAOC, FCK to Tampieri, n.p., September 11, 1923, copy.

76. AAOC, FCK to Mundelein, n.p., August 24, 1926, copy.

77. AAOC, FCK to Shannon, n.p., December 1, 1921, copy. See the New York *Times,* November 13, 1921, p. 13; and the *New World* (Chicago), November 18, 1921, p. 1.

78. AAOC, FCK to Bonzano, Rome, *ca.* October, 1915; FCK to James H. Blenk, n.p., January 21, 1916; FCK to Alexander Christie, n.p., January 21, 1916; FCK to Tiberghien, n.p., August 1, 1917; FCK to Muldoon, n.p., September 29, 1917 copies. AAC, 3-1916-M-299, FCK to Mundelein, n.p., July 26, 1916; 5-1919-M-137, same to same, Paris, April 25, 1919. EP, Gaetano De Lai to FCK, Rome, May 5, 1917.

79. AAOC, Calavassy to FCK, Constantinople, June 10, 1921.

80. AAOC, FCK to Tampieri, n.p., June 9 and December 6, 1923, copies.

81. New York *Times,* November 21, 1921, p. 16. FCK "Memories of Prince Edward Island," *The Maritime Advocate and Busy East* (Sackville, New Brunswick), XXX (May, 1940), 26-27, 47. MP, memorandum of Henry L. Mencken, n.p., September 9, 1941, copy. AAOC, FCK to Francisco Orozco y Jiménez, n.p., March

11, 1924; FCK to John L. Belford, n.p., March 14, 1942, copies. A tradition in Oklahoma preserves this postscript to the account of Mundelein's recommendation; namely, that FCK should be appointed to the Hawaiian Islands. In 1924, when the news of FCK's promotion to the episcopate broke in the press, Mundelein inquired, as the story goes, as to which diocese the priest was given. When he was told it was Oklahoma, the cardinal allegedly replied: "Not far enough away—it should have been Honolulu." Victor J. Reed to Raymond F. Harkin; interview with Harkin, Oklahoma City, October 20, 1975.

82. EP, Mundelein to the clergy of Chicago, Chicago, March 7, 1924, printed circular. AAOC, FCK to Tampieri, n.p., March 10, 1924, copy.

83. AAC, 8-1924-M-53, FCK to Mundelein, Chicago, March 31, 1924. AAOC, FCK to Charles A. O'Hern, n.p., April 1, 1924; FCK to Tampieri, n.p., April 23, 1924, copies.

84. AAOC, FCK to Tampieri, n.p., June 7, 1924, copy.

85. AAOC, FCK, "Address on Behalf of the Board of Governors . . . to their Cardinal-Chancellor" [Chicago, May 14, 1924], typed text corrected in FCK's hand; an edited version of FCK's address and Mundelein's reply appeared in *Extension Magazine,* XIX (July, 1924), 3-4. AAC, 8-1924-M-47, FCK to Mundelein, Chicago, May 15, 1924.

86. AAOC, FCK to Tampieri, n.p., June 28, 1924, copy. See also the *New World,* June 27, 1924, p. 1.

87. AAC, 8-1924-M-57, FCK to Mundelein, Washington, D.C., June 30, 1924. AAOC, FCK's secretary to Tampieri, n.p., June 30, 1924, copy.

88. AAOC, FCK to Tampieri, n.p., June 28, August 21, October 10, 1924; FCK to John W. Shaw, n.p., August 21, 1924; FCK to Joseph J. Quinn, n.p., August 21, 1924; FCK to O'Brien, n.p., January 16, 1941, copies. AAC, 8-1924-M-52, FCK to Mundelein, Chicago, September 22, 1924. Eugene J. McGuinness, "The Consecration of Bishop Kelley," *Extension Magazine,* XIX (November, 1924), 8, 38-39.

89. AAOC, FCK to Gustave Depreitere, n.p., September 5, 1924; FCK to Peter Guilday, n.p., May 1, 1933, copies. Interview with Archbishop John R. Quinn, Oklahoma City, November 4, 1977.

90. AAC, 8-1924-M-396, Mundelein's address at the Coliseum in Oklahoma City [October 15, 1942], typed and corrected in Mundelein's script; an edited version appeared in *Extension Magazine,* XIX (December, 1924), 1; and in *The Catholic Home* (Oklahoma City), November 1, 1924, pp. 18-19.

91. AAOC, FCK to Sheil, n.p., October 31, 1924, copy. See also FCK's personal acknowledgement in AAC, 8-1924-M-55, FCK to Mundelein, Oklahoma City, October 20, 1924.

92. EP, O'Brien to FCK, n.p., January 8, 1934, copy.

93. EP, O'Brien to FCK, n.p., March 1, 1943, copy; editorial in *Extension Magazine,* XIX (August, 1924), 1.

94. AAOC, FCK to Tampieri, n.p., April 9, 1925, copy.

CHAPTER VI

1. FCK, *The Forgotten God* (Milwaukee, 1932), 131. AAOC, Leslie to FCK, London, March 21, 1936, copy.

2. AAOC, FCK to Joseph T. Roche, n.p., September 11 and November 13, 1914; FCK to Tampieri, n.p., February 20, 1920, copies. A representative editorial was "A Suggestion to Those Who Love Peace" (*Extension Magazine,* IX [February, 1915], 4), which covered the preparedness controversy and condemned the two fringe positions—militarism and pacifism. Arthur S. Link thoroughly analyzes the factors that led Wilson to favor the British maritime system over that of Germany. See his *Wilson the Diplomatist: A Look at His Major Foreign Policies* (Chicago, 1965); and *Wilson: Campaigns for Progressivism and Peace* (Princeton, 1965), 337-38.

3. AAOC, FCK to Alfred E. Burke, n.p., April 17, 1916, copy.

4. New York *Times,* November 10, 1915, pp. 1-2. AAOC, FCK to John Farley, n.p. [February 28, 1916]; FCK to David Lawrence, n.p., January 31, 1917, copies.

5. AAOC, FCK to Burke, n.p., January 16, 1917, copy. Some details are given in a radio talk (December 26, 1938), the fifth in a series originating in Oklahoma and known as "In the Air Lanes: The Bishop Broadcasts."

6. AAOC, Tampieri to FCK, Rome, August 9, 1915.

7. Chicago *Tribune,* January 14, 1917, p. I-3. AAOC, FCK to Burke, n.p., January 16, 1917, copy.

8. FCK, "A Calamity Indeed," *Extension Magazine,* XI (March, 1917), 3; "War," *ibid.,* XI (May, 1917), 3.

9. AAOC, FCK to Tampieri, n.p., January 4, 1918, copy.

10. This theme is brilliantly explored in William Hardy McNeill, *The Rise of the West* (Chicago, 1963). FCK's views about the church's new responsibilities and opportunities, which will be discussed in chapter VII, are found in AAC, 5-1919-M-137, FCK to Mundelein, Paris, April 25, 1919.

11. FCK, "My Most Interesting Ten Weeks," 23-24. This is a typed manuscript (42 pp.) in the form of a journal (February 11-May 31, 1919), corrected in FCK's hand and hereafter cited as "Ten Weeks." Additional details in this section were supplied from Basil Henry Liddell Hart, *The Real War* (Boston, 1930).

12. "Ten Weeks," 24-26.

13. *Ibid.,* 26-28.

14. *Ibid.,* 28-29. *The Forgotten God,* 131-32. *Jots,* 244-45.

15. "Ten Weeks," 29-31.

16. Ellis, *Gibbons,* II, 261-62. New York *Times,* December 29, 1919, p. 9.

17. Gasparri to Mundelein, Rome, July 18, 1919, reprinted in "German-Americans in a Great Crisis," Mundelein, *Letters of a Bishop to His Flock* (New York, 1927), 184-97. The Central Verein was founded in Baltimore in 1855 and grew rapidly into a significant national society. Its programs included relief and insurance benefits, as well as political activity in behalf of parochial schools. At the outbreak of World War I its membership approached 150,000.

18. AAC, 5-1919-T-3, Mundelein to Tierney, Chicago, November 15, 1919, copy.

19. EP, MacDonald to FCK, Mons, Belgium, February 21, 1919, copy; Ledvina to Mundelein, Chicago, March 27, 1919.

20. AAOC, FCK to Burke, n.p., January 21, 1910, copy. New York *Times,* January 20, 1920, p. 17. FCK's bulletin appeared as an editorial in *Extension Magazine,* XV (July, 1920), 1.

21. FCK's "Rebuke," *Extension Magazine,* XV (October, 1920), 4. FCK was not alone in his outrage. Elliot Wadsworth, vice chairman of the American Red Cross, reported that in Vienna the daily food allowance amounted to only 900 calories, roughly half of what was required to survive. The little coal available had made heating and cooked meals scarce, and farmers would not sell to the government at fixed prices. Before the war, the U.S. dollar was equivalent to 5½ Austrian *kronen;* and after, it could be traded for as many as 250 *kronen.* New York

Times, May 9, 1920, VII-3. Another contemporary, Graham Lusk of the Cornell Medical College, uncovered revealing statistics appearing in an editorial of the *Wiener Arbeiterzeitung.* In February, 1920, Vienna had 1,894 births, while suffering 4,020 deaths—a net loss of some 2,100. In the capital, he added, citizens were eating a "meat substitute," consisting of potato and apple peels, potato bits, pine ash, and charcoal. Vienna, once the charming queen of an empire, was fast becoming a "city of the dead." New York *Times,* May 16, 1920, II-2.

Recent studies, however, have challenged FCK's blame on the decisions of the Paris peace conference. Reparations were to be scaled according to a formula based on the ability to pay. While, furthermore, Austria experimented with the notion of union with Germany, the republic tended to make so many conditions that such a union became less inviting to the Germans, who eventually welcomed the Paris ban on the *Anschluss.* Representative of this view is Karl R. Stadler, *Austria* (New York, 1971), 107-21.

22. AAC, 6-1920-H-202, Ledvina to Edward F. Hoban, Chicago, July 27, 1920. AAC, Piffl to FCK, Vienna, July 9, 1920. Joseph McGlinchey, Cardinal O'Connell's director of the Propagation, reported that the Boston *Pilot* had reprinted FCK's appeal, and this enabled him to raise a separate $3,000, which he forwarded to the American Relief Administration. AAOC, McGlinchey to FCK, May 28 and June 7, 1920. Even the unlucky Ambrose Petry, who had suffered business reverses, lauded FCK's ability "to produce that metallic sympathy so necessary for relief work." Petry would have enclosed a large contribution, he added, if he were not so urgently "tied up" with a new venture; and FCK appreciated the generous heart. AAOC, Petry to FCK, New York City, June 5, 1920.

23. AAOC, FCK to McGlinchey, n.p., June 11, 1920, copy.

24. *The Times* (London), July 10, 1920, p. 14.

25. FCK's reply to *The Times* is found in *Extension Magazine,* XV (November, 1920), 3-4.

26. AAC, 6-1920-M-244, FCK to Mundelein, Vienna, July 27, 1920; 6-1920-M-113, same to same, Chicago, October 25, 1920; 6-1920-M-174, FCK to Ledvina, Vienna, July 29, 1920.

27. AAOC, Dougan to FCK, Vienna, July 31 and August 4, 1920; Piffl to FCK, Vienna, August 12, 1920; R. Fuerlinger to Extension Society, Vienna, August 11, 1920; Charlotte Baynes to FCK, London, August 26, 1920; FCK to Baynes, London, September 8, 1920, copy. New York *Times,* October 31, 1920, VIII-4.

28. AAOC, Baynes to FCK, Vienna, October 2, 1920; "Précis of Conservation

with Mrs. Baynes on her work in Vienna" [London], January 6, 1921, p. 6, hereafter cited as "Précis." Caritas offered a satisfactory explanation regarding the 210 cases of milk sent to the cardinal's residence. This facility was intended to serve as a depot for delivering the milk to the rectories. AAOC, Fuerlinger to FCK, Vienna, October 26, 1920.

29. AAOC, Leslie to FCK, London, September 8, 1920, and March 21, 1936; Baynes to FCK, Vienna, October 9, 1920; FCK to Mundelein, n.p., October 11, 1920, copy; "Précis," 1-2.

30. "Précis," 6.

31. AAOC, FCK to Piffl, n.p., September 30, 1920, copy; FCK to Mundelein, n.p., October 11, 1920, copy, with attached draft; Gibbons to the Catholic people, Baltimore, November 19, 1920, printed circular. AAC, 6-1920-M-10, Mundelein to Messmer, Chicago, October 14, 1920; 6-1920-G-3, Mundelein to Gibbons, Chicago, October 21, 1920, copies. Mundelein indicated as his excuse in postponing the committee work Muldoon's departure from the United States soon after the bishops' meeting. The record of the bishops' meeting does not cite Mundelein's presentation or Gibbon's action. AAC, 6-1920-M-85, minutes of the second annual meeting of the American hierarchy, September 22, 1920.

32. AAC, 6-1920-M-113, FCK to Mundelein, Chicago, October 25, 1920; 6-1920-C-2, Mundelein to Bainbridge W. Colby, Chicago, December 11, 1920, copy; 6-1921-L-2, Mundelein to Ledvina, Chicago, February 19, 1921, copy. AAOC, Ledvina to Max Wittinghaff [Chicago], January 21, 1921, copy. "Rebuke," *Extension Magazine,* XV (October, 1920), 4. Board Minutes, II (November 10, 1920), 59-60.

33. AAOC, FCK to Baynes, n.p., October 25 and December 23, 1920, copies; Baynes to FCK, Vienna, October 25, November 27 and December 16 and 28, 1920.

34. "Précis," 1-6. AAOC, FCK to Franckenstein, London, December 20, 1920, and January 11 and 19, 1921; FCK to Ledvina, London, January 13, 1921, copies. AAC, 6-1921-M-153, Franckenstein to FCK, London, January 14, 1921.

35. AAC, 6-1921-M-210, FCK to Mundelein, London, January 14, 1921; 6-1921-M-199, Ledvina to Mundelein, Chicago, January 31, 1921. AAOC, Baynes to FCK, London, January 16 and February 8, 1921. Rempe reported to Mundelein his meeting with Mrs. Baynes. His refusal had been on the grounds that he had no instructions to purchase clothing in England. His tour of inspection likewise convinced him of other priorities in central Europe. AAC, 6-1921-M-35, Rempe to Mundelein, Cologne, Easter Monday [March 28], 1921, copy.

36. AAOC, FCK to Baynes, n.p., May 16, 1921, copy. AAC, 6-1921-M-201, Ledvina to Mundelein, Chicago, February 23, 1921.

37. AAOC, FCK to Frederick Schwager, S.V.D., n.p., July 5, 1921, copy.

38. AAOC, Edgar Prochnik to FCK, Washington, D.C., April 1, 1931.

CHAPTER VII

1. For an attractive review of the urban-rural antagonism, see William E. Leuchtenburg, *Perils of Prosperity: 1914-1932* (Chicago, 1958), 225-40.

2. *Jots,* 59.

3. AAOC, FCK to Burke, n.p., June 9 and 14, 1915, copies.

4. AAOC, FCK to Moeller, n.p., January 19, 1923, copy.

5. *Jots,* 242.

6. AAOC, Ledvina to FCK, n.p., April 1, 1919, copy.

7. AAOC, Tampieri to FCK, Rome, May 20, 1914, *personal.*

8. AAOC, FCK to Cerretti, n.p., March 8, 1920, copy. For amusing incidents illustrating FCK's conversational skills in French and Italian, see *Jots,* 71-72, 243-44, 317.

9. AAOC, FCK to Tampieri, n.p., January 4 and 9, 1923; FCK to Thomas B. Lawler, n.p., November 27, 1939, copies.

10. Recent surveys of the Roman Question appear in appropriate articles in the *New Catholic Encyclopedia.* An insightful review of the issues by John de Salis, British minister at the Holy See, appears in Thomas E. Hachey, ed., *Anglo-Vatican Relations,* 27-29.

11. E. Deboghel, *La question Romaine sous Pie XI et Mussolini* (n.p., n.d.), 14-15. FCK was actually in Rome when Rossi's pastoral on the Roman Question was published. From an interview with Merry del Val, he received a strong impression that the archbishop's proposal had either been inspired by the Vatican or received its blessing beforehand. FCK, "Ten Weeks," 31. FCK's published account on this subject was more cautious, omitting his opinion regarding the Vatican's connection with Rossi's pastoral. See *Jots,* 181.

12. AAOC, Edward L. Roe to FCK, Philadelphia, June 30, 1913; [James Slevin to] Merry del Val, Rome, July 6, 1913; FCK to A.P. Barnard, n.p., January 27, 1914; FCK to Joseph T. Brennan, n.p., March 12, 1914, copies.

13. AAOC, FCK to Tiberghien, n.p., May 17, 1916, copy.

14. A complete discussion of the Gibbons-Wilson connection at this stage is found in Ellis, *Gibbons,* II, 274-76.

15. Elvira Cerretti, *Il cardinale Bonaventura Cerretti, memoria* (Rome, 1939), 214, 231.

16. *Idem.* For Gibbons's messages to Mercier, see Ellis, *Gibbons,* II, 278-79.

17. For a splendid survey of the Fiume problem, see Edward M. House and Charles Seymour, eds., *What Really Happened in Paris: The Story of the Peace Conference, 1918-1919* (New York, 1921), 112-39.

18. AAOC, FCK to Charles Van Duerm, n.p., July 14, 1931, copy.

19. AAOC, FCK to Peter J. O'Callahan, C.S.P., n.p., November 23, 1918, copy; also FCK, "Ten Weeks," 1. Chapters XI and XII contain a fuller account of FCK's work regarding Mexico.

20. AAC, 2-1914-M-27, Cerretti to Mundelein, Washington, D.C., April 8, 1914. AAOC, Paschal Robinson, O.F.M., to FCK, Rome, December 6, 1921; Cerretti to FCK, Paris, March 13, 1922. FCK, "The New Nuncio," *Extension Magazine,* XVI (October, 1921), 3. Elvira Cerretti, *Cerretti,* 170-71, 205, 206-7. Hachey, *Anglo-Vatican Relations,* 15.

21. AAOC, FCK, "Ten Weeks," 7-9.

22. AAOC, FCK to House, n.p., May 6, 1919, copy. "Ten Weeks," 22-23, 31. FCK fleshed out his impressions of Colonel House in *Jots,* 265-66.

23. AAC, 5-1919-M-122, FCK to Mundelein, Rome, April 5, 1919; 5-1919-M-60, same to same, Paris, May 3, 1919. This treatment of FCK's involvement in the Roman Question is based largely on unpublished materials found in the AAOC, the same sources which FCK used for his classic account in *Jots,* 261-76.

24. "Ten Weeks," 26.

25. *Ibid.,* 26-27. AAOC, FCK to Mercier, n.p., May 19, 1919; FCK to Charles Van Duerm, S.J., n.p., July 14, 1931, copies.

26. "Ten Weeks," 31.

27. *Ibid.*, 32-33. AAOC, FCK, "Statement for [the] Holy See, 1929," 2; FCK to Francis J. Spellman, n.p., April 8, 1929, copy. This is the first draft of a statement which was published in "La Soluzione della Questione Romana nelle Conversazioni fra L'on. Orlando e Mons. Cerretti a Parigi nel Giugno del 1919," *Vita e Pensiero* (Milan) (June-July, 1929), 403-11; hereafter cited as "Statement."

28. "Ten Weeks," 33-35; "Statement," 2-5. AAOC, John Hughes to FCK, Evanston, Illinois, July 30, 1929.

29. AAOC, Brambilla to FCK, Paris, May 19, 1919, *strictly confidential.*

30. "Ten Weeks," 38-39; "Statement," 5-7.

31. "Ten Weeks," 39, 40-41; "Statement," 7. The press noted Cerretti's arrival in Paris, but he gave no interview. New York *Times,* May 28, 1919, p. 17.

32. AAC, 5-1919-M-265, Cerretti to Mundelein, Paris, May 30, 1919. "Statement," 7.

33. AAOC, FCK to Petry, n.p., June 19, 1919, copy.

34. "La Soluzione," 417. Cerretti, *Cerretti,* 231.

35. FCK had been contacted by an acquaintance, Vittorio Falorsi, who was an adviser at the Italian embassy. During the 1920s he served with the League of Nation's International Institute of Agriculture. He died in 1953, a distinguished professor of Romance languages at Ohio State University and perhaps a refugee from Fascism. AAOC, Harry I. Hazelton to FCK, Chicago, November 22, 1918. New York *Times,* August 26, 1953, p. 27.

36. AAOC, FCK to Cerretti, n.p., June 28 and September 11, 1919, copies; Cerretti to FCK, Rome, August 11, 1919; Robinson to FCK, Jerusalem, n.d; FCK to Robinson, n.p., November 19, 1919, copy.

37. AAC, 5-1918-M-150, McAdoo to Mundelein, Washington, D.C., December 10, 1918; 6-1920-M-102, Bonzano to Mundelein, Washington, D.C., February 24, 1920, "confidenziale." See also Paul R. Martin, *The First Cardinal of the West* [Chicago, *ca.* 1935], 121.

38. The Lateran Pacts consisted of a treaty, financial settlement, and concordat between the Holy See and the kingdom of Italy. The most important provision was Italy's recognition as fully sovereign and independent an enclave of 108.7 acres in Rome to be known officially as the "State of Vatican City." A summary of the provision may be found in the *New Catholic Encyclopedia* (New York, 1967), VIII, 410-11. A splendid on-the-spot review of the criticism against

the pope and Mussolini is given by Henry Getty Chilton, British minister to the Holy See, in his report to the Foreign Office, dated March 27, 1930, and reprinted in Hachey, *Anglo-Vatican Relations,* 166-67.

39. AAOC, FCK to Cerretti, n.p., January 21, 1929, copy.

40. *Daily Oklahoman* (Oklahoma City), March 31, 1929, p. 1. AAOC, FCK to Spellman, n.p., April 6, 1929; FCK to William D. O'Brien, n.p., April 9, 1929, copies.

41. Vittorio E. Orlando, "The First Agreement between Italy and the Holy See," *Saturday Evening Post,* CCI (May 4, 1929), 12-13, 206.

42. Public Record Office, London, Foreign Office Series 371.13686/116/3564, summary of Mussolini's speech to the Chamber of Deputies, Rome, May 13, 1929; 371.13686/116/3933, Ronald Graham to Austen Chamberlain, Rome, May 31, 1929. Hachey, *Anglo-Vatican Relations,* 167-68. E. Deboghel, *La question Romaine sous Pie XI et Mussolini,* 313, 316-18, 329. Mussolini's style in the Chamber of Deputies is reported by Arnaldo Cortesi in the New York *Times,* May 19, 1929, III-3.

43. "La Soluzione della Questione Roman nelle Conversazioni fra L'on. Orlando e Mons. Cerretti a Parigi nel Giugno del 1919," *Vita e Pensiero* (June-July, 1929), 403-11. AAOC, Cerretti to FCK, Rome, June 25, 1929.

44. AAOC, Dino Grandi to FCK, Rome, January 15 [1930]; John B. Tua to FCK, McAlester, Oklahoma, April 14, 1930. *Southwest Courier* (Oklahoma City), June 7, 1930, p. 1.

CHAPTER VIII

1. AAOC, FCK to Giuseppe Pizzardo, n.p., June 2, 1933, copy.

2. "German missions" and related phrases refer loosely to those missionary works which the Allied victors considered as belonging to German and Austrian religious societies or institutes. As former enemy aliens, their members were subject to the penalities provided in the Treaty of Versailles. Technically, a number of those also threatened with expatriation from overseas assignments were natives of neutral countries, such as Switzerland and the Netherlands, who had worked in these missions.

3. AAOC, FCK to Burke, n.p., December 2, 1916, copy. Four years later, a

pamphlet published by the society reported that after internment, the German mission staff had been expelled from Mozambique—14 priests, 10 brothers, and 15 sisters. *An Appeal to the Catholics of the World to Save the German Foreign Missions* (Techny, Illinois [1920?]), 12.

4. New York *Times*, May 8, 1919, p. 6. Public Record Office, London, Foreign Office Group (hereafter cited as FO) 371.4800/883/883, memorandum of Herbert W. Malkin [London], July 13, 1920.

5. Archives of the archdiocese of Westminster (hereafter cited as AAW), Roman Letters, IX, 31, Gasparri to Bourne, Rome, May 31, 1919. Public Record Office, Cabinet Group, 23/11/119-21, minutes of the meeting of the War Cabinet, London, August 13, 1919, *secret.*

6. AAOC, "Copy of the Draft of a Brief to the Conference of Peace, Paris, submitted by Mgr. Cerretti as representing the Holy See," eleven pages in FCK's hand and prefaced with the following: "Note: This is the original draft made by me for Mgr. Cerretti on the train from Rome to Paris and using notes & points in Card. Gasparri's handwriting." Cerretti's arrival was noted in the New York *Times*, May 28, 1919, p. 17. It was his third visit to Paris during the peacemaking.

7. AAOC, FCK [to Gibbons], n.p., September 23, 1920; FCK to Peter T. Janser, S.V.D., n.p., October 26, 1920, copies. Benedict XV's reservations are quoted in the New York *Times*, July 4, 1919, p. 10. Cerretti's compromise was stipulated in Arthur J. Balfour to Cerritti, Paris, June 6, 1919: "In those cases in which in accordance with the Treaty of Peace it will be found necessary to transfer the property of German missions to boards of trustees, the property of missions depending on the Holy See will be handed over to duly accredited persons of the Roman Catholic Church. In case it is found necessary according to the Treaty of Peace to exercise control over persons carrying on these missions, this can only be done after due consultation with the authorities of the respective religious denominations." AACC, Alfons Vaeth, S.J., "The Question of the German Catholic Missions," n.p., n.d., 14. FO 371.4897/3567/13065, draft statement regarding Balfour's explanation of article 438 of the Treaty of Versailles [December 4, 1920].

8. FO 371.4324/80831, Arthur Balfour to the Foreign Office [Paris], May 28, 1919.

9. AAW, Roman Letters, IX, 31, Willem van Rossum to Bourne, Rome, March 24, 1919. FO 371.4324/80831, report of John Wallace Ord Davidson [Guangzhou (Canton), China], June 9, 1919; 371.4324/90312, "Memo B: 'The Activities of German Missionaries in China' " [report of the Foreign Office of

Balfour, June 19, 1919]. The intervention of the United States in stopping the deportation of German missionaries from China is documented in the National Archives, Series 393.116/163-93, passim. While the British admitted that only ten German missionaries had been expelled, Catholic authorities set the number at twenty. *Ibid.*, 393.116/182½, James Gibbons to Frank L. Polk, Baltimore, June 6, 1919.

10. FO 371.4324/84832, Malcolm C. C. Seton to the Foreign Office, London, June 5, 1919, *urgent and confidential*. The clerk who scribbled the comment on this report was Hughe Montgomery Knatchbull-Hugessen. See also FO 371.4324/127118, John Edward Ferard to the Foreign Office, London, September 9, 1919.

11. FO 371.4324/88336, "German Mission in Africa" [report of the Colonial Office, June 13, 1919]; 371.4324/90312, "Memo A: The Political Activities of the Basle Mission" [report of the Foreign Office to Balfour, June 19, 1919].

12. FO 395.348/36/347, H. C. Watts to Alec W. G. Randall, n.p., March 26, 1920.

13. AAOC, FCK to Cerretti, n.p., April 3, 1920, copy. The mission-aid society was the Association of the Holy Childhood. "Crime of the Powers," *America*, XXII (April 3, 1920), 551-52. FO 395.348/36/169, comment of Alec W. G. Randall, dated April 22, 1920.

14. *An Appeal* . . . (Techny, Illinois [1920?]), 3-7, 10-17. The American edition of this pamphlet credited no author, but the French one identified him as J. Neuhausler, secretary general of the Ludwig Mission Society. FCK's foreword was virtually reprinted in "Internationalism or the Gospel?" *Extension Magazine*, XIV (April, 1920), 4. AAOC, FCK's confidential memorandum on his involvement in the Irish question (hereafter cited as "confidential memo on Irish question"), 1922, p. 1.

15. FCK, "Ten Weeks," 15-16. On April 30, 1919, Wilberforce was named assistant director of the British Library of Information and succeeded to the top post on October 1, 1920. His next assignment did not occur until April 1, 1941, when he was appointed to the ministry of information in London. Background on Wilberforce may be found in *Jots*, 283-84, and in Thomas E. Hachey, "Anglophile Sentiments in American Catholicism in 1940: A British Official's Confidential Assessment," *Records of the American Catholic Historical Society of Philadelphia*, LXXXV (March, June, 1974), 48-58. In his autobiography, FCK attributes the "diplomatic deafness" to Wilberforce's superior in Rome, Count John de Salis, who had died earlier in 1939. No doubt, this curious lapse regarding the facts was due

in part to the memoirist's intent to spare comments on the living, who at the time included Wilberforce.

16. FO 371.3827/31955, Colville Barclay to the Foreign Office, Washington, D.C., February 25, 1919; 371.4897/3657/5752, memorandum by Christopher J. Phillips [London], September 13 [1920].

17. FO 395.351/127/1378, memorandum of Christopher J. Phillips, dated November 11, 1920. The reasons for Bourne's strong reluctance to have FCK at his home are not altogether clear. The writer found no pertinent evidence in AAW. The Public Record Office registered four pieces related to the cardinal's invitation to FCK, but a search could not locate them. The standard biography of the English churchman is Ernest Oldmeadow, *Francis Cardinal Bourne,* 2 vols. (London, 1940-44).

18. AAOC, FCK to Mundelein, n.p., March 13 and April 3, 1920; FCK to Cerretti, n.p., April 3 and 14, May 28, June 7, 1920, copies; Cerretti to FCK, Rome, May 9 and June 30, 1920. FO 395.349/127/206, Wilberforce to William G. Tyrrell, New York City, April 12, 1920.

19. AAOC, FCK to Joseph F. McGlinchey, n.p., June 4, 1920, copy.

20. AAOC, FCK, "Memorandum for the Holy See on the German and Austrian Catholic Missions" Rome, August, 1920, a seven-page typed report of his discussions in London during the first three weeks of July, 1920, pp. 1-2; hereafter cited as "Memorandum for the Holy See."

21. AAOC, Leslie to FCK, London, March 21, 1936, copy. FCK, "Memorandum for the Holy See," pp. 2-3. A review of Tyrrell's fascinating life is found in the *Dictionary of National Biography, 1941-1950* (London, 1959), 893-96.

22. AAC, 6-1920-M-247, FCK to Mundelein, Downside Abbey, Stratton-on-the-Foss, near Bath, England, July 10, 1920. By 1858, the British government had evolved three "external" departments—the Foreign, Colonial, and India Offices, each with a secretary of state who was a member of the cabinet and responsible to Parliament. This arrangement lasted seventy years until the growing number of self-governing colonies prompted the establishment of the Dominions Office in 1925. The Foreign Office conducted the foreign policies of the British government. The Colonial and India Offices served generally as London's official medium of communication with the appropriate governments abroad, and it had the right of advising the veto of any act of a local legislature.

23. AAOC, FCK to Tyrrell, London, n.p., pp. 8-9, copy, Bourne file.

24. AAC, 6-1920-M-248, FCK to Mundelein, London, July 14, 1920; FCK,

"Memorandum for the Holy See," pp. 5-6, 7.

25. AAOC, press communiqués issued by the Government of India, November 22, 1919, and January 22, 1920.

26. AAOC, Richard H. Tierney, S.J., to FCK, New York City, June 26, 1920. See also, FCK to Wilberforce, n.p., June 11, 1920; FCK to McGlinchey, n.p., June 11, 1920, copies.

27. AAC, 6-1920-M-244, FCK to Mundelein, Vienna, July 27, 1920. AAOC, FCK to Wilberforce, Chicago, June 11, 1920, copy; Becker, "Aide-memoire for Msgr. Kelly [*sic*]," Rome, August 16, 1920; Becker, "Some notes on Assam for the Right Rev. Francis C. Kelly," Rome, August 19, 1920; Becker to FCK, Munich, September 5, 1920; J. B. Connolly to FCK, Clonmel, County Tipperary, Ireland, September 19, 1920. One should mention a splendid fifteen-page survey of German missions world-wide which was complied by one of the Jesuits at Bonn and given to Kelley. AAOC, Alfons Vaeth, S.J., "The Question of the German Catholic Missions."

28. AAOC, Pancratius Pfeiffer, S.D.S., to FCK, Rome, November 3, 1920.

29. FCK, "Memorandum for the Holy See." In an important defense of his activities to Propaganda a year later, Kelley dated these talks as occurring in July. AAOC, Kelley to Laurenti [Rome, February 15, 1921], copy. Yet, as he had explained to Mundelein, he was not scheduled to leave Vienna for Rome until July 29, and in his autobiography he recalled: "One thing was certain, we were likely to be at least two nights and two days on the road to Rome." AAC, 6-1920-M-244, FCK to Mundelein, Vienna, July 27, 1920. *Jots,* 317.

30. AAC, 6-1920-M-165, FCK to Mundelein, Rome, August 16, 1920. AAOC, Gasparri to FCK, Rome, August 20, 1920. The only reservation which Gasparri expressed concerning FCK's protocol was the cardinal's insistence that the formula—that is, the use of the ABCM as guarantor—applied *only* to Germans and other ex-enemy nationals working in missions in the British empire. No such arrangement would be acceptable for other groups.

31. AAC, 6-1920-M-165, FCK to Mundelein, Rome, August 16, 1920; 6-1920-M-245, same to same, Rome, August 31, 1920. Count Sir John Francis de Salis (1864-1939) was a scion of a Catholic family which had emigrated to England at the beginning of the eighteenth century from the Swiss Canton of Grisoni. The family retained the hereditary title of count of the Holy Roman Empire. De Salis was to give thirty-seven years to the British foreign service. After five years as minister to Montenegro, he was appointed as minister to the Vatican in 1916, where he served until his retirement in 1923. New York *Times,* January 15, 1939,

p. 38. Kelley remembered him in *Jots,* 177.

32. AAOC, FCK to Cerretti [London], September 8, 9, and 10, 1920; FCK to Schwager, London, September 9, 1920, copies; Frederick W. Duke to FCK, London, September 9, 1920; FCK to Duke, London, September 10, 1920, copy. FO 371.4840/6994/7174, Lord Milner to colonial governments (Fiji, Uganda, Malta, Cyprus, Ceylon, Hong Kong, Straits Settlements, Mauritius, British Guiana, Trinidad & Jamaica, Malay States, South Africa, and Zanzibar), London, September 22, 1920.

33. AAOC, FCK to Felix Couturier, O.P., London, September 9, 1920; FCK to Cerretti, n.p., September 30, 1920; FCK to Ernest R. Hull, S.J., n.p., October 5, 1920; FCK to Becker, n.p., October 11, 1920, copies.

34. FO 395.351/127/1378, memorandum of Christopher J. Phillips, November 11, 1920.

35. AAOC, FCK to Arthur P. Jackman, n.p., October 9, 1920; FCK to Christopher J. Phillips, n.p., October 27, 1920, copies. FO 371.4897/3657, comment by Percy Alexander Koppel.

36. AAOC, FCK to Cerretti, London, September 10, 1920, copy.

37. AAOC, FCK to [Gibbons], n.p., September 23, 1920; FCK to Denis O-'Connell, n.p., September 27, 1920, copies.

38. FO 395.351/127/1195, Wilberforce to Christopher J. Phillips, New York City, September 24, 1920, *confidential.*

39. AAOC, FCK to Cerretti, n.p., September 30 and October 11, 1920; FCK to Joseph H. McMahon, n.p., October 27, 1920, copies. The record of the meeting mentions simply that a letter from Kelley was read and received. AAC, 6-1920-M-85, minutes of the second annual meeting of the American hierarchy, September, 1920, p. 11.

40. FO 395.351/127/1378, Wilberforce to Tyrrell, New York City, October 28, 1920, *confidential.*

41. FO 395.351/127/1378, memorandum of Christopher J. Phillips, November 11, 1920.

42. AAOC, FCK, "confidential memo on Irish question," pp. 3-4.

43. FO 395.349/127/206, Wilberforce to Tyrrell, New York City, April 12, 1920. A summary of Cohalan's life is found in the New York *Times,* November 13, 1946, p. 27.

44. FO 395.351/127/1375, Wilberforce to Tyrrell, New York City, October 22, 1920. New York *Times,* June 20, 1920, p. 14; June 22, p. 25.

45. AAOC, FCK to Cerretti, n.p., October 11, 1920, copy.

46. AAOC, FCK to seventeen bishops by name, n.p., September 29, 1920, copies. McNeil to FCK, Toronto, October 4, 1920, two separate letters of the same date.

47. AAOC, FCK to Alfred A. Sinnott, n.p., October 26, 1920; FCK to Peter T. Janser, S.V.D., n.p., October 26, 1920; FCK to Cerretti, n.p., October 27, 1920, copies. Copies of twelve letters from Canadian bishops are filed in FO 395.353/127/1612. Additional duplicates were sent to the India and Colonial Offices.

48. AAOC, FCK to Cerretti, n.p., September 30 and October 27, 1920; FCK to Christopher J. Phillips, Chicago, October 27, 1920; FCK to Geddes, Chicago, October 27, 1920, with "suggestions" attached, copies.

49. AAOC, FCK to Couturier, London, September 9, 1920, copy. FCK appeared unaware of alleged criminal activity on the part of German Catholic missionaries in India, but the Foreign Office was, at this time, notified of charges of sedition against them. Accordingly, though unmolested at the beginning of World War I, the missionaries fomented unrest in Orissa, part of a province on the Bay of Bengal in east India, where the British were compelled to apply force. This action persuaded the government to repatriate the male religious, while leaving the sisters alone. "It was necessary & it was decided," the memorandum concluded, "not to permit their return after the war." FO 371.4897/3657/5752, memorandum [Tyrrell ?, September 13, 1920?].

50. AAOC, FCK to Phillips, n.p., November 24, 1920, copy; attached is the "exception to memorandums A & B" in FCK's script. British policy barring German missionaries had been promulgated by the India Office in a document entitled, "Admission into India of Aliens desiring to undertake Missionary, Educational or other Philanthropic Work in India after the War: Memorandum A. . .Memorandum B" [London], January, 1920. Kelley's formula was conceived as an "addendum" of exceptions to the two Memoranda. It was further assumed that if the India Office accepted the exceptions, the Colonial Office would promptly follow.

51. AAOC, FCK to Arthur P. Jackman, Chicago, November 10, 1920, copy.

52. AAOC, John Charles Walton to FCK, London, December 29, 1920; FCK to Cerretti, London [*ca.* January 3, 1921], copy.

53. AAOC, FCK to Cerretti, London [*ca.* January 2, 1921], January 5 and 10,

1921, copies; Hirtzel to FCK, London, January 3, 1921; FCK to Ledvina, London, January 13, 1921, copies.

54. AAOC, [Bourne to] Becker, Schwager, and Herman Doering, S.J., London, January 14, 1921, copies.

55. AAOC, Bourne's memorandum, London, December 23, 1920; "Report of Monsignor Francis C. Kelley to the Holy See on the subject of German and Austrian Missions in the British Empire" [Rome? *ca.* January 30, 1921], pp. 3-4; hereafter cited as "Report, 1921," copies. Hirtzel's adaptation of FCK's formula took the form of a "Memorandum B (suggested addendum)," which basically listed seven conditions which would regulate the return of the German missionaries. Attached to this addendum was a "form of application" to be completed by "former enemy aliens." FCK also supplied a lengthy argument regarding the merits of the formula in AAOC, FCK to Hirtzel, London, January 12, 1921, copy. Thus the addendum-application form and FCK's letter formed the package of documents mailed to the Government of India on January 20, 1921.

56. AAC, 6-1921-M-214, FCK to Mundelein, London, January 14, 1920. AAOC, FCK to Cerretti, London [*ca.* January 2, 1921], copy; Reading to FCK, London, January 10 [1921]; FCK to Reading [London], January 12, 1921, copy; FCK, "Interview with the Earl of Reading," attached to his "Report, 1921," copy.

57. AAOC, FCK to James Duhig, n.p., October 5, 1920, copy; Janser to FCK, Steyl, Holland, October 10, 1920, including the attached statement of Australian Prime Minister William P. Hughes to T. Ryan; FCK to Janser, n.p., October 26, 1920, copy; William Laumen, M.S.C., to FCK, memorandum on the mission of New Pomerania (later New Britain), Rome, February 5, 1921; FCK to Phillips, Rome, February 7, 1921, copy. By mid-1921, FCK learned that Australia ended its policy of expelling German missionaries from its mandates. FCK to Schwager, n.p., August 16, 1921; FCK to Wilberforce, n.p., November 1, 1921, copies.

58. AAOC, FCK to Read, London, January 20, 1921, copy; Read to FCK, London, February 4, 1921; FCK, "Report, 1921," pp. 15-17; FCK to Cerretti, n.p., September 30, 1920, copy; FCK to Mathias Fohrman, S.C.J., n.p., November 3, 1922, copy. Though German missionaries had been excluded from Africa, the Colonial Office had begun to readmit several in British colonies in the Americas. FCK, "Report, 1921," p. 16.

59. AAOC, FCK to Bourne, Rome, February 14, 1921; FCK to Moeller, Rome, February 15, 1921, copies. AAC, 6-1921-M-150, FCK to Mundelein, Rome, February 15, 1921.

60. AAOC, FCK to Laurenti, Rome, March 5, 1921, copy. AAC, 6-1921-M-

150, FCK to Mundelein, Rome, February 15, 1921.

61. FO 395.351/127/1378, memorandum of Christopher J. Phillips, November 11, 1920.

62. AAOC, FCK to Cerretti, Rome, February 15, 1921, copy; Moylett to FCK, Dublin, November 30, 1926; FCK to George Barnard, n.p., March 18, 1927, and September 15, 1934, copies. *The Times,* (London), August 30, 1921, p. 12. FCK, "Ireland," *Extension Magazine,* XVI (February, 1922), 3. Chicago *Tribune,* January 9, 1947, p. 30. New York *Times,* January 8, 1947, p. 24. Splendid surveys of the Anglo-Irish negotiations are found in Joseph M. Curran. "Lloyd George and the Irish Settlement, 1921-1922," *Éire-Ireland: A Journal of Irish Studies* (St. Paul, Minnesota), VII: 2 (1972), 14-46; and George Dangerfield, *The Damnable Question: A Study in Anglo-Irish Relations* (Boston, 1976), 319-50.

63. The publication of Bourne's pastoral and the criticism resulting from it are documented in the New York *Times,* February 13, 1921, p. 5; February 14, p. 10; February 18, p. 15; and March 20, p. 1. See also P. D. Murphy, "Cardinal Bourne and Ireland," *The Nation,* CXII (March 16, 1921) 398-99.

64. *The Irish Independent* (Dublin), April 1, 1921, p. 6. AAOC, FCK to the editor of *The Nation,* Chicago, July 20, 1921, signed copy; and appearing in *Extension Magazine,* XVI (November, 1921), 4.

65. AAW, Bourne Papers, Ireland 5/36a, Bourne to Lloyd George, London, April 6, 1921, copy. New York *Times,* April 7, 1921, p. 3. AAOC, FCK to John F. O'Beirne, n.p., November 27, 1939, copy.

66. AAOC, FCK to Moylett, n.p., December 23, 1926; FCK to Barnard, n.p., September 15, 1934, copies. Evidently, Moylett never published his memoirs. Henry Wickham Steed, editor of the *Review of Reviews,* had offered to publish them, but neither did they appear in this periodical nor are they listed in the *British Museum General Catalogue of Printed Books* (London, 1963).

67. AAOC, FCK to Cerretti, Rome, March 12, 1921; FCK to Moeller, Rome, March 19, 1921, copies; Gasparri to FCK, Rome, March 22, 1921. AAC, 6-1921-M-151, FCK to Mundelein, Rome, March 19, 1921.

68. FO 371.5785/3/10108, Cecil Dormer to Earl Curzon of Kedleston, Rome, May 9, 1921; 371.5785/3/11288, John de Salis to Curzon, Rome, May 26, 1921. AAOC, Becker to FCK, Rome, September 18, 1921.

69. FO 371.5785/3/17210, Dormer to Curzon, Rome, August 23, 1921; Dormer to Christopher J. Phillips; note by Curzon; 371.5785/3/19455, Dormer to Curzon, Rome, October 3, 1921.

70. AAOC, Becker to FCK, Rome, September 18, 1921; FCK to Becker, n.p., October 18, 1921, copy; FCK to Wilberforce, n.p., November 1, 1921, copy.

71. AAOC, FCK to Wilberforce, n.p., July 18, 1921, copy; Wilberforce to FCK, New York City, December 31, 1923, *private.*

CHAPTER IX

1. AAOC, Shahan to FCK, Washington, D.C., January 29, 1923.

2. AAOC, Kelley to "Roe," n.p. [1916], in the file of Edward L. Roe.

3. Before coming to Rome, Van Rossum (1854-1932) had spent most of his years as a seminary professor and rector in the Netherlands. His administration at Propaganda was highlighted by the publication of two papal letters on the missions and the creation of new districts, some of which received the expatriated German missionaries, whose return to prewar assignments Kelley had advocated. The prefect also reorganized mission-aid societies, including the Propagation. The latter's central offices were brought from France to Rome, a historic move which, in compensation, elevated the society to the rank of a pontifical institute. An authoritative survey of Van Rossum's life appears in *Analecta Congregationis SS. Redemptoris,* III (1924), 144-49; VIII (1929), 339-46; XI (1932), 264-69, 336-76; XIII (1934) 147-51. The writer is grateful to Harry Grile, C.Ss.R., of Mount Alphonsus Seminary, Esopus, New York, for having provided copies of this material. See also the *New Catholic Encyclopedia* (New York), 1967), XIV, 538; and *Compendio di Storia della Sacra Congregazione . . . "de Propaganda Fide," 1622-1972* (Rome, 1974), 214.

4. Hachey, *Anglo-Vatican Relations,* 14. AAOC, FCK, "Ten Weeks," 14.

5. *Ibid.,* 17, 18. AAC, 5-1919-M-122, FCK to Mundelein, Rome, April 5, 1919.

6. A careful distinction must be drawn between "Propaganda" and the "Propagation," two institutions intimately associated with Catholic missions. "Propaganda" refers to the *Congregation* for the Propagation of the Faith, or "de Propaganda Fide." Founded in 1622, this department of the Roman Curia directs the missionary activity of the universal church. Its chief officer, a prefect, is a cardinal who consults with the pope regularly twice a month. He is assisted by a secretary, an archbishop who, in Kelley's time, also had a bimonthly audience with the pontiff. The "Propagation," however, denotes the Society for the Propagation

of the Faith. Its foundation dates from 1822 in France, when a group of laity agreed to collect small sums for the foreign-missions. It thus began as a private association, whose rapid success eventually gave it a virtual monopoly of collecting and distributing mission funds the world over. Approved in Rome in 1823, the society was administered by lay officers, with central councils in Lyons and Paris.

7. AAOC [Kelley to Benedict XV, Rome, *ca.* April 9, 1919], copy.

8. AAOC, FCK, "Ten Weeks," 26.

9. AAOC, FCK to Van Rossum, n.p., July 11, 1919; FCK to Cerretti, New York City, July 11, 1919; FCK to John F. O'Hara, C.S.C., n.p., July 8, 1938; copies. Excellent summaries of the origins of the National Catholic Welfare Conference are found in the *New Catholic Encyclopedia* (New York, 1967), X, 225-29; and in Ellis, *Gibbons,* II, 298-308.

10. AAC, 5-1919-M-138, "Report of the Mission Section of a Special Advisory Committee to the Catholic Activities Committee of the American Hierarchy" [July, 1919]. AAOC, "Memoranda of discussion, which followed the reading . . . of a plan for the establishment of a Board for the direction of Catholic missions, home and foreign" [July, 1919]; FCK to Fréri, n.p., July 28, 1919; FCK to Van Rossum, n.p., July 28, 1919, copies.

11. AAOC, FCK, "Preliminary Statement" regarding the ABCM [Rome, *ca.* February 1, 1921], pp. 3-4, copy, hereafter cited as "Preliminary Statement."

12. AAOC, FCK to Van Rossum, n.p., October 4, 1919, copy. AAC, 5-1919-M-246, "Approved Plans of the American Board of Catholic Missions," printed text. Article V provides that the "Board will . . . divide the collections semi-annually between its Home and Foreign Sections. . . ." Further, it lists the nine members of the ABCM advisory committee as follows: Msgr. John E. Burke (Catholic Board for Mission Work Among the Colored People); Rev. Edward J. Knaebel, C.S.Sp. (Association of the Holy Childhood); Rev. Peter T. Janser, S.V.D. (Society of the Divine Word), Rev. Edward J. McCarthy (Chinese Mission Society, known popularly as the Columban Fathers); Very Rev. James A. Walsh (Maryknoll); Msgr. William H. Ketcham (Bureau of Catholic Indian Missions); Msgr. Joseph Fréri (Society for the Propagation of the Faith); Rev. Peter J. O'Callaghan, C.S.P. (Catholic Missionary Union); and Francis C. Kelley (Extension Society). See also *ibid.,* "Minutes of the first meeting of the advisory board. . . ," New York City, October 14-17, 1919; and "The Director-General's plan of campaign," printed texts. It should be noted, too, that Fréri's early attitude toward ABCM was ambiguous. A year after his acceptance of the vice-chairmanship of the executive committee, he claimed that he had accepted that position not in any official ca-

pacity but only as a private individual who wished to engage in the discussions. Archives of the Society for the Propagation of the Faith (hereafter to be cited as ASPF), Fréri to the Central Council in Lyons, New York City, October 30, 1920, *confidential and personal.*

13. AAOC, Van Rossum to FCK, Rome, August 3, 1919, *confidential;* FCK to Dougherty, n.p., September 5, 1919, *strictly confidential,* copy. AAC, 5-1919-M-138, FCK to Mundelein, Chicago, September 6, 1919.

14. AAOC, FCK to Van Rossum, n.p., September 10, 1919, copy. In spite of the harsh refusal of Hennessy's appeal, the society had always claimed a special indulgence for the United States. Its first overseas contribution had been given in 1822 to Bishop Louis William Dubourg's missions in Louisiana. *New Catholic Encyclopedia* (New York, 1967), XI, 844. See also Theodore Roemer, O.F.M. Cap., *Ten Decades of Alms* (St. Louis, 1942).

15. AAOC, Fréri to FCK, New York City, September 22 and October 7 and 9, 1919; FCK to Van Rossum, n.p., October 10, 1919; FCK to members of ABCM executive committee, n.p., Chicago, February 10, 1920, copies.

16. AAOC, FCK to Mundelein, Chicago, November 8, 1919; FCK to Sante Tampieri, n.p., November 17, 1919; FCK to Fréri, n.p., November 18, 1919; FCK to Van Rossum, n.p., November 19, 1919, copies. AAC, 5-1919-B-10 [Moeller, Mundelein, Hayes, Harty, and Canevin to] Bonzano, Chicago, November 11, 1919, copy. ASPF, Fréri to the Central Council, New York City, October 30, 1920, *confidential and personal.*

17. AAOC, Van Rossum to FCK, Rome, December 4, 1919; FCK to Van Rossum, n.p., December 30, 1919; ABCM to Van Rossum, n.p. [December 30, 1919].

18. AAOC, Tampieri to FCK, Rome, January 13, 1920; Tiberghien to FCK, Rome, January 28, 1920; Cerretti to FCK, Rome, February 16, 1920.

19. AAOC, "excerpts of a private letter from Rome," n.d., the original given to FCK on March 2, 1920.

20. FCK to Felix Couturier, n.p., February 13, 1920; FCK to Moeller, n.p., March 2 and 8, 1920; FCK to Hayes, n.p., March 2, 1920; FCK to Canevin, n.p., March 3, 1920; FCK to Mundelein, n.p., April 3, 1920, copies, Harty to FCK, Omaha, March 3, 1920; Moeller to FCK, Norwood, Ohio, March 4, 1920. AAC, 6-1920-M-39, Mundelein to Moeller, Chicago, March 2, 1920, copy.

21. AAOC, FCK, "Ten Weeks," pp. 14-22, passim; Gasparri to Mundelein, Rome, April 12, 1919, copy; Ledvina to FCK, n.p., April 28, 1919; FCK to Van

Rossum, n.p., July 28, 1919, FCK to Couturier, n.p., November 20, 1919, copies. AAC, 5-1919-M-54, Mundelein to Niccolò Marini, Chicago, June 21, 1919, copy. A good summary on the Oriental appears in the *New Catholic Encyclopedia* (New York, 1967), X 762-63. A note on the congregation's poverty is in order. The pope was at first forced to subsidize it "out of his own pocket," FCK told Mundelein; and the only other income then was the 250 Mass stipends which Extension sent. AAOC, FCK to Mundelein [Rome, *ca.* August 31, 1920], copy.

22. AAOC, FCK to Isaias Papadopoulos [Rome *ca.* August 29, 1920], copy; [Marini to] Moeller, Rome, August 31, 1920, copy. AAC, 6-1920-M-245, FCK to Mundelein, August 28, 1920.

23. AAOC, FCK to Papadopoulos, n.p., September 30, 1920; FCK to Cerretti, n.p., September 30, 1920; FCK to Merry del Val, n.p., September 30, 1920; FCK to Calavassy, n.p., October 27, 1920. AAC, 6-1920-M-85, minutes of the second annual meeting of the American hierarchy, Washington, D.C., September 22, 1920, p. 7.

24. AAOC, FCK to Moeller, n.p., October 1, 1920; FCK to Joseph F. McGlinchey, n.p., November 8, 1920; FCK to Cerretti, n.p., November 8, 1920; FCK to O'Connell, Chicago, December 4, 1920; FCK to Moeller, n.p., December 10, 1920, copies; Moeller to FCK, Norwood, December 6, 1920; clipping from the *New World* (Chicago), n.d. AAC, 6-1920-M-254, printed proof of the "Outline of Plan and Methods of the American Board of Catholic Missions," which includes the ABCM's constitution. New York *Times*, December 3, 1920, p. 15. ASPF, Fréri to Joseph Bruneau, S.S., New York City, December 4, 1920.

25. AAC, 6-1920-M-245, FCK to Mundelein, Rome, August 28, 1920; 6-1920-M-240, Galvin to Mundelein, Hanyang, Hubei (Hupeh) Province, China, December 28, 1920. AAOC, FCK to McGlinchey, n.p., October 1, 1920, copy; McGlinchey to FCK, Boston, October 6, 1920.

26. AAOC, extracts of Baudrillart's article (reprinted in *La Croix*, February 15, 1921) with FCK's comments [Rome, n.d.]; FCK, "Monsignor Baudrillart and the American Bishops," unfinished manuscript; FCK to Gaston Vanneufville, Rome, February 21, 1921; FCK to Moeller, Rome, March 1, 1921, copies.

27. AAC, 6-1921-M-80, Moeller to Mundelein, Norwood, January 24, 1921; Gasparri to Moeller, Rome, n.d., telegram copy. AAOC, FCK, "Preliminary Statement" [to Benedict XV, Rome, *ca.* February 2, 1921]; FCK to Van Rossum, Rome, February 2, 1921; FCK to Moeller, Rome, February 3, 1921, copies.

28. AAOC, FCK to Moeller, Rome, February 3 and 15, 1921; FCK to Camillo Laurenti, Rome, February 15 and March 5, 1921, copies. AAC, 6-1921-M-150,

FCK to Mundelein, Rome, February 15, 1921.

29. AAOC, FCK to Moeller, Rome, February 3 and 15, 1921.

30. AAOC, FCK to Donato Sbarretti, Rome, March 19, 1921; FCK to Moeller, n.p., April 18, 1921; FCK to Hayes, n.p., April 18, 1921; FCK to Alfred E. Burke, n.p., May 11, 1921, copies.

31. AAC, 6-1921-M-84, Van Rossum to Moeller, Rome, March 31, 1921, printed copy. AAOC, FCK to Merry del Val, n.p. April 29, 1921; FCK to Cerretti, n.p., April 29, 1921; FCK to Papadopoulos, n.p., May 16, 1921, copies.

32. AAOC, FCK to Dougherty, Chicago, May 3, 1921; FCK to Merry del Val, n.p., May 10, 1921, *confidential*, copies; George Calavassy to FCK, Constantinople, June 10 and July 18, 1921. Notice of Ledvina's promotion to Corpus Christi appeared a month before the actual appointment. See the New York *Times*, April 28, 1921, p. 12.

33. AAC, 6-1921-M-149, Moeller to Mundelein, Norwood, April 22, 1921; Moeller to Van Rossum, Norwood, April 22, 1921, copy; [Mundelein to] Van Rossum, n.p., n.d., copy. AAOC, Dougherty to FCK, Philadelphia, April 30, 1921; FCK to Moeller, n.p., May 27, 1921, copy.

34. AAC, 6-1921-M-200, FCK to Mundelein, Chicago, May 28, 1921. AAOC, FCK to Calavassy, n.p., August 9, 1921; FCK to Moeller, n.p., August 9, 1921, copies; Tampieri to FCK, Rome, June 5 and August 12, 1921.

35. AAC, 6-1921-M-84, Van Rossum [to each American bishop], Rome, August 1, 1921; 6-1921-M-154, Van Rossum to Moeller, Rome, August 12, 1921, copy. AACC, Merry del Val to FCK, Montecatini, Italy, July 17, 1921, *private;* FCK to Moeller, n.p., August 9, 1921; FCK to Papadopoulos, n.p., October 20, 1921, copies.

36. AAC, 6-1921-M-154, Moeller to Mundelein, Norwood, September 5, 1921. AAOC, Tampieri to FCK, Rome, August 12, 1921; Moeller to FCK, Norwood, September 15, 1921.

37. AAOC, Moeller, to FCK, Norwood, October 5, 1921; FCK to Calavassy, n.p., September 29, 1921; FCK to Cerretti, n.p., October 6, 1921; FCK to Moeller, n.p., October 7, 1921; FCK to Frederick Schwager, S.V.D., n.p., October 18, 1921; FCK to Papadopoulos, n.p., October 20, 1921. The NCWC does not possess the minutes of the meeting on September 21-22, 1921. Likewise, no reference to the ABCM appears either in the *NCWC Bulletin* (October, 1921) or in the 1921 annual report of the executive department, which is compiled by the chairman of the Administrative Committee. H. Warren Willis to the writer, Washington, D. C.,

January 10, 1978. The only extant record of the third endorsement of the ABCM by the American bishops is located in the archives of the archdiocese of Boston. There one may find the original handwritten resolution of Bishop Thomas F. Lillis of Kansas City, Missouri, which was given to Cardinal O'Connell for the official minutes. Evidently, however, these minutes were never compiled and distributed. The writer thanks Gerald P. Fogarty, S.J., and James O'Toole for this reference.

38. AAOC, Tampieri to FCK, Rome, October 19, November 29, and December 9, 1921, *confidential* and *most reserved;* FCK to Moeller, n.p., January 5 and 10, 1922, copies; Moeller to FCK, Norwood, January 7, 1922; Cerretti to FCK, Paris, March 13, 1922. EP, William D. O'Brien to Ledvina, n.p., January 12, 1922, copy. Edward John Hickey, *The Society for the Propagation of the Faith: Its Foundation, Organization and Success (1822-1922)* (Wash. D.C., 1922), 183-84.

39. AAOC, Cerretti to FCK, Paris, March 13, 1922.

40. AAOC, FCK to Cerretti, n.p., April 3, 1922, copy; Dougherty to FCK, Philadelphia, April 11, 1922. An account of the suppression of the NCWC may be found in John B. Sheerin, C.S.P., *Never Look Back: The Career and Concerns of John J. Burke* (New York, 1975), 67-82.

41. AAOC, Van Rossum to Moeller, Rome, May 2, 1922, printed copy; [Kelley] "Comments on the decree of May 2nd concerning the American Board of Catholic Missions," n.p., n.d.; FCK to Moeller, New York, City, September 25, 1922, copy.

42. AAC, 7-1922-M-133, Moeller to Mundelein, Norwood, July 10, 1922. AAOC, Moeller to members of the ABCM, Norwood, September 1, 1922, printed; Moeller to Pius XI, Cincinnati, November 4, 1922, copy; FCK to Francis Bourne, n.p., December 5, 1922, copy. After the 1922 meeting of the bishops, Dougherty ended his support of the original ABCM plan. When Moeller sent the three resolutions to the Holy See, the cardinal asked that his endorsement be dropped and that Rome be told that he was absent from the meeting. AAOC, Moeller to FCK, Norwood, November 20, 1922.

43. AAOC, Tampieri to FCK, Rome, December 12, 1922; FCK to Moeller, n.p., January 5, 1923, copy; FCK to Walsh, n.p., May 26, 1923, *personal and confidential,* copy.

44. AAOC, Tampieri to FCK, Rome, April 27 and May 3, 1923, *confidential.*

45. AAOC, Gasparri to Moeller, Rome, December 11, 1922, copy; Moeller to FCK, Norwood, January 2 and 3 and February 1, 1923; FCK to Moeller, n.p., January 9 and 19, 1923, copies. AAC, 7-1923-M-217, Fumasoni-Biondi to Moeller,

Washington, D.C., March 16, 1923, printed circular.

46. AAOC, FCK to James A. Walsh, n.p., May 10, 1923, copy.

47. AAOC, FCK to Tampieri, n.p., September 11, 1923, copy.

48. AAOC, FCK to Ledvina, n.p., February 7, 1923, copy.

CHAPTER X

1. AAOC, FCK to Tampieri, n.p., June 22, 1922; FCK to Ledvina, n.p., February 7, 1923, copies.

2. AAOC, Tampieri to FCK, Rome, May 3 and September 11, 1923; FCK to Moeller, n.p., June 9, 1923, copy; Fumasoni-Biondi to FCK, Washington, D.C., June 15, 1923; FCK to Fumasoni-Biondi, n.p., July 3, 1923, copy.

3. AAOC, FCK to Calavassy, n.p., October 20, 1923, copy.

4. AAOC, Francesco Marchetti-Selvaggiani to Tampieri, Rome, October 25, 1923; FCK to Eugene Phelan, C.S.Sp., n.p., November 21, 1923; FCK to Thomas F. Coakley, n.p., December 19, 1923, copy.

5. AAOC, Hughes to FCK, Washington, D.C., January 24, 1924.

6. AAOC, FCK to Hughes, n.p., January 30, 1924, copy.

7. AAOC, FCK to Frank A. Thill, n.p., February 8, 1924, copy; Marchetti-Selvaggiani to Tampieri, Rome, March 17, 1924. FCK's appointment to Oklahoma in 1924 removed him from further business with the exposition. AAC, FCK to Tampieri, n.p., December 15, 1924, copy. See also O'Brien, "Holy Year of 1925," *Extension Magazine,* XIX (January, 1925), 17, 29.

8. AAOC, Ledvina to the United States hierarchy, Corpus Christi, September 1, 1923; FCK to Ledvina, n.d., n.p., pp. 13-14, copies. AAC, 7-1923-M-163, FCK to Mundelein, New York City September 24, 1923.

9. AAOC, "mission resolutions" attached to Joseph H. Albers to FCK, Norwood, November 26, 1923.

10. EP, O'Brien to Ledvina, n.p., October 16, 1923. AAOC, FCK to Moeller, n.p., December 19, 1923, copies.

11. AAOC, Moeller to FCK, Norwood, January 22 and February 19, 1924;

FCK to Moeller, n.p., January 26 and March 10, 1924, copies.

12. AAOC, FCK to Tampieri, n.p., August 21, 1924, copy.

13. AAOC, FCK to Tampieri, n.p., October 10, 1924, copy.

14. NCWC, minutes of the sixth annual meeting of the American hierarchy, September 24-25, 1924, pp. 4, 14-16. *New World* (Chicago), October 3, 1924, p. 1. AAC, 8-1924-M-385, Van Rossum to Fumasoni-Biondi, Rome, November 17, 1924; 9-1925-M-30, Fumasoni-Biondi to the United State bishops, Washington, D.C. [December 3], 1924, copies.

15. AAOC, FCK to Tampieri, n.p., October 10, 1924, copy.

16. AAC, 13-1926-M-252, Mundelein's handwritten report on the ABCM for the 1926 meeting of the United States hierarchy [September, 1926].

17. AAC, 9-1925-A-6, minutes of the seventh annual meeting of the United States hierarchy, September 16 and 17, 1925, p. 5; hereafter cited as *Hierarchy's minutes (1925).*

18. Interviews with Charles J. Kerwin and John J. Fahey, Chicago, Illinois, October 5, 1976. Statistics published from 1924 to 1928 do not provide trustworthy comparisons between the archdioceses of New York and Chicago. By the latter date, nonetheless, Chicago had climbed to within 25,000 of the most populous diocese in the United States. Moreover, Mundelein's reputation with financiers is illustrated by the stir he caused when he undertook the funding of the construction of the new Pontifical Urban (Propaganda) College in Rome. The Holy See had purchased a ten-acre site on the Janiculum hill, close to the Vatican, for $500,000 through a loan from the Chase National Bank of New York. As an alumnus, Mundelein took a special interest in the project. In 1928 he devised an unusual arrangement in raising the $1.5 million needed for the buildings. This was done through the offering of twenty-year bonds backed by the "Catholic Bishop of Chicago, a Corporation Sole," and marketed through Halsey, Stuart & Company of Chicago. Made public in April, 1928, the offering was priced competitively to yield between 4.25 and 4.95 percent and succeeded in raising the capital for the college. New York *Times,* February 19, 1928, II-4; March 13, 1928, p. 5; March 18, 1928, III-3, and April 2, 1928, p. 43. AAOC, Eugene McGuinness to Dougherty, n.p., June 21, 1928, copy.

19. EP, O'Brien to Ledvina, n.p., April 20, 1922, copy. Mundelein retained a moderate interest in Nevada. In March, 1931, the Holy See created the diocese of Reno, naming as its first bishop a priest from Los Angeles, Thomas K. Gorman. When Gorman sought assistance at the Extension meeting in November,

Mundelein told him: "If Extension doesn't do anything for you write to me and I will see what can be done in the matter." Board Minutes, II (November 17, 1931), 183. In later years, however, Bishop Gorman acknowledged that the cardinal had given him no special help—perhaps because Nevada's bishop had originated from California and not from the Midwest. John Tracy Ellis to the writer, Washington, D.C., March 6, 1977.

20. *Hierarchy's minutes (1925)*, p. 9

21. Interview between Michael J. Curley and John Tracy Ellis, 1928; as noted in Ellis to the writer, Washington, D.C., March 6, 1977. EP, O'Brien to McGuinness, n.p., September 28, 1939, copy. The National Catholic Welfare Council had been changed into a "Conference" in 1923.

22. *Hierarchy's minutes (1925)*, p. 10. *Report of the American Board of Catholic Missions to the American Episcopate, from September, 1925, to June, 1928* [Chicago, 1928], 23, 27; hereafter the reports are cited as *ABCM Report (1925-1928)*.

23. AAC, 9-1925-M-30, minutes of FCK's meeting with Quinn and seven diocesan Propagation directors, New York City, November 16, 1925; 9-1925-K-32, Quinn to FCK, New York City, November 19, 1925.

24. *Hierarchy's minutes (1925)*, 9, 11. AAC, 9-1925-C-1, Gaetano De Lai to Dougherty, Rome, July 27, 1925; copy; Curley to Mundelein, Baltimore, November 21, 1925.

25. AAC, 9-1925-C-1, Mundelein to Curley, Chicago, December 3, 1925, initialed; 9-1925-M-30, FCK to Mundelein, Oklahoma City, December 8, 1925. AAOC, FCK to Dougherty, n.p., October 22, 1925, copy.

26. AAC, 13-1926-M-252, Mundelein's handwritten report to the United States hierarchy [September, 1926].

27. AAOC, FCK to eight missionary bishops, n.p., December 10, 1926, copy.

28. AAOC, Mitty to FCK, Salt Lake City, February 16, 1927.

29. AAOC, FCK to Ledvina, n.p., August 29, 1927, copy. See also AAOC, FCK to William Piani, n.p., August 31, 1927, copy.

30. AAOC, minutes of the ninth annual meeting of the American hierarchy, September 14 and 15, 1927, pp. 8-10.

31. AAOC, William O'Connell to FCK, Boston, November 4, 1927, copy.

32. AAOC, O'Connell to FCK, Boston, October 10, 1927, copy.

33. AAOC, FCK to O'Connell, n.p., November 4, 1927, copy.

34. AAOC, O'Connell to FCK, Boston, November 10, 1927, copy; O'Connell's italics.

35. AAOC, FCK to O'Connell, n.p., November 25, 1927, copy.

36. AAOC, minutes of the eighth meeting of the ABCM. . . , Chicago, November 9, 1927, pp. 7-9; McGuinness to FCK, Chicago, March 15, 1928.

37. AAOC, FCK to Ledvina, n.p., November 5, 1928, copy.

38. AAOC, minutes of the tenth annual meeting of the United States hierarchy, November 14 and 15, 1928, pp. 11-14.

39. *ABCM Report (1939-40),* 22-27.

40. EP, O'Brien to FCK, n.p., October 15 and November 9, 1926, copies.

41. AAOC, FCK to Charles M. Driscoll, O.S.A., n.p., May 15, 1923, copy.

42. AAOC, Piani to FCK, Manila, March 28 and July 30, 1927; FCK to Piani, n.p., August 31, 1927, copy; McGuinness to FCK, Chicago, August 23, 1927; FCK to McGuinness, n.p., August 29 and 30, 1927, copies.

43. EP, O'Brien to FCK, n.p., November 20, 1921, copy. See also EP, O'Brien to Ledvina, n.p., January 31, 1930; O'Brien to FCK, n.p., January 8, 1934, copies.

44. EP, FCK to O'Brien, Oklahoma City, April 11, 1936, See also AAOC, FCK to McGuinness, n.p., July 28, 1930, and EP, FCK to O'Brien, n.p., December 18, 1931, copies.

45. AAOC, FCK to Ledvina, n.p., September 16, 1942, copy.

46. AAC, 9-1925-M-263, John T. McNicholas, O.P., to Mundelein, Duluth, May 25, 1925.

47. AAOC, Corbett to FCK, Crookston, November 21, 1921. AAC, 7-1923-M-171, Corbett to Mundelein, Crookston, March 15, 1923.

48. AAOC, FCK to Corbett, n.p. [1928?], not sent; FCK to McGuinness, n.p., December 18, 1928, copy.

49. AAOC, FCK to Ledvina, n.p., January 7, 1929, copy.

50. EP, O'Brien to McGuinness, n.p., February 9, 1948, copy.

51. AAOC, FCK to Tampieri, n.p., June 28, 1924, copy.

52. AAOC, FCK to Dougherty, n.p., July 1, 1925; FCK to Mundelein, n.p., July 2, 1925, copies.

53. Simon A. Baldus, "Announcement," *Extension Magazine,* XXI (September, 1926), 1. EP, O'Brien to FCK, n.p., October 15, 1926, copy. It is likely that the money for expanding the magazine came from Mrs. Myles P. O'Connor of California. This notable Catholic philanthropist had arranged with Extension a large annuity. At her death, the principal was valued at $80,000 in bonds and passed at this time to the society. EP, O'Brien to FCK, n.p., May 3, 1926, copy. AAC, 13-1926-M-594, O'Brien to Mundelein, Chicago, May 11, 1926.

54. AAOC, FCK to Tampieri, n.p., December 15, 1924, copy. See also AAOC, FCK to O'Brien, n.p., December 31, 1924, copy; O'Brien to FCK, Chicago, April 4, 1925; FCK to Amleto G. Cicognani, n.p., December 7, 1939, copy.

55. AAOC, Tampieri to FCK, Rome, March 28 and May 15, 1924; FCK to Tampieri, n.p., June 7, 1924, copy.

56. AAOC, FCK to Tampieri, n.p., February 28, 1925, copy; Tampieri to FCK, Rome, March 18, 1928.

57. AAOC, FCK to Tampieri, n.p., April 9, 1925, copy.

58. AAOC, FCK to O'Brien, n.p., October 12, 1925, copy.

59. AAOC, FCK to Edward F. Hoban, n.p., November 24, 1930; FCK to Pietro Fumasoni-Biondi, n.p., December 31, 1930, copies.

60. Board Minutes, II (November 20, 1930), 175. AAOC, FCK to Hoban, n.p., November 24, 1930, copy.

61. AAOC, FCK to Hoban, n.p., November 24, 1930, copy.

62. AAOC, FCK to Fumasoni-Biondi, n.p., December 31, 1930, copy. FCK's comment on Extension's "reserves" referred to several Endowment Funds instituted under O'Brien. It did not include the Annuity Fund, which reached $1 million in 1928. This fund paid to subscribers a return of 6 percent of their investment, which reverted to the society's use only at their death. O'Brien, "Over the Million Mark." *Extension Magazine,* XXIII (August, 1928), 4, 46. *New World* (Chicago), June 12, 1931, p. 1.

63. AAOC, FCK to Fumasoni-Biondi, n.p., December 31, 1930, copy.

64. AAOC, Walsh to FCK, New York City, October 17, 1930; FCK to Walsh,

n.p., January 2, 1931, copy. FCK, "Catholic Missionary Activity in the United States of America: Confidential Study for Rev. Edmund A. Walsh, S.J., By the Bishop of Oklahoma" [Oklahoma City, January, 1931], pp. 4, 6, copy.

65. AAOC, FCK to Fumasoni-Biondi, n.p., December 31, 1930, copy.

66. AAOC, FCK to John F. Noll, n.p., December 14, 1932; FCK to O'Brien, n.p., September 17, 1934; FCK to McGuinness, n.p., November 28, 1938; FCK to Richard R. St. John, n.p., November 28, 1938; copies.

67. EP, O'Brien to FCK, n.p., November 20, 1931, copy.

68. EP, O'Brien to FCK, n.p., September 29, 1933; FCK to O'Brien, Oklahoma City, October 9 and November 4 and 9, 1933; O'Brien to Ledvina, n.p., September 20, 1934, copies. AAOC, FCK to McGuinness, n.p., November 25, 1938, copies.

69. EP, Ledvina to O'Brien, Corpus Christi, January 30, 1949; FCK to O'Brien, Oklahoma City, September 9, 1940. AAOC, O'Brien to FCK, Chicago, February 8, 1940; St. John to FCK, Chicago, September 14, 1940. Board Minutes, II (November 13, 1940), 254; II (November 18, 1941), 263; II (November 17, 1942), 273, 275; II (November 15, 1943), 281; III (November 18, 1946), 34; III (November 17, 1947), 42.

70. FCK, "Catholic Missionary Activity . . .: Confidential Study for Rev. Edmund A. Walsh . . ." [January, 1931], pp. 4, 5, copy.

71. AAOC, FCK to O'Brien, n.p., May 13, 1940, copy.

Index

INDEX